Evidentialism
Essays in Epistemology

Earl Conee and
Richard Feldman

CLARENDON PRESS · OXFORD

OXFORD
UNIVERSITY PRESS

Great Clarendon Street, Oxford OX2 6DP

Oxford University Press is a department of the University of Oxford.
It furthers the University's objective of excellence in research, scholarship,
and education by publishing worldwide in

Oxford New York

Auckland Bangkok Buenos Aires Cape Town Chennai
Dar es Salaam Delhi Hong Kong Istanbul Karachi Kolkata
Kuala Lumpur Madrid Melbourne Mexico City Mumbai Nairobi
São Paulo Shanghai Taipei Tokyo Toronto

Oxford is a registered trade mark of Oxford University Press
in the UK and in certain other countries

Published in the United States
by Oxford University Press Inc., New York

© in this volume Earl Conee and Richard Feldman 2004

The moral rights of the authors have been asserted
Database right Oxford University Press (maker)

First published 2004

All rights reserved. No part of this publication may be reproduced,
stored in a retrieval system, or transmitted, in any form or by any means,
without the prior permission in writing of Oxford University Press,
or as expressly permitted by law, or under terms agreed with the appropriate
reprographics rights organization. Enquiries concerning reproduction
outside the scope of the above should be sent to the Rights Department,
Oxford University Press, at the address above

You must not circulate this book in any other binding or cover
and you must impose this same condition on any acquirer

British Library Cataloguing in Publication Data
Data available

Library of Congress Cataloging in Publication Data
Data available

ISBN 0-19-925372-2
ISBN 0-19-925373-0 (pbk.)

1 3 5 7 9 10 8 6 4 2

Typeset by Newgen Imaging Systems (P) Ltd., Chennai, India
Printed in Great Britain
on acid-free paper by
Biddles Ltd., King's Lynn, Norfolk

Acknowledgments

"The Basic Nature of Epistemic Justification" (EC): copyright © 1988, *The Monist*, Peru, Ill. Reprinted by permission.

"Internalism Defended" (EC & RF): Hilary Kornblith (ed.), *Epistemology: Internalism and Externalism* (Oxford: Blackwell, 2001), 231–60.

"Evidentialism" (RF & EC): *Philosophical Studies*, 48 (1985), 15–34. Reprinted with kind permission of Kluwer Academic Publishers.

"Authoritarian Epistemology" (RF): *Philosophical Topics*, 23 (1995), 147–69.

"The Generality Problem for Reliabilism" (EC & RF): *Philosophical Studies*, 89 (1998), 1–29. Reprinted with kind permission of Kluwer Academic Publishers.

"The Ethics of Belief" (RF): *Philosophy and Phenomenological Research*, 60 (2000), 667–95.

"The Justification of Introspective Beliefs" (RF): John Greco (ed.), *Sosa and his Critics* (Oxford: Blackwell, forthcoming).

"Having Evidence" (RF): David Austin (ed.), *Philosophical Analysis* (Dordrecht: Kluwer Academic Publishers, 1988), 83–104. Reprinted with kind permission of Kluwer Academic Publishers.

"The Truth Connection" (EC): *Philosophy and Phenomenological Research*, 52 (1992), 657–69.

"Heeding Misleading Evidence" (EC): *Philosophical Studies*, 103 (2001), 99–120. Reprinted with kind permission of Kluwer Academic Publishers.

Contents

Introduction	1
Part I. General Issues	**9**
1. First Things First (EC)	11
2. The Basic Nature of Epistemic Justification (EC)	37
3. Internalism Defended (EC & RF)	53
Afterword	81
4. Evidentialism (RF & EC)	83
Afterword	101
Part II. Critical Discussions	**109**
5. Authoritarian Epistemology (RF)	111
6. The Generality Problem for Reliabilism (EC & RF)	135
Afterword	159
7. The Ethics of Belief (RF)	166
Part III. Developments and Applications	**197**
8. The Justification of Introspective Beliefs (RF)	199
9. Having Evidence (RF)	219
Afterword	241
10. The Truth Connection (EC)	242
Afterword	254
11. Heeding Misleading Evidence (EC)	259
12. Making Sense of Skepticism (RF & EC)	277
Works Cited	307
Index	315

Introduction

The essays included in this volume develop and defend evidentialism. As we understand it, evidentialism is a view about the conditions under which a person is epistemically justified in having some doxastic attitude toward a proposition. It holds that this sort of epistemic fact is determined entirely by the person's evidence. In its fundamental form, then, evidentialism is a supervenience thesis according to which facts about whether or not a person is justified in believing a proposition supervene on facts describing the evidence that the person has. It will be useful in this Introduction to distinguish the version of evidentialism we defend here from some other theses that might be confused with it and that may even sometimes go by the same name. It will also be useful to clarify the role we take justification to play in an epistemological theory. We will also provide brief summaries of the papers included in the volume.

1. Expressions of a generally evidentialist outlook can be found in the writings of many philosophers. Indeed, the two of us saw evidentialism as sufficiently obvious to be in little need of defense. When we noticed to our amazement that prominent contemporary epistemologists were defending theories that seemed incompatible with evidentialism, this prompted us to write our first paper explicitly on this topic, "Evidentialism" (Chapter 4 in this volume). We have been defending it ever since. We remain mildly amazed.

Among the historical precedents for evidentialism are the writings of John Locke and William K. Clifford. For example, Locke wrote:

Faith is nothing but a firm assent of the mind: which if it be regulated, as is our duty, cannot be afforded to anything, but upon good reason; and so cannot be opposite to it. He that believes, without having any reason for believing, may be in love with his own fancies; but neither seeks truth as he ought, nor pays the obedience due his maker, who would have him use those discerning faculties he has given him, to keep him out of mistake and error.[1]

On the assumption that good reasons and good evidence are the same thing, Locke's claim here is at least evidentialist in spirit. Clifford writes specifically of

---

[1] John Locke, *An Essay Concerning Human Understanding*, ed. A. C. Fraser (New York: Dover, 1959), IV. xvii. 24, pp. 413–14. We were led to this passage by Alvin Plantinga, who cites it in *Warrant: The Current Debate* (Oxford: Oxford University Press, 1993), 13.

Introduction

evidence in his well-known claim that "it is wrong always, everywhere, and for anyone, to believe anything upon insufficient evidence."[2] There is a distinctly moral tone to these pronouncements. The authors seem to be saying that it is morally wrong to fail to believe in accordance with one's evidence.

The evidentialism we defend makes no judgment about the morality of belief. Instead, it holds that the epistemic justification of belief is a function of evidence. It is possible that there are circumstances in which moral, or prudential, factors favor believing a proposition for which one has little or no evidence. In that case, the moral or prudential evaluation of believing might diverge from the epistemic evaluation indicated by evidentialism. It is consistent with our version of evidentialism that there are aspects of life in which one is better off not being guided by evidence. Thus, to take the obvious example, it is consistent with evidentialism that people are better off taking their religious beliefs on faith (rather than letting their beliefs on religious matters be guided by their evidence). Of course, if those beliefs are unsupported by evidence, then evidentialism implies that these beliefs are not epistemically justified. They may nevertheless retain whatever other non-epistemic virtues their defenders claim for them.

Another view sometimes called "evidentialism" implies that a belief is justified only if it can be defended by an argument.[3] An argument, of course, must have propositions as premises. Thus, this kind of evidentialism implies that all evidence is propositional evidence. Presumably, a mere proposition cannot do a person much good as evidence, so a plausible addition to this view is that all evidence is believed propositions. We reject this restricted view of evidence. Part of a person's evidence that it is a warm day might be her feeling warm. The feeling itself is part of her evidence. Perhaps one can diminish the difference between our view and the view with which we are contrasting it by allowing that arguments can have experiences as premises or by asserting that experiences take propositions as their objects. We will not here contest these somewhat contorted attempts to make some other views match the view we prefer. Instead, we wish merely to emphasize that our version of evidentialism allows that one's evidence includes one's feelings and one's experiences.

This understanding of what counts as evidence significantly affects the implications of the theory. Because one's evidence includes one's private experiences, it is not the case that all evidence is in any straightforward sense public

---

[2] W. K. Clifford, "The Ethics of Belief", *Contemporary Review* (1877); reprinted in Clifford's *Lectures and Essays* (London: MacMillan, 1879). The quotation is from p. 183.

[3] Alvin Plantinga seems to have this usage in mind when he discusses an *evidentialist* objection to belief in God in "Is Belief in God Properly Basic?", *Nous*, 15 (1981), 41–51.

Introduction

and capable of being shared. Of course, one person can tell another about his experiences, but this does not quite make them have the same evidence. And it may be that some experiential evidence can only be described in ways that fail to convey significant aspects of its content. Such evidence could not be put into an argument in any useful manner.

In decision theory, there is a view according to which the rational basis for all decisions is evidential. This kind of decision theory is typically contrasted with causal decision theory. Causal decision theorists contend that causal elements must be included separately in any acceptable theory about rational decisions. Defenders of evidentialist decision theory reject this contention, arguing that a condition of total knowledge will deal with the problems that critics have seen in their theory.[4] The evidentialism we defend has no implications for this debate. It is not a theory about rational action, but instead a theory about the justification of belief.

2. As we understand epistemic justification, it is an important necessary condition for knowledge. It is crucial that justification not be identified with whatever it is that, in addition to true belief, constitutes knowledge. We make this point in both "Evidentialism" and "Internalism Defended", but it is sufficiently important to warrant calling attention to it here.

According to evidentialism, a person is justified in believing a proposition when the person's evidence better supports believing that proposition than it supports disbelieving it or suspending judgment about it. Knowledge-level justification is stronger than this. We say something about strength of evidence in the Afterword to "Evidentialism" and in "Making Sense of Skepticism". We take it that the sort of justification we discuss is present in many of the ordinary beliefs that people have about the objects in the world around them. This justification is often sufficiently strong for knowledge, provided the other conditions for knowledge are met. But even when a person has a very strong justification for a believed proposition, the person can fall short of knowledge for three importantly different reasons: (i) the belief can be false; (ii) the person can fail to believe the proposition on the basis of the justifying evidence; and (iii) the justified belief can be true for reasons not properly related to the person's evidence (i.e., the person can be in a Gettier case).

When a belief is based on justifying evidence, then, in our terms, the belief is "well-founded". It is a necessary condition for knowledge. We discuss this

---

[4] See David Papineau, "Evidentialism Reconsidered", *Nous*, 35 (2001), 239–59, for a recent discussion of this dispute.

Introduction

concept in "Evidentialism" and in the Afterword to that paper. When a person is in a Gettier case, the person's belief is "externally defeated", with the result that the belief is not knowledge. Being undefeated is another necessary condition for knowledge. In our view, some recent epistemological discussions overlook the distinctions among these conditions on knowledge. We believe that philosophers who fail to pay careful attention to them run the risk of losing sight of a central epistemological concept.

3. Two papers are new to this volume: "First Things First" and "Making Sense of Skepticism". The rest have been published previously in journals or collections. The previously published papers have been reprinted as they were originally published. In some cases, we have added Afterwords to clarify, elaborate, or reply to objections.

Part I addresses large general issues, culminating in a statement and defense of our view of epistemic justification.

Chapter 1, "First Things First" (EC), is primarily about methodological issues. Philosophers have thought that there are insuperable limits to rationally opposing skepticism, to pursuing epistemological investigations without substantial presuppositions, or to explaining knowledge in general. It is argued that there are no such constraints on an evidentialist approach.

Chapter 2, "The Basic Nature of Epistemic Justification" (EC), seeks to reconcile foundationalism with coherentism, and internalism with externalism. The idea is that the main strengths of each are compatible, even synergistic. Though this is not emphasized in the paper, the evidentialism that we defend incorporates those strengths.

Chapter 3, "Internalism Defended" (RF & EC), endeavors to give a satisfactory account of the difference between internalist and externalist theories in epistemology. The internalist perspective, particularly in its evidentialist incarnations, is argued for and defended against recent objections. It is also suggested that epistemology is not best pursued by arguing about the boundaries of this division or by arguing about the merits of everything on either side.

In the Afterword, first we note how little in our defense of internalism depends on the particular account of internalism that we defend. In the second part, we note how little our view of internalism is affected if it turns out that all states of knowledge are internal. And thirdly, we discuss an objection to internalism stemming from an externalist view of mental content. We offer a slightly adjusted account of internalism to accommodate this concern.

Chapter 4, "Evidentialism" (RF & EC), is an outline of the view of justification we favor, a defense of the view against recent objections, and a presentation of

Introduction

advantages of the view over various rival approaches, including ones that emphasize deontological considerations and ones that emphasize reliability.

In the Afterword, first we state the heart of evidentialism as a supervenience thesis. We also discuss the notion of "fit" that we employ. Second, we distinguish evidentialism as we have defended it from an evidentialist account of the justification condition on knowledge. We also discuss the merits of an objection to a purely evidential account of the justification condition. Third, we assert two epistemic roles for the evidentialist notion of a well-founded belief. And fourth, we discuss an argument according to which the existence of any basic sources of knowledge enables people to know too easily that these sources are reliable.

Part II primarily criticizes non-evidentialist positions. Chapter 5, "Authoritarian Epistemology" (RF), takes on views that give a central role in the nature of epistemic justification to some kind of authority. These views are argued to have the sort of explanatory flaw that is famously discussed in Plato's *Euthyphro*.

Chapter 6, "The Generality Problem for Reliabilism" (EC & RF) argues that reliability approaches to justification are severely defective. They fail even to assert a necessary and sufficient condition for justification, much less a correct condition, if they do not identify the bearers of reliability. They fail to be credible if they identify bearers of reliability in a way that gives the theory grossly implausible results. We examine assorted attempts to respond to this difficulty. We find none with any promise of success.

The Afterword has five parts. In the first, we compare the generality problem for reliabilism to the reference class problem in probability theory. In the second, we comment on the prospects of solving the generality problem without identifying a unique relevant type of belief-forming process for each belief. In the third part we evaluate the idea that things other than processes or mechanisms are bearers of the reliability that is supposed to determine justification. We discuss in the fourth part our use of the basing relation in our account of well-founded belief. We reply to an objection alleging that this use incurs a generality problem for evidentialism. In the fifth and final part we discuss the suggestion that a fully developed version of evidentialism will in effect solve the generality problem for reliabilists.

Chapter 7, "The Ethics of Belief" (RF), discusses the merits of several versions of doxastic voluntarism; some are criticized, some supported. Various theses about the attitudes that we epistemically ought to have are critically discussed. An evidentialist thesis about the attitudes we epistemically ought to have is supported.

Introduction

Part III develops and applies evidentialism. Chapter 8, "The Justification of Introspective States" (RF), addresses an important challenge to any evidentialist view of the justification that conscious states provide. The challenge strongly suggests that something other than evidence plays a central role in epistemic justification, something like reliability or intellectual virtue. It is argued that nothing beyond evidence is needed.

Chapter 9, "Having Evidence" (RF), studies various conceptions of what constitutes a person's evidence. One view that is defended is that the evidence someone has at a time is limited to what the person is thinking at the time.

The Afterword argues that the problem of explaining what it is to have evidence is not a problem faced by evidentialism alone. All theories about justification and related concepts face a similar problem.

Chapter 10, "The Truth Connection" (EC), seeks to answer the question of how epistemic justification is distinctively related to truth. It is argued that the relation is this: epistemic justification of a proposition is evidence for the truth of the proposition.

The Afterword first clarifies the claim of the paper that rational inquiry is a pursuit of knowledge. The second part discusses a thesis in "The Ethics of Belief" about the attitudes that we epistemically ought to have.

Chapter 11, "Heeding Misleading Evidence" [EC], is about the following epistemic problem. Knowing a proposition appears to justify dismissing any evidence against that proposition as misleading. Yet a dismissal of evidence is dogmatic, and belief against sufficiently strong evidence is never epistemically justified. It is argued in response that the problem can be solved by applying an evidentialist view of the justification that is required for knowledge. Although knowledge includes evidence that helps to justify judgments to the effect that contrary evidence is misleading, we do not thereby become justified in disregarding contrary evidence.

Chapter 12, "Making Sense of Skepticism" (RF & EC), criticizes non-evidentialist theories of knowledge as they bear on external world skeptical arguments. The theories are held to provide no good way to understand the intuitive appeal of the arguments for skepticism. An evidentialist characterization is offered of the justification that is needed for knowledge. On the basis of this characterization, an account is given of the appeal of the skeptical arguments. The characterization also provides a basis from which to object to the arguments.

4. The order in which authors' names appear in our co-authored papers has no substantial significance. The papers are thoroughly collaborative efforts. Our practice for listing our names is to reverse the order each time we write a new

paper together, and we do not recall how we chose the ordering for our first joint paper.

5. Our thinking about the topics addressed in this volume has been greatly helped by the advice, comments, and objections raised by numerous friends, students, and colleagues. No doubt the list that follows leaves out some people to whom we are indebted. We apologize for those omissions. Among those to whom we would like to express our thanks are: John Bennett, David Braun, Roderick Chisholm, Stewart Cohen, Richard Foley, Richard Fumerton, Alvin Goldman, Hilary Kornblith, Peter Markie, Jim Pryor, Sharon Ryan, Ted Sider, Ernest Sosa, Jonathan Vogel, and Edward Wierenga.

Part 1
General Issues

1

First Things First
Earl Conee

Introduction

Epistemology is difficult enough without transcendental constraints. Evidentialist epistemology is unencumbered by unjustified presuppositions and intrinsic limitations of scope. This is illustrated here by addressing several issues that seem somehow primordial or ultimate. The first such issue is refuting skepticism without begging the question. This leads to the problem of the criterion: the contention roughly to the effect that all positions about the extent of our knowledge beg the question. Following that, three basic philosophical projects that some philosophers have thought cannot be accomplished are discussed. One such project is fully reflectively justifying the reliability of a source of knowledge. The others are giving reasons for thinking that our most basic reasons really are reasons, and giving a complete philosophical explanation of all knowledge. It is argued that in each case there is no insuperable limit to what an evidentialist approach can accomplish.

Refuting Skepticism, Inside and Out

Some philosophers think that the only good way to dispute a radical skeptical position without begging the question is to show that the skepticism refutes itself. Not so. We do not have to undermine a skeptical position by using its own resources, in order to avoid doing anything illegitimate. A better approach is to find reasons to deny the skeptical thesis that are stronger than the reasons that argue for it.

Earl Conee

1. First we should note some liabilities of an undermining response to skepticism. The broad idea of the response is that the skeptic's position includes assumptions or presuppositions that are sufficient to refute it. This in turn takes two main forms.

1a. One undermining response attempts to show that the skeptic, by arguing for the position, presupposes or tacitly acknowledges the falsity of that position. We can see that this is a bad tack to take by looking at an instance where the approach seems most likely to succeed. Universal skepticism about reasons is the thesis that there are no good epistemic reasons. Let us suppose that a universal reason skeptic presents an argument for her view. This presentation may seem to assume that the argument gives reason to accept its conclusion. Since the skeptical thesis is that there is no reason to believe anything, this apparent assumption denies the skeptic's view.

In fact, though, the skeptic's position either is immune to this problem, or can be readily recast to avoid it. She can use her argument as part of a *reductio ad absurdum* of the possibility of having good reasons. The argument would then have the following overall structure: if there were any good reasons to believe anything, then this argument would give conclusive reason to deny that there are any good reasons. Hence, there are none.

This argument gives no reason to believe its conclusion, according to the skeptic's own view. But that fact casts no doubt on the skeptic's thesis. One instance of poor reasoning does not so much as suggest that any good reason exists. Nor does this sort of skeptical argument rely on a premise asserting that any argument does give reason, and no premise in her argument need have that proposition in its defense. In this sort of skeptical effort, the reason-giving power of argument is only a *reductio* hypothesis. Nothing in this use of argument supports the conclusion that any argument supports its conclusion.

The psychological fact that a certain argument is found convincing may prompt a universal reason skeptic to present the argument. So the skeptic can offer the argument sincerely while not assuming or implying that it has any rational force. There may be a sense of "commitment" whereby the skeptic, just in virtue of presenting an argument, is committed to its cogency. This in turn may include a commitment to the rational defensibility of the argument's premises and form. If so, then these things are just conventional facts about the social role of offering an argument. And again, the skeptic may present the reasoning because she believes its premises and accepts its validity, without regarding any of it as reasonably believed. It is not entailed by someone's presenting an argument that the person asserts or implies that any of its premises, or its form, has some positive epistemic status.

First Things First

Thus, even a universal reason skeptic can argue for the view without implying anything incompatible with it. There is no reason to doubt that proponents of less sweeping skeptical theses can do so as well.

1b. The other sort of attempt to undermine skepticism consists in trying to show that the content of a skeptic's thesis, or the content of something in its defense, provides material to argue for its falsity. This is not impossible. If a skeptic denies all knowledge of the external world, and uses in defense of the thesis the known existence of perceptual illusions, or the known existence of empirically inadequate scientific theories, then this skeptic really must be wrong. If we know that some perceptual beliefs are not accurate, or we know that some scientific theory has failed some empirical test, then we know something about the external world.

This genuinely self-refuting sort of skepticism is understandably rare. There is no good ground to expect that a contrary assumption will be buried within other skeptical positions. In fact, it is easy for an external world skeptic to rely on the sort of evidence just mentioned while avoiding inconsistency. An assertion of knowledge of illusions, for instance, can be replaced by the claim that the existence of perceptual illusions is as reasonable to accept as is any proposition about the external world. The rest of the argument can be adjusted to go just as well as before. Or the proposition that we have knowledge of illusions can be inferred from the *reductio* assumption that some perceptual beliefs are known in the ordinary ways, in an attempt to conclude that ordinary ways do not yield knowledge. These skeptical claims may be false, or unjustified, or the reasoning may be fallacious. But these ways of arguing do not imply the falsity of their conclusions.

Thus, skeptical theses and positions should not be expected to refute themselves. Some philosophers use the term "self-refutation" in a way that can obscure this fact. Richard Fumerton considers whether some skeptical arguments are "epistemically self-refuting". By this he means that the truth of an argument's conclusion implies that at least one of its premises has no epistemic justification.[1] As Fumerton observes, a skeptical conclusion asserting that we have no epistemic reason to believe anything implies that we are without reason to believe its own premises.[2] So any argument for universal reason skepticism stands epistemically self-refuted.

The skeptical thesis itself is not thereby shown to be mistaken, though. Again, the implication that we have no reason to believe a premise in one

---

[1] Richard Fumerton, *Metaepistemology and Skepticism* (Lanham, Md.: Rowman and Littlefield, 1995), 44. [2] Ibid. 50.

argument does not show, or give reason to believe, that we have reason to believe anything else.[3]

Michael Huemer observes that a universal skepticism about justifying reasons might be the conclusion of a *reductio* argument.[4] Nonetheless, Huemer classifies this sort of universal skepticism as "self-refuting".[5] By this he means that the position cannot be rationally accepted.[6]

Maybe this skeptical view actually can be rationally accepted. For instance, it seems possible for such a skeptic to see rational force in some argument for her view, and thereby accept it, not noticing that the view entails that she is not thereby justified in believing it. This might be enough for a rational acceptance of the view. In any event, even if the view is not rationally acceptable, that would be no embarrassment for it and no weakness in it. Indeed, this result would be a confirming instance of universal reason skepticism. So the rational unacceptability of the view would have no tendency to show that it is untrue. Thus, even if its rational acceptance is impossible, this fact about it is not worthy of being classified as a refutation of the view.[7]

2. A skeptical position can be refutable without sowing the seeds of its own destruction. It need not be defended in a way that supports its own denial. We are still fully reasonable in denying the skepticism if we have better reasons to deny the thesis than to believe it. The skeptic need not supply these reasons. The reasons need not be entailed by the skeptic's conclusion, or its defense. Entailed objections are more convenient, more assuredly available, and perhaps rhetorically more effective. But they are not therefore stronger reasons.

If we have reasons that imply the falsity of a skeptic's conclusion, or the falsity of a premise leading to it, then these reasons are incompatible with that defense of skepticism. They are not worse reasons because they have this logical character. Crucially, although such reasons deny part of the skeptic's position, they are not thereby shown to be merely parochial reasons, not merely reasons from the non-skeptic's point of view. Rather, they are reasons that argue against the view. Reasonable skeptics who heeded them, and had no counterbalancing reason in reply, would not continue to rely on the skeptical view to infer their denial. They would change their view.

---

[3] In a similar spirit, Fumerton notes that when a skeptical position is subject to epistemic self-refutation, still, an anti-skeptic "cannot simply dismiss" the skeptical conclusion (ibid. 51).

[4] Michael Huemer, *Skepticism and the Veil of Perception* (Lanham, Md.: Rowman and Littlefield, 2001), 30.   [5] Ibid. 31.

[6] Ibid. 27.

[7] Huemer also calls the skeptical thesis "self-defeating," on the ground that it cannot be justified (ibid. 28). But even granting that it cannot be justified, this is no "defeat" for a universal denial of justification.

First Things First

This asymmetry would not obtain if reasons that go against skepticism were just beliefs. The skeptic would have skeptical beliefs, non-skeptics would have theirs, and there would be a mere clash of views. The clash could be avoided by holding to any consistent body of belief, skeptical or non-skeptical.

An evidentialist account of reasons is of assistance here. In an evidentialist view, reasons consist in evidence. A person has epistemic reason in support of a proposition wherever a person has evidence for the proposition. More substantially, it is reasonable to maintain that our evidence is not exhausted by our beliefs, and that it does not include all of them. It does not include beliefs for which we have no evidence. The evidence that a person has about a proposition consists in the indications that the person has concerning the truth-value of the proposition.

This abstract characterization of evidentialism about reasons could be applied directly to the meta-epistemological issues that we are discussing. A more specific evidentialist view will make clearer the merits of the approach. One credible version of evidentialism has it that positive evidence is supplied by seeming truth. The general idea is that someone's evidence about a proposition includes all that seems to the person to bear on the truth of the proposition. Call this "seeming evidentialism" (SE). What seem true are propositions. They seem true in virtue of the fact that we are spontaneously inclined to regard something of which we are aware as indicative of their truth. The substantial thesis about evidence of SE is that this sort of inclination defers to something that is in fact indicative of truth to us. What primarily strike us as indicating truth are conscious qualities, memories, and conceptual connections. Awareness of these is not belief. Some of our beliefs support others because among the conceptual connections we discern are deductive and inductive relations. When a proposition that seems true seems to imply another, and no doubt about the latter seems to arise, then the latter proposition seems true too. Thus, one proposition can seem true partly by seeming to follow from another.[8]

---

[8] Huemer advocates a principle that he calls "Phenomenal Conservatism": "(PC) If it seems to S as if P, then S thereby has at least prima facie justification for believing that P" (ibid. 99). SE is much in the same spirit. One relatively small difference concerns the positive epistemic status that seemings confer. "Prima facie justification" is intended to imply justification in the absence of any defeater (ibid. 100). SE holds instead that seemings confer epistemic reasons. This allows that they can be so weak as not to justify belief even if undefeated. Another difference is the use in PC of "as if P". This is most naturally read to mean: as things would seem, if P were true. This subjunctive clause makes trouble. For one thing, were P true, it might present some misleading or otherwise uncharacteristic appearance. The idea in SE is, rather, that when someone has an impression that strikes the person as indicating P's truth, P seems true to the person. This allows that, were P actually true, it might happen to make some

Earl Conee

Concerning any thought, our epistemically rational basis for our initial thinking about its truth is our initial evidence on the matter. On the present version of evidentialism, SE, this consists in how things initially seem to us. If the thought in question is a skeptical thesis, then any bases on which it seems false are reasons to deny it. This remains true as long as it really does seem false. It may well be that we do not find the skeptical thesis attractive, we are confident that it is untrue, and it would be difficult for us to believe. These facts are practical reasons to resist believing it. They are not bases on which its negation seems true.

On the other side, the fact that someone has asserted a skeptical thesis, or asserted a premise in defense of one, is not a reason to accept it.[9] This assertion does not nullify the rational capacity of evidence against the belief. If we offer the considerations that make the proposition seem false to us, then we have given our reasons for denying it. In order to demonstrate that this denial is correct, our reasons need not be already accepted by the skeptic, they need not persuade the skeptic, and they need not be reasons that a strategically astute defender of skepticism would acknowledge. They need only be reasons strong enough to refute the rational force of the skeptic's case.

Our reasons can rely on common ground, propositions conceded by the skeptic. This may make our case particularly effective psychologically. (And it may not—the skeptic may recoil at being undercut by her own concessions, and quickly retract them.) But equally, we may have reasons that skeptics have already denied. They may be good reasons, nonetheless. The denial may be groundless, or its grounds may be overridden by our reasons. This is unlikely to be conceded by skeptical opponents in a debate about skepticism. The strength of reasons is not measured by their efficacy in debate. It is measured by how good the evidence is that they provide.[10]

---

uncharacteristic impression. Also, Huemer counts all seemings as *prima facie* justification, but he does not count all seemings as evidence. SE counts them all. These differences should not obscure the strong affinity between SE and PC.

[9] On both sides, the cited facts may be part of a good reason. For instance, the skeptic may be an established source of otherwise reliable testimony. With that sort of additional evidence, the assertion of skepticism counts for something. Also, the skeptic's manner of assertion might cause the thesis to seem true, e.g., by expressing it in some revealing, accessible and credible formulation. The point is that none of the mentioned practical and rhetorical considerations is an epistemic reason on its own, according to SE, because none makes the thesis seem true.

[10] Richard Feldman and I pursue this strategy for refuting external world skepticism, in "Making Sense of Skepticism" (Ch. 12).

First Things First

Getting Started

"The Wheel", better known as "The Problem of the Criterion", can illustrate how a skeptical position is susceptible to a refutation that makes no contrary assumptions. The Wheel is a multifarious problem. Perhaps the central issue is best understood as the question: how is it possible to theorize in epistemology without taking anything epistemic for granted? We shall look at two specific versions of the Wheel.

1a. Roderick Chisholm addresses the topic by focusing on two pairs of questions:

(A)   What do we know? What is the extent of our knowledge?
(B)   How do we decide whether we know? What are our criteria of knowledge?[11]

Chisholm dubs as "methodists" those philosophers who think they have an answer to (B) and use it to answer (A), while "particularists" are philosophers who think they have an answer to (A) and use it to answer (B). In Chisholm's terminology the "skeptics" on this matter are philosophers who hold that any answer to (A) relies on an answer to (B), and vice versa, and who infer that neither question can be answered.[12]

Though Chisholm is a particularist, he declines to argue with methodists and skeptics about the correctness of the particularist approach to epistemology. He maintains that the problem of the criterion can be dealt with only by begging the question.[13]

A fourth approach is better than the three that Chisholm mentions. This other approach can be called "applied evidentialism", because that is what it is. Methodists, particularists, and skeptics all begin to construct and defend philosophical theses about knowledge on the assumption of an epistemic doctrine. The methodist doctrine is that a certain method of knowing succeeds, the particularist doctrine is that certain cases are examples of knowledge, and the skeptical doctrine is that each of these other two doctrines can be used in epistemology only an the basis of a legitimate reliance on the other.

The evidentialist view is that we proceed best by following our evidence. According to SE, this amounts to what seems to us to be known, how we seem to know it, and what seems to be needed in order to know the extent of our knowledge and the methods for acquiring it. In any evidentialist view, we start

---

[11] Roderick Chisholm, *The Problem of the Criterion* (Milwaukee: Marquette University Press, 1973), 12.
[12] Ibid. 14–15.   [13] Ibid. 37.

on the right track by relying on our evidence for what is known and how we know it, and following our evidence for how to improve our judgments about this. Then, guided by our evidence concerning how to proceed, we build a defense of doctrines concerning the extent of our knowledge and the methods for acquiring more of it.

Minimally, the evidentialist view is that epistemic justification consists in evidence. It does not recommend any procedure for theorizing, in epistemology or elsewhere. But we can have initial evidence about which procedures increase our justification in epistemic matters. According to SE, we have such evidence when it seems to us that some procedure increases this justification. The proposition that following those procedures will succeed is initially supported by this initial evidence that they yield increased justification. This proposition continues to be supported for as long as we have continuing evidence that they work.

This begs no questions. It does not take for granted any epistemic doctrine. This evidentialist view can be usefully compared to the method of reflective equilibrium. The relevant differences here are greater than the similarities. As in a pursuit of reflective equilibrium, in an evidentially justified pursuit of epistemology neither general principles nor particular cases are simply taken for granted. By pursuing reflective equilibrium, our initial beliefs about these things are compared, and a reconciling equilibrium is sought. By contrast, epistemology guided by evidentialism does not begin by endorsing any belief, and it need not seek equilibrium among beliefs. Our initial evidence for epistemological theory may concern both general propositions and specific cases. But the evidence need not consist in beliefs. Rather, in a plausible specification of SE the initial epistemological evidence consists in conceptual considerations and conscious states, including recollections and sensations, that seem to favor certain generalities and particular cases.

Evidentialism does not imply that an equilibrium will be the conclusion to the inquiry. The general doctrines and particular cases that go together most harmoniously may not be sufficiently justified by the evidence that we have at the time. For instance, there may be a tie in evidential support among sharply contrasting, incompatible, maximally harmonious aggregations of propositions, with no further evidence. Or a comprehensive equilibrium may not be achievable. It may be that intractable paradoxes prevent any real coherence among all epistemic propositions that continue to seem true. It may even be (contrary to how things now seem to many of us) that evidence turns up in the process indicating that coherence or "equilibrium" among propositions is not an epistemic factor in support of their truth.

1b. To those who are persuaded that the Wheel is bound to cast severe doubt on the existence of any reasoned starting point for an epistemological theory, this evidentialist approach may seem to be a form of methodism. Evidentialists, we may be told, simply take for granted that the method of adjusting beliefs to evidence produces justification and knowledge. This is just as much begging the question as assuming any other method.

In fact, though, the evidentialist view does not support beginning epistemology by taking for granted that evidentialism is true. The supported procedure for pursuing epistemology does not have us make any use of the thesis that evidence is what justifies. Rather, what potentially justifies belief in initial epistemic data and initial procedures of inquiry is the evidence itself. According to our illustrative evidentialist hypothesis SE, our evidence about the epistemic is how epistemic things seem to be. The view has it that whichever procedures of inquiry are thus supported as effective have precisely that epistemic virtue, and whichever epistemic beliefs about cases of knowledge or general principles initially seem correct are thereby supported as data for theorizing.

A proponent of SE would naturally endeavor to defend the claim that evidentialism itself is among the doctrines that are justified by how epistemic things have come to seem. But that claim about current support for evidentialism is entirely independent of assuming at the start the truth of evidentialism, or any version of it. No such assumption is required.

This point about not assuming a doctrine at the outset of epistemological theorizing may be granted by a partisan of the severity of the Wheel. Still, it may be replied, employing a procedure in which belief is counted as initially justified by evidentialism is as faulty a way to start as assuming a doctrine. This is "rule circularity". It is mere self-affirmation. What the employed procedure counts as justifying turns out to "justify" the doctrine that it is justifying. But this is merely "justification" by its own standards. In light of this, employing a procedure that is sound according to evidentialism is no better epistemically than employing tarot card reading and counter-induction on their own behalf.

Let us assume that these procedures all affirm their own capacity to produce justification and knowledge. So they are equally self-affirming. There is a vital difference, however. If evidentialism is defended in a way that succeeds by its own standard, then it is not defended on the basis that it is self-affirming. It is defended by evidence that it is true. This is epistemic reason to think it true. There is no good reason to think that a tarot card reading, or a counter-inductive inference, provides good reason for its outcome.

The last claim would be contested by entrenched defenders of the latter two procedures. But this is not to say that the entrenched have good reasons.

There is no rational standoff. In the absence of any cogent skeptical ground to question this, we know that their reasons are no good. This is not merely assuming anything or merely disagreeing. It is arguing on the basis of the reasons that we have to doubt that tarot card reading and counter-induction supply rational support.

The substantial merits of evidentialism matter here. The same pattern of claims can be made to no good effect. Let us call "conjecturalism" the view that intentionally guessing that a proposition is true is a good reason to believe that it is true. Conjecturalists too can claim that they have a solution to the Wheel that begs no questions, and is not merely self-affirming. Conjecturalists can claim that some propositions about what we know are merely guessed, and thereby justified and known, simply by being guessed on purpose, without presupposing any methods or examples. A conjecturalist can further claim that although conjecturalism is self-affirming—he himself has guessed its truth—the resulting epistemic support arises not from the sheer fact of self-affirmation, but rather from the good reason that guessing provides. Conjecturalists can even add that a further conjecture establishes that evidence does not give good reasons.

None of this makes conjecturalism a credible view, much less a solution to any problem associated with the Wheel. This is not because conjecturalism is committed to a structurally defective initial method. It is because we have ample reason to doubt that intentional guesses can provide epistemic reasons.

The same goes for reliabilism. The method of beginning by employing what are in fact reliable relevant kinds of belief-forming processes would not be structurally defective by dint of unjustified presuppositions or circularity. Rather, the method would have the liabilities of reliabilism about reasons. For instance, it would count pure guesses as good reasons if guessing were properly reliable. Yet, intuitively, guesses are not epistemic reasons, no matter what.

The crucial difference is that evidentialism is supported by evidence, and evidence does give good reasons. Again, this is not a mere proclamation, easily matched by any other approach. It is supported by reasons, according to our best understanding of reasons.

2. Chisholm introduces the problem of the criterion with the following paraphrase from Montaigne. It describes a different question from those raised by Chisholm's two pairs of questions, (A) and (B). Evidentialism might seem ill suited to answer this other question.

To know whether things really are as they seem to be, we must have a *procedure* for distinguishing appearances that are true from appearances that are false. But to know whether our procedure is a good procedure, we have to know whether it really *succeeds* in distinguishing appearances that are true from appearances that are false. And we cannot know whether it really does succeed unless we already know which appearances are *true* and which ones are *false*. And so we are caught in a circle.[14]

This paraphrase of Montaigne states a problem that purportedly arises in attempting to go beyond appearances. It is a problem of knowing, from among the ways things appear to be, which ways things really are. Yet our present version of evidentialism, SE, relies on how things seem. So something more than this evidentialism seems to be required for a solution to Montaigne's problem.

The paraphrase of Montaigne raises a new question, which asks us to identify our ways of knowing that some things really are a particular way, given that they appear to be that way.

No addition to our evidentialist view is needed. According to SE, our reasons for accepting answers to this question consist in what seems to be required, beyond how external things appear, in order to know how they really are, the ways in which we seem able to acquire what is needed, and the examples in which it seems clear that we have done so. When we proceed as seems reasonable, we find more or less powerful justification for accepting the success of certain procedures for knowing when appearances are in accord with reality, and we find more or less powerful justification for accepting various cases as examples of such knowledge.

Or perhaps our evidence will not turn out to be so reassuring. Evidentialism does not guarantee that we can know how things really are. In its SE version it says that what we are justified in believing about this at any stage of the inquiry depends on what then seems needed and what we then seem to have. The balance of evidence at some point may indicate that we know only how external things appear to be, not how they are. So a skeptical phase of this inquiry is possible, as is a skeptical outcome.

The basic evidentialist response is that in order to come to have justified beliefs about sorting appearance from reality, we need not start with the assumption that some procedure is effective, or the assumption that a certain collection of cases includes only successful ones. In an evidentialist view, the evidence for the accuracy of a procedure is not that it correctly classifies antecedently identified cases of knowledge. In the current version, the evidence may be that the procedure seems to get right seeming cases of knowledge. There may also be purely conceptual evidence for a procedure, yielded by analyzing memory, or perception, or whatever the apparent source of knowledge may be.

---

[14] This is Chisholm's paraphrase of Montaigne, ibid. 3.

Accepting the success of a source on the basis of seemingly accurate outputs is not to be taking the status of those cases for granted, even tentatively. According to SE, it is having evidence that they are cases of knowledge, and evidence that the source yields them. Further consideration of the topic may alter this. Perhaps reflection on apparently possible errors will cast grave doubt on either the status of the examples or the judgment that the source yields them. Or perhaps reflection will reveal new reasons to affirm initial impressions.

In this reliance on evidence, nothing epistemic is assumed. We can gain reasoned answers to Montaigne's question by beginning with nothing more than the seeming answers and the seeming ways to improve them. Or at least, no good reason to doubt this has emerged.

Circles

William Alston and Paul Moser are united in thinking that we can have justification and knowledge of propositions whose epistemic status is challenged by skeptics, without inevitably arguing in a defective way. But they are also united in contending that there is a sort of positive epistemic status for propositions subject to skeptical challenge that we are barred from achieving, on pain of employing some variety of circular reasoning.

1. Alston's work in this area is intricate. His topic is the epistemic defensibility of what he succinctly expresses as follows

(II) Sensory experience is a reliable source of perceptual beliefs.

(II) abbreviates

(i) We and the world around us are so constituted that beliefs about the immediate physical environment, that are based on sense experience in the way that such beliefs usually are, and that are formed in the kinds of situations in which we typically find ourselves, are or would be generally true.[15]

Alston argues that all the available support for this proposition is "epistemically circular". By this he means that premises in good arguments for the proposition are justified by processes employing sensory experience. This Alston characterizes as assuming the conclusion "in practice"—that is, proceeding in belief formation "as if" the proposition is true.[16]

---

[15] William Alston, "Epistemic Circularity", *Philosophy and Phenomenological Research*, 47 (1996), 2, 4.
[16] Ibid. 9.

Alston argues that this epistemic circularity does not prevent an argument which exemplifies it from "showing" or "establishing" that (II) is true.[17] Yet Alston contends that epistemic circularity "really does render an argument useless for some purposes.... [A]n epistemically circular argument cannot be used to rationally produce conviction."[18] This sounds like a significant epistemic liability. It also seems virtually to contradict his previous conclusion that an epistemically circular argument can "establish" its conclusion. Why could this establishing not produce rational conviction? After all, an epistemically circular argument does not require any prior conviction of its conclusion. It requires only assuming it "in practice"—forming beliefs as if the conclusion is true. In contrast, what is established for a person is thereby made rational for the person to believe.

It immediately emerges that Alston does not mean to deny any of this. What he says next is this:

> At least [an epistemically circular argument] cannot be used to rationally move a person from a condition of not accepting the conclusion *in any way*, to a condition of doing so. For if the person does not already, at least practically, accept the conclusion he cannot be justified in accepting the premises.[19]

This last claim does not deny that the propositions asserted by the premises can be justified to the person by sensory experience. It is just that someone who does not accept the reliability of sensory experience "in practice" is someone who does not form beliefs on the basis of sensory experience. So such a person does not accept the premises (or accepts them on some other basis, which does not justify them). Alston earlier describes this person as one who "wholeheartedly denied or doubted" the reliability of sensory perception.[20] But this is not to say that the person has reason to deny that it justifies. This sheer refusal to accept the beliefs usually induced by sensory perception is the only reason why one who does not accept the conclusion "in any way" cannot be rationally moved to accept the conclusion of an epistemically circular argument.

Clearly, the fact that someone who refuses to accept an argument's premises is not rationally persuaded by that argument is no epistemic liability for the argument. It shows a lack of persuasion, but not a lack of reason. So this much shows no epistemic significance in the fact that some arguments are in Alston's sense "epistemically circular".

Alston virtually agrees with this assessment.[21] But he goes on to contend that there is a substantial epistemic limit on what can be accomplished in defense of (II).[22] The sort of limit he discusses is similar in spirit to the Wheel.

[17] Ibid. 15.   [18] Ibid.   [19] Ibid.   [20] Ibid. 9.   [21] Ibid. 19.
[22] Ibid. 19–20.

Earl Conee

Alston argues that (II) cannot be "fully reflectively justified" (FRJ). This epistemic status is the goal of full critical reflection on one's justification. Alston takes this reflection to require finding justification by argument for all of the premises used in justifying a belief.[23] He argues that in the course of attempting to be FRJ in believing (II), an argument exhibiting "logical circularity" is bound to be required. That is, some argument will be needed that contains a premise asserting the reliability of sensory experience.

Alston's first argument that (II) cannot be FRJ is explicitly dependent on an assumption with two important halves. The first half of the assumption is that beliefs are justified by satisfying some condition, C, only if the beliefs are reliably formed when C holds. This half of the assumption can be called "the reliability constraint". The second half of Alston's assumption is that, when it is asserted that for a belief to satisfy condition C justifies the belief, "part of what is asserted" is the reliability condition.[24]

The second half of the assumption—call it "the assertion constraint"—does the crucial work in Alston's argument that (II) cannot be FRJ. The process of becoming FRJ seeks arguments as justification, but (II) makes an empirical claim. Argument for it must use empirical premises. These must include perceptual beliefs, or beliefs justified partly by derivation from perceptual beliefs. To become FRJ, these perceptual beliefs must be defended by argument. Alston plausibly contends that, at some point in this pursuit of becoming FRJ, a general sufficient condition on the justification of a perceptual belief will have to be used as a premise.[25] This premise asserts that some condition justifies the perceptual belief. So, from the assertion constraint it follows that (II) is part of what the premise asserts. This renders an argument relying on that premise logically circular.[26]

Three things are notable about this argument. First, the reliability constraint is not part of all theories of justification. In particular, it is no part of the evidentialist view applied here. Alston acknowledges that without the reliability constraint "epistemic circularity is even more benign" than he is claiming.[27] There is no general proof here that being FRJ in believing (II) is unavailable. It remains to be seen whether logical circularity can be found in all pursuit of becoming FRJ in believing (II), if either half of Alston's assumption is incorrect.

Second, the reliability constraint by itself does not require logical circularity in becoming FRJ in believing (II). We can take it for granted, and grant too Alston's claim that some general sufficient condition for the justification of a perceptual belief will show up as a premise in some justifying argument

---

[23] Ibid. 23. [24] Ibid. 21. [25] Ibid. 21–2. [26] Ibid. 22. [27] Ibid.

First Things First

along the way. It follows only that this premise implies (II), in the sense that it is true only if (II) is true. This implication need not be at all obvious. We may require other premises to gain reason to derive (II), for instance, premises justified by extensive reflective inquiry concerning what is necessary for justification. It is the assertion constraint that gains Alston his efficient derivation of logical circularity.

And third, the assertion constraint is not credible. If a reliability requirement is defensible, that fact must emerge from philosophical argument. It cannot be present in the content of justification claims themselves. Alston says that he argues elsewhere for the assertion constraint.[28] Argument is not what is needed, though. If a reliability requirement were "part of what is asserted" in asserting a sufficient condition for justification, then this constraint would need only to be pointed out. It would not need to be argued for. The assertion would have to contain the requirement explicitly, in order for an argument with the assertion as a premise and (II) as a conclusion to be logically circular. To make this true, the reliability requirement would have to be obvious. It would have to be manifest to any comprehending maker of the assertion. It manifestly does not have that status.

Finally, though, becoming FRJ of (II) without logical circularity is not available to us. It is unavailable for any proposition. Alston sketches a good argument for this, which goes essentially as follows.

Becoming FRJ requires justification by argument for anything that justifies a belief. Each new argument to justify a premise previously used has at least one premise. The premise is either identical to a previous premise, or not. If it is identical, then the procedure is logically circular in an incontestable way. If it is not identical, then it is a new proposition. Eventually we will run out of all the propositions that we ever consider, much less use as premises. So eventually there will be an argument with a premise that we have not justified by a logically noncircular argument.[29]

This is nearly enough right about being FRJ.[30] But it imposes no epistemic limit. Alston thinks that it refutes the traditional philosophical aspiration expressed by the maxim: the unexamined principle is not worth accepting. Alston writes: "Not everything can be subject to the test of critical examination, or we shall be bereft of all belief."[31]

---

[28] Ibid. 25. [29] Ibid. 26.
[30] There is a complication concerning arguments with no premises in a natural deduction system. It does not affect the point to be made about the epistemic insignificance of the limit on becoming FRJ. [31] Ibid. 28.

25

Earl Conee

This is a mistake. We can critically reflect on principles. A principle might be justified, or known, by support from the evidence we have obtained through this critical scrutiny. This is all of the "critical examination" that it is reasonable to seek. Our having no argument for a principle is compatible with its having any positive epistemic status for us. It can be supported by evidence that justifies it, and enables us to know it, and it can sustain this epistemic status through a thorough critical examination.

Alston also holds that the impossibility of becoming FRJ without logical circularity rules out "the *total* explicit rationalization of belief".[32] This has a true reading, but it states no epistemic limit. Every consideration relevant to the justification and knowledge of any proposition can be made quite explicit. All of the connections by which those considerations justify or yield knowledge also can be made explicit. What cannot be done is to state a "total rationalization" for a belief, in the sense of stating some justification which consists entirely in arguments. None of our beliefs is justified by an endless argument or a logically circular argument, so no truth is left out by not being able to state a total rationalization.[33]

It is logical circularity, not an epistemic variety, that plays a role in Alston's argument against the possibility of becoming FRJ in believing (II). The only epistemic barrier that Alston attributes to epistemic circularity in this discussion is the one that we have seen: it prevents one who refuses to use perception to accept the premises of an epistemically circular argument from thereby justifying belief in (II). We have also seen that this is not an epistemic limit.

Alston contends that a much greater rational restriction is imposed by epistemic circularity. He reaffirms that epistemic circularity does not stop an argument from "showing" that (II) is true.[34] He acknowledges that even simple track record arguments for the reliability of sensory experience can justify that conclusion. Nonetheless, he proceeds to use the epistemic circularity of an argument to disqualify candidate arguments from showing that sensory experience is any more reliable than crystal ball gazing.

Alston argues for this disqualifying role of epistemic circularity. First he describes his acknowledgment of the utility of epistemically circular arguments for (II) as admitting nothing more than the conditional fact that if sense

---

[32] Ibid.

[33] If we had the capacity for an endless justification by argument, we might well have had the wherewithal to make it all explicit. Either both are impossible, or neither is.

[34] William Alston, *The Reliability of Sense Perception* (Ithaca, NY: Cornell University Press, 1993), 16.

First Things First

perception is reliable, a track record argument will show that it is.[35] Then he asserts that "we can say the same of any belief forming practice whatever, no matter how disreputable".[36] He takes this last point to show that we cannot use epistemically circular track record arguments to "discriminate" the ones that can "reasonably be trusted".[37] Alston concludes: "Hence I shall disqualify epistemically circular arguments on the grounds that they do not serve to discriminate between reliable and unreliable doxastic practices."[38]

There are three important mistakes here. The first is an error in self-attribution. What Alston acknowledges about the epistemic capacities of epistemically circular arguments is the unconditional fact that they can show that (II) is true. And this is no slip-up. It is a fully warranted acknowledgment. Recall that epistemic circularity implies only that the process of belief formation that the conclusion asserts to have some epistemic merit is used to accept premises in the argument. As Alston observes, this allows that the process is in fact justifying and knowledge-conferring. In the case of the best sorts of arguments for (II) that employ perceptual experience in defense of premises, Alston presents no reason to deny that they are indeed strong enough arguments to yield knowledge.

Second, and more importantly, it is not the case that just any method of forming beliefs can be *shown* to be reliable by use of the method, if it is in fact reliable. Sheer reliability does not justify belief. Showing requires having known premises, and this entails more than just believing the premises by what is in fact a reliable method. It may be, for instance, that we have strong though misleading reason to deny the method's reliability. Then the premises are not even justified.

By contrast, sensory perception in particular does not have this liability. In an enormous variety of cases, there is a track record argument for (II), with perceptually acquired premises, and we have no good reason to doubt those premises.

Third, and most importantly, Alston's rejection of all epistemically circular arguments for (II) is entirely unwarranted. There are epistemically circular arguments that do not show their conclusions to be true. Counter-inductive arguments for the truth of future counter-inductively drawn conclusions are like this. So epistemic circularity is not sufficient for showing a conclusion to be true. Such circularity is also not sufficient for justifying that conclusion, as the counter-induction example also makes plain. Thus, Alston is correct that the feature of having a reliability that is derivable by an epistemically circular argument does not select out doxastic practices that can be reasonably trusted.

---

[35] Ibid. 17.   [36] Ibid.   [37] Ibid.   [38] Ibid.

However, this insufficiency does not imply that there is something defective or inadequate about every epistemically circular argument, as Alston infers in "disqualifying" them. Again, we are given no reason to deny that some epistemically circular arguments show their conclusions to be true. An epistemically circular argument may also have a form that we know to be demonstrative, and premises that we know to be true. There need not be anything wrong with it. Thus, Alston errs in inferring that epistemic circularity is a disqualifying feature of an argument for reliability. There is no epistemic weakness at all that is implied by this feature.

Even a prospect of logical circularity need not impede justification. Genuine logical circularity makes for a bad argument. But this does not exclude a kind of justification that can appear to be accurately represented by a logically circular argument of the very simplest sort. It is quite plausible that there are cases in which, by just considering a proposition, we gain justification for believing it. Any thought that seems quite obviously true, just in virtue of what it says, is like this. For instance, there is thought

P1:   Each thing is one thing.

P1 can be seen to be true by those who understand it. This seeing is acquiring evidence. It might appear to involve circularity. It might be thought that for a proposition to provide evidence for itself would require that the proposition argue for its own truth. If so, this would be rightly represented by an argument of the form X, therefore X, which is as circular as reasoning can be.

Taking an optimal view of what the evidence is here, that form of argument is not the real nature of the evidence in such cases. Part of the evidence is background information about attribution in general. The evidence that is specific to P1 is acquired by considering P1. In virtue of that fact, it may be accurate to describe the proposition as "self-evident". But this evidence is not the proposition itself. The evidence consists in what is discerned when considering P1 about the concepts employed and the relationships asserted by P1 to hold among the things to which the employed concepts apply. A description of the evidence we might acquire for P1 by considering it would be something like this: "the proposition makes a claim that addresses each thing singly, and the claim made is simply to attribute being one thing." So a premise asserting the evidence for P1 would make this sort of structural claim, rather than just asserting P1 itself. And the specific evidence for such a premise would also not be the premise itself. That premise would be supported by the awareness, induced by considering P1, of these concepts and their roles in P1. In terms of the version of evidentialism that has been applied here, this awareness is one way for the proposition to seem true. Thus, even something worth calling self-evidence is possible without involving any reasoning that has a circular structure.

2. Paul Moser discusses "moderate realism", the humble doctrine that some of our beliefs are objectively true.[39] He is concerned that certain skeptical questions about moderate realism pose a "dangerous obstacle" to this claim.[40] The form of skepticism that Moser has in mind challenges the moderate realist to provide non-question-begging support for a certain proposition. It is not moderate realism itself. With Alston, Moser acknowledges that there is no circularity in justifying, or knowing, moderate realism on the basis of some combination of grounds involving considerations such as perception, memory, coherence, and predictive success.[41] The threat of begging the question is supposed to arise when a skeptic asks this question: "What non-question-begging epistemic support have we to claim that [such a ground of belief] is actually indicative of what is objectively the case?"[42] Moser holds that for a moderate realist simply to appeal to the same sort of basis for believing moderate realism would be to beg this question. Yet grounds of this sort seem to Moser to exhaust our reasons for holding that some of our beliefs are objectively true.[43]

Appealing to perception, coherence, or the like, would not beg the question that Moser is discussing. Rather, it would fail to answer the question. One belief that a moderate realist might well defend as objectively true is that there are dogs. A good argument for this belief would have to appeal to some combination of perception, memory, coherence, and the like. But the truth of the belief is not questioned by the skeptic whom Moser is discussing. The skeptic is asking for reason to think, not that the belief is true, but rather that the cited grounds are actually indicative that the belief is true. To respond by just reiterating those grounds fails entirely to answer the skeptic's question about their capacity to indicate the truth of the matter.

SE asserts that we gain justification from how things seem to us. According to SE, this provides evidence for how things are. A somewhat lengthier expression of this latter claim would say that the grounds are "indicative" of how things "objectively" are. In the case of this question about grounds indicating truth, the seeming consists in an intuitive application of the concept of evidence or the concept of a reason. In particular, perceptions apparently of dogs, with cohering memories, testimony, and the like, seem to constitute evidence

---

[39] Paul Moser, "Realism, Objectivity and Skepticism", in John Greco and Ernest Sosa (eds.), *The Blackwell Guide to Epistemology* (Oxford: Blackwell, 1999), 71.
[40] Ibid. 73. [41] Ibid. 74. [42] Ibid. 75. [43] Ibid.

that dogs exist. It is plausible that these grounds provide reason to think that dogs exist. A good deal more epistemology is needed in order to have a full account of what the evidence-giving relation really is, and to show that it holds in this case. But the mere fact that the cited grounds seem to be evidence gets us started. It is an initial reason to hold that the grounds are indicative of the truth of the belief.

Nothing in this claim begs the question. The support we are asked to identify is support for the proposition that such grounds indicate that there are dogs. The claim that this is an intuitively correct application of the concept of an indication (or a reason, or evidence) does not assert, presuppose, or otherwise assume that the grounds are such support. It answers the question by stating a reason for thinking that they are.

A final, new skeptical question can be asked:

What non-question-begging reason have we for the claim that what intuitively seems to be a correct application of a concept really is indicative of what is objectively the case?

It may be that our only good answer to this question reports a conscious response that arises in considering the claim. According to the version of evidentialism that we are applying, SE, this response can be put succinctly: it seems so. And it might be thought that this answer, finally, surely, begs this new question.

But no. Once again, the question is of the form: Why think that X is related to Y by relation R? Specifically, the question is: Why think that an intuitive appearance that perceptual experiences and the like are evidence for the existence of dogs indicates that the former really is evidence for the latter? The answer—it seems so—is not of the question-begging form: R is a relation of X to Y. The claim is not that the appearance that the grounds are evidence simply is a reason to think that they are. Rather, the answer is that there is further evidence. It is the appearance that this last claim is true, the answer of the reason-giving form: A reason, consisting in an appearance, is offered to think that R relates X to Y.

Stroud's Generality Problem

Barry Stroud does not argue that epistemology must be started in a defective way. He argues, rather, that a fundamental epistemological project is defective from the start in a way that dooms it to failure.[44] He describes the doomed

---

[44] Barry Stroud, "Understanding Human Knowledge in General", repr. in Hilary Kornblith (ed.), *Epistemology: Internalism and Externalism* (Oxford: Blackwell, 2001), 126–46; *idem*, "Skepticism, 'Externalism', and the Goal of Epistemology", in Keith DeRose and Ted A. Warfield (eds.), *Skepticism: A Contemporary Reader* (Oxford: Oxford University Press, 1999), 292–304. See also Ernest

First Things First

project as seeking to achieve "a philosophical understanding of how human knowledge is possible".[45]

1. Stroud argues for the impossibility of success at this project in two phases. In the first phase, he attacks what he regards as a traditional approach to achieving a philosophical understanding of knowledge in a given domain.[46] This approach has two key components. The first is the thesis that some sources of knowledge are elements of a domain that has "epistemic priority" over knowledge in another domain. Elements of the former domain are the basis, or grounds, or source, of the latter knowledge.[47]

The second key component of the project is the thesis that a subject must have epistemically prior knowledge of a linking principle. The idea intended appears to be that a subject gains knowledge in a domain, D, by at least tacitly deriving it from elements in a prior domain, using prior knowledge of how those elements suffice to confer the knowledge in D. So, one thing a subject needs in order to know something in a domain, D, is epistemically prior knowledge of a principle asserting that certain elements of a domain epistemically prior to D are sufficient for the knowledge in D.

The approach has it that, by finding these two components, we gain an understanding of how a person's knowledge of propositions in D is possible. We have found a basis for knowing, a basis consisting in elements of some domain that is epistemically prior to D. And we have found that the subject possesses epistemically prior knowledge of the sufficiency of those elements for

---

Sosa's excellent discussion, with which the present work is largely in accord, "Philosophical Skepticism and Epistemic Circularity", in DeRose and Warfield (eds.), *Skepticism*, 93–114.

[45] Stroud, "Understanding Human Knowledge in General", 127. In fairness to Stroud, it should be mentioned that he sometimes limits his conclusion to the conditional: if certain "almost effortlessly natural ways of thinking embodied in the traditional enterprise" are affirmed, then the project is doomed (ibid. 145). Stroud sees no assurance that we can avoid these ways of thinking, however.

[46] By "domain" Stroud means something like a general classification of the content of the knowledge: e.g., external world propositions, propositions about the past, and propositions allegedly open to *a priori* knowledge.

[47] There is a small but important complication here. Typically a source of knowledge in a domain that is epistemically prior to knowledge in another domain will be *propositions* of some classification that places them outside the latter. For instance, propositions about behavior may be in a domain that is epistemically prior to those in a domain containing propositions about other minds. But another traditional possibility is that an epistemically prior domain contains propositions that report experiences by the subject. The way in which things in that domain yield knowledge in other domains need not be that the person knows the appropriate propositions. It may be enough that the person has the appropriate experiences. Stroud never quite says this. But it seems clearly to be his intention when he writes about " 'sense data' " or " 'experiences' " (Stroud's scare-quotes) being epistemically prior to knowledge of material objects (ibid. 131).

31

knowing propositions in D. So we see what grounds the knowledge, and we see how the person is in a position to use those grounds to gain the knowledge.

One problem that Stroud finds for this approach is essentially the following. However well the project works for limited domains, it cannot succeed for all of human knowledge. To see this, first we should note that epistemic priority is to be a transitive, asymmetric relation. Though there need not be a temporal ordering from prior to posterior domains, there is supposed to be a conferring of epistemic status upon elements of the posterior domain by elements of the prior domain that either have the status or do not need it. The prior elements could not do this if they had to receive their epistemic status in a way that involved elements of the epistemically posterior domain having that status. Finally, given the modest assumption that the beliefs and experiences that are elements of the domains are finite in number, we have it that only finitely many domains are epistemically prior to any given belief.

In any application of this approach to knowledge in a domain, there will always be at least one item of knowledge that has not been explained by the domains already cited. This is so even if the elements of the epistemically prior domain are not further factual knowledge that requires explanation. For instance, perhaps knowledge in the domain of external world propositions can be explained on the basis of experiences, together with knowledge of a linking principle saying that the experiences are sufficient for the knowledge. Perhaps having the experiences is enough, and knowing that they are had is not required. But still, there is also the needed knowledge of a linking principle. The approach requires knowledge of that principle to be explained by citing its source in an epistemically prior domain, together with knowledge of an epistemically prior linking principle. And then the knowledge of this second linking principle must also be explained, if all human knowledge is to be explained. The approach requires that a new epistemically prior domain be found to explain it, and to explain the further linking principle connecting elements of that new domain to the last linking principle. Since the domains are finite, eventually there will be no domain left.

So this project cannot be completed for all knowledge. We shall see that this fact places no limit on what can be explained in epistemology.

2. A less demanding approach exists to understanding human knowledge. On this other approach, the subject need not know any principle linking the source of the knowledge to what is known. The subject need not even have reason to believe such a principle. It is enough if there is a fact to the effect that pertinent elements of the epistemically prior domain are sufficient for the knowledge in the domain in question. Stroud terms this approach "externalism".

This sort of externalism is not subject to the argument for incompleteness just presented. It allows that there is an ultimate, epistemically prior domain for factual knowledge. The ultimate domain may contain no factual knowledge. It may contain only experiences. No epistemically prior knowledge of a linking principle is required. Nothing in this externalism requires infinitely many new domains.

The second phase of Stroud's argument against the possibility of understanding how all human knowledge is possible attacks the adequacy of this other approach. To study its workings, Stroud considers a lightly sketched reliabilist view of how knowledge and good reasons are acquired.[48] We are given nothing more about the reliabilist view than that it counts beliefs as known, and backed by good reasons, when they are reliably caused. Let's call this view "R". According to R, no fact about a source of knowledge need be known by the subject, or even supported by good reason. So, in particular, the subject need not know, or have reason to believe, any fact about the sufficiency of elements of an epistemically prior domain for knowledge of a posterior proposition.

Stroud finds it difficult to articulate fully the obstacle that he sees to the success of externalism. But a rough outline of his objection is accessible enough. Stroud observes that R implies that we have plenty of knowledge about the external world, if common sense and science are at least roughly right about the causes of our beliefs. Stroud does not question that they are right. He holds that trouble emerges when it comes to knowledge and good reasons pertaining to R itself. He grants that *if* R is true, then the externalist has such knowledge and good reasons. But for Stroud, this is a big "if".

Stroud contends that the externalist can do no more to defend her having knowledge of R than to argue for such conditionals. When we have knowledge of nothing stronger than the conditional—if R is true, then the externalist knows R—we have what Stroud calls an "unwitting understanding" of the knowledge. He claims that even if R is true, unwitting understanding is "the most that the 'externalist' philosophical theorist of knowledge could be said to have of his own knowledge".[49] Stroud proposes that the philosophical quest for understanding how human knowledge is possible seeks something better—a witting understanding of the knowledge.[50]

Attempting to articulate the inadequacy that he sees in the externalist approach, Stroud repeatedly asks for some good reason to believe the theory, rather than merely something that is good reason to believe the theory *if* the theory is true.[51] Finally, his best effort at describing the inadequacy is this: "Perhaps

---

[48] Ibid. 140ff.   [49] Ibid. 143.   [50] Ibid.   [51] Ibid. 140, 142, 143.

it is best to say that the theorist has to see himself as having good reason to believe his theory in some sense of 'having good reason' that cannot be fully captured by an externalist account."[52]

This is Stroud's case against externalism. It does not identify a problem for externalism in general. This "externalism" includes diverse epistemic theories. What they have in common is that they explain knowledge and good reason without requiring that we know a source of some knowledge or reason to be its source, in order to have that knowledge or reason. Externalism implies no restriction on how the views in its category can be rationally defended. In particular, externalism does not imply that some externalist theory can be supported simply by being numbly applied to belief in itself.

Any theory is open to defense by giving what actually are good reasons to believe it. This remains true when a theory is about good reasons. An externalist theory of good reasons is open to support from its intuitive plausibility, its agreement with reflective judgments about the presence or absence of good reasons in hypothetical cases, and arguments for it from well-supported premises. Our evidence about reasons tells us that these are good reasons to believe a theory. The fact that good reasons are the topic of the theory does not affect that.

Stroud may have been misled by using R as his paradigm externalist theory. A reliability view of good reasons does not seem credible. At least initially, reasons and their epistemic quality appear to be determined entirely internally. An unrefined reliability theory also does a poor job at capturing reflective judgments about hypothetical cases. For instance, it seems inescapable that some kinds of mental states and events stand no chance of being good epistemic reasons for believing. To repeat an earlier example, an intentional guess at the truth is not a good reason to believe what is guessed. This would remain the case, no matter how strongly the relevant type of the guess tended toward truth. So reliabilism seems hopelessly wrong about the potential of this sort of event for giving a good reason. No good argument for reliabilism about good reasons is available, either. So it may well have appeared to Stroud that the most a proponent can do in support of R is to point out that R, applied to our actual circumstances as we ordinarily take them to be and as science tells us that they are, counts belief in R as belief that is backed by good reason.

Self-affirmation is not a good reason. That is, the fact that a theory, applied to itself under actual conditions, implies that is has some positive epistemic status, is no good reason to think that it does have that status. Quite generally, the mere fact that a theory, in conjunction with facts or reasonable beliefs, has

[52] Ibid. 143.

First Things First

a particular implication, is not a good reason to believe the theory. An implication can be part of a good reason, if the implied proposition itself has some positive epistemic status. Then its implication can confirm the theory. But an implication does not acquire any positive epistemic status just by being implied. So if this sort of self-support is the most that a proponent of R can find in favor of R, then there is no good reason to believe R. Indeed, if a theory counts this sort of self-support as good reason, that classification disconfirms the theory.

Actually, even this self-applying sort of pseudo-support for R is probably lacking. The relevant mechanism, or process type, causing belief in R is quite obscure. But clearly R is a product of philosophical theorizing. If that fact turns out to be dominant in determining the relevant reliability, then it is doubtful that the reliability is high. Philosophical theorizing has a poor track record.

This cumulative weakness of R may have led Stroud to think, mistakenly, that externalism in general is incapable of being well supported. But again, externalism about good reasons can be defended, as can any theory. An evidentialist version illustrates the availability of good reasons for an externalist theory. An evidentialist view of good reasons for believing a proposition holds that they are evidence for the proposition. The evidentialist who is, by present standards, an externalist adds that someone who has the evidence need not know, or have good reason to believe, that it is a good reason. That much "externalism" seems wise. It is plausible that, in order for a consideration to be a good reason to believe P, it must be available to guide belief by someone who is being reasonable about the truth of P. The consideration need not actually be counted as a good reason—much less known to be one—in order to have that status.

This nominally externalist evidentialism has the support of good reasons. For one thing, the view is intuitively plausible. The epistemic reasons that a person has for believing a proposition seem to be considerations the person has that support the truth of the proposition. Those considerations are at least part of the person's evidence concerning the proposition. Differences in the quality of reasons appear to be settled by their internal character, in a way that matches differences in the strength of someone's evidence. The view does well at matching reflective hypothetical judgments, though providing detailed support for this last claim would be a huge undertaking. Reasonable argument can be given for the view.[53]

---

[53] For instance, see the evidentialist application of the argument from examples for internalism in "Internalism Defended" (Ch. 3).

Earl Conee

Thus, there is nothing common to the theories that Stroud terms externalist that makes them all vulnerable to his objections. In particular, nothing evident at the outset bars externalist evidentialism from providing an understanding of how all human knowledge is possible.

Conclusion

Evidence is an epistemic first cause. Non-doxastic evidence can constitute an epistemic reason on its own. So it can provide us with initial reasons in the most fundamental or universal inquiries, while we take nothing for granted. There is no methodological limit to the content of propositions that it can support, including propositions about evidence. It can guide critical reflections on the propositions that it initially supports. So we can reasonably challenge the fruits of our initial reasons. It makes possible a wholly reasonable and universal epistemology.

2
The Basic Nature of Epistemic Justification
Earl Conee

The leading approaches to the nature of epistemic justification are the sides taken in two controversies: coherentism versus foundationalism, and externalism versus internalism. The former dispute has time-tested durability; the latter threatens to become equally persistent. Nevertheless, it will be argued here that these controversies have satisfactory resolutions. It will be argued that each of the four approaches is fundamentally right. Each has a plausible core that combines consistently with the others. This paper offers a prolegomenon. Its goals are to clear away apparent obstacles to a reconciliation among the approaches and to outline the resulting inclusive view.

Coherentism and Foundationalism

1. What makes coherentism seem right? The best grounds derive from considerations such as these: The research practices of natural science obviously enhance the justification of beliefs based on such research. The effect is strongest and most obvious when explanatory theories and experimental observations fit together. Standard examples of scientific progress make the point. A scientist begins with, say, beliefs about the shapes of the known planets' orbits and the planets' masses, belief in a theory of gravitation, beliefs entailing a predominantly gravitational influence on the shapes of planetary orbits, and beliefs about the way telescopes yield observations of distant bodies. By accepting the existence of a new planet having a certain mass and orbit, the scientist can explain the previous telescopic observations and predict new ones.

Earl Conee

Once the scientist gains observational beliefs that match the predictions, all of the mentioned beliefs cohere in a system of explanation, prediction, and confirmation.

The scientist's epistemic situation seems to include the following features. Each belief is epistemically supported by its coherence with the others in the system. No belief within the system is merely a source of support for others. Nothing outside of the system is needed for coherence to play this role as a justifying factor. In particular, the support provided by mutual coherence in an explanatory system does not depend on any self-justifying belief inside or out of the system.

These considerations defend two coherentist theses: First, explanatory coherence contributes to epistemic justification. And second, no autonomously justified belief is necessary for the beliefs in a coherent system to be supported by their mutual coherence. There may be other factors relevant to epistemic justification, and the nature of explanatory coherence is by no means obvious. But surely this core of coherentism is at least part of the truth about justification.

This sort of coherentist proposal is not too modest to have a critic. John Pollock objects.[1] His objection is somewhat indirect. To see what it is, we should be clear about the fact that our topic is epistemically *justified* belief. This is to be distinguished from the topic of epistemically *well-founded* belief. A well-founded belief is justified and also believed in a way that appropriately "derives from" its justification.[2] In effect, Pollock argues that what has just been identified as the core of coherentism about justified belief cannot be extended to an adequate theory of well-founded belief, and thus the core of coherentism is unacceptable. Pollock begins his argument by assuming that a belief is well-founded only if it is at least partly *caused* by its justification. He contends that, in a coherentist view, this implies that if a new belief is well-founded then the cohering of the newly believed proposition with other beliefs must help to cause the proposition to be believed:

In order for [well-founded] belief to be possible on such a view, the coherence relation (whatever it is) must be such that P's cohering with B *can* cause one (in an appropriate way) to believe B.[3]

---

[1] John Pollock, "A Plethora of Epistemological Theories," *Justification and Knowledge*, George Pappas, ed. (Dordrecht: D. Reidel, 1979), pp. 104–5.

[2] In Pollock's terms, this is the distinction between 'warranted' and 'justified' beliefs, respectively. "Derives from" is Pollock's phrase, and he too puts it in scare-quotes. Richard Feldman and I discuss the epistemic role of this distinction in section 4 of "Evidentialism," *Philosophical Studies*, 48 (1985), pp. 15–34 [Ch. 4 in this volume].   [3] "A Plethora of Epistemological Theories," p. 104.

Basic Nature of Epistemic Justification

Pollock points out that well-founded beliefs are virtually never brought about by any belief to the effect that the new belief coheres. The plain fact is that people acquiring justified beliefs very very rarely think about coherence. Pollock then asks how the mere coherence itself of a proposition with current beliefs could help to cause the proposition to be believed. After expressing doubt that this could happen given either of two existing proposals about the nature of coherence, he concludes by finding it quite unlikely that the requisite causation by coherence occurs.[4]

There is no insurmountable trouble here for the core of coherentism. Rational belief formation can be reasonably held to involve causation by coherence. It is quite credible to suppose that rational belief formation at least partly consists in adopting beliefs because they fit well with other things that the person thinks or is aware of. Pollock gives no reason to doubt that this happens. He may be right that existing views about coherence do not provide for this sort of causal role. But if so, that counts against these existing views. It does not refute the causal efficacy of coherence.

Pollock has identified a constraint on an acceptable theory of justification. It must tell part of the truth about well-founded belief, since any well-founded belief is a belief that is justified, plus something else. But Pollock gives no reason to think that the core of coherentism violates this constraint.

The basic coherentist views remain quite plausible: Coherence among beliefs contributes to their justification. No autonomously justified beliefs are required for this to occur.

2. What makes foundationalism seem right? The best grounds derive from considerations such as these: Our cognitive access to the world is initiated by sensory experience. To employ a convenient example, a conspicuous epistemic difference between my justified belief that there is a *Bic Stic* pen in my hand, and my unjustified belief that the pen still holds plenty of ink to finish this draft, is that my sensory experiences and occurrent memories lend credence to the former and not to the latter. (The ink looks pretty low in the transparent plastic barrel of the pen.) Quite generally, it seems beyond reasonable doubt that epistemically justified belief is constrained by what is experienced. In fact, experience can override what otherwise would be sufficient coherence among beliefs with the result that the beliefs are unjustified. If you somehow managed to believe in the presence of your current experiences that a large blue balloon is in your hands, and this belief fit into a system of theoretical and observational beliefs that you also got yourself to accept, nevertheless the balloon belief

---

[4] Ibid., pp. 104–5.

would fail to be epistemically justified. It would be rendered unreasonable by your entirely unballoonish experiences. Also, coherence with other beliefs cannot justify attributing to oneself experiences that are not actually undergone. If you added to the concocted system of beliefs about a balloon in your hands the belief that it appears to you as though a large blue balloon is in your hands, this belief would fail to be justified in spite of its coherence with the others. It would patently conflict with what you really do experience.

Such considerations defend three basic foundationalist views: The epistemic justification of beliefs requires a suitable substantiation by experience. Sensory experience does not in turn require substantiation by beliefs in order to act as a constraint on justified belief. And coherence among beliefs is insufficient to justify those beliefs in the face of recalcitrant experience, even if the system includes beliefs attributing to oneself what would be appropriate experiences if one had them.

Again we have reasonable considerations on behalf of certain basic elements of an approach to the nature of epistemic justification. Again there may be more that contributes to justification, and the nature of the substantiation that experience can provide is by no means obvious. But surely this core of foundationalism is part of the truth about justification.

This core of foundationalism too is not too modest to have a critic. Michael Williams argues against there being any epistemic role for sheer sensory experience.[5] Williams discusses what he calls "the sensuously given." He reasons from the assumption that it is a nonpropositional, unconceptualized sort of awareness. This can be granted.[6] He quotes with approval C. I. Lewis's claim that the given elements in experience and conceptual thought are such that "neither limits the other."[7] From this Williams infers that any such given element

...cannot provide a rational check on anything, cannot favor one hypothesis over another.[8]

It may be that experience places no insuperable *causal* limit on what can be believed. But this is not a problem for the core foundationalist thesis that

---

[5] Michael Williams, *Groundless Beliefs* (Oxford: Basil Blackwell, 1977), pp. 28–9, 102, 174.

[6] There is no need for present purposes to contest Williams's characterization of the sort of thing that is counted here as the plausible foundation of justified beliefs. But it is defensible to maintain that sensory experience consists in apprehending certain propositions, those that the person having the experience can express by the sentence "I am thus," where 'thus' has as its content the experience of a certain phenomenal quality. (This sort of account could be given without invoking propositions in terms of self-attributions of the properties designated by 'thus'.) [7] *Groundless Belief*, p. 29.

[8] Ibid., p. 102.

Basic Nature of Epistemic Justification

experience sets a *rational* limit: the character of experience limits which beliefs can be justified. Why does Williams doubt this? In some passages it seems that he infers an incapacity of the given to provide a rational check on belief directly from the nonpropositional nature of the given.[9] This inference is puzzling. Fortunately Williams provides a linking premise at one point.[10] There, the reasoning begins with the assumption that any epistemic foundation for beliefs about the external world must be premises from which the beliefs follow by some good deductive or inductive argument. The other assumption is that the content of any nonpropositional sort of awareness cannot serve as a premise, because only propositions have logical relations. It follows that nonpropositional sensory experience cannot supply an epistemic foundation for external world beliefs.

This reasoning is objectionable. There is no good reason to accept its first assumption that foundations must be propositions with deductive or inductive logical relations to any justified belief. The expression "substantiation" has been used here in order to convey the sort of support that a sensory foundation can provide to perceptual beliefs. This terminology is far from completely clear. But it is a serviceable pretheoretical expression for a relation which is thoroughly familiar, however imperfectly it is understood.[11] Again, it seems obvious that experience somehow constrains justified belief.[12] What is not obvious is the exact nature of the constraint. As Williams's second assumption asserts,

---

[9] E.g., ibid. See note 6 above for a suggestion regarding how sensory awareness might take propositional objects. This possibility requires a revision in Williams's argument, since the suggestion gives experiences the right sort of ontological status to serve as premises. It is likely that Williams would contend that the given *cannot* be propositional in structure. He seems to think that propositional thought is "conceptualized," and that it follows directly that it is not merely given. (Ibid.) On the suggestion in note 6 though, sensory experience is propositional without being conceptual in any problematic way. For instance, the suggestion does not imply that a person who is having a sensory experience must be applying some classifying rule. Rather, the "concepts" constituting the experiential propositions are identical to the qualities experienced. The person grasps these "concepts" sufficiently to apprehend the propositions experienced simply by being aware of the qualities.

[10] Ibid., p. 174.

[11] I have tried to say something precise about the nature of the epistemic support relation of tending to confirm in "Propositional Justification," *Philosophical Studies*, 38 (1980) pp. 65–8. Tending to confirm as defined there is an epistemic relation between propositions. But I would offer the same account of what I am calling here "substantiation," after making straightforward modifications to allow that what does the substantiating may be events of sensory awareness or other conscious states (see note 16) and perhaps therefore not propositions (but see note 6).

[12] I am far from the first to take this as a secure starting point. To cite just two recent examples, Ernest Sosa relies on experience having such a role in his case against a version of coherentism in "The Raft and the Pyramid," *Midwest Studies in Philosophy*, vol. V, French, Uehling and Wettstein, eds. (Minneapolis, MN: University of Minnesota Press, 1980). James van Cleve finds it "initially obvious" that experience has a justifying role. See "Epistemic Supervenience and the Circle of Belief," *The Monist*, vol. 68, no. 2, p. 95.

nonpropositional sensory experiences cannot be premises in a deductive or inductive demonstration of any external world belief. Premises must be propositions. Putting this point together with the previous one, it follows that experience can substantiate external world beliefs by virtue of an epistemic support relation other than deductive and inductive validity.[13] This amounts to a denial of the first assumption in Williams's reasoning. Experiences can provide foundations without being premises.

This basis for objecting to Williams's argument is not contentious. Coherentists and foundationalists concur about the existence of some sort of epistemic support in addition to the logical relations of deductive and inductive validity. Coherence itself is to be such a relation.[14] Indeed, it may be that Williams did not intend finally to defend a conclusion precluding the *possibility* of any rational check by the given on belief. When he explicitly addresses a view which is virtually the same as the one identified here as the core of foundationalism, he does not renew his contention that nonpropositional awareness *cannot* provide a rational check on belief. Rather, he observes that a view according to which there is some unspecified sort of nonpropositional rational check leaves us

...completely in the dark as to *how* the alleged foundation of knowledge is supposed to perform the task demanded of it.[15] [emphasis added]

This observation is surely well taken. The *nature* of the justificatory constraint provided by experience does call for explanation. But the *existence* of the relation is not rendered dubious by anything in Williams's work. We have been offered no reason to believe that the foundationalist approach has a hollow core.

In fact, this epistemic relation is a topic where a combination of coherentism and foundationalism is particularly promising. Substantiation by experience calls for an explanation, and so does coherence among beliefs. There is no need to think that these are *two* problematic relations. It may be that the only basic

---

[13] Roderick Chisholm argues for the existence of such an additional relation of epistemic support in *Theory of Knowledge*, 2nd ed. (Englewood Cliffs, NJ: Prentice-Hall, 1977), pp. 64–7.

[14] Williams himself appears to believe in a kind of explanatory coherence that is a relation of epistemic support other than deductive or inductive validity. (*Groundless Belief*, pp. 104–5.) He might take his own position to be exempt from the trouble that he finds for experiences as foundations, since coherence as he conceives of it is a relation holding exclusively among propositions. Thus, on his account coherence at least relates the right sort of thing to be involved in arguments. But to take this line would be in effect to concede that epistemic support need not take any inductive or deductive form, contrary to his first premise. Once this is conceded, there does not appear to be any reason for thinking that the supporting entities must nonetheless be of a kind suitable for being premises of an argument. And even if a reason were found, it could be accommodated by the suggestion of note 6 above.

[15] Ibid., p. 178.

Basic Nature of Epistemic Justification

epistemic support relation is a sort of coherence that can hold both among beliefs in a system and between a system of beliefs and constraining experiences. If so, then the best theory of justification would combine the core of coherentism with the core of foundationalism and have it that a belief is epistemically justified exactly when it is in a coherent system that coheres with the person's experiences.[16]

3. Thus characterized, the fundamental views of coherentism and foundationalism are compatible. It might appear otherwise, since the core of coherentism asserts that a cohering system of justified beliefs requires no autonomously justified belief, while the core of foundationalism asserts that a cohering system of beliefs is unjustified without appropriate experiential substantiation. There is no inconsistency in this. The core of coherentism denies a need for foundational *beliefs*. The core of foundationalism affirms a need for foundational *experiences*. Both can be true because experiences need not either consist in beliefs or be a topic of beliefs. A source of needless dispute between coherentists and foundationalists is the difficulty of classifying experiences within doxastic categories such as belief, judgment, and knowledge. The plausible part of each approach is not jeopardized by any reasonable classification. Reformulation always rehabilitates the core considerations. For instance, suppose what seems worst for the reconciling effort undertaken here: suppose that experiencing is always believing. This seems worst because the core of foundationalism counts such beliefs as necessary foundations while the core of coherentism denies any need for foundational beliefs. But if experiencing is believing, it must be believing of a very special sort. In typical straightforward cases of belief, a belief is a stable dispositional state that a person can express in language that he or she understands. Yet experiences seem to be undergone by as languageless and conceptually limited a being as a newborn kitten. Even among human adults, experiences are ordinarily fleeting events. Few sensory details can be recalled minutes later. Thus, if all experiences are beliefs, then some beliefs are extremely atypical. They are highly transitory states that can be undergone without the capacities to use language and to form judgments.

With these classificatory points in mind, consider what is plausible about the coherentist denial of a need for foundational "beliefs." The plausible basis for this denial is that there can be cohering systems of justified beliefs without any

---

[16] "Experience" is a handy generic term for conscious events of all sorts. It is worth mentioning that it would not be most reasonable simply to assume that only sensory events are foundational. For instance, justification in mathematics may be substantiated by some sort of nonsensory apprehension, and justification of moral judgments may be substantiated by apprehension of certain emotive responses.

external support consisting of beliefs of the *ordinary* sort. A person need not reflect on his or her experiences or formulate judgments about them in order to have a system of justified beliefs. There is no similar plausibility to the claim that a cohering system of beliefs would be justified, even if one's atypical, *experiential* beliefs fail to lend credence to the system. Suppose that a certain Mr. Jones has a system of cohering beliefs including that he sees just black and white objects illuminated by a white light, and that he is not hallucinating or otherwise deceived. Suppose too that Jones has a visual experience of phenomenal blue. Under these circumstances, the perceptual beliefs in Jones's system are not justified. Whether or not Jones has adopted any ordinary sort of belief about the experience of phenomenal blue, it renders unjustified his belief that all he sees is black or white.

Similarly, any foundationalist requirement to the effect that a justified belief have some appropriate doxastic foundation is defensible only if the foundation can be supplied by atypical, experiential beliefs. Certainly, not all clear cases of justified belief are reasonably thought to be accompanied by any standard belief about the contents of experience. The plausible sort of candidate for an experientially constituted necessary condition on justified belief is a condition met by ordinary experiences, which may be regarded as extraordinary beliefs.[17]

4. Would such a reconciliation retain everything plausible in coherentism and foundationalism? It might seem not. It might seem that the coherentist point of view essentially includes the doctrine that cohering beliefs are justified without any sort of foundation, while the foundationalist point of view essentially includes the doctrine that a belief with a proper foundation is justified even in the absence of any coherence with other things.

Coherentism and foundationalism are sometimes formulated to have conflicting implications. But their inclusion is not justified by what is plausible about the approaches.[18] The cases that indicate a role for coherence in the justification of a belief never contain experiences that are clearly unsuited to substantiate the cohering system. It is difficult to conceive of the bizarre

---

[17] Pollock makes a similar proposal about the epistemic role of experience (ibid., pp. 99–100). This strength of the foundationalist approach can be obscured by formulating foundationalism so as to require foundational *beliefs*. See e.g., Hilary Kornblith, "Beyond Foundationalism and the Coherence Theory," *The Journal of Philosophy*, 77 (October 1980), p. 600.

[18] On occasion, the conflicting implications have been added purely for the sake of insuring a conflict. For instance, James Cornman rejects a schema proposed by Keith Lehrer to isolate distinctively coherentist theories. Cornman's sole reason for the rejection is that the schema permits a cohering system to include what Cornman counts as foundational beliefs. (Lehrer's proposal is in *Knowledge* (Oxford: Oxford University Press, 1974), p. 162. Cornman's rejection of the proposal is in *Skepticism, Justification, and Explanation* (Dordrecht: D. Reidel, 1980), p. 132.)

possibilities where there are sufficient observational beliefs to constitute a convincingly coherent system while experience does not at least largely fit with the system. There is a strong inclination to smuggle appropriate experiences into the case by counting them as "observational beliefs" within the system. When we do what we can to consider a case where appropriate experiences really are absent, there is no credibility to the claim that the cohering beliefs are justified. Any such system fails to make sense of the person's own sensory states. Because of this, the system has the epistemic status of a fantasy.

Similarly, when an example clearly indicates a crucial role for experiential foundations in justification, it never contains justified beliefs in plainly incoherent combinations. Again it is difficult to evaluate the bizarre possibilities required. Only fairly elaborate systems of beliefs about the external world are clearly coherent or clearly incoherent.[19] All that the core of coherentism requires is that a justified belief be in *some* cohering system. Every belief is also in many motley sets of the person's beliefs, sets that do not constitute cohering systems. Furthermore, it is not plausible to require that a belief cohere with the members of the set of all of the other beliefs that the person has, in order to be in a cohering system that helps to justify the belief. Some people who are otherwise reasonable fall prey to superstitions without undermining the justification of all of their other beliefs. When superstitions are appropriately isolated from serious inquiries, the latter can yield coherent and justified systems of belief. Even a devout adherence to astrology does not ruin the justification of, say, a biologist's beliefs about heritability, unless astrological views are tangled into every line of defense that the biologist has for the biological beliefs.

These considerations render suspect any example about which it is claimed that experiential substantiation for a belief is present, coherence is absent, and yet the belief is justified. Suppose that Mr. Jones believes that the lights in his room are on. He is undergoing ordinary visual experiences of an illuminated room with no windows. So far, the belief appears to be justified. But suppose that Jones also believes that there is no power available to supply electricity,

---

[19] External-world beliefs are the main topic of the dispute between coherentists and foundationalists. It might seem that in the case of beliefs about the *internal* world, unalloyed foundationalism is most plausible. For instance, it might seem that no coherence is needed to justify a belief ascribing to oneself awareness of some phenomenal quality. After all, it was claimed above (pp. 39–40) as part of the core of foundationalism that coherence among beliefs is neither necessary for experience to constrain which beliefs are justified nor sufficient to justify ascription to oneself of an experience that is not actually undergone. But even first-person phenomenal quality beliefs are not plausibly held to be justified in the absence of all coherence. Any plausible view will imply that such beliefs are justified only when they cohere with an experience of the phenomenal quality, thus requiring at least a minimal "coherent system" (in the broad sense indicated on p. 43 above).

and that the lights are electrical. These three beliefs do not form a coherent system. But this is not a conclusive fact about the coherence of Jones's beliefs about lights in the room. The presence or absence of the right sort of coherence also depends on what else Jones thinks. Suppose that he also thinks that there are lights on when things look as they do to him and his eyes are working normally, that his eyes are working normally, and that he may be wrong about the power. Then it is clear enough that Jones is justified in thinking that the lights in his room are on. But this case is not evidence against a need for coherence to justify such a belief. The latter beliefs may supply the main elements of a coherent system. Suppose therefore that Jones does not have the latter beliefs, nor any replacements that link his experiences to the belief that the lights are on. It is no longer clear that his visual experiences, or anything else, suffices to justify the belief. Why does Jones conclude that the lights are on rather than, say, that illuminating rays are issuing from his eyes? In ordinary cases the answer would involve at least tacit cognizance of linking propositions about conditions under which vision is possible when outdoor light sources are obstructed. But to impute any such tacit beliefs would undermine our attempt to assure ourselves that there is no cohering system of beliefs supporting the judgment that the lights are on. Yet in the absence of linking assumptions the case is not sufficiently clear-cut to offer evidence for the possibility of experiential justification of a belief without a coherent belief system.

The example illustrates the general point that the cases that support the foundationalist approach do not really show that foundational experiences can justify external world beliefs in the absence of coherence with other beliefs. More generally, when one approach is supported by a case, the other approach is not threatened. In order for a theory to capture all that is right about both coherentism and foundationalism, it must imply that both coherence with some system of belief and a foundation in experience are separately necessary and jointly sufficient for the justification of a belief.

We have seen ways to overcome the main apparent obstacles to a theory that incorporates what is plausible about coherentism and foundationalism. It is time to seek the same for the other two principal contemporary approaches to the nature of epistemic justification.

Externalism and Internalism

1. The externalist approach locates some important feature of a belief's justification outside the mind of the one whose belief is justified. For instance,

the simplest reliabilist sort of external theory has it that a belief is justified whenever it is produced by a belief-forming mechanism that reliably produces true beliefs.[20] The fact that a reliable mechanism has produced a given belief may be something that the person has no grounds to believe. Still, according to simple reliabilism this external fact implies the belief to be justified.

The internalist approach consists in requiring that a person whose belief is justified have cognitive access to a justification for the belief. The justification is "internal" to the person's mental life. For instance, a Cartesian sort of internalist theory has it that a belief is justified only when the belief provides its own justification or the person apprehends a proof of the belief from self-justifying premises. The justification is wholly accessible to reflective inquiry.

Again there is the appearance of a conflict between two approaches to the nature of justification. If a justification can depend on external features of the case, how can it also be that every justified belief has a cognitively accessible justification? We have a reconciling answer to this question if justification is determined by both external and internal factors with enough allowed to be external to bear out externalism and enough required to be internal to bear out internalism. To see how external and internal contributions are most plausibly held to be distributed, let us try to identify the strongest grounds for adopting each approach.

The best support for externalism derives from considerations like these: Ordinary people routinely acquire numerous justified perceptual beliefs. But if some normal nonphilosopher, e.g., Mr. Jones, were asked to provide some justification for thinking that a certain one of his perceptual beliefs is true, very likely he would be at a loss about what to use and how to use it. If he sees and recognizes a table under favorable observation conditions, then it is quite plausible that he is justified in believing that he sees a table. But there need not be anything that he regards as his justification for the belief. Yet he may not think that it needs none. In all likelihood Jones has no opinion at all on such matters, nor does he have a view about some epistemic link between the sensory experiences that give rise to his belief and the belief itself, nor about how well the belief coheres with others that he has. Such examples make it reasonable to

---

[20] The classic statement of this sort of view is by Alvin Goldman in "What Is Justified Belief?" *Justification and Knowledge*, George Pappas, ed. (Dordrecht: D. Reidel 1979), pp. 1–24. As will become evident, the simple reliabilism that I have just described goes way beyond what I count as the plausible core of externalism about justification. But it is noteworthy that there is no need to dispute here the theory that Goldman ultimately defends in this paper. On p. 18 he asserts that he offers reliability conditions to explain, not justified belief, but rather what we take to be justified belief. Such a thesis is independent of the facts about what actually justifies belief, and only the latter is the topic of the present paper.

conclude that a belief can be justified while the person has no idea what does the justifying, or how. These epistemic facts can be external to the mental life of someone whose beliefs are justified.

Lawrence BonJour appears in effect to dispute this externalism.[21] In BonJour's view, the principle that generates the best epistemic regress argument is this: A person's belief is epistemically justified only if the person justifiably believes premises that constitute a justifying argument for the belief. BonJour endorses this principle. Indeed, it is fundamental to his attack on foundationalist theories. Thus, he requires anyone who has a justified belief to be in a position to offer an argument for the belief. This appears to preclude the possibility that the person is ignorant of what justifies the belief, and thus to conflict with the externalism defended here.

The best epistemic regress arguments do not rely on BonJour's principle. There is no reason to suppose that *every* justified belief depends for its justification on justified premises. Epistemic regresses loom only in those cases where it appears that a justified belief does depend for its justification on other things that must also be justified. All it takes to stop any such regress in a reasonable way is to identify a condition that both is sufficient for any belief's justification and does not include any endless sequence. We have found this in the justification provided by coherence with other beliefs and experiences. In such a view, each justified belief is justified in virtue of its coherence with the rest of these clearly finite elements. A person can have a belief that is thus justified without being cognizant of this sort of epistemic fact. So the externalism defended here is not jeopardized by a problematic regress.[22]

The best grounds for accepting internalism derive from considerations like these: A person has a justified belief only if the person has reflective access to

---

[21] "Can Empirical Knowledge Have a Foundation?", *American Philosophical Quarterly*, 15 (1978) p. 7.

[22] The externalism advocated here is compatible with the most plausible *interpretation* of BonJour's regress-generating principle. So even those who find the principle plausible need not contest this externalism. Note that BonJour himself holds that the relevant justifying argument may only be "available" to the person; he denies that everyone who has a justified belief need rehearse some such argument or even need be able to identify one without substantial reflective investigation (ibid., p. 2). If we add to these sensible qualifications two other broadening conditions that have been advocated above, the resulting reading of the principle allows a person's justification to include all of the defended external elements. We need add only that the premises may assert "beliefs" in a sense in which all experiencing is believing, and that the "argument" may support a justified belief in virtue of an epistemic relation beyond deductive and inductive validity. The resulting reading of the principle allows that a justification is not regarded as such and not otherwise epistemically appreciated. The reading allows experiences to be beliefs that are justified by arguing for themselves and help to justify external world beliefs by arguing for them in concert with the support afforded by the beliefs' presence in a cohering system of beliefs. So construed, BonJour's principle does not conflict with what has been held here to be plausible about externalism.

evidence that the belief is true. A telling epistemic difference between my justified belief that I see a pen and my increasingly unjustified opinion that the pen contains plenty of ink to finish this draft is that I am aware of things that give me good evidence that I see a pen, while I have no good evidence that much ink remains in it. (The transparent plastic barrel now looks clear of ink all the way down.) Perhaps my judgment about ample ink happens to have been caused by a mechanism that reliably produces true beliefs.[23] Still, I am not epistemically justified in making this judgment because I have no good evidence that it is true. Such examples make it reasonable to conclude that there is epistemic justification for a belief only where the person has cognitive access to evidence that supports the truth of the belief. Justifying evidence must be internally available.

This gives short shrift to reliabilism. That is appropriate here, because reliabilism is not a plausible form of externalism. It is not even initially credible to claim that a belief-producing mechanism's reliability always contributes to a resulting belief's justification. One way to see this implausibility is to compare the justificatory contributions of pure reliability with those of some egregious appeal to authority. Even the worst appeals to authority advert to someone who at least appears to be an authority about something, thus providing some epistemic excuse for heeding the appeal. In contrast to this, a reliably formed belief may provide no excuse for believing it. It can be a pure shot in the dark. The person who holds the belief need not have epistemic grounds for accepting the belief. The sheer reliability of the cause of a belief provides no epistemic support for taking the proposition to be true, though of course a person who has evidence that the cause is reliable does have that epistemic support for the belief. This epistemic role of *confirmed* reliability is all that reliability is plausibly held to contribute to epistemic justification. Since this paper advocates a reconciliation among approaches to the nature of epistemic justification by identifying what is plausible in each, and there is nothing plausible about distinctively reliabilistic forms of externalism, the reconciling view has no place for them.[24]

David Annis appears in effect to dispute the evidential internalism advocated here.[25] He maintains that there are contexts where no reasons at all are required

---

[23] This is not likely. The sorry fact is that I cling to my belief that ample ink remains in the pen on the practical ground that it gives me some slight comfort, while its denial would bother me. Replacing the pen would—I should rather say "will soon"—necessitate an inconvenient excursion. (It did.)

[24] For a more extensive illustration of the implausibility of reliability as a factor contributing to justification, see Lawrence BonJour's "Externalist Theories of Empirical Knowledge," *Midwest Studies in Philosophy*, vol. 5 (1980); Stewart Cohen's "Justification and Truth," *Philosophical Studies*, vol. 46 (1984), pp. 279-95.

[25] See "A Contextualist Theory of Epistemic Justification," *American Philosophical Quarterly*, 15 (1978), pp. 213-19.

in order for certain beliefs to be justified. To defend this view, he offers the example of Jones looking in a furniture store for a new red chair:

Mr. Jones who has the necessary perceptual concepts and normal vision, points at a red chair a few feet in front of him and says "here is a red one."[26]

Annis claims that Jones thereby asserts a justified belief.

It should be conceded that Jones is justified in believing the chair he designates to be red, even though he may lack any reason for believing it. This can be consistently acknowledged by one who accepts the advocated core of internalism. Having reasons is one thing; having evidence is another, independent thing. The reasons that a person has for holding a belief in the sense in which Jones obviously has none are the considerations taken by the person to count in favor of holding the belief. With reasons thus understood, it is clear that in the example Jones may have no reason for his belief. He need not regard himself as having any support for it. But the internalism defended here does not imply that justified beliefs are backed by such reasons. All that is required is cognitive access to evidence which in fact epistemically supports the belief. The justifying evidence need not be taken as such, and so it need not be a reason for holding the belief. Jones does have justifying evidence in the example. He has the visual evidence of seeing a red chair. (Annis does not actually say that Jones ever sees the chair, but surely that is supposed to be part of the example.) Thus, both Annis's ascription of justification to Jones in this example, and his general point about the possibility of justification without reasons, are compatible with the defended core of internalism.

2. The best way to combine the strengths identified in externalism and internalism is straightforward. What can be external to the mind of a person whose belief is justified, i.e., inaccessible to the person by reflection, are epistemological facts about what evidence provides the person's justification and about the nature of the epistemic link of the belief to its justifying evidence. What must be internal, i.e., accessible to the person by reflection, is evidence that does in fact suffice to justify the belief.

3. Again it might seem that the proposed reconciliation leaves out something basic to one or the other of two rival approaches. Is it not basic to the externalist point of view that all justifying factors might be wholly external? Is it not basic to the internalist point of view that all justifying factors must be internal?

---

[26] See "A Contextualist Theory of Epistemic Justification," *American Philosophical Quarterly*, 15 (1978), p. 216.

Basic Nature of Epistemic Justification

The stronger views suggested by these questions go beyond what makes each approach seem right. It is an implausible excess to allow that justification might be entirely external. The examples supporting external justifying factors are ones where someone is unable to recognize and use evidence to argue for the truth of a justified belief. In all such cases internal factors, especially sensory events, give every appearance of playing a justifying role. These same examples show that it would be excessively internalistic to insist that a belief is justified only when the person can identify and explain its justification. What supports the core of internalism is the correlation between cases of justified belief and cases where the person has justifying evidence which is cognitively accessible. It is reasonable to conclude that the apportioning of internal and external factors that has been proposed here captures what is plausible in internalism and externalism.

A Comprehensive Unification

We have seen the way that coherentism and foundationalism are best combined and the way that externalism and internalism are best combined. It is time to determine how the two combined views—call them "foundational coherentism" and "external internalism"—are best combined. Foundational coherentism is about a structural property of the relation of a belief to its justification. It asserts that a justified belief must be in a cohering system of beliefs that coheres with experience. External internalism is about the position occupied by justifying factors in or out of the mind. It asserts that the mental life of a person who has a justified belief must include justifying evidence, though the person need not have cognitive access to the epistemic facts about what does the justifying and how it works. These two views are best combined on the basis of three plausible claims about interrelationships. The first claim makes room for externalism, asserting that the presence of an appropriate coherence does not imply that the person is able to become aware of it or aware of its capacity to justify. The second claim makes room for foundational coherentism, asserting that justifying evidence always consists in some portion of a cohering system of beliefs and experiential foundations. The third claim concedes to internalism that we can discover by reflection those of our mental states that are in fact a justification for each of our justified beliefs. The first claim insures that the epistemic fact that a justification is afforded by certain evidence and the epistemic facts about how the evidence justifies can be inaccessible by reflection. The second and third claims imply that a justifying coherence exists within

Earl Conee

systems of belief and between such systems and experiences exactly when the person has reflective access to what is in fact justifying evidence for the beliefs in the system.

Foundational coherentism and internal externalism thus can be plausibly accommodated in a single theory.[27]

---

[27] I am grateful for comments on previous drafts from Robert Audi, John Bennett, Eva Bodanszky, Richard Feldman, Hilary Kornblith, Stefan Sencerz, Ernest Sosa, and participants in a colloquium at Hobart and William Smith Colleges.

3
Internalism Defended
Earl Conee and Richard Feldman

Internalism in epistemology has been getting bad press lately. Externalism is ascendant, partly because insurmountable problems for internalism are supposed to have been identified.[1] We oppose this trend. In our view the purported problems pose no serious threat, and a convincing argument for internalism is untouched by the recent criticism.

Our main goal here is to refute objections to internalism. We begin by offering what we think is the best way to understand the distinction between internalism and externalism. We then present a new argument for internalism. We proceed to consider and reject defenses of internalism based on the premise that epistemic justification is a deontological concept. This frees internalism from what we regard as suspect deontological underpinnings. Finally we reply to what we take to be the most significant objections to internalism.

In our view the primary strength of internalism consists in the merits of a specific internalist theory, evidentialism, which holds that epistemic justification is entirely a matter of internal evidential factors. We shall not concentrate on evidentialism here, however, beyond making an occasional positive observation about it. We respond to the objections largely on behalf of internalism in general. It is a resourceful perspective that makes room for a variety of reasonable responses to the objections.

An earlier version of this paper was presented at The Creighton Club, where William Alston commented, and to the University of Rochester philosophy department. We are grateful to Alston and to both audiences for their comments.

[1] For a summary of the current state of epistemology that illustrates this sort of view, see Philip Kitcher, "The Naturalists Return," *The Philosophical Review*, 101 (1992): 53–114.

Earl Conee and Richard Feldman

1. What is Internalism?

Internalism and externalism are views about which states, events, and conditions can contribute to epistemic justification—the sort of justification that, in sufficient strength, is a necessary condition for knowledge. Use of the terms "internalist" and "externalist" to classify theories of justification is a recent development, and the terms are routinely applied to theories that predate their use. Thus, many proponents of theories of justification have not classified their views as internalist or externalist. The recent literature is therefore the best source of information about the nature of the distinction. Here are a few examples of how internalism has been identified. Laurence BonJour writes:

> The most generally accepted account... is that a theory of justification is *internalist* if and only if it requires that all of the factors needed for a belief to be epistemically justified for a given person be *cognitively accessible* to that person, internal to his cognitive perspective.[2]

Robert Audi writes:

> Some examples suggest that justification is grounded entirely in what is internal to the mind, in a sense implying that it is accessible to introspection or reflection by the subject—a view we might call *internalism about justification*.[3]

Alvin Plantinga writes:

> The basic thrust of internalism in epistemology, therefore, is that the properties that confer warrant upon a belief are properties to which the believer has some special sort of epistemic access.[4]

Matthias Steup characterizes internalism as follows:

> What makes an account of justification internalist is that it imposes a certain condition on those factors that determine whether a belief is justified. Such factors—let's call them "J-factors"—can be beliefs, experiences, or epistemic standards. The condition in question requires J-factors to be *internal to the subject's mind* or, to put it differently, *accessible on reflection*.[5]

---

[2] Laurence BonJour, "Externalism/Internalism," in Jonathan Dancy and Ernest Sosa, eds., *A Companion to Epistemology* (Oxford: Blackwell Publishers, 1992), p. 132.

[3] Robert Audi, *Epistemology: A Contemporary Introduction to the Theory of Knowledge* (New York: Routledge, 1998), pp. 233–4. Emphasis in the original.

[4] Alvin Plantinga, *Warrant: The Current Debate* (Oxford: Oxford University Press, 1993), p. 6. A very similar formulation appears in William Harper, "Paper Mache Problems in Epistemology: A Defense of Strong Internalism," *Synthese*, 116 (1998): 27–49. See p. 28.

[5] Matthias Steup, *An Introduction to Contemporary Epistemology* (Upper Saddle River, NJ: Prentice-Hall, 1996), p. 84. Emphasis in the original.

Internalism Defended

John Pollock writes that:

Internalism in epistemology is the view that only internal states of the cognizer can be relevant in determining which of the cognizer's beliefs are justified.[6]

Finally, Ernest Sosa characterizes one version of internalism this way:

Justification requires only really proper thought on the part of the subject: if a believer has obtained and sustains his belief through wholly appropriate thought, then the believer is justified in so believing—where the appropriateness of the thought is a matter purely internal to the mind of the subject, and not dependent on what lies beyond.[7]

We find two distinct but closely related characterizations of internalism in passages such as these. One characterization uses a notion of access. What we shall call "accessibilism" holds that the epistemic justification of a person's belief is determined by things to which the person has some special sort of access. BonJour calls this access a "suitable awareness."[8] Audi says that the access is through "introspection or reflection." Others say that the access must be "direct."[9]

The quotations from Steup, Pollock, and Sosa suggest a somewhat different account. They suggest that internalism is the view that a person's beliefs are justified only by things that are internal to the person's mental life. We shall call this version of internalism "mentalism."[10] A mentalist theory may assert that justification is determined entirely by occurrent mental factors, or by dispositional ones as well. As long as the things that are said to contribute to justification are in the person's mind, the view qualifies as a version of mentalism.

We think it likely that philosophers have not separated mentalism from accessibilism because they have tacitly assumed that the extensions of the two do not differ in any significant way. They have assumed that the special kind of access on which many internalist theories rely can reach only mental items, and

---

[6] John Pollock, "At the Interface of Philosophy and AI," in John Greco and Ernest Sosa, eds., *The Blackwell Guide to Epistemology* (Malden, MA: Blackwell, 1999), pp. 383–414. The quotation is from p. 394.

[7] Ernest Sosa, "Skepticism and the Internal/External Divide," *The Blackwell Guide to Epistemology*, pp. 145–57. The quotation is from p. 147. Sosa goes on to describe another version of internalism that highlights accessibility.

[8] Laurence BonJour, "The Dialectic of Foundationalism and Coherentism," *The Blackwell Guide to Epistemology*, pp. 117–42. The quotation is from p. 118.

[9] William Alston, "Internalism and Externalism in Epistemology," reprinted in William Alston, *Epistemic Justification: Essays in the Theory of Knowledge* (Ithaca, Cornell University Press, 1989), pp. 185–226. See p. 186.

[10] Steup describes internalism as both mentalism and accessibilism in the passage quoted. Pollock does not make explicit that the internal states to which he refers must be mental states. However, it is reasonable to assume that this is what he has in mind.

perhaps all mental items, or at least all that might be counted as playing a role in justification.

We think that simplicity and clarity are best served by understanding internalism as mentalism. "Internalism" is a recent technical term. It has been introduced to refer to a variety of theories in epistemology that share some vaguely defined salient feature. Any definition of the term is to some extent stipulative. Mentalism codifies one standard way in which the word has been used.

Somewhat more precisely, internalism as we characterize it is committed to the following two theses. The first asserts the strong supervenience of epistemic justification on the mental:

S   The justificatory status of a person's doxastic attitudes strongly supervenes on the person's occurrent and dispositional mental states, events, and conditions.

The second thesis spells out a principal implication of S:

M   If any two possible individuals are exactly alike mentally, then they are alike justificationally, e.g., the same beliefs are justified for them to the same extent.[11]

(M) implies that mental duplicates in different possible worlds have the same attitudes justified for them. This cross world comparison follows from the strong supervenience condition in (S).[12] Externalists characteristically hold that differences in justification can result from contingent non-mental differences, such as differing causal connections or reliability. Theories that appeal to such factors clearly deny (S) and (M). Thus, our way of spelling out the internalism/externalism distinction properly classifies characteristically externalist views.

(M) implies that mental duplicates in two different possible worlds have the same beliefs justified for them. The significance of this can be illustrated by considering a view William Alston has defended. Alston held that for a belief

---

[11] It has become standard to distinguish between an existing belief (or other attitude) being justified and a person being justified in believing (or having another attitude toward) a proposition whether or not the person actually believes it (or has that attitude). We shall use phrases such as "justified belief" to refer to beliefs that are justified and we shall say of a person that he or she is justified in believing a proposition when we mean to say that the latter relation obtains. This distinction will not play a significant role in the discussion that follows. As stated, (S) and (M) are about the justification of existing attitudes. They could easily be reformulated to state internalist constraints on the conditions under which a person is justified in having a particular attitude.

[12] Whether (M) implies (S) depends upon details of the supervenience relation which we will not discuss here.

to be justified the believer must have internal grounds that make the belief "objectively probable."[13] If actual frequencies of association, or something else external to the mind and contingent, can make Alston's objective probability vary while the internal grounds remain the same, then his theory is a kind of externalism by our standards. But if it is necessary that the same grounds make the same beliefs objectively probable, then Alston's theory conforms to (M) and qualifies as a version of internalism. This seems exactly right: it is internalism if and only if contingent factors external to the mind cannot make an epistemic difference.

One advantage of our way of understanding the distinction between internalism and externalism in epistemology is that it closely parallels the counterpart distinctions in the philosophy of mind and ethics.[14] In the philosophy of mind case, the main idea is to distinguish the view that the contents of attitudes depend entirely on things within a person's own cognitive apparatus from the view that there are factors external to the person that help to determine attitudinal content. Mind internalism is naturally rendered as a supervenience thesis. Roughly, the thesis is that a person's mental content supervenes on the person's "purely internal" states, conditions, and events. The relevant supervenience base cannot be specified as "the mental," as we have done for epistemic internalism, since a person's mental states, events, and conditions are trivially sufficient for the person's attitudes with their specific contents. But the root idea is the same. The mind internalist is trying to exclude such plainly external factors as the environmental causal origins of the person's attitudes and their social milieu. Likewise, the epistemic internalist is principally opposed to the existence of any justification determining role for plainly external factors such as the general accuracy of the mechanism that produces a given belief or the belief's environmental origin. Mentalism bears this out.

What internalism in epistemology and philosophy of mind have in common is that being in some condition which is of philosophical interest—being epistemically justified in certain attitudes, or having attitudes with certain contents—is settled by what goes on inside of cognitive beings. The condition of interest is in this sense an "internal" matter, thus justifying the use of the term. Mentalism obviously captures this feature of internalism. Accessibilism

---

[13] William Alston, "An Internalist Externalism," in *Epistemic Justification: Essays in the Theory of Knowledge*, pp. 227–45. See esp. p. 232.

[14] Not all philosophers who make this sort of comparison seek an account of internalism with this advantage. James Pryor takes internalism to be accessibilism, notes that internalism in the philosophy of mind is a supervenience thesis, and concludes that the two kinds of internalism are dissimilar. See "Highlights of Recent Epistemology," *British Journal for the Philosophy of Science*, 52 (2001): 95–124.

captures it only when conjoined with the further thesis that what is relevantly accessible is always internal to something, presumably, the mind.[15]

Internalism in ethics is analogous, but significantly different. It is roughly the view that accepting a moral obligation to act in a certain way entails being motivated to act in that way.[16] This cannot be understood as a supervenience thesis concerning what is inside a person. Being motivated is an internal state on all accounts. Rather, ethical internalism holds that the motivation is "inside" of something much less extensive, namely, the accepting of a moral obligation. The pertinent supervenience thesis is consequently about a much narrower supervenience base. The thesis is roughly the claim that any individuals under any possible circumstances who accept that they have a moral obligation to act in a certain way have some motivation to act in that way.

One modest asset of viewing internalism as mentalism is that it renders readily intelligible the nominal connection of epistemic internalism to mind internalism and ethical internalism. A much stronger consideration in favor of mentalism itself is that it turns out to be entirely defensible, as we shall try to show.

It is worth noting the methodological neutrality of the internalism/externalism distinction as we interpret it. With internalism understood as mentalism, there is no direct connection between internalism and any view about *a priori* knowledge. In particular, internalism does not imply that epistemic principles are *a priori*.[17] This same methodological independence goes the other way as well. Externalists hold that some justificatory differences have an extramental basis. This does not imply that we must discover empirically which extramental factors make that difference.

II. A Defense of Internalism

Our argument for internalism focuses on pairs of examples that we take to be representative. Either in one member of the pair someone has a justified belief in a proposition while in the other someone else's belief in that proposition is not justified, or the one person's belief is better justified than the other's.[18]

---

[15] In "Skepticism and the Internal/External Divide," Sosa considers and rejects an argument that has mentalism as a premise and accessibilism as its conclusion. See pp. 146–8.

[16] See David Brink, *Moral Realism and the Foundations of Ethics* (Cambridge: Cambridge University Press, 1989), pp. 37–50 for details and references.

[17] Some internalists do believe that epistemology is entirely an *a priori*, or at least an armchair, matter. See most notably Roderick Chisholm, *Theory of Knowledge*, 3rd edition (Englewood Cliffs, NJ: Prentice-Hall, 1989), pp. 76–7.

[18] Some of the examples contrast what one person is justified in believing with what another person is justified in believing.

Internalism Defended

We contend that these contrasts are best explained by supposing that internal differences make the epistemic difference. Here are the examples.

Example 1   Bob and Ray are sitting in an air-conditioned hotel lobby reading yesterday's newspaper. Each has read that it will be very warm today and, on that basis, each believes that it is very warm today. Then Bob goes outside and feels the heat. They both continue to believe that it is very warm today. But at this point Bob's belief is better justified.

Comment: Bob's justification for the belief was enhanced by his experience of feeling the heat, and thus undergoing a mental change which so to speak "internalized" the actual temperature. Ray had just the forecast to rely on.

Example 2   After going out and feeling very warm, Bob goes back in and tells Ray of the feeling. Here are two versions of relevant details:

(2a) Bob is in fact a pillar of integrity, but Ray has no reason to think so. As far as Ray can tell, it is just as likely that Bob is trying to deceive him as that Bob is telling the truth.

(2b) Bob is a pillar of integrity, and Ray has observed and recalls many examples of Bob's honesty and none of dishonesty.

In example (2b) Ray's belief that it is very warm becomes more strongly justified after he hears from Bob. In example (2a) hearing from Bob does not affect the strength of Ray's justification for his belief.

Comment: Bob's honesty, something out of Ray's ken in (2a), has become "internalized" by Ray in (2b). Bob's integrity made no justificatory difference to Ray's belief until it was suitably brought into Ray's mind.

Example 3   A novice bird watcher and an expert are together looking for birds. They both get a good look at a bird in a nearby tree. (In order to avoid irrelevant complexities, we can assume that their visual presentations are exactly alike.) Upon seeing the bird, the expert immediately knows that it is a woodpecker. The expert has fully reasonable beliefs about what woodpeckers look like. The novice has no good reason to believe that it is a woodpecker and is not justified in believing that it is.

Comment: The epistemic difference between novice and expert arises from something that differentiates the two internally. The expert knows the look of a woodpecker. The novice would gain the same justification as the expert if the novice came to share the expert's internal condition concerning the look of woodpeckers.

Earl Conee and Richard Feldman

Example 4 A logic TA and a beginning logic student are looking over a homework assignment. One question displays a sentence that they both know to express a truth and asks whether certain other sentences are true as well. The TA can easily tell through simple reflection that some of the other sentences express logical consequences of the original sentence and thus she is justified in believing that they are true as well. The student is clueless.

Comment: Again there is an internal difference between the two. The difference is that the TA has justification for her beliefs to the effect that certain propositions validly follow from the original one. She is expert enough to "see" that the conclusions follow without performing any computations. This case differs from example 3 in that here the mental difference concerns cognizance of necessary truths of logic whereas in example 3 the expert was cognizant of contingent facts about visual characteristics of woodpeckers. But just as in example 3, relevant internal differences make the difference. The beginning student could come to share the epistemic state of the TA by coming to share the TA's familiarity with the logical consequence relation.

Example 5 Initially Smith has excellent reasons to believe that Jones, who works in his office, owns a Ford. Smith deduces that someone in the office owns a Ford. The latter belief is true, but the former is false. Smith's reasons derive from Jones pretending to own a Ford. Someone else in the office, unknown to Smith, does own a Ford. The fact that Jones is merely simulating Ford ownership keeps Smith from knowing that someone in his office is a Ford owner, but it does not prevent Smith from being justified or diminish his justification. At a later time Smith gains ample reason to believe that Jones is pretending. At that point Smith is not justified in believing either that Jones owns a Ford or that someone in his office owns a Ford.

Comment: Again the epistemic change occurs when a suitable external fact—this time, the fact that what Smith has seen is Jones pretending to own a Ford—is brought into Smith's mind. The difference between Smith being justified in believing that Jones owns a Ford (and that someone in the office owns a Ford) in the one case and not in the other is an internal change in Smith.

Example 6 Hilary is a brain in a vat who has been abducted recently from a fully embodied life in an ordinary environment. He is being stimulated so that it seems to him as though his normal life has continued. Hilary believes that he ate oatmeal for breakfast yesterday. His memorial basis for his breakfast belief is artificial. It has been induced by his envatters. Here are two versions of relevant details.

(6a) Hilary's recollection is very faint and lacking in detail. The meal seems incongruous to him in that it strikes him as a distasteful breakfast and he has no idea why he would have eaten it.

(6b) Hilary's recollection seems to him to be an ordinary vivid memory of a typical breakfast for him.

Comment: Although in both (6a) and (6b) Hilary's breakfast belief is false and its basis is abnormal, the belief is not well justified in (6a) and it is well justified in (6b). Hilary in (6a) differs internally from Hilary in (6b). His mental states in (6b) include better evidence for the belief in (6b) than he has in (6a).

In the first five of these examples the location of a relevant item of information—in the mind of a subject or outside of it—makes the epistemic difference. In the sixth example, a purely internal difference is decisive. It is reasonable to generalize from these examples to the conclusion that every variety of change that brings about or enhances justification either internalizes an external fact or makes a purely internal difference. It appears that there is no need to appeal to anything extramental to explain any justificatory difference. These considerations argue for the general internalist thesis that these epistemic differences have an entirely mental origin. In each case, the mental difference is a difference in the evidence that the person has. Variations in its presence or strength correspond to the differences in justification. Evidentialism thus provides the best explanation of the epistemic status of beliefs in these pairs.

We have no proof that there is no exception to the pattern exhibited by our examples. The argument does not establish that internalism or evidentialism is true. It does support these views. Further support will emerge from successful replies to objections. We shall soon turn to those objections and replies.

III. Internalism and Deontology

According to deontological conceptions of epistemic justification, one has a justified belief in a proposition when one deserves praise (or does not deserve blame) for having the belief or when it is one's duty or obligation to believe that proposition (or believing it violates no duty or obligation). Alvin Goldman, Alvin Plantinga, William Alston, and other leading critics of internalism have thought that the central argument for internalism relies on the premise that epistemic justification is a deontological concept. Plantinga speaks for many of these critics when he writes, "It is really this deontological feature of the classical conception of justification that leads to the internalist result."[19] We deny

---

[19] Plantinga, *Warrant: The Current Debate*, p. 15.

that internalism depends on a deontological conception of justification. In describing and assessing the beliefs in the examples of section II, we did not say anything about what the individuals had a duty or obligation to believe, what they were permitted to believe, or what they might be praised or blamed for believing. There might be deontological truths of these sorts. What we are rejecting are arguments for internalism based on the idea that epistemic concepts are to be analyzed in these deontological terms. In this section we will briefly address three versions of such arguments.[20]

Goldman criticizes an argument that is supposed to establish internalism partly on the basis of a premise asserting the deontological nature of justification.[21] The argument he discusses goes approximately as follows:

Justification is a matter of not violating any epistemic duties. One can have duties only if the facts that make it the case that one has these duties are facts that one can know. Therefore these facts must be internal facts, since one might not be in a position to know external facts. Thus, the justifiers[22]—roughly, the facts that make a belief justified—must be internal facts.

It is difficult to find much to recommend in this argument. One can know external facts. So, as Goldman points out, the premise that duties depend upon what one can know does not rule out the possibility that they can depend on external facts.[23] Furthermore, since on all accounts knowledge depends on external factors such as the truth of the known proposition, people internally alike can know different things. The assumption that one's duties depend upon what one knows does not imply that people who are internally alike must have the same duties. This leaves open the possibility that different things are justified for people who are internally alike. Thus, we agree with Goldman that no good argument for internalism can be found among these considerations.

It might be thought that these problems can be avoided by framing the argument in terms of justification, avoiding reference to knowledge. The new argument begins with the assumption that one has a duty to do something if and only if one is justified in believing that one has the duty. With the added

---

[20] We suspect that deontological arguments for internalism are more the work of internalism's critics than its supporters. However, one can find defenses of versions of the arguments below in Carl Ginet's *Knowledge, Perception, and Memory* (Dordrecht: D. Reidel, 1975), pp. 36–7 and in Mathias Steup's "A Defense of Internalism," in Louis Pojman, ed., *The Theory of Knowledge: Classical and Contemporary Readings*, 2nd edition (Belmont, CA: Wadsworth, 1999), pp. 373–84. See esp. pp. 375–6.

[21] Alvin Goldman, "Internalism Exposed," *The Journal of Philosophy*, 96 (1999): 271–93. See section I.

[22] Though it does not affect our assessment of this argument, the term "justifiers" can make trouble. We discuss the potential problem in section IV part A.

[23] Goldman, "Internalism Exposed," p. 288.

Internalism Defended

premise the beliefs in the same duties are justified for those who are internally alike, it follows that those who are internally alike have the same duties. Making use of the deontological assumption that justification is a matter of not violating any epistemic duties, it can be inferred that the same beliefs are justified for those who are internally alike.

The premise in this argument asserting that beliefs in the same duties are justified for those who are internally alike needs some defense. Why would beliefs specifically about duties always be justified on purely internal grounds? In the absence of a special reason, this assumption seems acceptable only as an implication of the full generality that people internally alike are justified in believing the same things. So as it stands this argument depends for its cogency on the characteristic internalist claim that people internally alike have the same justified beliefs. The argument therefore relies on internalism rather than establishing it.

A third and final deontological argument for internalism focuses on blame.[24] It might be assumed that epistemic justification is a matter of blameless belief, and that people who are internally alike are alike in what they can be blamed for. So, people who are internally alike will have the same blameless beliefs, and thus the same justified beliefs.

This argument's initial assumption is clearly incorrect. Blameless belief is not always justified. Someone who innocently held a belief as a result of external manipulation or psychological compulsion would be blameless in holding this belief.[25] Nevertheless, if the belief is induced directly and the person has good reason to deny the belief and no reason to believe it, then it is clearly not a justified belief.[26] Also, justified beliefs are not always blameless. Someone who, for barely adequate epistemic reasons, accepts that a friend has been malicious is epistemically justified in that belief. But such a person may be blameworthy for having insufficient trust in the friend.

We agree with the critics that there is no cogent argument for internalism that relies on deontological premises. However, the failure of these arguments

---

[24] In some passages Plantinga seems to have an argument like this in mind. See Plantinga, *Warrant: The Current Debate*, chapter 1, section IV.

[25] We also doubt that people are to be blamed for their beliefs in more routine cases of unjustified belief. This depends in large part upon whether blame applies only in cases of voluntary action and whether belief is voluntary in such cases. It may be that ordinary unjustified beliefs are often results of processes that are irresistible, at least in the short term, and consequently the resulting beliefs are not blameworthy.

[26] The assumption that people internally alike are to be blamed for the same things is also questionable. Two people could end up in the same internal state as a result of different factors. One might have gotten there through negligence, such as not pursuing important leads concerning some significant proposition. Some internalists would say that the negligent one might deserve blame for the resulting belief. We note also that (M) allows internalists to make justificatory use of historical mental states. The people in this example need not be classified as internally alike, since they differ mentally at earlier times.

shows no weakness in internalism. The internalist position is independently well supported. In our view the case for internalism rests primarily on the strengths of its best versions, and as we say, our favorite candidate is evidentialism. These strengths include its explanatory capacities, such as its capacity to account for the epistemic differences in the pairs of examples discussed in section II, and its resistance to objections.

IV. Objections and Replies

The objections that we shall consider fall into two broad and overlapping categories. One sensible general description of internalist theories is that they say that a belief B is justified just in case there is some combination of internal states—typically featuring an experience or another justified belief—that is suitably related to B. Objections of the first sort focus on the existence of internal states that are supposed to justify beliefs, arguing that there are some justified beliefs for which there are no internal justifying states. Objections in the second group focus on the connections between candidate internal justifiers and the beliefs they are supposed to justify, arguing that internalists inevitably run into insurmountable difficulties when they attempt to say anything definite about the nature or status of the connections.

While some internalist theories may have trouble dealing with some of these objections, there are several internalist approaches that can deal adequately with all of them. We concentrate primarily on two approaches, one that limits justifying states to currently conscious mental states and one that also includes as potential justifiers whatever is retained in memory. Since theories of each sort surmount all of the objections, the internalist approach is in no danger of a general refutation.

A. Are there Enough Internal Justifiers?

A1. Impulsional Evidence

Alvin Plantinga's objection focuses on evidentialist versions of internalism.[27] But the same sort of objection seems equally applicable against any initially plausible internalist view. Plantinga asserts that there are three views evidentialists can hold concerning what constitutes evidence, and he argues that each view

---

[27] Alvin Plantinga, "Respondeo ad Feldman," in Jon Kvanvig, ed., *Warrant in Contemporary Epistemology: Essays in Honor of Plantinga's Theory of Knowledge* (London: Rowman and Littlefield, 1996), pp. 357–61.

renders evidentialism unsatisfactory. The three possibilities are: (1) evidence consists only of other beliefs (all evidence is propositional); (2) evidence consists only of beliefs and sensory states (all evidence is propositional or sensory); (3) evidence can also include the sense of conviction or confidence that accompanies beliefs (all evidence is propositional, sensory, or impulsional).

Plantinga uses knowledge of simple arithmetical facts to defend his objection. He asserts that we do not believe that $2 + 1 = 3$ on the basis of propositional or sensory evidence. So, if evidentialists adopt alternatives (1) or (2), their theory implies that this belief is not justified. Yet, of course, we do know that $2 + 1 = 3$. Plantinga claims that there is a "felt attractiveness" about the content of that belief, and he says $2 + 1 = 5$ "feels wrong, weird, absurd, eminently rejectable."[28] He calls the "felt attractiveness" an "impulse" and classifies it as "impulsional evidence." So internalists might take Plantinga's third alternative and claim that this impulsional evidence is the internal factor that justifies simple mathematical beliefs.

Plantinga argues that there is a problem with this account. He claims that necessarily all beliefs would have similar justification: "You have impulsional evidence for p just in virtue of believing p... It isn't even possible that you believe p but lack impulsional evidence for it: how could it be that you believe p although it does not seem to you to be true?"[29] He infers that on this view of evidence, the internalist justification condition for knowledge that consists in having evidence is implied by the belief condition. If Plantinga is right about this, then evidentialists who take alternative (3) are stuck with the unacceptable conclusion that all actual beliefs are justified. The other initially plausible internalist views, for instance, those that appeal to epistemic responsibility as the key to a belief's justification, seem equally susceptible to this sort of objection. The "felt attractiveness" seems equally to render believing the epistemically responsible alternative to take. So, again, all beliefs would be justified.[30]

Plantinga's objection is multiply faulty, however. First, even if he were right in claiming that the evidence for beliefs like $2 + 1 = 3$ is impulsional, he would be mistaken in thinking that all beliefs have any similar sort of evidential support. There are several internal states to distinguish here. Perhaps we feel attracted to the proposition that $2 + 1 = 3$ and we feel impelled to believe it.

[28] Plantinga, "Respondeo," p. 359.   [29] Plantinga, "Respondeo," p. 360.

[30] Plantinga's premises establish at most that if a person believes a proposition, then the person has impulsional evidence for that proposition. Plantinga assumes that this evidence justifies the person's belief. However, even if the evidence is strong enough to justify believing the proposition, the person may fail to believe the proposition on the basis of this justifying evidence. In the body of the paper we question the claim that the impulsional evidence is always strong enough to justify believing the proposition and we ignore issues having to do with the basis of the belief.

Earl Conee and Richard Feldman

Not everything we believe feels attractive in this way or any other. For instance, some known propositions are believed reluctantly, on the basis of reasons, in spite of their seeming distinctly unattractive and implausible. Some beliefs result from fears. They need not seem in any way attractive. Correspondingly, the denials of things we believe do not always feel "weird" or "absurd," even if we think that they are false. There may be a "sense of obviousness" that accompanies belief in some propositions. This sense may contribute to their evidential support. But quite plainly not all believed propositions share that feature, or anything that resembles it. So it is not true that there is "impulsional evidence" for every believed proposition.

Furthermore, even if there were impulsional evidence for each belief, it would not follow that each belief satisfies any plausible evidential version of the justification condition for knowledge. The existence of a bit of supporting evidence is clearly not enough. A plausible evidential condition for knowledge requires something more, such as strong evidence on balance, or at least evidence undefeated by other evidence. An impulse to believe would not always qualify as strong evidence on balance, or undefeated evidence. Moreover, even if there were some impulsional evidence for all beliefs, it would not follow that all beliefs are justified to any degree. In some cases anything like impulsional evidence is decisively outweighed by competing evidence. Therefore, the existence of impulsional evidence for all beliefs would not render redundant a plausible evidential condition on knowledge and would not saddle internalists with the unacceptable result that all beliefs are justified.

Finally, even with regard to the simplest of mathematical beliefs, impulsional evidence of the sort Plantinga mentions is not our only evidence. We have evidence about our success in dealing with simple arithmetical matters and knowledge of the acceptance that is enjoyed by our assertions about these matters. So, we have these additional reasons to think that our spontaneous judgments about simple mathematical matters are correct. Furthermore, we know that we learned these sorts of things as children and we have not had our more recent assertions about them contradicted by others. If we had been making mistakes about these kinds of things, it is very likely that problems would have arisen and we would have been corrected. Moreover, at least according to some plausible views, we have a kind of *a priori* insight that enables us to grasp simple mathematical propositions. This insight provides us with some evidence for the truth of simple mathematical truths. Much of this evidence is retained in memory; some of it is conscious whenever such propositions are consciously apprehended. So there seems to be plenty of additional evidence, whether or not justifiers are restricted to conscious states. Indeed, the suggestion that our

Internalism Defended

only evidential bases for simple arithmetical beliefs are impulses to believe is extremely implausible.

Thus, Plantinga's objection makes no real trouble for evidentialism. Any other reasonable internalist view clearly has similar responses available to the counterpart objections. Our epistemic responsibilities, for instance, can be credibly held to stem in part from the discerned practical and social reinforcement of our mathematical beliefs, rather than from just our impulses with regard to them.

A2. Stored Beliefs

Alvin Goldman argues that internal states cannot account for the justification of stored beliefs.[31] The problem is this. At any given moment almost nothing of what we know is consciously considered. We know personal facts, facts that constitute common knowledge, facts in our areas of expertise, and so on. Since we know all these things, we believe them. These are stored beliefs, not occurrent beliefs. Since we know them, they are justified beliefs. But on what internalist basis can these beliefs be justified? As Goldman says, "No perceptual experience, no conscious memory event, and no premises consciously entertained at the selected moment will be justificationally sufficient for such a belief."[32] Internalists are stuck with the unacceptable result that these beliefs are not justified, unless something internal that justifies them can be found.

In formulating this objection Goldman assumes two propositions, either of which internalists can sensibly reject. On the one hand, he assumes that virtually all justified beliefs are stored beliefs. On the other hand, he assumes that internalists must find something conscious to serve as their justification. But internalists have good reason to reject this conjunction of propositions. One alternative is to argue that, in the most central sense, almost all justified beliefs are occurrent and very few stored beliefs are justified. The second option is to argue that other non-occurrent internal states can contribute to the justification of non-occurrent beliefs.

The first response relies on the idea that there are occurrent and dispositional senses of "justified," just as there are occurrent and dispositional senses of "belief." In the most fundamental sense of "justified" a belief can be justified for a person only by the person's current evidence, and one's current evidence is all conscious. In this sense, non-occurrent beliefs are typically not justified. However, in the same way that there are stored beliefs, one can have "stored

[31] Goldman, "Internalism Exposed," p. 278.   [32] Goldman, "Internalism Exposed," p. 278.

67

justifications" for these beliefs. That is, one can have in memory reasons that justify the belief.[33] Beliefs like this are dispositionally justified.[34] Thus, although stored beliefs are seldom justified in the most fundamental sense, they are often dispositionally justified.

Goldman objects to a proposal along these lines that one of us made previously.[35] He takes the general idea behind the proposal to be that a disposition to generate a conscious evidential state counts as a justifier. He then raises the following objection:

Suppose a train passenger awakes from a nap but has not yet opened his eyes. Is he justified in believing propositions about the details of the neighboring landscape? Surely not. Yet he is *disposed*, merely by opening his eyes, to generate conscious mental states that would occurrently justify such beliefs.[36]

The idea behind the current proposal is not what Goldman criticizes here. It is not that any conscious mental state that one is disposed to be in counts as evidence. The idea is that some non-occurrent states that one is already in, such as non-occurrent memories of perceptual experiences, are stored evidence. Presently having this stored evidence justifies dispositionally some non-occurrent beliefs that one already has. The train passenger does not have the evidence that he would receive were he to open his eyes. The dispositional state that he is in, his disposition to see the landscape by opening his eyes, is not stored evidence for propositions about the landscape. It is a potential to acquire evidence, and that is crucially different.

The second solution to the problem of stored beliefs does not invoke a distinction between occurrent and dispositional justification. Internalists can plausibly claim that if we have numerous ordinary justified beliefs that we are not consciously considering, then there is no reason to exclude from what justifies these beliefs further stored beliefs or other memories. These stored

---

[33] It may be that if one were to become conscious of the belief, one would also bring to mind some stored justification that one has for it. Thus, if these stored beliefs were occurrent, they would be justified in the fundamental sense. Whether this justification would happen to accompany an occurrent consideration of a belief does not seem crucial. What may be crucial to having a stored epistemic justification for a stored belief is being capable of recalling a conscious justification, or at least being capable of recalling the key confirming evidence in such a justification.

[34] Though it is possible for a stored belief to be justified by one's current evidence, in the usual case, one's evidence for a stored belief will also be stored. It is also possible for an occurrent belief to have only dispositional justification.

[35] Richard Feldman, "Having Evidence," in David Austin, ed., *Philosophical Analysis* (Dordrecht: Kluwer, 1988), pp. 83–104 [Ch. 9 in this volume].

[36] Goldman, "Internalism Exposed," pp. 278–9.

Internalism Defended

justifications are internalist by the standard of (M) and they are plausibly regarded as evidence that the person has.[37]

The description presented here of the second internalist approach leaves open important questions about which stored internal states can justify beliefs and what relation those stored states must have to a belief to justify it. No doubt these are difficult questions. Versions of internalism will differ concerning which stored states they count as justifiers.[38] But there is no reason to think that internalism lacks the resources to provide satisfactory answers to these questions. There is a difficulty here only if people internally alike can nevertheless differ with respect to which stored states are justifiers. We see no reason to admit such a possibility.

However, one might think that external factors having to do with the actual source of a memory belief can affect its justification. In fact, Goldman himself describes something similar to our second internalist approach and claims that it fails for just this reason.[39] We turn next to this objection.

A3. Forgotten Evidence

Several authors have raised objections involving forgotten evidence.[40] We will focus on an example Goldman provides:

Last year Sally read about the health benefits of broccoli in a *New York Times* science-section story. She then justifiably formed a belief in broccoli's beneficial effects. She still retains this belief but no longer recalls her original evidential source (and has never encountered either corroborating or undermining sources). Nonetheless, her broccoli belief is still justified, and, if true, qualifies as a case of knowledge.[41]

This example illustrates something that must be conceded to be common. We now know things for which we have forgotten our original evidence.

---

[37] It is, in the typical case, an internal state that is accessible to the believer, so accessibilist versions of internalism can accept this approach as well. We suspect that many internalists will find the second sort of approach to the problem of stored beliefs more appealing. By limiting evidence to current conscious states, the former view limits severely the number of justified beliefs a person has at any time. We do not regard this limitation as clearly unsatisfactory, given the availability of a dispositional notion of justification to account for the favorable epistemic status of many stored beliefs. We shall continue to present both approaches in the remainder of this paper.

[38] For example, they can differ with respect to how readily accessible those states must be. It is also possible to hold that the degree of justification provided by a state is partly determined by how readily accessible it is. [39] Goldman, "Internalism Exposed," p. 279.

[40] See, for instance, Sosa, "Skepticism and the Internal/External Divide," pp. 145–57. The relevant example appears on pp. 152 f. Goldman cites Gilbert Harman, Thomas Senor, and Robert Audi as having raised similar objections. See Gilbert Harman, *Change in View* (Cambridge: MIT Press, 1986); Thomas Senor, "Internalist Foundationalism and the Justification of Memory Belief," *Synthese*, 94 (1993): 453–76; and Robert Audi, "Memorial Justification," *Philosophical Topics*, 23 (1995): 31–45.

[41] Goldman, "Internalism Exposed," p. 281.

Earl Conee and Richard Feldman

The problem for internalism arises most clearly if we assume that Sally's original evidence is irretrievably lost and not part of any stored justification that Sally might have. In other words, let us assume that Sally is occurrently entertaining her justified belief about broccoli and that the facts about the original source of the belief are not part of any internalist justification of it. Externalists might argue that the contingent merits of the external source of this belief account for its justification. How can internalists explain why this belief is currently justified?

One internalist answer to this question is that Sally's justification consists in conscious qualities of the recollection, such as its vivacity and her associated feeling of confidence. We see no fatal flaw in this response. It will be most attractive to internalists who hold that only what is conscious can justify a belief. We note that not all memory beliefs are justified according to this theory. Some memory beliefs are accompanied by a sense of uncertainty and a lack of confidence. Other memory beliefs are accompanied by a recognition of competing evidence. This competing evidence can render vivacious memory beliefs unjustified. These are plausible results, so this restrictive version of internalism does have the resources to deal with forgotten evidence.

Another defensible answer is available to internalists who think that not all evidence is conscious. If Sally is a normal contemporary adult, she is likely to have quite of a bit of readily retrievable evidence supporting her belief about broccoli. The healthfulness of vegetables is widely reported and widely discussed. Furthermore, her belief about broccoli is probably not undermined by any background beliefs she is likely to have. Finally, she, like most people, probably has supporting evidence consisting in stored beliefs about the general reliability and accuracy of memory. She knows that she is generally right about this sort of thing. So Sally would have justification for her broccoli belief, though it is not her original evidence. If Sally lacks any supporting background information and also lacks any reason to trust her memory, then we doubt that her belief about the broccoli really is justified.

Goldman considers and rejects this second response on the basis of a new version of the example about Sally. The new example resembles one that Ernest Sosa presents involving a generally reasonable person who believes a conclusion as a result of a "tissue of fallacies" which, however, has now been forgotten.[42] Sosa thinks this origin renders the belief unjustified, no matter what the person now thinks about the source of her belief or her general capacities. The crucial feature of Goldman's revised example is also that a belief originally came from a disreputable source. Sally has the same belief about broccoli and

---

[42] Sosa, "Skepticism and the Internal/External Divide," p. 153.

the same background beliefs about the reliability of her relevant capacities. But now it is part of the story that Sally obtained the belief about broccoli from an article in the *National Inquirer*, a source Goldman assumes to be unreliable. Goldman claims that

> Sally cannot be credited with justifiably believing that broccoli is healthful. Her past acquisition is still relevant, and decisive. At least it is relevant so long as we are considering the "epistemizing" sense of justification, in which justification carries a true belief a good distance toward knowledge. Sally's belief in the healthfulness of broccoli is not justified in that sense, for surely she does not know that broccoli is healthful given that the *National Inquirer* was her sole source of information.[43]

We agree that Sally does not know that broccoli is healthful under these conditions. We also agree that facts about her acquisition of the belief determine this result. However, it does not follow that Sally's belief is not justified. The "epistemizing" sense of justification is said by Goldman to be a sense according to which a belief that is justified is one that has been carried "a good distance toward knowledge." This fits with our initial characterization of epistemic justification as the sort that is necessary for knowledge. But from the fact that Sally's belief falls short of knowledge, it does not follow that it has not been carried a good distance toward knowledge. Thus, an initial weakness in this objection is that its concluding inference is invalid.

A second fault is that the alleged unjustified belief is actually a Gettier case. We endorse the following rule of thumb for classifying examples of true beliefs that are not knowledge:

RT   If a true belief is accidentally correct, in spite of its being quite reasonably believed, then the example is a Gettier case.

RT helps to show that the second version of the example about Sally is a Gettier case. Sally believes that broccoli is healthful. She believes (presumably justifiably) that she learned this from a reliable source. She is wrong about her source but, coincidentally, right about broccoli. This fits exactly the pattern of Gettier cases, and RT classifies it as such. It is a quite reasonable belief on Sally's part which, in light of its unreliable source, is just accidentally correct. It is a justified true belief that is not knowledge. Similar remarks apply to Sosa's example.

Our view has an implication that may initially seem odd. When Sally first came to believe that broccoli is healthful, the belief was unjustified because Sally had reason to distrust her source. Yet we seem to be saying that simply

---

[43] Goldman, "Internalism Exposed," pp. 280–1.

because she has forgotten about that bad source, the belief has become justified. We are not quite saying that. As we see it, when she forgets about the source she has lost a defeater of a justification for her broccoli belief. Assuming that Sally knows herself normally to be judicious about her sources, all beliefs she retains thereby have considerable internal support. Whatever beliefs she retains are justified by this, unless they are defeated. A belief is defeated in any case in which she has indications that impeach what it is reasonable for her to take to be the source of her belief. But when she no longer possesses any such indication, as in the present Sally case, the otherwise generally good credentials of her memorial beliefs support the belief and are undefeated.

Some confirmation of our analysis comes from comparing the case as described to a case in which Sally does remember the unreliability of her source but retains the belief anyway. It is clear that there would be something far less reasonable about her belief in that situation. This suggests that forgetting the source does make the belief better justified.

Further confirmation emerges from contrasting the example with yet another variation. Suppose Sally believes both that broccoli is healthful and that peas are healthful. Suppose that her source for the former is still the *National Inquirer* but her source for the latter belief is the reliable *New York Times*. Again she has forgotten her sources, but she correctly and reasonably believes that she virtually always gets beliefs like these from trustworthy sources. Goldman's objection requires differentiating these two beliefs in an unacceptable way. It counts the former belief as unjustified, on the basis of the unreliability of its forgotten source. Yet from Sally's present perspective, the two propositions are on a par. It would be completely unreasonable for her to give up one belief but not the other. The best thing to say is that both are justified, but the broccoli belief does not count as knowledge because it is a Gettier case.

We conclude that internalism does not have any difficulty finding adequate justification in cases of forgotten evidence.

A4. *Concurrent Retrieval*

Another problem that Goldman poses for internalism is the problem of concurrent retrieval.[44] The problem purports to affect only those internalist views that are versions of holistic coherentism. Holistic coherentism says that a belief is justified only if it coheres with one's whole corpus of beliefs, including stored beliefs. This leads to a problem for the coherentist who also accepts the deontologically defended claim that one can always find out whether a belief

---

[44] Goldman, "Internalism Exposed," pp. 281–2.

is justified. Ascertaining whether one belief coheres with the rest by bringing them all consciously to mind at once is well beyond the capacities of any person.

This is a problem only when holistic coherentism is conjoined with the deontologically defended thesis just mentioned. A holistic coherentist need not accept a deontological conception of epistemic justification, and can simply deny that epistemic status is something that one always can find out. The holist can also respond to Goldman's objection by denying that finding out epistemic status so as to comply with any relevant duty requires the simultaneous retrieval of all that the status depends on. It might be held to be sufficient for complying with a duty to find out whether a belief, B1, coheres with one's other beliefs simply to form a true belief, B2, that B1 coheres, as long as B2 itself coheres with the rest of one's beliefs.

In any case, problems peculiar to holistic coherentism cast no doubt on internalism generally. There are, however, related questions concerning the accessibility of stored beliefs that might be raised for other internalist theories, including evidentialism. Here is one of them. Suppose that someone has a conscious belief that is supported by some currently conscious evidence. Suppose further that the person also has a large number of stored beliefs whose conjunction implies the falsity of the conscious belief. This conjunction is too complex for the person to entertain. Under these circumstances, what is the epistemic status of the current belief and can internalism properly account for that status?

This case does not jeopardize internalism. Consider first internalists who say that stored beliefs are among the mental items relevant to justification. Suppose beliefs that are contradicted by some huge conjunction of stored beliefs are not justified. These internalists can easily explain this result. They can hold that any conjunction of the stored beliefs can serve as a defeater of the justification of current beliefs, regardless of whether the individual can consciously consider the conjunction. If, on the other hand, beliefs such as those under consideration here are justified, internalists who hold that stored beliefs affect justification can also explain this result. They can say that justification supervenes on a restricted class of stored mental items. Perhaps items that are too complex to be retrieved are excluded. In that case, an unbelievably complex conjunction of stored beliefs would not be a defeater. Perhaps only combinations of stored beliefs whose negative relevance to the belief in question have been, or could readily be, noticed or appreciated count as defeaters. Perhaps, as accessibilists hold, only mental items that are in one way or another accessible can be defeaters.

Consider next internalists who hold that only currently accessed evidence is relevant to the epistemic status of occurrently believed propositions. Suppose that the beliefs under discussion are justified. These internalists can easily explain this result, since it is stipulated in the example that the currently accessed evidence does support the belief. The potentially defeating combinations of beliefs that are not accessed would not undermine justification. Internalists who limit sources of justification to what is conscious could not accept the view that these beliefs are not justified. They must instead argue that any appearance of defeat by a combination of merely stored beliefs is illusory. Since it is far from clear that there is any such defeat, the position of such internalists is not untenable.

Some of these approaches seem to us to be more promising than others. For present purposes it is not necessary to defend any particular view. We are arguing here for the explanatory power and credibility of internalist theorists. The devil may lurk in the details, for all that we have shown. But in the absence of any good reason to think that internalists must make *ad hoc* or indefensible claims about stored beliefs, there is no reason to think that there is a general problem here.

B. Links and Connections

We turn next to a set of objections concerning the connections between perceptual experiences or other justified beliefs and the beliefs they are supposed to justify. There are difficult questions about exactly how these states manage to justify the beliefs they support. These are problems of detail, and internalists have reasonable choices concerning how to work out the details. As we shall show by responding to several related objections, there are no unresolvable problems here.

B1. *The Need for Higher Order Beliefs*

William Alston has argued that the considerations that support internalism equally support the imposition of what he calls a "higher order requirement" on justification. The idea is that if the argument that leads to the conclusion that only internal factors can serve as justifiers is sound, then there is also a sound argument to the conclusion that for a belief to be justified the believer must be able to tell which factors justify the belief. Alston writes:

Suppose that the sorts of things that can count as justifiers are always accessible to me, but that it is not accessible to me which items of these sorts count as justifications for which beliefs. I have access to the justifiers but not to their justificatory efficacy. This will take away my ability to do what I am said to have an obligation to do just as surely as the lack of access to the justifiers themselves. To illustrate, let's suppose that experiences can function as justifiers, and that they are accessible to us. I can always tell what sensory experiences I am having at a given moment. Even so, if I am unable to tell what belief about the current physical environment is justified by a given sensory experience, I am thereby unable to regulate my perceptual beliefs according as they possess or lack experiential justification.[45]

Alston goes on to argue that this higher level requirement is one that few of us are able to satisfy, and he rejects the requirement partly for this reason. Since the argument for the higher order requirement is clearly unsound, Alston concludes that the original argument for internalism is unsound as well.

The argument Alston considers relies on a deontological conception of justification according to which justification is a matter of conforming to duties one must be in a position to know about. As we have noted, internalists are free to reject that conception. They need not defend an identification of justification with duty fulfillment. They need not defend anything that makes having justified beliefs depend on having some way to know what justifies what. To cite our favorite instance, evidentialists hold that the possession of the right evidence by itself secures the justification of the corresponding beliefs. The justification supervenes on the internal possession of appropriate evidence. Neither epistemic evaluations nor duties need enter in at all.

It might be thought that evidentialism should be formulated in ways that require for justification not only supporting evidence but also knowledge of higher level principles about the justificatory efficacy of this evidence. Some internalists do seem to impose such a requirement.[46] We agree with Alston that any such theory is implausible, implying that few people have justified beliefs. However, we see no reason to think that evidentialists must endorse any higher order requirement. Having evidence can make for justification on its own.

The appearance that justifying relations pose a problem for internalism arises partly from formulating the debate between internalists and externalists as a debate over whether all "justifiers" are internal. Indeed, that is exactly how some epistemologists do formulate the debate. For example, Goldman takes internalists to require that all "justifiers" must be in some suitable way accessible.[47] This way of formulating the issue is problematic. Suppose that a person who believes q on the basis of believing p has a justified belief in q. We might then say, as a first approximation, that the justifiers for q are (i) the belief that

---

[45] Alston, "Internalism and Externalism in Epistemology," p. 221.
[46] See, for example, Laurence BonJour, "Externalist Theories of Empirical Knowledge," *Midwest Studies in Philosophy*, 5 (1980): 55. In "Highlights of Recent Epistemology" James Pryor calls the view that endorses the higher order requirement "Inferential Internalism" and identifies several of its proponents.
[47] Goldman, "Internalism Exposed," section I.

p together with its justification, and (ii) the fact that p supports q. The fact in (ii) is not itself an internal state, and so it might be thought that internalists are faced with the difficult task of finding some internal representation of this state to serve as a justifier.[48]

There is a sense in which p's support for q is a "justifier." It is part of an explanation of the fact that the person's belief in q is justified. But this does not imply that internalists are committed to the view that there must be some internal representation of this fact. It may be that a person's being in the state described by (i) is sufficient for the belief that q to be justified. If so, then all individuals mentally alike in that they share that state are justified in believing q. The fact in (ii) may help to account for the justification without the person making any mental use of that fact.

General beliefs that relate evidence to a conclusion sometimes do make a justificatory difference. This occurs in some of the examples in our argument for internalism. But the sort of connecting information that the examples suggest to be necessary is non-epistemic information that justified believers typically have. The logic TA, for example, had justification for beliefs about implication relations that the student lacked. The expert bird watcher had justification for beliefs about what woodpeckers look like. This might take the form of various generalizations, e.g., any bird that looks like that is a woodpecker, any bird with that sort of bill is a woodpecker, etc.[49] The student and the novice bird watcher lacked these justifications. It would be a mistake, however, to argue from these cases to any universal "higher order requirement," especially to a higher order requirement to have epistemic information about what justifies what.

A fully developed internalist theory must state whether linking information of the sort possessed by the logic TA and the expert bird watcher is required in the case of simpler connections. Suppose that a person has a justified belief in some proposition, p. Suppose further that q is an extremely simple and intuitively obvious (to us) logical consequence of p. For the person to be justified in believing q, must he have additional evidence, analogous to the TA's additional evidence, for the proposition that q follows from p?

One possible view is that the answer is "No." According to this view, there are certain elementary logical connections that are necessarily reflected in epistemic connections. The best candidates for this relation include cases where

---

[48] See, for instance, Michael Bergmann, "A Dilemma for Internalism," in Thomas Crisp, Matthew Davidson, and Dave Vanderlaan (eds.), *Knowledge and Reality: Essays in Honor of Alvin Plantinga* (Dordrecht: Kluwer, forthcoming).

[49] Internalists who hold that all evidence is conscious can point to evidence such as the expert's feeling of confidence and sense of familiarity while making the judgment.

Internalism Defended

one proposition is a conjunction of which the other is a conjunct. The general idea is that some propositions, p and q, have a primitive or basic epistemic connection. If p and q have this connection, then, necessarily, if a person has a justified belief in p, then the person is also justified in believing q. Perhaps it is part of understanding p that one grasps the connection between p and q. There is, then, no need for additional information about the link between p and q that a person who is justified in believing p might lack. By the test of the supervenience thesis asserted by (M), internalists can accept this answer.

Internalists can also hold that the answer to the question above is "Yes." In this case, there is something resembling a higher order requirement. However, it is not any implausible requirement that one have information about justification. It is merely a requirement that one have evidence that there is a supporting connection—for instance, the logical consequence relation—between what is ordinarily regarded as one's evidence and what it is evidence for. This evidence can come from direct insight or from any other source. This is evidence that people normally have in a variety of normal situations.[50]

A similar question arises concerning perceptual beliefs about the qualities of the objects one is perceiving. We said above that the expert bird watcher has background information about the look of woodpeckers that justified the belief that he saw a woodpecker. The novice lacked that information. The new question concerns simpler qualities such as redness. Must a person with a clear view of a red object have evidence about the look of red things in order to be justified in believing that there is something red before him or is the mere experience of redness (in the absence of defeaters) sufficient for justification?

Again, it is not crucial to answer this question here. What is important for present purposes is that internalists have plausible options. If an experience of the phenomenal quality corresponding to redness automatically justifies the proposition (absent any defeater), then people internally alike in that they share the experience will be justified in believing the same external world proposition. If information about the look of red objects is required, then people internally

---

[50] There is a non-evidentialist view that some internalists find attractive. The idea is that a mental fact about people is that they have fundamental inferential abilities. Perhaps this view could also be described in terms of the ability to see connections. But this view denies that this ability is, or leads to, differences in evidence. This is a mental difference, but not an evidential difference.

These two views can also be applied to the original example about the logic student. We said the TA can see that the original sentence has consequences that the student can't see. This is what accounts for the differences in what is justified for them. As we described the case, we interpreted these facts in an evidentialist way, taking the difference in what they can see as an evidential difference. The non-evidentialist internalist alternative agrees that there is a mental difference between the two, but it characterizes that difference in terms of an inferential skill rather than a difference in evidence. It is not essential to a defense of internalism to select between these alternatives.

alike in that they share this information as well as the experience of red will have the same external world proposition justified. There is a problem for internalism here only if there is some reason to think that internal differences are inadequate to account for some difference in justification. We see no threat of that.

B2. *Computational Operations*

Goldman poses another objection similar to the one just considered. This objection concentrates on the justifying relations themselves, rather than any epistemic fact about the relations. He uses foundationalist versions of internalism to illustrate the point.[51] Foundationalists identify a limited class of basic justified propositions, usually propositions very closely linked to experiences. To avoid skeptical consequences, foundationalists typically assert that the rest of our justified beliefs are justified by being in appropriate relations to the basics. Candidates usually involve formal relations of logic and probability, among others. Goldman points out that the existence of a formal relation between propositions is not an internal state. He infers that foundationalists who are internalists cannot simply declare that beliefs that are suitably formally related to basics are thereby justified. Such a declaration would yield an unsatisfactory theory anyway, since many unjustified propositions are related to basics by formal relations such as implication.[52] Yet some non-basic beliefs must be justified somehow, or there will be grave skeptical implications.[53]

Goldman considers ways in which internalists might try to solve this problem. The one that he calls "the natural move" proposes that a belief is justified if and only if the fact that it has "appropriate logical or probabilistic relations" to the basics can be ascertained by performing "selected computational operations."[54] Goldman contends that serious problems exist for this way of avoiding skeptical implications. He claims that there is no satisfactory way to identify the admissible computational operations.

There is, however, no need for internalists to identify admissible computational operations. Goldman may be thinking that the relations of basics to further beliefs are justifiers and that all justifiers must be somehow internalized. As we discussed above, this is not the case. What must be internal are sufficient conditions for justification, not facts about their sufficiency. The root internalist idea is that the mental states one is in determine what one is justified in believing. As noted in the previous section, it may be that some ultra-simple

---

[51] Goldman, "Internalism Exposed," pp. 282–6.
[52] For example, distant and complex logical consequences of the basics may not be justified.
[53] Goldman, "Internalism Exposed," pp. 282–6. [54] Goldman, "Internalism Exposed," p. 283.

Internalism Defended

logical consequences of justified beliefs are automatically justified, perhaps by the understanding required to have the entailing beliefs. If that is the case, then these simple logical consequences of the basics are justified no matter what additional information about logical consequences one has. Internalism as characterized by (M) allows this. If, on the other hand, even simple logical consequences are justified only after the implications have been noticed, accepted, or understood, then internalists are in a position to say that only consequences meeting this further mental condition are justified. It is immaterial whether the satisfaction of this further condition results from computation, direct insight, testimonial evidence, or etc.

B3. Justification of Introspective Beliefs

Ernest Sosa raises a problem about how experiences justify introspective beliefs:

Some experiences in a certain sense "directly fit" some introspective beliefs. But not all experiences directly fit the introspective beliefs that describe them correctly. Thus my belief that at the centre of my visual field there lies a white triangle against a black background would so fit the corresponding experience. But my belief that my visual field contains a 23-sided white figure against a black background would *not* fit that experience.[55]

The question, then, is this: Why does having a suitable experience of a triangle justify the introspective belief that one is having that experience, while no experience of a 23-sided figure justifies for us the belief that one is having that experience?

Internalism has the resources to explain why the two experiences have different epistemic consequences. We can best explain the relevant internal features through consideration of some hypothetical person who does have the ability to identify 23-sided figures in his visual field and contrasting this person with ordinary people who lack that ability. According to one internalist option, someone who has the ability has an experience qualitatively different from those who lack that ability. We will call the quality that underlies the ability "recognition." It can plausibly be held that recognition makes a justificatory difference. When our visual field contains a triangle that contrasts clearly with its surroundings, we recognize it as such. We do not similarly recognize 23-sided figures. The recognition is not a true belief linking the experience to a belief about its content.[56] It is, instead, a feature of experience itself. This

---

[55] Ernest Sosa, "Beyond Scepticism, to the Best of our Knowledge," *Mind*, 97 (1988): 153–88. The quotation is from p. 171.

[56] The term "recognize" implies that the classification is accurate. There is no need to insist on an infallible capacity here. If there is some such phenomenon as seemingly recognizing a conscious quality while misclassifying it, then it is a seeming recognition which supplies the conscious evidence for the classification.

experiential feature is what makes it true that triangles optimally viewed are generally seen as triangles, while 23-sided figures, even when optimally viewed, are not generally seen as being 23-sided. It is this aspect of the experience that provides evidential support for the corresponding belief. For most of us, this sort of feature is present when we experience clearly discriminable triangles and not present when we experience 23-sided figures. But a person who did have that remarkable ability would have an experience unlike ours.

Rather than appealing to any qualitative difference in experience, internalists can appeal instead to background information. Ordinary people have learned that the property of being a 3-sided image is associated with a certain sort of visual appearance. They have not learned which sorts of visual appearances are associated with being a 23-sided image. On this view, only by learning some such association could a person have justification from experience for making these sorts of classifications of images. Internalists can plausibly appeal to this sort of background information as the internal difference that accounts for differences in justification in these cases. As in the cases considered in section B1, the information here is not epistemic information about what justifies what, information people typically lack. It is simply information about properties that are associated with experiences of certain types.

We conclude that Sosa is right to say that some but not all experiences lead to justification of introspective beliefs that correctly describe them. But internal differences, either in the experiences themselves or in background information, are available to account for the difference between those that do lead to justification and those that do not.

VII. Conclusion

We have defended internalism not just to praise it, but to move the debate beyond it. No genuine problem for this category of theories has been identified. We have seen that even versions of internalism that depend on only conscious elements have not been refuted. Various less restrictive views about what determines justification have emerged entirely unscathed as well. But on any account of internalism, including the one we recommend, internalism is nothing more than a broad doctrine about the location of the determining factors for epistemic justification. Having argued that internalist views stand in no jeopardy of being generally refuted, we recommend that epistemological attention focus on more specific accounts that are more informative.

Internalism Defended

Afterword

1. Though we give reasons to prefer mentalism to accessibilism, our defense of internalism does not turn on any difference between the two accounts of what internalism is. The one possible exception concerns the hypothesis we discuss that a belief might be defeated by some huge conjunction of separately stored beliefs that is too complex to be considered as a whole. Perhaps this conjunction is not "accessible" because it cannot be considered in one thought. It is not sufficiently clear what might count as "access" to judge this conclusively. Perhaps considering the conjuncts serially is enough to "access" the conjunction. If it is indeed inaccessible, then an accessibilist cannot include it as a defeater, since there is no access to it. A mentalist can say that the conjunction defeats because its capacity to defeat supervenes on the presence of all of the separate mental states that contain the conjuncts. This would be a small point of difference, in any event, since it is implausible that the unbelievable conjunction really is a defeater. Otherwise, our defense of internalism is fully available to accessibilists.

2. Timothy Williamson has resourcefully defended the thesis that knowledge is a mental state.[57] Mentalism, our version of internalism, includes any mental state in the supervenience base of epistemic justification. Knowledge seems to be a partly external state, at least when the content of the knowledge is an external world fact. So it might be thought that if Williamson is correct that knowledge is a mental state, then some embarrassment must be implied for our view that internalism is mentalism.

There is an embarrassment for our thesis only if including states of knowledge as mental states allows some external condition to make a justificatory difference. This is not implied. It may seem peculiar to regard everything that is justified by states of knowledge as internally justified. We think that this reaction derives from doubts that knowledge is actually a mental state. Our version of internalism is in trouble only if there is trouble for the thesis that if knowledge is a mental state, then knowledge is an internal state. We see no good reason to doubt that conditional.

It might be thought that knowing a proposition justifies believing, concerning any contrary evidence one receives subsequently, that it is misleading. By contrast, believing a proposition with justification does not even appear to justify such beliefs about new contrary evidence. It might be thought that in this way including knowledge among the mental states affects what a mentalist must acknowledge

---

[57] *Knowledge and its Limits* (Oxford: Oxford University Press, 2000). See especially chs. 1–4.

to be justified. But knowing does not actually justify disregarding new contrary evidence. This is argued in "Heeding Misleading Evidence" (Chapter 11 below).

3. Externalists about the propositional content of attitudes may reject internalism as we characterize it on the grounds that two people who are internally alike can be justified in believing different propositions due to differences in their external circumstances. The relevant notion of what is internal is primarily spatial—the interiors of the two people are the same in their intrinsic qualities. For example, S and his Twin Earth counterpart S', might be internally alike in this way, yet S is justified in believing that water exists while S' is justified in believing that twater exists, and not vice versa.

We will not debate the merits of content externalism here. If it is correct, then internalism about justification can be modified without abandoning the spirit of the view. The modification will appeal to "counterpart propositions". If, according to the content externalist, two people who are internally alike believe a proposition that each could express by the same sentence, then the proposition that the one believes is a counterpart of the proposition that the other believes. If they are believing different propositions due to external differences, then the two propositions are counterpart propositions for those two people at the time. If they are believing the same proposition, then that proposition is a counterpart of itself for them at the time.

Using this notion of a counterpart proposition, we can characterize internalism about justification as the thesis that if two individuals are internally alike, then one is justified in believing a proposition exactly to the extent that the other is justified in believing that person's counterpart proposition.

Intuitively the idea is this: content externalism is the thesis that external factors partly determine which proposition one is in a position to have attitudes toward. Epistemological internalism is the thesis that internal factors determine justification. If external factors place people who are internally alike in a position to have attitudes toward different propositions, still, internal factors determine which of those propositions the person is justified in believing. And in the presence of the same internal factors, the justified propositions differ at most in ways that are externally determined. For example, internal factors determine the extent of anyone's justification for believing whichever proposition the person would express by "Water exists", while external factors help to determine what proposition that is.

4
Evidentialism
Richard Feldman and Earl Conee

1

We advocate evidentialism in epistemology. What we call evidentialism is the view that the epistemic justification of a belief is determined by the quality of the believer's evidence for the belief. Disbelief and suspension of judgment also can be epistemically justified. The doxastic attitude that a person is justified in having is the one that fits the person's evidence. More precisely:

EJ   Doxastic attitude D toward proposition p is epistemically justified for S at t if and only if having D toward p fits the evidence S has at t.[1]

We do not offer EJ as an analysis. Rather it serves to indicate the kind of notion of justification that we take to be characteristically epistemic—a notion that makes justification turn entirely on evidence. Here are three examples that illustrate the application of this notion of justification. First, when a physiologically normal person under ordinary circumstances looks at a plush green lawn that is directly in front of him in broad daylight, believing that there is something green before him is the attitude toward this proposition that fits his evidence. That is why the belief is epistemically justified. Second, suspension of judgment is the fitting attitude for each of us toward the proposition that an even number of ducks exists, since our evidence makes it equally likely that the number is odd. Neither belief nor disbelief is epistemically justified when our evidence is equally balanced. And third, when it comes to the proposition that

---

[1] EJ is compatible with the existence of varying strengths of belief and disbelief. If there is such variation, then the greater the preponderance of evidence, the stronger the doxastic attitude that fits the evidence.

sugar is sour, our gustatory experience makes disbelief the fitting attitude. Such experiential evidence epistemically justifies disbelief.[2]

EJ is not intended to be surprising or innovative. We take it to be the view about the nature of epistemic justification with the most initial plausibility. A defense of EJ is now appropriate because several theses about justification that seem to cast doubt on it have been prominent in recent literature on epistemology. Broadly speaking, these theses imply that epistemic justification depends upon the cognitive capacities of people, or upon the cognitive processes or information-gathering practices that led to the attitude. In contrast, EJ asserts that the epistemic justification of an attitude depends only on evidence.

We believe that EJ identifies the basic concept of epistemic justification. We find no adequate grounds for accepting the recently discussed theses about justification that seem to cast doubt on EJ. In the remainder of this paper we defend evidentialism. Our purpose is to show that it continues to be the best view of epistemic justification.

II

In this section we consider two objections to EJ. Each is based on a claim about human limits and a claim about the conditions under which an attitude can be justified. One objection depends on the claim that an attitude can be justified only if it is voluntarily adopted, the other depends on the claim that an attitude toward a proposition or propositions can be justified for a person only if the ability to have that attitude toward the proposition or those propositions is within normal human limits.

Doxastic Voluntarism

EJ says that a doxastic attitude is justified for a person when that attitude fits the person's evidence. It is clear that there are cases in which a certain attitude toward a proposition fits a person's evidence, yet the person has no control over

---

[2] There are difficult questions about the concept of fit, as well as about what it is for someone to *have* something as evidence, and of what kind of thing constitutes evidence. As a result, there are some cases in which it is difficult to apply EJ. For example, it is unclear whether a person has as evidence propositions he is not currently thinking of, but could recall with some prompting. As to what constitutes evidence, it seems clear that this includes both beliefs and sensory states such as feeling very warm and having the visual experience of seeing blue. Some philosophers seem to think that only beliefs can justify beliefs. (See, for example, Keith Lehrer, *Knowledge* (Oxford: Oxford University Press, 1974), pp. 187–8.) The application of EJ is clear enough to do the work that we intend here—a defense of the evidentialist position.

Evidentialism

whether he forms that attitude toward that proposition. So some involuntarily adopted attitudes are justified according to EJ. John Heil finds this feature of the evidentialist position questionable. He says that the fact that we "speak of a person's beliefs as being warranted, justified, or rational... makes it appear that... believing something can, at least sometimes, be under the voluntary control of the believer."[3] Hilary Kornblith claims that it seems "unfair" to evaluate beliefs if they "are not subject" to direct voluntary control.[4] Both Heil and Kornblith conclude that although beliefs are not under *direct* voluntary control, it is still appropriate to evaluate them because "they are not entirely out of our control either".[5] "One does have a say in the procedures one undertakes that lead to" the formation of beliefs.[6]

Doxastic attitudes need not be under any sort of voluntary control for them to be suitable for epistemic evaluation. Examples confirm that beliefs may be both involuntary and subject to epistemic evaluation. Suppose that a person spontaneously and involuntarily believes that the lights are on in the room, as a result of the familiar sort of completely convincing perceptual evidence. This belief is clearly justified, whether or not the person cannot voluntarily acquire, lose, or modify the cognitive process that led to the belief. Unjustified beliefs can also be involuntary. A paranoid man might believe without any supporting evidence that he is being spied on. This belief might be a result of an uncontrollable desire to be a recipient of special attention. In such a case the belief is clearly epistemically unjustified even if the belief is involuntary and the person cannot alter the process leading to it.

The contrary view that only voluntary beliefs are justified or unjustified may seem plausible if one confuses the topic of EJ with an assessment of the *person*.[7] A person deserves praise or blame for being in a doxastic state only if that state is under the person's control.[8] The person who involuntarily believes in the presence of overwhelming evidence that the lights are on does not deserve praise for this belief. The belief is nevertheless justified. The person who believes that he is being spied on as a result of an uncontrollable desire does not deserve to be blamed for that belief. But there is a fact about the belief's

---

[3] See 'Doxastic agency', *Philosophical Studies*, 43 (1983), pp. 355–64. The quotation is from p. 355.

[4] See 'The psychological turn', *Australasian Journal of Philosophy*, 60 (1982), pp. 238–53. The quotation is from p. 252.   [5] Kornblith, *op. cit.*, p. 253.

[6] Heil, *op. cit.*, p. 363.

[7] Kornblith may be guilty of this confusion. He writes, "if a person has an unjustified belief, that person is epistemically culpable", *op. cit.*, p. 243.

[8] Nothing we say here should be taken to imply that any doxastic states are in fact voluntarily entered.

epistemic merit. It is epistemically defective—it is held in the presence of insufficient evidence and is therefore unjustified.

Doxastic Limits

Apart from the questions about doxastic voluntarism, it is sometimes claimed that it is inappropriate to set epistemic standards that are beyond normal human limits. Alvin Goldman recommends that epistemologists seek epistemic principles that can serve as practical guides to belief formation. Such principles, he contends, must take into account the limited cognitive capacities of people. Thus, he is led to deny a principle instructing people to believe all the logical consequences of their beliefs, since they are unable to have the infinite number of beliefs that following such a principle would require.[9] Goldman's view does not conflict with EJ, since EJ does not instruct anyone to believe anything. It simply states a necessary and sufficient condition for epistemic justification. Nor does Goldman think this view conflicts with EJ, since he makes it clear that the principles he is discussing are guides to action and not principles that apply the traditional concept of epistemic justification.

Although Goldman does not use facts about normal cognitive limits to argue against EJ, such an argument has been suggested by Kornblith and by Paul Thagard. Kornblith cites Goldman's work as an inspiration for his view that "having justified beliefs is simply doing the best one can in the light of the innate endowment one starts from..."[10] Thagard contends that rational or justified principles of inference "should not demand of a reasoner inferential performance which exceeds the general psychological abilities of human beings".[11] Neither Thagard nor Kornblith argues against EJ, but it is easy to see how such an argument would go: A doxastic attitude toward a proposition is justified for a person only if having that attitude toward that proposition is within the normal doxastic capabilities of people. Some doxastic attitudes that fit a person's evidence are not within those capabilities. Yet EJ classifies them as justified. Hence, EJ is false.[12]

We see no good reason here to deny EJ. The argument has as a premise the claim that some attitudes beyond normal limits do fit someone's evidence. The

---

[9] See 'Epistemics: The regulative theory of cognition', *The Journal of Philosophy*, 75 (1978), pp. 509–23, esp. p. 510 and p. 514.

[10] 'Justified belief and epistemically responsible action', *The Philosophical Review*, 92 (1983), pp. 33–48. The quotation is from p. 46.

[11] Paul Thagard, 'From the descriptive to the normative in psychology and logic', *Philosophy of Science*, 49 (1982), pp. 24–42. The quotation is from p. 34.

[12] Another version of this argument is that EJ is false because it classifies as justified for a person attitudes that are beyond *that person's* limits. This version is subject to similar criticisms.

fact that we are limited to a finite number of beliefs is used to support this claim. But this fact does not establish the premise. There is no reason to think that an infinite number of beliefs fit any body of evidence that anyone ever has. The evidence that people have under ordinary circumstances never makes it evident, concerning every one of an infinite number of logical consequences of that evidence, that it is a consequence. Thus, believing each consequence will not fit any ordinary evidence. Furthermore, even if there are circumstances in which more beliefs fit a person's evidence than he is able to have, all that follows is that he cannot have at one time all the beliefs that fit. It does not follow that there is any particular fitting belief which is unattainable. Hence, the premise of the argument that says that EJ classifies as justified some normally unattainable beliefs is not established by means of this example. There does not seem to be any sort of plausible evidence that would establish this premise. While some empirical evidence may show that people typically do not form fitting attitudes in certain contexts, or that some fitting attitudes are beyond some individual's abilities, such evidence fails to show that any fitting attitudes are beyond normal limits.

There is a more fundamental objection to this argument against EJ. There is no basis for the premise that what is epistemically justified must be restricted to feasible doxastic alternatives. It can be a worthwhile thing to help people to choose among the epistemic alternatives open to them. But suppose that there were occasions when forming the attitude that best fits a person's evidence was beyond normal cognitive limits. This would still be the attitude *justified* by the person's evidence. If the person had normal abilities, then he would be in the unfortunate position of being unable to do what is justified according to the standard for justification asserted by EJ. This is not a flaw in the account of justification. Some standards are met only by going beyond normal human limits. Standards that some teachers set for an 'A' in a course are unattainable for most students. There are standards of artistic excellence that no one can meet, or at least standards that normal people cannot meet in any available circumstance. Similarly, epistemic justification might have been normally unattainable.

We conclude that neither considerations of doxastic voluntarism nor of doxastic limits provide any good reason to abandon EJ as an account of epistemic justification.

III

EJ sets an epistemic standard for evaluating doxastic conduct. In any case of a standard for conduct, whether it is voluntary or not, it is appropriate to speak of 'requirements' or 'obligations' that the standard imposes. The person who has overwhelming perceptual evidence for the proposition that the lights are on, epistemically ought to believe that proposition. The paranoid person epistemically ought not to believe that he is being spied upon when he has no evidence supporting this belief. We hold the general view that one epistemically ought to have the doxastic attitudes that fit one's evidence. We think that being epistemically obligatory is equivalent to being epistemically justified.

There are in the literature two other sorts of view about epistemic obligations. What is epistemically obligatory, according to these other views, does not always fit one's evidence. Thus, each of these views of epistemic obligation, when combined with our further thesis that being epistemically obligatory is equivalent to being epistemically justified, yields results incompatible with evidentialism. We shall now consider how these proposals affect EJ.

Justification and the Obligation to Believe Truths

Roderick Chisholm holds that one has an "intellectual requirement" to try one's best to bring it about that, of the propositions one considers, one believes all and only the truths.[13] This theory of what our epistemic obligations are, in conjunction with our view that the justified attitudes are the ones we have an epistemic obligation to hold, implies the following principle:

CJ Doxastic attitude D toward proposition p is justified for person S at time t if and only if S considers p at t and S's having D toward p at t would result from S's trying his best to bring it about that S believe p at t iff p is true.

Evaluation of CJ is complicated by an ambiguity in 'trying one's best'. It might mean 'trying in that way which will in fact have the best results'. Since the goal is to believe all and only the truths one considers, the best results would be obtained by believing each truth one considers and disbelieving each falsehood one considers. On this interpretation, CJ implies that believing each truth and disbelieving each falsehood one considers is justified whenever believing and disbelieving in these ways would result from something one could try to do.

On this interpretation CJ is plainly false. We are not justified in believing every proposition we consider that happens to be true and which we could believe by trying for the truth. It is possible to believe some unsubstantiated proposition in a reckless endeavor to believe a truth, and happen to be right. This would not be an epistemically justified belief.[14]

[13] See *Theory of Knowledge*, 2nd ed. (Englewood Cliffs, NJ: Prentice-Hall, 1977), especially pp. 12–15.

[14] Roderick Firth makes a similar point against a similar view in 'Are epistemic concepts reducible to ethical concepts', in *Values and Morals*, edited by Al. L. Goldman and J. Kim (D. Reidel, Dordrecht, 1978), pp. 215–29.

It might be contended that trying one's best to believe truths and disbelieve falsehoods really amounts to trying to believe and disbelieve in accordance with one's evidence. We agree that gaining the doxastic attitudes that fit one's evidence is the epistemically best way to use one's evidence in trying to believe all and only the truths one considers. This interpretation of CJ makes it nearly equivalent to EJ. There are two relevant differences. First, CJ implies that one can have justified attitudes only toward propositions one actually considers. EJ does not have this implication. CJ is also unlike EJ in implying that an attitude is justified if it would result from *trying* to form the attitude that fits one's evidence. The attitude that is justified according to EJ is the one that as a matter of fact does fit one's evidence. This seems more plausible. What would happen if one tried to have a fitting attitude seems irrelevant—one might try but fail to form the fitting attitude.

We conclude that the doxastic attitudes that would result from carrying out the intellectual requirement that Chisholm identifies are not the epistemically justified attitudes.

Justification and Epistemically Responsible Action

Another view about epistemic obligations, proposed by Hilary Kornblith, is that we are obligated to seek the truth and gather evidence in a responsible way. Kornblith also maintains that the justification of a belief depends on how responsibly one carried out the inquiry that led to the belief.[15] We shall now examine how the considerations leading to this view affect EJ.

Kornblith describes a case of what he regards as "epistemically culpable ignorance." It is an example in which a person's belief seems to fit his evidence, and thus it seems to be justified according to evidentialism. Kornblith contends that the belief is unjustified because it results from epistemically irresponsible behavior. His example concerns a headstrong young physicist who is unable to tolerate criticism. After presenting a paper to his colleagues, the physicist pays no attention to the devastating objection of a senior colleague. The physicist, obsessed with his own success, fails even to hear the objection, which consequently has no impact on his beliefs. Kornblith says that after this, the physicist's belief in his own theory is unjustified. He suggests that evidentialist theories cannot account for this fact.

---

[15] Kornblith defends this view in 'Justified belief and epistemically responsible action'. Some passages suggest that he intends to introduce a new notion of justification, one to be understood in terms of epistemically responsible action. But some passages, especially in section II, suggest that the traditional analysis of justification is being found to be objectionable and inferior to the one he proposes.

Crucial details of this example are left unspecified, but in no case does it provide a refutation of evidentialism. If the young physicist is aware of the fact that his senior colleague is making an objection, then this fact is evidence he has against his theory, although it is unclear from just this much detail how decisive it would be. So, believing his theory may no longer be justified for him according to a purely evidentialist view. On the other hand, perhaps he remains entirely ignorant of the fact that a senior colleague is objecting to his theory. He might be 'lost in thought'—privately engrossed in proud admiration of the paper he has just given—and fail to understand what is going on in the audience. If this happens, and his evidence supporting his theory is just as it was prior to his presentation of the paper, then believing the theory does remain justified for him (assuming that it was justified previously). There is no reason to doubt EJ in the light of this example. It may be true that the young physicist is an unpleasant fellow, and that he lacks intellectual integrity. This is an evaluation of the character of the physicist. It is supported by the fact that in this case he is not engaged in an impartial quest for the truth. But the physicist's character has nothing to do with the epistemic status of his belief in his theory.

Responsible evidence-gathering obviously has some epistemic significance. One serious epistemological question is that of how to engage in a thoroughgoing rational pursuit of the truth. Such a pursuit may require gathering evidence in responsible ways. It may also be necessary to be open to new ideas, to think about a variety of important issues, and to consider a variety of opinions about such issues. Perhaps it requires, as BonJour suggests, that one "reflect critically upon one's beliefs."[16] But everyone has some justified beliefs, even though virtually no one is fully engaged in a rational pursuit of the truth. EJ has no implication about the actions one must take in a rational pursuit of the truth. It is about the epistemic evaluation of attitudes given the evidence one does have, however one came to possess that evidence.

Examples like that of the headstrong physicist show no defect in the evidentialist view. Justified beliefs can result from epistemically irresponsible actions.

Other Sorts of Obligation

Having acknowledged at the beginning of this section that justified attitudes are in a sense obligatory, we wish to forestall confusions involving other notions of obligations. It is not the case that there is always a *moral* obligation to believe in accordance with one's evidence. Having a fitting attitude can bring about

---

[16] Laurence BonJour, "Externalist theories of empirical knowledge," *Midwest Studies of Philosophy*, 5 (1980), p. 63.

disastrous personal or social consequences. Vicious beliefs that lead to vicious acts can be epistemically justified. This rules out any moral obligation to have the epistemically justified attitude.[17]

It is also false that there is always a *prudential* obligation to have each epistemically justified attitude. John Heil discusses the following example.[18] Sally has fairly good evidence that her husband Burt has been seeing another woman. Their marriage is in a precarious condition. It would be best for Sally if their marriage were preserved. Sally foresees that, were she to believe that Burt has been seeing another woman, her resulting behavior would lead to their divorce. Given these assumptions, EJ counts as justified at least some measure of belief by Sally in the proposition that Burt has been seeing another woman. But Sally would be better off if she did not have this belief, in light of the fact that she would be best served by their continued marriage. Heil raises the question of what Sally's prudential duty is in this case. Sally's *epistemic* obligation is to believe that her husband is unfaithful. But that gives no reason to deny what seems obvious here. Sally *prudentially* ought to refrain from believing her husband to be unfaithful. It can be prudent not to have a doxastic attitude that is correctly said by EJ to be justified, just as it can be moral not to have such an attitude.

More generally, the causal consequences of having an unjustified attitude can be more beneficial in *any* sort of way than the consequences of having its justified alternative. We have seen that it can be morally and prudentially best not to have attitudes justified according to EJ. Failing to have these attitudes can also have the best results for the sake of *epistemic* goals such as the acquisition of knowledge. Roderick Firth points out that a scientist's believing against his evidence that he will recover from an illness may help to effect a recovery and so contribute to the growth of knowledge by enabling the scientist to continue his research.[19] William James's case for exercising "the will to believe" suggests that some evidence concerning the existence of God is available only after one believes in God in the absence of justifying evidence. EJ does not counsel against adopting such beliefs for the sake of these epistemic ends. EJ implies

---

[17] This is contrary to the view of Richard Gale, defended in 'William James and the ethics of belief', *American Philosophical Quarterly*, 17 (1980), pp. 1–14, and of W. K. Clifford who said, 'It is wrong always, everywhere, and for every one, to believe anything upon insufficient evidence' (quoted by William James in 'The will to believe', reprinted in *Reason and Responsibility*, edited by J. Feinberg (Belmont, California, Wadsworth Publishing Co., 1981) p. 100).

[18] See 'Believing what one ought', *Journal of Philosophy*, 80 (1983), pp. 752–65. The quotation is from pp. 752 ff.

[19] See 'Epistemic merit, intrinsic and instrumental', *Proceedings and Addresses of The American Philosophical Association*, 55 (1981), pp. 5–6.

that the beliefs would be unjustified when adopted. This is not to say that the believing would do no epistemic good.

We acknowledge that it is appropriate to speak of epistemic obligations. But it is a mistake to think that what is epistemically obligatory, i.e., epistemically justified, is also morally or prudentially obligatory, or that it has the overall best epistemic consequences.

IV

Another argument that is intended to refute the evidentialist approach to justification concerns the ways in which a person can come to have an attitude that fits his evidence. Both Kornblith and Goldman propose examples designed to show that merely *having* good evidence for a proposition is not sufficient to make believing that proposition justified.[20] We shall work from Kornblith's formulation of the argument, since it is more detailed. Suppose Alfred is justified in believing p, and justified in believing if p then q. Alfred also believes q. EJ seems to imply that believing q is justified for Alfred, since that belief does seem to fit this evidence. Kornblith argues that Alfred's belief in q may still not be justified. It is not justified, according to Kornblith, if Alfred has a strong distrust of *modus ponens* and believes q because he likes the sound of the sentence expressing it rather than on the basis of the *modus ponens* argument. Similarly, Goldman says that a person's belief in q is not justified unless the belief is caused in some appropriate way.

Whether EJ implies that Alfred's belief in q is justified depends in part on an unspecified detail—Alfred's evidence concerning *modus ponens*. It is possible that Alfred has evidence against *modus ponens*. Perhaps he has just seen a version of the Liar paradox that seems to render *modus ponens* as suspect as the other rules and premises in the derivation. In the unlikely event that Alfred has such evidence, EJ implies that believing q is *not* justified for him. If rather, as we shall assume, his overall evidence supports *modus ponens* and q, then EJ does imply that believing q is justified for him.

When Alfred has strong evidence for q, his believing q is epistemically justified. This is the sense of 'justified' captured by EJ. However, if Alfred's basis for believing q is not his evidence for it, but rather the sound of the sentence expressing q, then it seems equally clear that there is some sense in which this state of believing is epistemically "defective"—he did not arrive at the belief in the right way.

---

[20] See Kornblith's 'Beyond foundationalism and the coherence theory', *The Journal of Philosophy*, 77 (1980), pp. 597–612, esp. pp. 601 f. and Goldman's 'What is justified belief?' in *Justification and Knowledge*, George S. Pappas, ed. (D. Reidel, Dordrecht, 1979), pp. 1–24.

Evidentialism

The term 'well-founded' is sometimes used to characterize an attitude that is epistemically both well-supported and properly arrived at. Well-foundedness is a second evidentialist notion used to evaluate doxastic states. It is an evidentialist notion because its application depends on two matters of evidence—the evidence one *has*, and the evidence one *uses* in forming the attitude. More precisely:

WF S's doxastic attitude D at t toward proposition p is well-founded if and only if
(i) having D toward p is justified for S at t; and
(ii) S has D toward p on the basis of some body of evidence e, such that
   (a) S has e as evidence at t;
   (b) having D toward p fits e; and
   (c) there is no more inclusive body of evidence e' had by S at t such that having D toward p does not fit e'.[21]

Since the evidentialist can appeal to this notion of well-foundedness, cases in which a person has but does not use justifying evidence do not refute evidentialism. Kornblith and Goldman's intuitions about such cases can be accommodated. A person in Alfred's position *is* in an epistemically defective state—his belief in q is not well-founded. Having said this, it is reasonable also to affirm the other evidentialist judgment that Alfred's belief in q is in another sense epistemically right—it is justified.[22]

V

The theory of epistemic justification that has received the most attention recently is reliabilism. Roughly speaking, this is the view that epistemically

---

[21] Clause (ii) of WF is intended to accommodate the fact that a well-founded attitude need not be based on a person's whole body of evidence. What seems required is that the person base a well-founded attitude on a justifying part of the person's evidence, and that he not ignore any evidence he has that defeats the justifying power of the evidence he does base his attitude on. It might be that his defeating evidence is itself defeated by a still wider body of his evidence. In such a case, the person's attitude is well-founded only if he takes the wider body into account.

WF uses our last main primitive concept—that of *basing* an attitude on a body of evidence. This notion is reasonably clear, though an analysis would be useful. See note 22 below for one difficult question about what is entailed.

[22] Goldman uses this sort of example only to show that there is a causal element in the concept of justification. We acknowledge that there is an epistemic concept—well-foundedness—that appeals to the notion of basing an attitude on evidence, and this may be a causal notion. What seems to confer epistemic merit on basing one's belief on the evidence is that in doing so one *appreciates* the evidence. It is unclear whether one can appreciate the evidence without being caused to have the belief by the evidence. But in any event we see no such causal requirement in the case of justification.

justified beliefs are the ones that result from belief-forming processes that reliably lead to true beliefs.[23] In this section we consider whether reliabilism casts doubt on evidentialism.

Although reliabilists generally formulate their view as an account of epistemic justification, it is clear that in its simplest forms it is better regarded as an account of well-foundedness. In order for a belief to be favorably evaluated by the simple sort of reliabilism sketched above, the belief must actually be held, as is the case with WF. And just as with WF, the belief must be "grounded" in the proper way. Where reliabilism appears to differ from WF is over the conditions under which a belief is properly grounded. According to WF, this occurs when the belief is based on fitting evidence. According to reliabilism, a belief is properly grounded if it results from a belief-forming process that reliably leads to true beliefs. These certainly are *conceptually* different accounts of the grounds of well-founded beliefs.

In spite of this conceptual difference, reliabilism and WF may be extensionally equivalent. The question of equivalence depends on the resolution of two unclarities in reliabilism. One pertains to the notion of a belief-forming process, and the other to the notion of reliability.

An unclarity about belief-forming processes arises because every belief is caused by a sequence of particular events which is an instance of many types of causal processes. Suppose that one evening Jones looks out of his window and sees a bright shining disk-shaped object. The object is in fact a luminous frisbee, and Jones clearly remembers having given one of these to his daughter. But Jones is attracted to the idea that extraterrestrials are visiting the Earth. He manages to believe that he is seeing a flying saucer. Is the process that caused this belief reliable? Since the sequence of events leading to his belief is an instance of many types of process, the answer depends upon which of these many types is the relevant one. The sequence falls into highly general categories such as perceptually-based belief formation and visually-based belief formation. It seems that if these are the relevant categories, then his belief is indeed reliably formed, since these are naturally regarded as "generally reliable" sorts of belief-forming processes. The sequence of events leading to Jones's belief also falls into many relatively specific categories such as night-vision-of-a-nearby-object

---

[23] The clearest and most influential discussion of reliabilism is in Goldman's 'What is justified belief?' One of the first statements of the theory appears in David Armstrong's *Belief, Truth and Knowledge* (Cambridge University Press, Cambridge, 1973). For extensive bibliographies on reliabilism, see Frederick Schmitt's 'Reliability, objectivity, and the background of justification', *Australasian Journal of Philosophy*, 62 (1984), pp. 1–15, and Richard Feldman's 'Reliability and justification', *The Monist*, 68 (1985), pp. 159–74.

Evidentialism

and vision-in-Jones's-precise-environmental-circumstances. These are not clearly reliable types. The sequence is also an instance of this contrived kind: process-leading-from-obviously-defeated-evidence-to-the-belief-that-one-sees-a-flying-saucer. This, presumably, is an unreliable kind of process. Finally, there is the maximally specific process that occurs only when physiological events occur that are exactly like those that led to Jones's belief that he saw a flying saucer. In all likelihood this kind of process occurred only once. Processes of these types are of differing degrees of reliability, no matter how reliability is determined. The implications of reliabilism for the case are rendered definite only when the kind of process whose reliability is relevant is specified. Reliabilists have given little attention to this matter, and those that have specified relevant kinds have not done so in a way that gives their theory an intuitively acceptable extension.[24]

The second unclarity in reliabilism concerns the notion of reliability itself. Reliability is fundamentally a property of kinds of belief-forming processes, not of sequences of particular events. But we can say that a sequence is reliable provided its relevant type is reliable. The problem raised above concerns the specification of relevant types. The current problem is that of specifying the conditions under which a kind of process is *reliable*. Among possible accounts is one according to which a kind of process is reliable provided most instances of that kind until now have led to true beliefs. Alternative accounts measure the reliability of a kind of process by the frequency with which instances of it produce true beliefs in the future as well as the past, or by the frequency with which its instances produce true beliefs in possible worlds that are similar to the world of evaluation in some designated respect, or by the frequency with which its instances produce true beliefs in all possible worlds.[25]

Because there are such drastically different ways of filling in the details of reliabilism the application of the theory is far from clear. The possible versions of reliabilism seem to include one that is extensionally equivalent to WF. It might be held that all beliefs are formed by one of two relevant kinds of belief-forming process. One kind has as instances all and only those sequences of events leading to a belief that is based on fitting evidence; the other is a kind of process that has as instances all and only those sequences leading to a belief

---

[24] For discussion of the problem of determining relevant kinds of belief-forming processes, see Goldman, 'What is justified belief?', Schmitt, 'Reliability, objectivity, and the background of justification', Feldman, 'Reliability and justification', and Feldman, 'Schmitt on reliability, objectivity, and justification', *Australasian Journal of Philosophy*, 63 (1985), pp. 354–60.

[25] In 'Reliability and justified belief', *Canadian Journal of Philosophy*, 14, (1984), pp. 103–14, John Pollock argues that there is no account of reliability suitable for reliabilists.

that is not based on fitting evidence. If a notion of reliability can be found on which the former sort of process is reliable and the latter is not, the resulting version of reliabilism would be very nearly equivalent to WF.[26] We do not claim that reliabilists would favor this version of reliabilism. Rather, our point is that the fact that this *is* a version shows that reliabilism may not even be a rival to WF.[27]

Evaluation of reliabilism is further complicated by the fact that reliabilists seem to differ about whether they *want* their theory to have approximately the same extension as WF in fact has. The credibility of reliabilism and its relevance to WF depend in part on the concept reliabilists are really attempting to analyze. An example first described by Lawrence BonJour helps to bring out two alternatives.[28] BonJour's example is of a person who is clairvoyant. As a result of his clairvoyance he comes to believe that the President is in New York City. The person has no evidence showing that he is clairvoyant and no other evidence supporting his belief about the President. BonJour claims that the example is a counter-example to reliabilism, since the clairvoyant's belief is not justified (we would add: and therefore ill-founded), although the process that caused it is reliable—the person really is clairvoyant.

The general sort of response to this example that seems to be most commonly adopted by reliabilists is in effect to agree that such beliefs are not well-founded. They interpret or revise reliabilism with the aim of avoiding the counter-example.[29] An alternative response would be to argue that the reliability of clairvoyance shows that the belief *is* well-founded, and thus that the example does not refute reliabilism.[30]

We are tempted to respond to the second alternative—beliefs such as that of the clairvoyant in BonJour's example really are well-founded—that this is so clear an instance of an ill-founded belief that any proponent of that view must have in mind a different concept from the one we are discussing. The clairvoyant has no reason for holding his belief about the President. The fact that the belief was caused by a process of a reliable kind—clairvoyance—is a significant

---

[26] This version of reliabilism will not be exactly equivalent to WF because it ignores the factors introduced by clause (ii) of WF.

[27] It is also possible that versions of reliabilism making use only of natural psychological kinds of belief-forming processes are extensionally equivalent to WF. Goldman seeks to avoid evaluative epistemic concepts in his theory of epistemic justification, so he would not find an account of justification satisfactory unless it appealed only to such natural kinds. See 'What is justified belief?', p. 6.

[28] See 'Externalist theories of empirical knowledge', p. 62.

[29] See Goldman, 'What is justified belief?, pp. 18–20, Kornblith, 'Beyond foundationalism and the coherence theory', pp. 609–11, and Frederick Schmitt, 'Reliability, objectivity, and the background of justification'.

[30] We know of one who has explicitly taken this approach. It seems to fit most closely with the view defended by David Armstrong in *Belief, Truth and Knowledge*.

Evidentialism

fact about it. Such a belief may merit some favorable term of epistemic appraisal, e.g., "objectively probable." But the belief is not well-founded.

There are, however, two lines of reasoning that could lead philosophers to think that we must reconcile ourselves to the clairvoyant's belief turning out to be well-founded. According to one of these arguments, examples such as that of Alfred (discussed in Section IV above) show that the evidentialist account of epistemic merit is unsatisfactory and that epistemic merit must be understood in terms of the reliability of belief-forming processes.[31] Since the clairvoyant's belief is reliably formed, our initial inclination to regard it as ill-founded must be mistaken.

This argument is unsound. The most that the example about Alfred shows is that there is a concept of favorable epistemic appraisal other than justification, and that this other concept involves the notion of the *basis* of a belief. We believe that WF satisfactorily captures this other concept. There is no need to move to a reliabilist account, according to which some sort of causal reliability is *sufficient* for epistemic justification. The Alfred example does not establish that some version of reliabilism is correct. It does not establish that the clairvoyant's belief is well-founded.

The second argument for the conclusion that the clairvoyant's belief is well-founded makes use of the strong similarity between clairvoyance in BonJour's example and normal perception. We claim that BonJour's clairvoyant is not justified in his belief about the President because that belief does not fit his evidence. Simply having a spontaneous uninferred belief about the whereabouts of the President does not provide evidence for its truth. But, it might be asked, what better evidence is there for any ordinary perceptual belief, say, that one sees a book? If there is no relevant epistemological difference between ordinary perceptual beliefs and the clairvoyant's belief, then they should be evaluated similarly. The argument continues with the point that reliabilism provides an explanation of the crucial similarity between ordinary perceptual beliefs and the clairvoyant's belief—both perception and clairvoyance *work*, in the sense that both are reliable. So beliefs caused by each process are well-founded on a reliabilist account. The fact that reliabilism satisfactorily explains this is to the theory's credit. On the other hand, in advocating evidentialism we have claimed that perceptual beliefs are well-founded and that the clairvoyant's belief is not. But there appears to be no relevant evidential difference between these beliefs. Thus, if the evidentialist view of the matter cannot

---

[31] We know of no one who explicitly defends this inference. In 'The psychological turn', pp. 241 f., Kornblith argues that these examples show that justification depends upon "psychological connections" and "the workings of the appropriate belief forming process." But he clearly denies there that reliabilism is directly implied.

be defended, then reliabilism is the superior theory and we should accept its consequence—the clairvoyant's belief is well-founded.

One problem with this argument is that reliabilism has no satisfactory explanation of *anything* until the unclarities discussed above are removed in an acceptable way: What shows that perception and clairvoyance are relevant and reliable types of processes? In any event, there *is* an adequate evidentialist explanation of the difference between ordinary perceptual beliefs and the clairvoyant's belief. On one interpretation of clairvoyance, it is a process whereby one is caused to have beliefs about objects hidden from ordinary view without any conscious state having a role in the causal process. The clairvoyant does not have the conscious experience of, say, seeming to see the President in some characteristic New York City setting, and on that basis form the belief that he is in New York. In this respect, the current version of clairvoyance is unlike ordinary perception, which does include conscious perceptual states. Because of this difference, ordinary perceptual beliefs are based on evidence—the evidence of these sensory states—whereas the clairvoyant beliefs are not based on evidence. Since WF requires that well-founded beliefs be based on fitting evidence, and typical clairvoyant beliefs on the current interpretation are not based on any evidence at all, the clairvoyant beliefs do not satisfy WF.

Suppose instead that clairvoyance does include visual experiences, though of remote objects that cannot stimulate the visual system in any normal way. Even if there are such visual experiences that could serve as a basis for a clairvoyant's beliefs, still there is a relevant epistemological difference between beliefs based on normal perceptual experience and the clairvoyant's belief in BonJour's example. We have collateral evidence to the effect that when we have perceptual experience of certain kinds, external conditions of the corresponding kinds normally obtain. For example, we have evidence supporting the proposition that when we have the usual sort of experience of seeming to see a book, we usually do in fact see a book. This includes evidence from the coherence of these beliefs with beliefs arising from other perceptual sources, and it also includes testimonial evidence. This latter point is easily overlooked. One reason that the belief that one sees a book fits even a child's evidence when she has a perceptual experience of seeing a book is that children are taught, when they have the normal sort of visual experiences, that they are seeing a physical object of the relevant kind. This testimony, typically from people whom the child has reason to trust, provides evidence for the child. And of course testimony from others during adult life also gives evidence for the veridicality of normal visual experience. On the other hand, as BonJour describes his example, the clairvoyant has no confirmation at all of his clairvoyant beliefs. Indeed, he has evidence

Evidentialism

against these beliefs, since the clairvoyant perceptual experiences do not cohere with his other experiences. We conclude, therefore, that evidentialists can satisfactorily explain why ordinary perceptual beliefs are typically well-founded and unconfirmed clairvoyant beliefs, even if reliably caused, are not. There is no good reason to abandon our initial intuition that the beliefs such as those of the clairvoyant in BonJour's example are not well-founded.

Again, reliabilists could respond to BonJour's example either by claiming that the clairvoyant's belief is in fact well-founded or by arguing that reliabilism does not imply that it is well-founded. We turn now to the second of these alternatives, the one most commonly adopted by reliabilists. This view can be defended by arguing either that reliabilism can be reformulated so that it lacks this implication, or that as currently formulated it lacks this implication. We pointed out above that as a general approach reliabilism is sufficiently indefinite to allow interpretations under which it does lack the implication in question. The only way to achieve this result that we know of that is otherwise satisfactory requires the introduction of evidentialist concepts. The technique is to specify the relevant types of belief-forming processes in evidentialist terms. It is possible to hold that the relevant types of belief-forming process are believing something on the basis of fitting evidence and believing not as a result of fitting evidence. This sort of "reliabilism" is a roundabout approximation of the straightforward evidentialist thesis, WF. We see no reason to couch the approximated evidentialist theory in reliabilist terms. Moreover, the reliabilist approximation is not exactly equivalent to WF, and where it differs it appears to go wrong. The difference is this: it seems possible for the process of believing on the basis of fitting evidence to be unreliable. Finding a suitable sort of reliability makes all the difference here. In various possible worlds where our evidence is mostly misleading, the frequency with which fitting evidence causes true belief is low. Thus, this type of belief-forming process is not "reliable" in such worlds in any straightforward way that depends on actual frequencies. Perhaps a notion of reliability that avoids this result can be found. We know of no such notion which does not create trouble elsewhere for the theory. So, the reliabilist view under consideration has the consequence that in such worlds beliefs based on fitting evidence are not well-founded. This is counterintuitive.[32]

In this section we have compared reliabilism and evidentialism. The vagueness of reliabilism makes it difficult to determine what implications

---

[32] Stewart Cohen has made this point in 'Justification and truth', *Philosophical Studies*, 46 (1984), pp. 279–95. Cohen makes the point in the course of developing a dilemma. He argues that reliabilism has the sort of flaw that we describe above when we appeal to worlds where evidence is mostly misleading. Cohen also contends that reliabilism has the virtue of providing a clear explanation of

the theory has and it is not entirely clear what implications reliabilists want their theory to have. If reliabilists want their theory to have approximately the same extension as WF, we see no better way to accomplish this than one which makes the theory an unnecessarily complex and relatively implausible approximation to evidentialism. If, on the other hand, reliabilists want their theory to have an extension which is substantially different from that of WF, and yet some familiar notion of "a reliable kind of process" is to be decisive for their notion of well-foundedness, then it becomes clear that the concept they are attempting to analyze is not one evidentialists seek to characterize. This follows from the fact that on this alternative they count as well-founded attitudes that plainly do not exemplify the concept evidentialists are discussing. In neither case, then, does reliabilism pose a threat to evidentialism.

VI

Summary and Conclusion

We have defended evidentialism. Some opposition to evidentialism rests on the view that a doxastic attitude can be justified for a person only if forming the attitude is an action under the person's voluntary control. EJ is incompatible with the conjunction of this sort of doxastic voluntarism and the plain fact that some doxastic states that fit a person's evidence are out of that person's control. We have argued that no good reason has been given for thinking that an attitude is epistemically justified only if having it is under voluntary control.

A second thesis contrary to EJ is that a doxastic attitude can be justified only if having that attitude is within the normal doxastic limits of humans. We have held

---

how the epistemic notion of justification is connected with the notion of truth. A theory that renders this truth connection inexplicable is caught on the second horn of Cohen's dilemma.

Although Cohen does not take up evidentialism as we characterize it, the second horn of his dilemma affects EJ and WF. They do not explain how having an epistemically justified or well-founded belief is connected to the truth of that belief. Evidentialists can safely say this much about the truth connection: evidence that makes believing *p* justified is evidence on which it is *epistemically* probable that *p* is true. Although there is this connection between justification and truth, we acknowledge that there may be no analysis of epistemic probability that makes the connection to truth as close, or as clear, as might have been hoped.

Cohen argues that there must be a truth connection. This shows no flaw in EJ or WF unless they are incompatible with there being such a connection. Cohen does not argue for this incompatibility and we know of no reason to believe that it exists. So at most Cohen's dilemma shows that evidentialists have work left to do.

that the attitudes that are epistemically justified according to EJ are within these limits, and that even if they were not, that fact would not suffice to refute EJ.

Some philosophers have contended that believing a proposition, p, is justified for S only when S has gone about gathering evidence about p in a responsible way, or has come to believe p as a result of seeking a meritorious epistemic goal such as the discovery of truth. This thesis conflicts with EJ, since believing p may fit one's evidence no matter how irresponsible one may have been in seeking evidence about p and no matter what were the goals that led to the belief. We agree that there is some epistemic merit in responsibly gathering evidence and in seeking the truth. But we see no reason to think that epistemic justification turns on such matters.

Another thesis conflicting with EJ is that merely having evidence is not sufficient to justify belief, since the believer might not make proper use of the evidence in forming the belief. Consideration of this claim led us to make use of a second evidentialist notion, well-foundedness. It does not, however, provide any good reason to think that EJ is false. Nor do we find reason to abandon evidentialism in favor of reliabilism. Evidentialism remains the most plausible view of epistemic justification.

Afterword

1. Our bedrock epistemic view is a supervenience thesis. Justification strongly supervenes on evidence. More precisely, a whole body of evidence entirely settles which doxastic attitudes toward which propositions are epistemically justified in any possible circumstance. That is,

ES   The epistemic justification of anyone's doxastic attitude toward any proposition at any time strongly supervenes on the evidence that the person has at the time.

The use of EJ to formulate evidentialism in our paper "Evidentialism" has its advantages. For one thing, ES says less than EJ. EJ implies that all and only "evidence-fitting" doxastic attitudes are justified, while ES does not say what relation to evidence justifies an attitude. But, on the other hand, "fit" in EJ is vague at best. This makes non-trivial trouble, as is illustrated by cases like this. Suppose that Smith receives apparently sincere testimonial evidence to the effect that Jones, a person whom Smith has long regarded as a close friend, has been spreading malicious gossip about Smith. If the evidence from the testimony is strong enough, Smith's evidence may favor the conclusion that Jones has been maliciously gossiping about Smith. Yet it may be that the loyalty Smith owes to Jones morally requires him to resist such a conclusion until his evidence is more conclusive than the evidence that he currently has. What attitude toward the proposition that Jones has been maliciously gossiping about him then "fits" Smith's evidence? The answer is not clear. Perhaps belief is the attitude that "epistemically fits" Smith's evidence, and suspension of judgment is the attitude that "morally fits", and there is no summary notion of fit. Or perhaps moral considerations always override in conflicts of fit. If the latter is true, then EJ makes the mistake of counting Smith as not justified in believing that Jones has been maliciously gossiping about Smith.

This mistake would be an accident arising from our use of the term. We could have said, albeit more obscurely, that the justified attitude is the one that is "epistemically fitting". Also, there is something nearly equivalent to EJ that we could have expressed in a more cumbersome way. We could have said this:

EC   Believing is the justified attitude when the person's evidence on balance supports a proposition, disbelieving is the justified attitude when the person's evidence on balance supports the negation of a proposition, and suspension of judgment is the justified attitude when the person's evidence on balance supports neither a proposition nor its negation.

EC avoids "fit" altogether. But it closes some options that we would prefer that our general thesis leave open. One such option is that when someone's evidence on balance just barely supports a proposition, a suspension of judgment is justified. EJ leaves open the possibility that suspending judgment as well as believing "fits" the evidence, and thus that each attitude is justified. It also leaves open the possibility that only suspending judgment fits such meager evidence. A second option worth leaving open is that no doxastic attitude is justified when a person's evidence supports a proposition that the person does not understand. This problem could be avoided by restricting EC to justification for propositions that the person does understand. But then EC leaves out some justified attitudes, if understanding is not required. A third option worth leaving open is that there are many more doxastic attitudes than the three just mentioned, because there are degrees of belief and disbelief. A given strength of evidence would fit with a corresponding degree of belief or disbelief.

The formulation in terms of "fit" or "epistemic fit" nicely avoids clear implications about any of those options. In any event, as we say, ES is bedrock evidentialism.

Evidentialism

2. Jeremy Fantl and Matthew McGrath have recently argued against what they call evidentialism.[33] Their target is this thesis:

EK For any two subjects, S and S′, necessarily, if S and S′ have the same evidence for/against p, then S is justified in believing p iff S′ is, too.[34]

Someone is "justified in believing p", as Fantl and McGrath intend the phrase, just when the person has evidence that is good enough to know that p.[35] They argue that there is a pragmatic element in the justification needed for knowledge. Roughly, this element is how important the truth-value of the proposition is to the person. Fantl and McGrath oppose EK by arguing that there can be cases in which subjects have the same evidence about a proposition, while the pragmatic element differs, with the result that in only one case is that evidence good enough for knowledge of the proposition. Fantl and McGrath cite the present work as a defense of EK.[36] But our work is noncommittal with regard to EK, given the way that Fantl and McGrath interpret "justified". Our work is a defense of EJ. EJ is subject to the misgivings expressed above, and perhaps our view is clarified by ES. As EJ and ES bear on belief, they are about the epistemic justification that a person may have for believing a proposition (or the degree of belief that is justified). They hold that this justification is entirely determined by the evidence that the person has. They do not imply anything about how justification relates to knowledge. In particular, they do not imply that the strength of justification that is needed for knowledge is the same in all cases.

There would be a counter-example to EJ and ES if there were a case in which two people are unequally justified in some attitude while possessing the same evidence. Fantl and McGrath do not so much as seek to establish that this is a possibility. In opposing what they call evidentialism, namely EK, they seek only to show that the justification condition on knowledge of a given proposition is not always met by someone who has the same evidence as a person who does meet the justification condition on knowledge of the proposition. Again, nothing in our paper commits us to denying that. Fantl and McGrath's topic is an epistemic classification of a belief for which epistemologists often use the term "justified" in a relatively technical way. Someone's belief is thus "justified" when the belief is well enough justified for the person to know the proposition. EJ and ES are compatible with this status *not* being entirely determined by evidence. It is compatible with EJ and ES to hold that whether or not someone's epistemic justification for believing a proposition is good enough for

---

[33] "Evidence, Pragmatics, and Justification", *Philosophical Review*, 111 (2002), 67–94.
[34] Ibid. 68.   [35] Ibid. 67.   [36] Ibid. 68.

knowledge is partly determined by something other than how strongly justified the proposition is for the person. EJ and ES are compatible with Fantl and McGrath's view that the practical significance to the person of the truth-value of the proposition makes a difference to what strength of justification is sufficient for the person to know the proposition.

This is not a suitable place for a full discussion of the relation of the strength of epistemic justification to knowledge. (We give our view about that in "Making Sense of Skepticism", Chapter 12 below.) Here we will respond very briefly to Fantl and McGrath's position. The practical significance to someone of a proposition's truth does not seem to us to contribute to when the person is well enough justified to know it. Rather, it seems to us that this practical factor may exert influence on how readily an attribution of knowledge is made, both by the knower and by others. We deny that knowing entails knowing that one knows, or even reasonably believing that one knows. One reason for this denial is that people can make reasonable mistakes about whether their justification is strong enough for knowledge. When the evidence is strong enough, generally there is nothing inescapably manifest about that fact. So even when it is strong enough, people can reasonably doubt that their evidence gives them knowledge, and when the truth matters enough to them, they can reasonably seek better evidence. (This sort of vulnerability to error is discussed further in the final main section of "Making Sense of Skepticism".) Lastly, a variety of factors can affect whether a person prudentially, morally, or in some other way *ought* to get additional evidence regarding a proposition. Possibly judgments about this affect our willingness to ascribe knowledge to someone, without affecting whether the person has knowledge.

3. The notion of a well-founded belief makes a cameo appearance in "Evidentialism". It serves only to accommodate the intuition that there is something epistemically defective about drawing justified conclusions for bad reasons. Such beliefs are ill-founded, in virtue of not being based on justifying evidence.

We think that WF is an acceptable evidentialist account of the pre-theoretical notion of a well-founded belief. This is a good place to state our view that the notion has at least two significant epistemic roles to play.

First, and most simply, one useful epistemic role for an account of a well-founded belief concerns theorizing about what it is to be reasonable. A reasonable person is, among other things, one who has an inclination to base her beliefs on undefeated justifying reasons. That is, a reasonable person must have an inclination toward well-founded beliefs. WF seems to us to impose the right requirements on reasonableness. And second, knowledge of P requires a well-founded belief in P. If a belief is justified and otherwise apt for knowledge, but not well-founded, then the belief is accidentally correct in a way that somewhat resembles what occurs in the classic Gettier cases. But, unlike in classic Gettier cases, there is nothing epistemically defective about the connection between the person's justification for P and a fact making P true. The belief itself is not held in light of the justification, though. It is held dogmatically, or from wishful thinking, or on some other epistemically faulty basis. Knowing a proposition to be true requires a well-founded belief in the proposition.

This necessary condition for knowledge requires a fairly broad notion of a basis for a belief. For example, in many cases of knowing by remembering, the person has forgotten her original basis for the belief. (We discuss cases of this sort in section A3 of "Internalism Defended", Chapter 3.) In such cases, her current justification derives partly from background evidence she has that she sufficiently tends to acquire true beliefs on subject matters that are similar enough to that of the remembered proposition. This evidence in the background distinguishes knowledge by memory, when the original source is forgotten, from fortunately accurate recollective beliefs that are not thereby known. The need for a broad notion of basing arises because this sort of background contribution to the justification is almost never a conscious part of knowing by remembering. Yet it is an essential part of the evidence by which the belief is currently justified. So it must be part of the basis for the belief if the belief is to be well-founded and thereby known.

4. Stewart Cohen has raised an issue about how basic sources of knowledge provide evidence.[37] Evidentialists seem required to say something implausible about what is justified. To illustrate the problem, we can suppose that simple perceptual experiences all by themselves provide justification for some simple corresponding beliefs about the external world. For example, one might hold the following principle:

RED If S seems to see something red (S is appeared-to-redly), then S is justified in believing that there is something red before S provided S has no defeaters for this proposition.[38]

---

[37] See Stewart Cohen, "Basic Beliefs and the Problem of Easy Knowledge", *Philosophy and Phenomenological Research*, 65 (2002), 309–29.

[38] Defeaters of the sort mentioned in RED are parts of one's overall evidence that defeat one's justification. They are "internal" defeaters. They differ from the external defeaters of justified true beliefs that disqualify the beliefs from being knowledge.

Analogous principles might be defended for other simple sensory qualities. A corresponding principle might be advanced concerning memory. We will say that any property for which any such principle is true is a property that "directly justifies" belief in the relevant external world proposition.

If there are any properties that directly justify belief in the relevant external world propositions, then it seems that one can all too easily come to know facts about one's visual accuracy. Suppose that RED is true. And suppose one wonders whether one's visually formed beliefs that things are red are usually correct. That is, one wonders whether things really are red when one judges that there is something red on the basis of seeming to see something red. If RED is true, then one seems to be all set to construct a good inductive argument for the accuracy of one's judgments that things are red. The argument would have as premises such propositions as:

Now (when I am seeming to see something red) I believe that something is red, and I am right.

Each such judgment is justified. The first conjunct is justified, we assume, because one knows what one visually experiences and what one believes. And, given RED, the second conjunct is justified as well. If one can combine enough such premises, one gets what looks like a good inductive argument for a general conclusion that affirms the accuracy of one's beliefs that something is red. Yet, one does this without needing any general information about one's perceptual abilities. Nothing more is needed than the truth of RED and one's realization that one is believing that something is red on the relevant experiential basis. This is an implausibly easy way to justify the conclusion that one is making uniformly true color judgments.

We believe that this argument helps to bring out challenging issues about how experiences justify beliefs. We do not think that the accuracy of one's color judgments can be so easily supported by inductive argument. In our view, RED is false, as are other principles of the same structure. It might be thought that if RED is false, then the nearest true principle is one according to which the experience of redness must be combined with a justified general principle about the reliability of one's perceptions of red in order to have justification for the belief that there is something red before one. It is difficult to see how one could acquire justification for the general principle without prior justification for specific beliefs. Cohen advocates a holist view according to which, at some point in intellectual development, both the individual belief and the general belief first become justified.[39]

---

[39] See Cohen, "Basic Beliefs and the Problem of Easy Knowledge", section VI.

Evidentialism

One can reject RED without resorting to Cohen's holism. The experience of redness all by itself does not justify to any degree the corresponding external world belief. Perhaps very young children and newly sighted adults can have the experience of redness without being justified at all in believing that there is something red before them. They may even lack the requisite concepts. People learn to respond to particular kinds of experiences with the judgment that there is something red present. Exactly what it is in this learning that equips people for justified color judgments is not clear. One learns not to make the judgments in response to any and all episodes where one is appeared-to-redly. It is reasonable to think that one must learn something about distinguishing sufficiently apt environments for visual color judgments and perhaps also something about signs of perceptual abnormalities. Evidence acquired in this learning makes it true that people can be justified in believing that something red is present. If an account along these lines is correct, then what is learned need not be some general proposition about the reliability of one's redness judgments. This is supported by the fact that people can know that things are red without having the sophistication required for knowing any such generalization. Children who have learned their colors can know that there is a red object before them without having any such general knowledge.

Though we believe that the evidentialist approach to this matter that we have sketched is correct, the details must await another occasion.

Part II
Critical Discussions

5
Authoritarian Epistemology
Richard Feldman

One traditional problem in epistemology concerns the relation that must hold between a body of evidence and a proposition for it to be rational (or reasonable or justified) for a person having that body of evidence to believe that proposition. The problem manifests itself in many ways. For example, familiar questions about our knowledge of the external world turn in part upon whether our experiential evidence makes our ordinary beliefs about the world justified. Similarly, the problem of induction is in part the question of whether evidence concerning observed regularities justifies belief in unobserved regularities. Comparable questions can be raised about the epistemic value of moral "intuitions" for beliefs about morality, for the epistemic value of religious experience for beliefs about religion, and for the epistemic value of experimental and observational evidence for theoretical beliefs in science.

The general question, of which all of these are instances, then, can be framed this way:

Q. What relation must hold between evidence E and proposition P for it to be epistemically rational for a person whose evidence is E to believe P?

In this paper I will discuss several seemingly diverse recent answers to (Q). I will argue that they all share a common feature, in spite of their superficial diversity. I hope to show that each of these answers is a kind of "authoritarian epistemology" and that each succumbs to an objection as old as that found in Plato's *Euthyphro*.

1

Before turning to the authoritarian epistemologies that are the main topic of this paper. I will, in this section, consider several points that will help to clarify (Q) and in the next section briefly discuss some other proposed answers to (Q).

Richard Feldman

First, (Q) asks about the conditions under which believing a proposition is *epistemically* rational. The point of this qualification is to make clear that it is rationality (or justification) of an epistemic sort that is in question. There can be cases in which believing a proposition is beneficial, and thus perhaps prudentially rational or justified, but not epistemically rational. Some beliefs about one's future success may be of this sort. Perhaps some beliefs are morally justified when they somehow add moral value to the world. But this has nothing much to do with epistemic rationality or justification.

Second, it can be epistemically rational for a person to believe a proposition even if the person fails to believe it. The question raised by (Q) concerns the *propositions* that are rational for the person to believe. It does not concern the *beliefs* that are justified. The question is thus analogous to ethical questions about what a person is justified in doing, what it would be acceptable (or obligatory) for the person to do, rather than which of the person's deeds are justified.[1]

Third, I assume that evidence is not necessarily restricted to other believed propositions. The experiences a person has can be counted as part of the person's evidence. So, for example, my current visual experiences may be part of the evidence relevant to the assessment of the rationality of my now believing that there are people in the room. Memory experiences and the feelings of confidence (or the lack thereof) that go with them can also count as evidence.

Fourth, by the phrase "a person whose evidence is E" I mean a person whose total (or total relevant) evidence is E. Some epistemologists believe that one's total evidence supports a proposition provided some portion of that evidence prima facie supports it and nothing in the rest of the evidence undermines or defeats that support. Although I will not discuss this matter further here, nothing in this paper is incompatible with the idea that the relation of epistemic support is best understood in this way.

Finally, (Q) is formulated in evidentialist terms. That is, the question presupposes that a relation between the evidence a person has and a proposition determines whether believing that proposition is rational for that person. Some philosophers, such as reliabilists, may think that framing the question this way rules out their answer from the start. It does strain the language a bit to fit reliabilist views into this framework, but one could give a reliabilist answer to (Q)

---

[1] There are nontrivial questions about the connections between the conditions in which a person is justified in believing something and the conditions in which a person has a justified belief. For example, it will not do to say that if a proposition is justified for a person and the person believes that proposition, then that belief is justified. The reason for this is that a person may believe a proposition that is justified for him but believe it for all the wrong reasons. Such a belief is not justified, even though it is a belief in a proposition that the person is justified in believing.

Authoritarian Epistemology

along the following lines: Evidence E makes believing P rational just in case there is a reliable process leading from (belief in) E to the belief that P.[2]

II

One might think that the epistemic-support relation that (Q) asks about can be understood in terms of familiar logical relations. One might propose a deductivist account according to which evidence supports a proposition only if the proposition can be deduced from the evidence. This view is excessively restrictive, implying that the evidence in all the examples mentioned at the outset of this paper is insufficient.[3] A more plausible view is "inductivism," according to which a body of evidence makes believing a proposition rational provided the proposition is deducible from or inductively supported by the evidence.

One problem with inductivism arises from the third point listed in section I. If one's evidence can include nonpropositional items such as perceptual experiences or current feelings, then it is not clear that familiar logical notions properly capture the relation that holds between evidence and the propositions that evidence justifies. There's no clear sense to the claim that a proposition is deducible from or inductively supported by an experience.[4]

Rather than attempt to solve this problem, for present purposes I will simply adopt some terminology that masks it. Let us say that an experience necessitates a proposition if the experience is such that necessarily, if the experience occurs, then the proposition is true. And let us say that an experience makes a proposition probable provided the experience is such that if it occurs, then the proposition is probably true.[5] A body of evidence can then be said to necessitate

---

[2] Although the way (Q) is formulated may suggest to some that it must be given a foundationalist answer, I am making no such assumption. We can take coherentism to be the view that one's evidence includes everything else one believes and that a further belief is supported by one's evidence provided it coheres with that evidence. Thus, a legitimate answer to (Q) could be given in coherentist terms.

[3] The argument against deductivism has two main premises: (*i*) in all the familiar cases the propositions we believe cannot be deduced from our evidence, and (*ii*) in at least some of those cases our beliefs are rational. The first premise is more difficult to establish than one might imagine, since it is possible for deductivists to contend that our evidence includes conditionals linking our basic evidence to the conclusions we wish to draw from that evidence. I believe, however, that deductivists will have a hard time explaining why these conditionals are justified, and thus I think that the argument against deductivism is sound.

[4] Perhaps one can attempt to establish logical relations between experiences and propositions by arguing that experiences have propositional content.

[5] There are, no doubt, serious problems with the concepts described here. If experiences have their intrinsic characteristics only contingently, then they necessitate or make probable very little. One might want to say, for example, that my current experience of seeming to see a teacup necessitates the

a proposition just in case the proposition must be true if the propositions in the evidence are true and the experiences it includes occur. And a body of evidence makes probable a proposition provided the proposition is probably true if the propositions in it are true and the experiences in the evidence occur. Making use of these notions, we can formulate the inductivist answer to (Q) as follows:

I. If a person, S, has evidence E, then it is epistemically rational for S to believe P if and only if either E necessitates P or E makes P probable.

There are difficult questions about how to interpret "probable" in this context. On an epistemic interpretation, to say that E makes P probable is to say that having E as evidence makes it epistemically rational to believe P. So interpreted, (I) is empty.[6] Other interpretations of (I) appeal to frequency or logical interpretations of probability. I will describe below, briefly, some problems associated with (I) given such interpretations. A full investigation of this topic would require detailed treatment of the various interpretations of probability, something well beyond the scope of this paper.

What is crucial to note here is that there appear to be counterexamples to (I) in both directions, given a standard nonepistemic interpretation of "probable." That is, sometimes one's evidence necessitates or makes probable something, but believing that thing is not rational. And, it is widely thought, sometimes it is rational to believe something even if one's evidence does not imply it or make it probable.

The following example shows that the conditions in (I) are not sufficient for rationality. Suppose a beginning logic student has learned the axioms of some axiomatic system but knows little more about the system. The student is looking through the back of the logic text and notices a list of complex formulas. The list is part of an exercise set to which the following explanation is attached: "Exactly half of the formulas listed below are theorems. Which of them are theorems?" The student looks over the formulas, understands some of them, and thinks that one of them seems true. So, he believes it. He does not have any decent reason to think that the formula can be derived from the axioms, and the fact that it is listed in the book does not give him testimonial or inductive evidence that it is a theorem, since half the formulas listed there are nontheorems.

---

proposition that I seem to see a teacup and makes probable the proposition that I do see a teacup. But if that experience could have been very different than it actually is, then it does not necessitate or make probable these propositions.

[6] I argue below that the fact one's evidence necessitates a proposition is not sufficient for it to be rational for one to believe the proposition. If that argument is sound, then under the interpretation being discussed (I) is false. But the second conjunct simply restates the concept we are attempting to analyze.

He also has no reason to trust his hunches or inclinations on these matters. Suppose, however, that he's right; the formula is a theorem.

Among the student's evidence in this case are axioms which do imply the theorem. So, according to (I) it is rational for him to believe the theorem. But, quite clearly, that is a mistaken result. He's not yet justified in accepting that theorem. Coming to understand the proof, or at least getting good testimonial evidence that it's a theorem, is surely required. The mere fact that there is a complicated derivation from the axioms plainly does not make belief in the theorem rational for him. From an epistemological point of view, all the formulas in the list at the back of the book—the theorems and the nontheorems—are on a par. With no other evidence to go on, suspending judgment about all of them is the rational thing to do. Believing some of them, but not others, is not made rational by the mere fact that some of them happen to be logically derivable from the axioms. The fact that a body of evidence necessitates a conclusion does not guarantee that it is reasonable for anyone who has that evidence to believe that conclusion.

Essentially the same point applies to propositions that are merely made probable by one's evidence. Alvin Goldman has made this point while objecting to a theory he calls "Evidential Proportionalism."[7] He describes a case in which a detective knows facts which make probable a conclusion about which suspect is guilty of a crime. But the line of reasoning from those known facts to that conclusion is a very complex statistical one and not at all understood by the detective. Just as in the case of the logic student, believing the conclusion is not made rational by the mere fact that there exists this probabilistic relation between the evidence and the conclusion. The fact that the evidence does make it more probable that one of the suspects is guilty is not epistemically relevant to the statistically naive believer. A logical or probabilistic connection of this sort is not sufficient for epistemic support.

The examples discussed so far show that having evidence which implies or makes probable a proposition is not sufficient to make believing that proposition rational. Is having such support necessary? Many philosophers think the answer is "No." The reason for this can best be brought out in terms of an example. Consider the average person who sees something that looks like a tree and believes that the thing is a tree. We typically take such beliefs to be rational. However, it is widely argued, the inductivist cannot ultimately defend such a claim. If we take the person's relevant evidence to be limited to his perceptual

---

[7] Alvin Goldman, *Epistemology and Cognition* (Cambridge, Mass.: Harvard University Press, 1986), 89–93.

experience or to the proposition that he sees something that looks like a tree, then, it is claimed, the evidence bears no logical or probabilistic relation to the conclusion. To get a probabilistic relation one must also have as evidence something like the proposition that, usually, when a thing looks like a tree the thing is a tree.

Perhaps this expanded evidence does make probable the conclusion. However, it is questionable whether defenders of (I) have any adequate basis for thinking that typical believers have the generalization available as evidence. Roderick Chisholm writes:

> To see that there is something wrong with this account of perception, we have only to ask: what was the nature of those earlier experiences wherein we found that a tree-like experience was accompanied by the apprehension of an external, physical tree? How was it made known to us then that there was a tree there? ... The inductive theory transfers the question to those earlier experiences wherein we were able to correlate tree-appearances [things looking like trees] with the perception of external trees. And then it leaves the question unanswered.[8]

Richard Fumerton writes:

> [Hume] correctly concludes that one could never inductively establish sensations as evidence for the existence of physical objects for one could never observe the necessary correlations between sensations and objects necessary to get knowledge of the premises of an inductive argument.[9]

I will not challenge these objections to (I) here, although I am not entirely convinced that they are correct. They rest on the assumptions that the generalization is needed in the evidence for there to be a probabilistic relation to the conclusion and that the generalization can only be established by *observing* that sensations of a certain sort are regularly correlated with the presence of objects of a certain kind. This is rightly said not to be within our power. However, both assumptions warrant further scrutiny.

Another answer to (Q), which I will call the "traditional view," holds that there are irreducible nonlogical epistemological facts to the effect that certain bodies of evidence support certain propositions. Thus, for example, the fact that a thing looks red just does provide good evidence for the proposition that it is red. One doesn't need to justify independently some inductive generalization for

---

[8] Roderick Chisholm, *Theory of Knowledge*, 3d ed. (Englewood Cliffs, N.J.: Prentice-Hall, 1989), 45–6.

[9] Richard Fumerton, "Metaepistemology and Skepticism," in *Doubting: Contemporary Perspectives on Skepticism*, ed. Michael Roth and Glenn Ross (Dordrecht: Kluwer, 1990), 60–1.

the conclusion to be justified. Epistemological facts are a kind of quasi-logical fact, in that they depend on epistemological relations that obtain independently of what anyone thinks or does. But, for the reasons mentioned above, epistemological relations are distinct from familiar logical and probabilistic relations.

I believe that Stewart Cohen and Keith Lehrer had something like the traditional view in mind when they wrote:

> According to foundationalist theories, like Chisholm's and Pollock's, the justification articulated in epistemic principles is just a brute epistemic fact. It is a brute epistemic fact, postulated in the principles cited above, that under certain conditions of appearing or believing a person is justified in believing a specified proposition. When such justification is defeated, it is again a brute epistemic fact that the justification is defeated.[10]

Richard Fumerton, with great reluctance, endorses a similar view when he suggests that we "can be directly and immediately acquainted with facts of the form E makes P probable."[11]

Many contemporary philosophers are likely to deny the existence of brute epistemological facts. It is tempting to think that if some body of evidence does provide epistemic support for a proposition, it must do so either because epistemic support can be reduced to (or analyzed in terms of) some nonepistemic concepts or because epistemic-support relations hold in virtue of some other relation that holds between the evidence and the proposition. The idea is that epistemic facts must somehow depend upon nonepistemic facts. (Analogies to ethics should be clear.) An adequate answer to (Q) would describe these other relations and facts.

If (Q) cannot be answered by appeal to familiar logical and probabilistic relations or by appeal to brute epistemic facts, then one wonders how it can be answered at all. In the remainder of this paper I want to examine several recent theories, of varying degrees of plausibility and influence, all of which attempt to explain the basis of epistemic rationality in nonlogical terms. They thus purport to provide alternatives to inductivism and the traditional view. I will argue against them, in an effort to suggest that we would do well to return to either inductivism or the traditional view.

---

[10] Stewart Cohen and Keith Lehrer, "Justification, Truth, and Coherence," in *Human Knowledge: Classical & Contemporary Approaches*, ed. Paul Moser and Arnold Vander Nat (New York: Oxford University Press, 1987), 331.

[11] Fumerton, op. cit., 67–8. Fumerton attributes the view to John Keynes in *A Treatise on Probability* (London: Macmillan, 1921).

Richard Feldman

III

The authoritarian theories I want to examine hold that relations of epistemic support depend on the beliefs, behavior, or intentions of some individuals. Roughly, the theories hold that if a person has evidence E, then believing P is justified if and only if some designated individual or group—an epistemic authority—approves of believing P on the basis of E. The theories differ with respect to who the designated authority is and with respect to the ways in which such an authority must approve of the belief. All theories that fit this pattern are versions of what I will call "authoritarian epistemology." I will describe three such theories, as well as a fourth theory that is similar in some respects but does not quite fit the pattern.

1 Individual Subjectivism

Richard Foley's theory makes epistemic rationality a function of an individual's own "deepest epistemic standards." He takes these standards to be revealed by what the person would accept if he or she were to reflect in an appropriately epistemic way. He writes:

[I]t is epistemically rational for an individual to be persuaded of the truth of just those propositions that are the conclusions of arguments that he would regard as likely to be truth preserving were he to be reflective and that in addition have premises that he would uncover no good reason to be suspicious of were he to be reflective.[12]

Foley's view is a kind of individual subjectivism according to which the epistemic rationality of a person's beliefs depends upon what that person thinks of his or her arguments for those beliefs. But Foley's view is not a simplistic and naive subjectivism, according to which it is one's actual beliefs about available arguments that determine rationality. Rather, his theory advocates a kind of reflective subjectivism, according to which it is what conforms to one's own deepest epistemic standards that determines rationality. This is important since one's actual beliefs and practices need not conform to one's deepest standards. Lack of attention, carelessness, fears, desires, and many other factors could cause there to be a difference. Analogously, one might have deep views about what's morally right and wrong but behave in ways and have transient and unreflective beliefs about such matters that don't conform to those beliefs. It is

---

[12] Richard Foley, *The Theory of Epistemic Rationality* (Cambridge, Mass.: Harvard University Press, 1987), 5.

Authoritarian Epistemology

the deep epistemic standards, not the transient thoughts and actions, that Foley appeals to. We can formulate his theory this way:

F. If S has evidence E, then it is rational for S to believe P iff if S were sufficiently reflective, then S would believe that the argument from E to P is sufficiently likely to be truth preserving and that the premise (i.e., E) of that argument is true.

Foley makes clear that his fundamental idea is that rational beliefs are beliefs that conform to one's deepest epistemic standards. He spells out one's deepest epistemic standards in terms of the arguments one would endorse if one were sufficiently reflective in the appropriate way. Now, these are two separable elements of his theory, and, I believe, the counterfactual analysis of one's deepest standards is a distraction from the real heart of the theory.[13]

So, I propose that we eliminate the counterfactual from Foley's theory and take the best version of individual subjectivism to be something like this:

F1. If S has evidence E, then it is rational for S to believe P iff S's own deepest epistemic standards approve of the inference from E to P (i.e., according to S's deepest epistemic standards, the inference from E to P is a good one).

(F1) differs from (F) in that (F1) drops the counterfactual and replaces it by a straightforward appeal to the agent's own standards. Notice the similarity of (F1) to the following view endorsed by John Pollock. Pollock writes:

[W]e can give an entirely adequate analysis of epistemic justification as follows:

a person's belief is justified if and only if he holds it in conformance to his epistemic norms.[14]

Thus, it appears that both Foley and Pollock endorse versions of individual subjectivism.

---

[13] I argued for this point in "Foley's Subjective Foundationalism," *Philosophy and Phenomenological Research*, 50 (1989): 149–58. It seems to me that what Foley's theory declares to be rational is, roughly, what would be rational on reflection. But what would be rational on reflection may well differ from what is in fact rational. There are arguments that are not rational for you to accept now. Their premises do not now provide adequate support for their conclusions for you. But, if you were reflective you would come to see the merits of the arguments and then, but only then, it would be rational for you to believe the conclusions. Foley's theory mistakenly declares it actually rational for you to believe those conclusions. Furthermore, there are arguments that are rational for you to accept, given the apparent plausibility they have and the approval they get from others. But, if you were to reflect, you would then (but only then) come to see their flaws. Foley's theory mistakenly declares such arguments no good for you. But it has this result only because it includes in its assessment of current rationality attitudes and insights you would have only if you were reflective.

[14] John Pollock, *Contemporary Theories of Knowledge* (Totowa, N.J.: Rowman and Littlefield, 1986), 168.

Richard Feldman

There are numerous questions one might raise about (F1).[15] For example, it is not at all clear that people regularly have deep epistemic standards. They may simply have a set of dispositions to believe various things under various circumstances and to accept or reject various inferences. So, it isn't clear that the theory has implications regarding all the cases it should. However, I will not pursue this sort of question about Foley's theory here. Instead I will turn to some other theories that are superficially quite unlike Foley's but which, I will argue, are in some respects quite similar and which all fall victim to one line of criticism.

2 Expertism

A second version of authoritarian epistemology has been proposed by Stephen Stich and Richard Nisbett. (Stich no longer accepts it.) They see their theory as a modification of a view proposed earlier by Nelson Goodman. Stich and Nisbett make justification depend on the practices of those one regards as experts on inferential practice. They write:

On our amended view, an attribution of justification to a rule of inference can be unpacked as a claim that the rule accords with the reflective inductive practice of the people the speaker takes to be appropriate. ... So, on the view we are urging,

Rule r is justified

is to be analyzed as

Rule r accords with the reflective inferential practice of the (person or) group of people I (the speaker) think appropriate.[16]

We can call the person an agent thinks appropriate to assess rules of inference the agent's epistemic authority and then reformulate Stich and Nisbett's proposal as the following answer to (Q):

SN.   If S has evidence E, then it is rational for S to believe P iff inferring P from E conforms to the reflective practice of S's epistemic authority.

There are many problems of detail with this proposal, but I will mention only one.[17] It is possible, indeed likely, that many people do not have epistemic

---

[15] I discuss some of these objections in "Foley's Subjective Foundationalism."

[16] Stephen Stich and Richard Nisbett, "Justification and the Psychology of Human Reasoning," *Philosophy of Science*, 47 (1980): 188–202; the quotation is from 201.

[17] Some of the points mentioned here are developed in greater detail in Earl Conee and Richard Feldman, "Stich and Nisbett on Justifying Inference Rules," *Philosophy of Science*, 50 (1983): 326–31.

authorities. Depending upon exactly how we deal with nonreferring singular terms in instances of (SN), it will have no implications for such cases or it will imply that such a person has no rational beliefs. That result is clearly unsatisfactory.

One can easily imagine variants on Stich and Nisbett's version of expertism. (SN) makes justification depend upon the practices of those individuals a believer regards as expert. Other views could appeal to the stated views of the experts rather than their practices. It is also possible to appeal to the practices or views of the socially recognized experts. But rather than discuss these variations on the theme, I will look next at a theory that appeals to an expert of a different sort.

3 Supernaturalism

The first two theories we have looked at are individualistic, in the sense that they make rationality relations dependent upon factors that can vary from one individual to another. There is, according to these theories, no nonrelative or "objective" fact about whether some evidence makes some belief rational. Rather, some evidence makes believing a proposition rational for a person depending upon certain facts about that individual. As a result, you and I could have similar, perhaps identical, evidence concerning some proposition and it may be rational for one of us to believe it but not rational for the other to believe it. Alvin Plantinga's version of authoritarian epistemology differs in this respect. His view is a kind of supernaturalism, the leading idea being that a belief is justified when it results from the proper functioning of one's cognitive system. He explains proper function in theological terms: A system is functioning properly when it functions the way its designer, God, intended it to function. So, on this view, if two people have the same evidence, the same propositions are rational for them.[18]

Plantinga writes:

[A] belief has warrant for me only if (1) it has been produced in me by cognitive faculties that are functioning properly (functioning as they ought to, subject to no cognitive dysfunction) in a cognitive environment that is appropriate for my kinds of cognitive faculties, (2) the segment of the design plan governing the production of that belief is aimed at the production of true beliefs, and (3) there is a high statistical probability that a belief produced under those conditions will be true.[19]

---

[18] The claim here relies on the assumptions that the two people have the same cognitive design and that the relevant parts of the cognitive system are designed to respond only to evidence. Plantinga may not accept these assumptions, especially the second one.

[19] Alvin Plantinga, *Warrant and Proper Function* (Oxford: Oxford University Press, 1993), 46–7.

Richard Feldman

A variety of factors lead Plantinga to complicate his basic story, which is expressed in the first clause. The main one, for our purpose, is this. One's cognitive system has many goals and is designed to achieve a variety of purposes. It may be that one of its goals is to give people true beliefs about their environment. But there are times when true beliefs are detrimental to some other significant end. For example, there are times when it is good to be optimistic—to believe that one will succeed or thrive—even though one's evidence does not support that belief. It seems that our cognitive system is designed to allow, or even encourage, such beliefs in at least some circumstances. However desirable those beliefs may be, they are not epistemically rational beliefs. This is the reason for the second clause in the passage just quoted. The third condition is intended to assure that the system is in general a reliable one. A simple rendition of Plantinga's theory is:

P. *S*'s belief that *p* is rational iff *S*'s belief that *p* results from the proper functioning of the segment of *S*'s cognitive system that is aimed at producing true beliefs. (The system is functioning properly when it is functioning the way God intended it to. The aim of a segment of the system is determined by God's reason for including it.)

As formulated, Plantinga's theory concerns the rationality of actual beliefs, not the conditions under which believing a proposition is rational. However, it can be modified to be a theory of the latter sort, and thus more directly useful as an answer to (Q). The modification yields:

P1. If *S* has evidence *E*, then it is rational for *S* to believe *P* iff if the segments of *S*'s cognitive system that are aimed at producing true beliefs were to function properly (i.e., as God intended them to function), then (working from evidence *E*) they would produce the belief that *P*.

As was the case with individual subjectivism and expertism, there are many questions one might raise about the details of this theory. For example, one might wonder whether our cognitive systems have all the "segments" that Plantinga mentions and whether these segments can plausibly be said to be "aimed at producing true beliefs."[20] Again, I will not go into these objections here. Instead, I'll turn in the next section to what I see as the common element of the three theories just described.

---

[20] I develop objections along these lines, as well as others, in "Proper Functionalism," *Nous*, 27 (1993): 34–50.

IV

With only a little bit of harmless distortion, we can characterize the three theories described in section III as special cases of one general kind. Roughly, the theories all say that a body of evidence justifies belief in a proposition provided that inferring that conclusion from that evidence gets the approval of the appropriate person—oneself on reflection, one's epistemic authority, or God. We can state the general pattern this way:

AE. If S has evidence E, then it is rational for S to believe P iff the inference from E to P is approved by——.

To get Foley's individual subjectivism, fill in the blank with "S after careful reflection" (or "S's deepest epistemic standards"). To get Stich and Nisbett's expertism, fill in the blank with "S's epistemic authorities." To get Plantinga's supernaturalism, fill in the blank with "God."

There is, as I said, some harmless distortion in describing these theories as instances of (AE). Stich and Nisbett don't speak of experts approving of an inference. Rather, what matters to their theory is whether the experts follow the inference. However, we can say that they express their approval by making the inference. Plantinga doesn't speak of God approving an inference. Instead, he speaks of God designing a cognitive system to make an inference. However, it isn't stretching things too far to say that God is approving of an inference by designing our systems to make it. So, his theory is close enough to the pattern to warrant discussion under its heading.

V

The problem I want to raise for (AE) has its roots in Plato's *Euthyphro*.[21] There Socrates is discussing Euthyphro's view that what's pious is what's loved or approved of by the gods. Socrates asks Euthyphro whether the pious is loved by the gods because it is pious or pious because it is loved by the gods. The point, I think, is that it might be true that all and only pious things are loved by the gods, but that the gods love those things because they are pious (or, better, because they realize they are pious). But if that's the case, then there must be some other feature of these things that makes them pious and which makes the gods love them. It is this other property that properly defines piousness and that should be described in our account of piousness. The authoritarian definition of

---

[21] Plato, *Euthyphro, Apology, Crito*, trans. F. J. Church (New York: Bobbs-Merrill, 1956); see 12–13.

piousness fails. Similar objections, I think, apply to ideal observer theories in ethics. And, I believe, a similar objection applies to all versions of authoritarian epistemology.

To accept individual subjectivism is to hold that believing a proposition is rational provided believing that proposition conforms to the believer's epistemic standards, no matter how bizarre or misguided those standards happen to be. To accept expertism is to hold that believing a proposition is rational provided believing it conforms to the standards of one's experts, no matter how confused or muddled those experts happen to be. To accept Plantinga's supernaturalism is to hold that a belief is rational provided believing it conforms to the design plan covering the believer, no matter how inept the designer happened to be[22] and what purposes the designer has for the system. (Of course, when you add that the designer is perfect, the problem may seem less severe.)

When put the way I just put them, each of these theories seems quite implausible. However, it is fairly easy to see why one might be led to accept them. Why would one think that what's rational is what one approves of upon reflection (or what's supported by one's deep epistemic standards)? Because one thinks that people on reflection are able to identify good inferences (or their deep standards are apt to be good ones). Why think that what's rational is what the experts (or those one regards as experts) approve of (or do)? Because the experts are especially likely to evaluate (or make) inferences properly. Why think that good reasoning is reasoning that follows patterns prescribed by God? Because God knows what good reasoning is and designed us to reason well.

In my view, there is an independently identifiable thing that counts as good reasoning or justified belief and the theories described here attempt to characterize it in a roundabout way. They identify some person or system that will, in suitable circumstances, properly identify good reasoning as good reasoning. And then the theories say that good reasoning is reasoning so identified by those people or systems. There may well be some biconditional in the ballpark of each of these theories that is true. To take the simplest example, good inferences may well be the ones God endorses. But if it is true that God endorses them because they are good, then it must be that there is a philosophically more illuminating theory of good reasoning to be sought. The same goes for the other theories.

We can construct an authoritarian or expert-evaluator theory of almost anything. I think that criticism of such theories will typically come in three

---

[22] This claim may be somewhat unfair, given the third condition, which requires a kind of general reliability, that Plantinga builds into his account. Still, I don't think this undermines the general point raised in this section.

Authoritarian Epistemology

stages. To illustrate this, consider the suggestion that a person, S, is in country X if and only if some designated authority would think, in appropriate circumstances, that S is in country X. An individual subjectivist version of this idea would be:

C. S is in country X iff if S were to reflect on her whereabouts, S would conclude that she is in country X.

(C) will have many true instances since, for the most part, people will be right about their locations. However, the first and most obvious sort of criticism of (C) is that it is false. There are decisive counterexamples to it. People who have been kidnapped and brainwashed may have mistaken reflective views about where they are.

One could attempt to patch up this analysis by packing more things into the antecedent of the conditional. One could attempt to specify conditions that guarantee that people will have correct beliefs about where they are. For example, one might try:

C'. S is in country X iff if S had a correct belief about which country S is in, then S would believe that S is in country X.

This too is false, since there are possible cases in which S would only have a correct belief about her location if she were in a place other than she actually is. A further revision suggests itself:

C". S is in country X iff if S were in the same place S actually is and S had a correct belief about which country S is in, then S would believe that S is in country X.

(C") is true, but objectionably circular. So, the second sort of criticism of authoritarian analyses is that, if they are immune to counterexamples, they are circular.

It is not entirely clear that every counterexample-free authoritarian analysis must be circular. Some are at least not explicitly circular. For example, consider:

C'''. S is in country X iff God believes that S is in country X.

I will ignore worries about the theism assumed by this principle. It is not overtly circular. Some believe that it is true. Still, no one would say that it provides the desired sort of account of what it is to be in a particular country. It does not identify the basis or analysis of that concept. It does not provide an account of what it is to be in a country.

My contention is that the authoritarian epistemological theories described above are subject to similar criticism. My first line of objection to each of the theories is that there are counterexamples to the equivalences they imply. For example, Foley's idea that rationality consists in conformity to one's own deep epistemic standards seems quite implausible when you consider the possibility of a person having absurd standards. There's also some question about why he picked one's deep standards. Why not appeal instead to one's not so deep standards or to one's most readily available standards? For that matter, why not appeal to my Uncle Al's standards? The answer, I suspect, rests on the realization that the theory is apt to have more plausible implications when it appeals to one's deep standards, since one's less deep standards can be, and my Uncle Al's standards were, rather peculiar.

Expertism also seems to have obviously mistaken implications. For example, you might agree that someone is the leading expert on inferences, but if that person did not accept a rule you favored, you would sooner withdraw your evaluation of the person than you would reject the rule. This will be especially problematic if your expert has made a serious mistake. (SN) has the bizarre implication that a person who knew the truth about the rule the expert mistakenly endorsed would be justified in believing conclusions supported by the fallacious rule and unjustified in refraining from believing those conclusions.[23]

Plantinga's supernaturalism is also subject to numerous potential objections. Some turn on the possibility of poorly designed systems. The theory seems to imply that such systems acquire justified beliefs by conforming to their poor designs, even if they are designed to believe contrary to their evidence and to violate elementary rules of logic. (It may be that the third clause of Plantinga's proposal helps to deal with such cases.) Furthermore, the theory seems to imply that a believer who violates its design plan by improving upon it, and following evidence when it is designed not to, cannot thereby get justified beliefs. This strikes me as a clear mistake.

Defenders of these theories may find some of these objections unpersuasive and they may find ways to patch up the theories to get true biconditionals. Thus, for example, with suitable qualifications and additions, one might be able to construct a version of, say, Foley's theory that gets things right. There are

---

[23] Stich and Nisbett themselves point out such a case when they describe the work of a Professor Coppee whose logic text endorses the gambler's fallacy. They quote Coppee as follows: "Thus, in throwing dice, we cannot be sure that any single face or combination of faces will appear; but if, in very many throws, some particular face has not appeared, the chances of its coming up are stronger and stronger, until they approach very near to certainty. It must come; and, as each throw is made and it fails to appear, the certainty of its coming draws nearer and nearer." (See Stich and Nisbett, op. cit., 196.)

some conditions such that I would approve of just those beliefs of mine that are justified. Thus, consider:

F2. If S has evidence E, then it is rational for S to believe P iff if S were a perfect identifier of which propositions it is actually rational for S to believe, then S would believe that it is rational for him to believe P.

This, or something very close to it, is true. But (F2) obviously fails as an analysis, due to circularity. Similar points may be true of the other theories.

Now, I can't prove that every authoritarian epistemological theory is either false or circular. But the case for the view that they are is fairly compelling. Under almost any circumstances I can imagine, anybody will be open to making bad judgments about the rationality of inferences or beliefs.[24] The only way to eliminate that possibility is to characterize the person and the circumstances in a way that amounts to saying that the person in those circumstances must have correct judgments about rationality. And if you say that in the analysis, it is circular.

Even if one can come up with an analysis that's neither false nor circular, it will still fail some additional condition that we set for theories of this sort. A correct analysis of justification—and an acceptable answer to (Q)—should identify the basis of rationality, the property that makes belief rational. Authoritarian epistemologies fail to do that.

Any alleged authority—oneself on reflection, experts, God—will have a reason for using or favoring a particular pattern of inference or for endorsing a particular belief. Assume for the sake of discussion that we were designed by God. When God designed our cognitive system, or the truth-seeking part of the system, he had a goal for that system. There was something it was supposed to do. Being omniscient and omnipotent and benevolent, he had lots of options he could have implemented, but he chose the one he did. He must have had a reason. That reason must have been that, given various other considerations, the system he chose was the best option. That is, it did the best job of achieving the goal—getting true beliefs or knowledge. But then the fact that God chose this system, and intended us to reason this way, isn't what makes reasoning this way good reasoning. What makes it good reasoning is whatever it is about this sort of reasoning that led God to choose it in the first place.

Basically the same point applies to the other theories. When you carefully reflect on arguments and declare some to be good and some to be bad, those are not whimsical judgments. There is something about the arguments that you

---

[24] A version of expertism that makes God everyone's expert may avoid this problem.

see, or think you see, that leads you to evaluate them as you do. It is this other property, what you see or think you see in the argument, not your assessment of it, that determines rationality. Some evidence for this comes from the fact that if you learned that you had previously misperceived the argument and that it didn't have the properties you previously thought it had, you would conclude that it was always a bad argument. You would not conclude that it used to be good, because you used to approve of it when you reflected, but that now it is bad because you've changed your mind. What you are thinking about, when you assess the rationality of a past belief, is not what you would have thought about that belief on reflection but rather something about the merits of the reasons you had for the belief. Past or present reflective judgments about the merits of those reasons may be useful guides to the belief's epistemic status, but they are not determinants of that status.

Similarly, inferential rules aren't good ones simply because experts use them. Rather, experts are good guides to good rules simply because they have the best insight into the matter.

Thus, it seems to me that even if there is a version of (AE) that is true and not explicitly circular, it would still be unsatisfactory as an account of rational belief. That's because it would only get at that concept in an indirect way and it would fail to explain or illuminate the basis of rationality.

VI

There's another theory that bears a similarity to the authoritarian theories we've just examined, although it does not characterize rationality in terms of the views or practices of any alleged expert. This is a naturalistic variant of Plantinga's supernaturalism; it holds that rational beliefs are beliefs formed in the way one is naturally designed to form beliefs. Although I know of no one who explicitly endorses this theory, William Lycan comes close to endorsing it.[25] Something similar has been defended by L. J. Cohen, who contends that "Human reasoning cannot be held to be faultily programmed: it sets its own standards."[26]

One formulation of the theory suggested by these remarks is:

N. If S has evidence E, then it is rational for S to believe P if and only if people (or S) are naturally designed to believe P when they have evidence E.

---

[25] See William Lycan, *Judgement and Justification* (Cambridge: Cambridge University Press, 1988), ch. 7, esp. 148 f.

[26] L. J. Cohen, "Can Human Irrationality be Experimentally Demonstrated?," *Behavioral and Brain Sciences*, 4 (1981): 317–70; the quotation is from 317.

Authoritarian Epistemology

One needn't read anything supernatural into (N). It makes sense to say that the human heart is designed to pump blood in certain ways. This does not imply that there is any designer. Similarly, it makes sense to say that our cognitive systems are designed for us to form beliefs in a certain way.

There are problems with (N) comparable to the problems with the other theories examined here. For one thing, there is a problem in separating epistemic evaluations from other evaluations. In my view, it is a good idea to believe things when so believing is, all things considered, likely to be beneficial. So, for example, sometimes being optimistic and engaging in wishful thinking is a good thing. We may be naturally designed to believe in those ways in certain circumstances. But, of course, wishful thoughts are not *epistemically* justified. The problem, then, is to identify which aspects of our natural design lead to the formation of epistemically justified beliefs. Where Plantinga had some hope of dealing with this issue by appealing to the aims God had for segments of the design plan, naturalists must find a naturalistic counterpart. I see little hope for success, but I will not pursue this point here.

What is most relevant to present concerns is that this sort of naturalism is subject to exactly the same sort of objection as are the authoritarian theories discussed above. Why think that it is rational to believe what one is naturally designed to believe? Because nature has as a matter of fact designed us to be rational. But to accept naturalism is to accept something well beyond the claim that we are in fact designed to be rational. It is to hold that believing a proposition is rational provided one is naturally designed to believe that proposition, no matter what factors shaped one's design and no matter what the designer, "Mother Nature," was trying to accomplish. There's little plausibility in that claim. It may be that nature makes us reason well, but our beliefs don't count as rational simply because they are the ones nature leads us to have.

VII

Some defenders of some versions of authoritarian epistemology may not be moved by my objection. I believe that as an objection to authoritarian theories about one's location, the sort of objection I've raised is decisive. So, defenders of authoritarian epistemologies must think that there is some important and relevant way in which epistemic propositions differ from location propositions that makes authoritarian epistemologies immune to the objection. I will briefly consider four possible defenses in this final section.

Richard Feldman

1 Rejecting Epistemic Objectivity

Some epistemologists may believe that there are no objective standards of epistemic evaluation. On their view, there is no truth about what "really" justifies what. Instead, there are simply the beliefs and practices of various individuals and cultures. Just as some people think that there are no standards on matters of taste or beauty apart from the beliefs and practices of various individuals and groups, there are those who may be inclined toward a rejection of independent standards in epistemology. Rationality, they might say, is dependent upon the attitudes of the relevant group or individual.

A view such as the one just described hardly constitutes a defense of any version of authoritarian epistemology. Indeed, it seems to be a rejection of all such theories. It implies that people can have their differing beliefs and differing inferential practices, and even their differing beliefs about what entails or makes probable what, but that there is no truth of the matter about what is "really" justified for them. There is, then, no correct answer to (Q) and so authoritarian answers are not correct. So, a rejection of epistemic objectivism will not provide support for any version of authoritarian epistemology.

2 Evolutionary Considerations

Defenders of some versions of (AE) may find hope in Quine's remark that "Creatures inveterately wrong in their inductions have a pathetic but praiseworthy tendency to die before reproducing their kind."[27] Extrapolating wildly, one might think that we must tend toward rational beliefs since we have survived. Hence, to form beliefs as we naturally do is to form rational beliefs. So, some version of naturalism or perhaps some version of individual subjectivism is true.

Evolutionary considerations may show that we are naturally disposed to reason in ways that are conducive to our survival. This conclusion is not the same as the desired one, that we are naturally disposed to form epistemically rational beliefs. Whether the further conclusion is true depends upon how significant having epistemically rational beliefs is to our survival. In other words, we may have reason to think that we must in general be disposed to form beliefs in ways that are conducive to survival. But whether we are entitled to the further claim that we are in general disposed to form beliefs that are epistemically

---

[27] W. V. O. Quine, "Natural Kinds," in his *Ontological Relativity and Other Essays* (New York: Columbia University Press, 1969), 126.

Authoritarian Epistemology

justified depends upon whether such beliefs are conducive to survival. And that is an issue not addressed in the argument suggested by Quine's remark.[28]

Even if there were a sound evolutionary argument for the conclusion that we are naturally disposed to form beliefs that are epistemically justified, that conclusion would be a far cry from the conclusion needed to support the naturalistic version of (AE). It is at least a conceptual possibility that there is a species of naturally bad reasoners. They might be in the process of becoming extinct. If we are not in that unfortunate situation, then that we are not is at best a contingent truth. So, these evolutionary considerations can't show that (N) is true. To accept (N) is to accept the idea that no matter how we happened to be naturally disposed to form beliefs, beliefs so formed would be epistemically justified. That thesis receives no support from contingent facts about our own evolutionary situation.

3 An Analogy to Language

Another line of thought might lead some to accept (N) or something like it. Consider by analogy the rules of a language. It is not implausible to think that the right way to speak English is somehow determined by the ways in which people actually do speak English. Whatever rules there are, are some sort of generalization on or extrapolation from the things people say and write. The language is, in this respect, a socially constructed thing. This might lead one to think that an analogue of (N), stating the conditions under which it is linguistically correct to utter a certain sentence, would be true.

Whatever the merits of this analogue of (N), I think that we ought not be induced to accept (N) itself. Rational belief is not, as I see it, a social phenomenon in the same way proper English usage is. Language is arbitrary and conventional. We could use any symbols to refer to any objects we like. No doubt some possible languages are less effective means of communication than others, but as long as we share a language, we are able to communicate. We are speaking properly when we follow the patterns we have adopted. Rational belief is not an arbitrary and conventional matter. We can't, by agreement, turn bad reasoning into good reasoning.

L. J. Cohen proposes a competence-performance distinction for our reasoning abilities similar to the distinction frequently invoked in discussions of linguistic ability. Cohen argues that "any normative analysis of everyday reasons—any statement that such and such lay judgments of deducibility or probability are

---

[28] I don't mean to suggest that Quine was arguing for this further conclusion.

Richard Feldman

correct, or incorrect, as the case may be—must in the end rely for its defense on the evidence of relevant intuitions."[29] His point is that our theory of rational inference is ultimately a matter of systematizing our intuitions about cases. But, he goes on,

> where you accept that a normative theory has to be based ultimately on the data of human intuition, you are committed to the acceptance of human rationality as a matter of fact in that area, in the sense that it must be correct to ascribe to normal human beings a cognitive competence—however often faulted in performance—that corresponds point by point with the normative theory.[30]

Cohen's point seems to be that since our intuitions are the source of both our theoretical judgments of rationality and of our rational competence, there must be a correspondence between our theory of what constitutes a rational inference and our natural inclinations to make inferences. This suggests that a theory along the lines of (N) must be true.

Notice that variants of Cohen's argument might be used to defend individual subjectivism or expertism. Cohen seems to think that the intuitions on which a theory of rationality are based are the collective intuitions of nonexperts. Hence, he gets the conclusion that those people must have a corresponding rational competence. However, one who thought that the theory of rationality for each person must be based on that person's intuitions might use the argument to defend a version of individual subjectivism. One who thought that our theory of rationality must be based on the intuitions of experts might use the argument to defend some version of expertism. I'll discuss only Cohen's version of the argument below. Similar comments apply to the other versions.

Cohen's argument raises a host of interesting issues. If he's right in thinking that our theory of rationality is based on our intuitions, then he may be right in thinking that in some sense our theory must in the end correspond to our intuitions. Perhaps it is correct to put this point by saying that we have a natural "competence" for rational inference. However, this is a competence for identifying which inferences are rational ones, which is a rather different matter from a natural competence to make good inferences. Furthermore, his conclusion is that our competence must correspond to our *theory* of rationality, not that we must actually be rational. His negative answer to his title question—"Can Human Irrationality be Experimentally Demonstrated?"— leaves open the possibility that humans can be systematically irrational, even if that fact can't be demonstrated. So, I think that Cohen's argument, even if sound, fails to

---

[29] Cohen, op. cit., 320.   [30] Ibid., 321.

Authoritarian Epistemology

establish anything quite like (N). Comparable arguments for other authoritarian theories fail for similar reasons.

4 The Egocentric Predicament

I will consider one final line of thought that presents a more promising defense of the individual subjectivist version of authoritarian epistemology. Foley suggests a rationale for his view that

> arises out of the egocentric predicament. You need a way to make sense of the world from your own perspective, a way in which it is appropriate for you to proceed, given your own lights. You cannot simply read off from the world what is true, and it is equally unhelpful for you to be told to use only reliable methods. Part of your predicament is to determine from your own perspective what methods are reliable. In exactly the same way, it is unhelpful... to suggest... that you are to believe only that for which you have objectively adequate grounds, grounds that in fact make probable what you believe. For once again, part of your predicament is that of determining from your perspective what grounds are objectively adequate....
>
> So, how are you to proceed? There is only one possible way to proceed, given the nature of the predicament. You must marshal your own resources.... [Y]ou do so by using your own current beliefs and your own epistemic standards. If in terms of these a proposition P is defensible, then believe it. My further suggestion is this: if under these conditions you do believe P, then in one important sense you will be believing just what it is rational for you to believe.[31]

While I agree with Foley that there is some sense in which the egocentric predicament makes it true that all one can do is proceed by one's own lights, I don't see here any reason to think that whatever one comes up with by one's own lights is therefore in any important sense rational. As William Alston notes, conforming to one's own standards might make one "consistent, well integrated, or single minded,"[32] but that's not the same as being epistemically rational.

Furthermore, Foley's own remarks undermine his claims in the passage just quoted. He says that the reflections that determine believers' deep epistemic standards are reflections "from a purely epistemic point of view" and this requires that they "abstract away from potentially distorting features of their current psychological states."[33] He says this because he realizes that reflections

---

[31] Richard Foley, "Reply to Alston, Feldman, and Swain," *Philosophy and Phenomenological Research*, 50 (1989): 169–88; the quotation is from 171–2.

[32] William Alston, "Foley's Theory of Epistemic Rationality," *Philosophy and Phenomenological Research*, 50 (1989): 135–47; the quotation is from 46.

[33] Foley, "Reply to Alston, Feldman, and Swain," 181.

that are not from a purely epistemic point of view might yield appraisals that don't lead to epistemically rational beliefs. That is, a theory that appealed to standards produced by less than purely epistemic reflection might be subject to counterexamples because those reflections would yield bad standards. Perhaps by appealing to epistemic standards one would accept from a purely epistemic point of view Foley avoids some such objections, but the result is that his theory fails to come to grips with the problem brought on by the egocentric predicament. It is quite unhelpful to be told to make my beliefs conform to the standards I would have from a purely epistemic point of view from which all distorting features of my current psychology are eliminated. It is every bit as much a troublesome part of my current predicament to figure out what those standards are as it is to figure out what objectively adequate grounds are. I conclude that we can't get a sound defense of individual subjectivism out of these considerations of the egocentric predicament.

VIII

The authoritarian epistemologies I've examined in this paper all attempt to characterize epistemic rationality in terms of the beliefs, preferences, or actions of some individual or group. I have argued that all such theories fail. As formulated, they are open to seemingly decisive counterexamples. Although it may be possible to reformulate them to avoid these examples, the theories remain open to the charge that at best they identify epistemic rationality in an indirect and uninformative way. They identify some circumstances and some individual or group who would believe rationally or prescribe rational beliefs in those circumstances, and then they identify rational belief with beliefs or prescriptions like those. An acceptable theory of rational belief would say what it is about those beliefs or prescriptions that make them rational.[34]

---

[34] Earlier versions of this paper were presented at the Conference on Epistemology and Philosophy in Dubrovnik and at West Virginia University. I am grateful to audiences there for helpful discussion. As always, I am indebted to Earl Conee for his comments on drafts of this paper.

6
The Generality Problem for Reliabilism
Earl Conee and Richard Feldman

1. Introduction

A. Reliabilism and the Generality Problem

Reliabilism is the most widely discussed contemporary epistemological theory. The most widely discussed version of reliabilism is process reliabilism, which makes the processes that cause and sustain beliefs epistemically crucial. The central idea of process reliability theories of epistemic justification is this:

RJ. A belief is justified if and only if it is produced by a process that reliably leads to true beliefs.[1]

A fully articulated reliabilist theory must identify with sufficient clarity the nature of the processes it invokes. In doing so, the theory confronts what has come to be known as 'the generality problem'.[2]

---

[1] Some authors discuss process reliability accounts of knowledge rather than accounts of epistemic justification. No point will be made below that turns on the differences between knowledge and justification.

[2] Alvin Goldman in "What is Justified Belief?" in G. S. Pappas (ed.), *Justification and Knowledge* (Dordrecht, Holland, Reidel, 1979) and *Epistemology and Cognition* (Cambridge, MA, Harvard University Press, 1986) defends process reliabilist accounts of epistemic justification. In those works he recognizes the existence of the generality problem. See especially "What is Justified Belief?", p. 11 and *Epistemology and Cognition*, pp. 49–51. The problem is emphasized in Richard Feldman's "Reliability and Justification", *The Monist*, 68 (1985): 159–74. It is also discussed by John Pollock in "Reliability and Justified Belief", *Canadian Journal of Philosophy*, 14 (1984): 103–14. For responses to the problem, see the works of William Alston, Ralph Baergen, Mark Heller, Frederick Schmitt, Ernest Sosa, and Charles Wallis cited and discussed below.

A simple example will show the nature of the problem. Suppose that Smith has good vision and is familiar with the visible differences among common species of trees. Smith looks out of a house window one sunny afternoon and sees a plainly visible nearby maple tree. She forms the belief that there is a maple tree near the house. Assuming everything else in the example is normal, this belief is justified and Smith knows that there is a maple tree near the house. Process reliabilist theories reach the right verdict about this case only if it is true that the process that caused Smith's belief is reliable. And one might think that the process is obviously reliable. However, before accepting this conclusion, we should think carefully about exactly what that process is and what its reliability consists in.

Light reflects from the tree and its surroundings into Smith's eyes. Optic neural events result, and these produce further neural events within Smith's brain. Particular concrete occurrences, involving sensory neural simulation in combination with complex standing conditions in Smith's brain, result in Smith forming the belief. This sequence of concrete events is the process that caused the belief. So, if we take the process that must be reliable to be composed of causally active events that bring about the belief, then reliabilism requires for justification that a sequence of concrete events is reliable.

However, reliability is a kind of tendency. The notion of reliability applies straightforwardly only to enduring mechanisms, such as an eye or a whole visual system, and to repeatable types of processes, such as the type: visually initiated belief formation. Reliability does not apply in any obvious way to the particular sequence of concrete events that caused Smith's belief on this occasion. Each event in the sequence happens only once and the sequence causes whatever beliefs result just on that occasion. Process reliabilists who realize this have sought the requisite reliability in the *types* of process of which particular causal sequences are tokens.[3]

As many reliabilists have recognized, each token process that causes a particular belief is of numerous different types of widely varying reliability. The token event sequence in our example of seeing the maple tree is an instance of the following types, among others: visually initiated belief-forming process, process of a retinal image of such-and-such specific characteristics leading to

---

[3] It is possible to construct a version of process reliabilism which is only about process tokens and does not confront the generality problem. It faces a considerable problem in making sense of the claim that a token sequence of events has some tendency toward producing beliefs whose truth-ratio would constitute its "reliability". Furthermore, the problems that affect (NS3) below, in virtue of types having just one belief content in their outputs, also affect reliability theories that locate a sort of reliability in process tokens.

The Generality Problem for Reliabilism

a belief that there is a maple tree nearby, process of relying on a leaf shape to form a tree-classifying judgment, perceptual process of classifying by species a tree located behind a solid obstruction, etc. The number of types is unlimited. They are as numerous as the properties had by the belief-forming process. Thus, process reliability theories confront the question of which type must be reliable for the resulting belief to be justified. It is clear that the answer to this question will significantly affect the implications of the theory. For instance, while visually formed beliefs in general seem to be fairly reliable, processes that use a characteristically maple-leafish visual experience to judge that a maple tree is near seem much more highly reliable, and perceptual processes leading to a belief that a tree, which is behind a solid obstruction, is of a particular species seem generally unreliable, in spite of the fact that in some of their instances, such as the present case, the obstruction is transparent. The process token is of endlessly many other types as well, types of extremely varied reliability. So, which type has to be sufficiently reliable?

Process reliabilists must solve this generality problem. A solution identifies the type whose reliability determines whether a process token yields justification.[4] This type is "the relevant type" for that token. Thus, it is not the causally active process token that has to be sufficiently reliable, according to reliabilists. It is the relevant type of the process. We need to know what determines this sort of relevance.

Without a specification of the relevant type, process reliabilism is radically incomplete. Only when a bearer of reliability has been identified does the theory have any implications about the justification of beliefs in particular cases. Philosophers often overlook this. They purport to determine whether or not a given belief is justified according to reliabilism using nothing more than one description of the process causing the belief. No such inference is acceptable. The theory must first be elaborated at least enough to imply exactly what process type has to be reliable in the case in question. A fully general reliabilist theory of justification has to do this for all cases in which there is a fact of the matter.

A second necessary task for process reliabilists is to specify which situations of a process type's operation determine whether or not the type is reliable. Strength of reliability might be settled by the frequency with which the process actually produces true beliefs or rather by its truth-to-falsehood output ratio in

---

[4] There may not always be a fact of the matter. In the examples used here the belief is either definitely justified or definitely unjustified. The reliability of relevant types for process tokens that lead to beliefs whose epistemic status is unclear will be of less value to present concerns, since such cases are less useful in assessing epistemological theories.

certain counterfactual circumstances. The generality problem arises no matter how this question about reliability is answered. William Alston's sensible specification of what determines the reliability of a process type will do for present purposes:

R. A process type is reliable if and only if it would yield a high proportion of truths over a wide range of situations of the sort we typically encounter.[5]

B. Necessary Conditions for a Solution to the Generality Problem

A solution to the generality problem must meet the following three conditions.

First, it must be principled. Given the multiplicity of belief-forming process types and their variations in reliability, it is easy to make *ad hoc* case-by-case selections of types that match our intuitions. But case-by-case selection of relevant types does not constitute working out a reliabilist theory of justification.

The claim that the reliability of "the relevant type" of the belief-forming process is what determines a belief's justification is analogous to the claim that "the suitable type" of a horse is what produces victory in a horse race. In the absence of further explanation, this use of 'suitable' has no definite content. On its own, the phrase 'the suitable type of horse' tells us nothing about what makes horses win races. If there is no further explanation but rather we are offered case-by-case choices of "suitability-making properties", choices made on the basis of knowing which horses are the winners, then the claim is no closer to having any definite content. Clearly, a general basis for identifying suitability is required for the claim to say more than just that something or other makes each winning horse win its race. Analogously, we have an informative reliabilist theory of knowledge or justification only after we are told what determines "the relevant type" in general.

---

[5] "How to Think about Reliability", *Philosophical Topics* (Spring 1995): 1–29. The proposal mentioned here appears on p. 10. If a satisfactory solution to the generality problem existed, it would be worth addressing difficulties with details of this proposal. For one thing, it is not clear who "we" are supposed to be: all of humanity, or all sentient life on earth, or sentient life everywhere in the universe, or etc. And for another thing, it is unclear which belief-forming situations are "typical". Presumably, bizarre psychology lab situations are atypical. But is perception during space travel atypical, no matter how common it becomes? Are situations of fatigue, intoxication, and excitement atypical? Another difficulty is that we may be specially perceptive during rare emergency conditions. If these are atypical situations, then the justified beliefs from these perceptions might turn out not to be of generally reliable types. In any event, if the present work is correct in its main thesis, then these difficulties are not worth pursuing because the generality problem is insoluble.

The Generality Problem for Reliabilism

Although a solution must be principled, it need not state necessary and sufficient conditions for relevance that are either precise or always determinate. Claims to the effect that a belief is "epistemically justified" might be vague and they might be context-sensitive in various ways. A solution must be universal only in that it must specify the relevant type whenever there are definite facts about justification.

The second requirement for solving the generality problem is that the rule must make defensible epistemic classifications. Stating a general rule of relevance that merely assigns some type or other to each process token does not constitute an adequate solution to the generality problem.[6] The types identified must have a reliability that is plausibly correlated with the justification of the resulting beliefs.

Finally, a solution must remain true to the spirit of the reliabilist approach. We are addressing process reliability theories.[7] So, the rule of relevance must somehow implement the basic idea that it is the reliability of a process of belief formation, specified in nonepistemic terms, that settles the epistemic status of the belief. Process reliabilists characteristically think that a belief is justified because the workings of the process that produced it (or sustained it) are sufficiently conducive to generating true beliefs. A solution to the generality problem would specify those workings so as to bear out this idea. A solution thus cannot identify the relevant type for a process in a way that merely smuggles a non-reliabilist epistemic evaluation into the characterization of relevant types. For instance, one could develop a form of "reliabilism" that just restates an evidentialist theory of justification in a roundabout way. Pseudo-reliabilism of this sort holds that there are only two relevant types of belief-forming process.

---

[6] In some passages in "How to Think about Reliability" Alston seems to construe the generality problem somewhat differently. For his purposes, a solution need only show that there are "objective, psychological facts of the matter that pick out a unique type as the one of which a particular process is a token" (p. 5). Thus, he is content to identify relevant types, leaving as a different matter the question of the acceptability of the resulting reliabilist theory. The problem discussed here is that of getting the theory stated *and getting it right*. Any rule of relevance that selects one type for each token will generate some reliabilist theory or other, most of them preposterous.

[7] Reliabilist theories that make use of the reliability of indicators or mechanisms of belief formation are thus not our topic. But the problems for the theory of relevance (NS3) below carry over straightforwardly to many reliable indicator theories. Also, there is a problem similar to the generality problem concerning "the mechanism" that produces a given belief. For instance, when a visual judgment relies on only black-and-white discrimination, is the person's whole visual apparatus the relevant mechanism, or is it the black-and-white sensitive portion of that apparatus, or is it only the active part of that portion? Does "the mechanism" for remembered beliefs include parts of the brain active in forming the belief, or just parts active in storing it and recovering it? These questions may have answers that are attractive to reliabilists, but as with the generality problem, the challenge is to identify a principle that implies all and only the correct answers to such questions.

One type is "belief based on adequate evidence" and the other type is "belief based on inadequate evidence". Assuming that the first of these is reliable and the second is not, this version of reliabilism will get plausible results (or at least results that an evidentialist would find plausible).[8] But this theory is only verbally a version of reliabilism. It mentions the processes of belief formation only in order to characterize the quality of the evidence for the belief. This is obviously incompatible with the spirit of process reliabilism.

C. Our Thesis

Our thesis is that the prospects for a solution to the generality problem for process reliabilism are worse than bleak. We will investigate the merits of approaches exemplified by several recent proposals. There is no significant progress in any of these approaches, singly or in combination. The basic process reliabilist idea just does not pan out.

It is reasonable to look for a solution to the generality problem in three places: common sense, science, and context. Common sense is the likeliest source. As we shall soon see, Alvin Goldman's early account of reliabilism draws much of its initial attraction from the *prima facie* correlation between justified beliefs and beliefs produced by common sense types of processes that are probably reliable. Goldman immediately realized that some refinement of these common sense types is needed, for reasons that we shall illustrate below. But at first glance the thought is appealing that common sense process types like "careful perception", "vivid memory" and the like are reliable. So, it makes sense to pursue the reliabilist idea that these types of process produce justified beliefs because of their reliability. In contrast, common sense belief-forming process types like "guessing" seem to be unreliable and seem to yield unjustified beliefs.

If, as we shall argue, common sense types will not do, then the next likeliest source of relevance is scientific classification. Scientific types of belief-forming processes are types that correspond to the predicates that enter into the laws and explanations of science. We shall next investigate the possibility of solving the generality problem by identifying relevant types with these scientific types.

---

[8] The results of this theory may be implausible in "demon worlds" in which a demon sees to it that believing in accord with one's evidence does not reliably lead to truths. Whether this is a decisive objection to our evidentialist pseudo-reliabilism depends in part on how reliability is measured. The objection as it is often described makes the challengeable assumption that a process is reliable in a world only if it regularly leads to truths in that world. In contrast, see for instance William Alston's proposal, stated as (R) above. It does not imply that unreliability in a demon world entails a lack of justification. What (R) makes decisive is roughly the truth-ratio of belief production in more typical situations.

The Generality Problem for Reliabilism

Another reasonable thought is that different types are relevant to justification in different contexts, just as different comparison classes determine the application of terms like 'small' and 'far' in different contexts and just as different reference classes determine the truth value of probability judgments in different contexts. Thus, we shall consider next the merits of contextualist solutions to the generality problem.

We shall argue that none of these approaches works out. This might raise the concern that our way of posing the generality problem for reliabilism is somehow ill-conceived. It might be thought that the relevant types are obvious when the question is properly understood, or that no general solution is actually needed. We shall take up this line of thinking as well.

That exhausts the reasonable philosophical approaches to the generality problem. If they all fail, then so does process reliabilism.

II. Common Sense Types

In his pioneering defense of process reliabilism, Alvin Goldman appeals to common sense process types in an effort to convey the plausibility of the theory. He writes,

> ... what kinds of cause confer justifiedness? We can gain some insight into this problem by reviewing some faulty processes of belief-formation, i.e., processes whose belief-outputs would be classed as unjustified. Here are some examples: confused reasoning, wishful thinking, reliance on emotional attachment, mere hunch or guesswork, and hasty generalization. What do these faulty processes have in common? They share the feature of *unreliability*: they tend to produce *error* a large proportion of the time. By contrast, which species of belief-forming (or belief-sustaining) processes are intuitively justification-conferring? They include standard perceptual processes, remembering, good reasoning, and introspection. What these processes seem to have in common is *reliability*.[9]

Thinking of reliabilism in terms of these types gives the theory its initial appeal.

However, common sense types have two liabilities as the basis for a solution to the generality problem. First, there are far too many common sense types to provide a unique identification of the relevant type for each process token. In our initial example, Smith's visually formed maple tree belief results from a process instantiating all the following common sense types: visual process, perceptual process, tree-identifying process, daytime process, indoor process, etc., etc. These types differ widely in their reliability. So, we still need to be told which one determines the justificatory status of the resulting belief.

---

[9] "What is Justified Belief?", pp. 10–11.

Earl Conee and Richard Feldman

The other main problem with the types Goldman mentions is that not all beliefs resulting from any one such type are even approximately equally justified. Consider another common sense type that Goldman refers to, brief and hasty scanning. Sometimes, on the basis of a brief and hasty scanning we can get extremely well justified beliefs, as when we see in a glance that there is a tree in the backyard. Other times brief and hasty scanning does not yield a justified belief, as when the belief concerns exactly how many leaves are on the tree. Simple common sense classifications are thus too broad to make the right epistemic distinctions among beliefs.

In a recent discussion of the generality problem, William Alston sometimes calls what he proposes as the relevant types "habits" of belief formation.[10] Likewise, Charles Wallis appeals to "strategies" of belief formation.[11] Habit and strategy are common sense classifications of some of the ways we form beliefs. In classifying trees by species, an expert naturalist has identifying routines that differ considerably from those of novice and ill-informed tree classifiers, even though all of them may judge by experiencing the same views of the trees. The expert is better justified. So there is some initial plausibility in the idea that it is the "routine", the "habit of mind", the "strategy", employed in forming a given belief that determines its level of justification.[12] This suggests:

H. The relevant type for any belief-forming process token is the habit of mind, or belief-forming strategy, that it instantiates.

For a large class of cases, it is doubtful that (H) serves to identify a single relevant type. This is because many process tokens are instances of more than one habit. Smith, our maple tree identifier, may have a habit of concentrating while making careful visual judgments, a habit of calling to mind types of trees known to be in the area when making species classifications, and a habit of counting points on leaves for identifying deciduous trees. Some of her belief-forming process tokens result from the employment of all three habits. So there

---

[10] "How to Think about Reliability", pp. 13 f.

[11] Charles Wallis, "Truth-Ratios, Process, Task, and Knowledge", *Synthese*, 98 (1994): 243–69. See especially p. 266. Wallis relies on belief-forming strategies as part of his response to problems that he discusses for reliability theories of knowledge. It is not clear that he is attempting to solve the generality problem that is the topic of this essay. One reason for this unclarity is that Wallis is working on a concept of knowledge that is relativized to the specification of a task, unlike the traditional concept which is our topic. In any case, we do not intend to attribute to him a simple reliance on strategies as a full solution.

[12] What follows is a possible solution to the generality problem, suggested by some of Alston's language, that merits a brief look. It is not what Alston proposes. His proposals will be taken up shortly.

would be no such thing as "the habit" employed on those occasions, and thus no relevant type by the present proposal.

There are, furthermore, cases in which justified beliefs are formed in a way that is in no intuitive sense "habitual", or "routine", or "strategy-employing". For instance, Smith might happen to notice a cardinal on a branch of the maple tree, and be thereby justified in believing that a cardinal is there. She is not employing any strategy, or habit, or routine, in forming this belief. Thus, a theory that requires a high enough reliability for the relevant type here would conclude that the belief is not justified, since there is no habit or strategy that is either reliable or unreliable. Yet in many such cases the belief clearly is justified.

Also, the same belief-forming habit can produce some justified beliefs and some unjustified ones. Jones might make a habit of judging the theme of a philosophy article by reading only its concluding paragraph. Sometimes the theme is clearly presented there and Jones will be justified. Other times the final paragraph does not make clear the point of the paper and Jones will not gain justification by employing this procedure.

Another approach using common sense classifications would be to hold that the solution to the generality problem is to classify together processes that produce equally general beliefs:

G. Two process tokens are of the same relevant type if and only if they generate beliefs at the same level of generality.

(G) has no promise as a solution to the generality problem. The problem of finding the relevant type does not reduce to that of finding the right level of generality for the contents of the resulting beliefs. It is often not clear what "level of generality" a belief has. But if there is any merit in the approach that (G) represents, then two judgments will be at the same level of generality if their contents consist in classifying an individual by species. Thus, the following visually based beliefs are all at the same level of generality: this is a mountain-goat, this is a giraffe, this is a crocodile, this is an alligator. (G) implies that all such classificatory beliefs result from the same relevant type, and hence all are equally justified. But clearly this is not so. For instance, some such beliefs are based on more justifying perceptible features than others. To ordinary observers, nearby giraffes are pretty obvious, while nearby crocodiles are easily mistaken for alligators. Processes generating equally general beliefs are not all equally justifying.

A similar idea would be to distinguish processes in terms of the identity of their particular output beliefs, so that the different beliefs just mentioned would result from different relevant types of processes. This has numerous unacceptable results too, however. Clearly there are both justified and unjustified examples of belief in the same proposition.

There is no reason to think that any appeal to simple common sense types will solve the generality problem. Their main liability is that they are too broad to differentiate properly among the justification levels of our various beliefs. Less simple types can be constructed by conjoining together the broad common sense classifications that we have been discussing. These can be much narrower, for instance: visual process causing a belief that classifies by species a close, unobstructed, opaque object, in bright sunlight. But the members of such types still vary in their degree of justification depending on such things as whether the viewer is familiar with the visual appearance of the species from the viewing angle, has normal vision, is intoxicated, is expecting visual trickery, is emotionally distraught, etc. There is no good reason to believe that even such narrow kinds will include only equally justified beliefs, however elaborately they are specified, as long as they use only common sense nonepistemic categories.[13]

Common sense types thus do not stand scrutiny as candidates to provide a satisfactory solution to the generality problem.

III. Science

It is in keeping with the "naturalistic" spirit of reliabilist theories to look for classifying help from natural science. One tempting line of thought is that reliabilists can count on cognitive psychology to identify the types of belief-forming

---

[13] In "What is Justified Belief?" Goldman introduced a distinction between belief-dependent belief-forming processes and belief-independent belief-forming processes. The former processes take beliefs, as well as other factors, as inputs and yield new beliefs as outputs. The latter processes do not take prior beliefs as inputs. Belief-dependent processes are reliable when, over a suitable range of cases, they yield true beliefs if their input beliefs are true. Furthermore, a belief resulting from a belief-dependent process is justified only if the input beliefs are themselves justified. One might hope to appeal to this distinction to help deal with some of the examples discussed in this section and elsewhere in this paper. For example, if one's background beliefs are part of the cause of one's animal classifying beliefs, then the differences in the degree of justification for the beliefs mentioned here might be attributable to differences in the degree of justification of the beliefs upon which they depend. One might therefore be able to maintain the claim that one relevant type is responsible for all the species classifying beliefs.

Defenders of reliabilism have not made significant use of the belief-dependent/belief-independent distinction in their efforts to solve the generality problem. There are good reasons for this. First, it is likely that virtually all beliefs that adult humans form are partially caused by other beliefs. Hence, virtually all our beliefs result from belief-dependent processes. It is therefore doubtful that there is any acceptable way for reliabilists to account for the differing epistemic status of the background beliefs in the examples under discussion. Furthermore, some account of the reliable types for belief-dependent processes is needed. If they are identified in terms of, say, patterns of inference, then process reliabilism turns out to be equivalent to the view that a belief is justified if it results from an inference that is

processes that will be useful to their theory. Suggestions of such a view can be found in writings by Alston, Goldman, and Ralph Baergen.[14]

A. Natural Kinds

Alston's mention of habits of mind is not his theoretical proposal for coping with the generality problem. Rather, he suggests that belief-forming process tokens belong to natural kinds and that these kinds are the types to which reliabilists ought to appeal. He writes:

> With a process token, as with any other particular, any of its properties can be said to be correlated with a type to which it belongs ... Even if it is true that you and I belong to indefinitely many classes, such as *objects weighing more than ten pounds, objects that exist in the twentieth century, objects mentioned in this paper*, etc. etc., it is still the case that membership in the class of human beings is fundamental for what we are in a way that those others are not, just because it is the natural kind to which we belong. I shall suggest that something analogous is true of belief-forming processes—that there are fundamental considerations that mark out, for each such process token, a type that is something like its "natural kind".[15]

Although this is not Alston's final account of the matter, it is important to see that more is needed. Merely citing the fact that each belief-forming process falls into a natural kind does not provide an adequate rule of relevance. To see this, note the inadequacy of the following solution to the generality problem.

NS1. The relevant type for any belief-forming process token is the natural kind to which it belongs.

Process tokens may belong to natural kinds. Still, there is no good reason to think that each token belongs to just a single natural kind, and hence no reason to think that (NS1) provides a solution to the generality problem. What the natural

---

likely to be truth preserving from justified beliefs. This familiar view violates the spirit of process reliabilism since it uses processes only as an indirect way to refer to inferential relations. Finally, it is difficult to see just how to make use of the belief-dependent/belief-independent distinction in conjunction with the specific proposals discussed here. Consider, for example, (G). According to (G), the relevant type is determined by the level of generality of the resulting belief. Thus, according to (G), if two people end up believing that there is a giraffe nearby, they have used processes of the same relevant type. None of the details of the routes by which they got to that belief play any role in determining which type they used. One could be making an invalid inference from justified premises while the other is making an accurate classification based on background knowledge. A theory employing (G) incorrectly evaluates the two beliefs the same way.

As the solutions proposed in the existing literature are discussed below, the reader is invited to note that, like (G), they do not give any role to the difference between belief-dependent and belief-independent processes.

[14] Alston's and Baergen's implementations of this idea are discussed below. Goldman mentions this sort of approach in *Epistemology and Cognition*, p. 50.   [15] "How to Think about Reliability", p. 11.

kinds of belief-forming processes are is up for grabs, but every belief-forming process token is categorized in multiple ways by laws in each of several sciences. These all seem to be natural kinds of the process, according to current science. Reasonable candidates for natural kinds of a typical visual belief-forming process include electrochemical process, organic process, perceptual process, visual process, and facial-recognition process. All belief-forming process tokens are thus in a multiplicity of natural kinds. So (NS1) does not single out a relevant type for any such process. These natural kinds differ widely in their reliability. So, (NS1) does not solve the generality problem.

B. Psychological Realism

Process tokens thus belong to numerous natural kinds. Alston contends, however, that for each belief-forming process token there is only one type that is "psychologically real". His suggestion is that this type is the relevant type.

According to Alston, every process token instantiates what he calls a "function". He stipulates that this term is to have its mathematical sense. In the case of beliefs formed on the basis of perceptual experience, these functions take as inputs features of experience to which we are responsive and yield beliefs as outputs. Alston is aware that each particular input/output pair is in the extension of many mathematical functions, but he claims that there is only one such function that any belief-forming process actually is an "activation" of. Only this one is psychologically real.[16]

The intended solution to the generality problem seems to be:

NS2. The relevant type for any process token is the natural psychological kind corresponding to the function that is actually operative in the formation of the belief.

(NS2) does narrow the set of candidates for relevant types. Furthermore, psychology does aspire to provide psychological explanations of at least all normally acquired beliefs.[17] If this aspiration is met, there will be psychological types of belief-forming process for all such beliefs.

If (NS2) provides a solution to the generality problem, it must be that there is only one actually operative "psychologically real" type for each belief-forming

---

[16] "How to Think about Reliability", section vi.

[17] Philosophers often invoke examples in which beliefs result from blows to the head or tumors. It may be that such beliefs do not result from any *psychological* belief-forming process type. Perhaps the explanations of such beliefs must come from a different science or perhaps psychology must be inclusive enough to account for them too, simply because they are mental effects. If some beliefs lack any psychological cause, that would present a problem for (NS2), since even these beliefs can be assessed for justification, and hence they must have a relevant type.

process. In apparent support of this, while discussing the application of (NS2) to beliefs resulting from vision, Alston emphasizes that there is a fact about which elements of a visual scene a person responds to in forming a belief about what is present. Thus, in our example about Smith and the maple tree, Smith might form her belief on the basis of noticing certain features of leaf shape. The token process therefore goes from these input features to that belief. In other examples, when presented with the same scene Smith might pick up on features such as the tree's overall shape or bark texture, rather than leaf shape. These considerations show that the relevant type in the original case must be one that corresponds to a function having as an input/output pair the leaf-shape features to which Smith responds and the belief that she forms.

This may limit somewhat the candidates for relevant types, but in Smith's case there still are numerous overlapping functional relations, and corresponding psychological process types, that include the input/output pair we've identified. There is a very narrow function that goes from just the leaf shape that Smith notices as input to just the output of Smith's particular belief that a maple tree is nearby. There is another function, one that maps a variety of fairly similar inputs, including the particular shape that Smith noticed, onto some belief or other to the effect that there is a maple tree nearby, including the belief Smith forms. There is a broader function, one that maps a variety of somewhat similar inputs, all involving visual shapes, onto either the belief that there is a maple tree nearby or the belief that there is an oak tree nearby or the belief that there is an elm tree nearby, etc. There are still broader types that include the original pair, and add new inputs involving various other sensory cues. In many cases, all these functional causal relations, and many others as well, would be actually operative in forming Smith's belief. Smith's disposition to form the particular belief that she did on the basis of the particular shape that she saw is part of these broader classifying dispositions. The one event of belief formation manifests them all. Thus, in this and other typical cases, there are a multitude of actually operative psychological types.

An example from another domain may help to make this point clearer. Suppose that a certain pot of water at sea level is brought to a boil. There occurred a certain sequence of concrete events leading to the boiling of the water. This sequence instantiates any number of types, all "physically real". We can identify these types in terms of the functions that describe their final stage. At any given pressure, there is a function that maps water onto a certain temperature—its boiling point. This corresponds to the process "bringing water to a boil at sea-level atmospheric pressure". There is a broader type, "bringing water to a boil". The function corresponding to this second type takes water and varying pressures as inputs, and yields a boiling point for water at each temperature. A still broader function takes as inputs triples of temperatures, pressures, and types of liquid and yields the boiling point for each. This corresponds to the type "bringing liquids to a boil". The token process in our example is an instance of all these types. It is not the case that only one is "physically real". All of them accurately characterize what occurred in the pot. Similarly, far too many functions are "psychologically real". They all correspond to natural psychological kinds. So, (NS2) fails to identify the relevant type.

C. Maximum Specificity and Narrow Causal Types

Alston also suggests that his psychological realism implies, or at least is compatible with, a different specification of relevant types, one that relies on completely causally specific functions. He assumes that "the functions in question are maximally specific, in that any difference in input that is registered by the function indicates a different function".[18] Making use of this idea of maximal specificity is one way of trying to make good on the idea that only one function is "operative" in the formation of any belief.[19]

In any case where a person forms a belief on the basis of a perceptual experience, some features of the experience contribute to a belief-forming causal sequence that starts with the experience. Other features of the experience play no causal role. The same goes for subsequent events in the sequence leading to the belief. Some features of these events help to cause the belief, others do not. The maximum specificity proposal is the idea that the relevant type includes all and only process tokens with the same causal features: they all begin with experiences with the same causally active features, are followed by subsequent events with the same causal features, and have the same belief as output. At one time, Alvin Goldman suggested a very similar solution to the generality problem.[20] We can formulate this proposal as follows:

NS3. The relevant type for any belief-forming process token t is the natural kind that includes all and only those tokens sharing with t all the same causally contributory features from the input experience to the resulting belief.[21]

---

[18] "How to Think about Reliability", p. 26.

[19] Throughout this section, when we speak of maximally specific functions or types, we mean the maximally specific *psychological* functions or types.   [20] *Epistemology and Cognition*, p. 50.

[21] Theories can differ over exactly what counts as the input. The process type could begin at the surface of the skin, or farther in at some point where conscious experience begins, or farther out in an external cause of the experience. Alston favors perceptual experiences as the initial step (pp. 12. f). He does not defend this selection. No point made here depends on any particular beginning for the causal sequence that constitutes the process.

(NS3) does yield a unique type for each process token. But the reliabilist theory of justification that employs (NS3) is seriously defective. (NS3) classifies into the same relevant type only beliefs that share *all* internal causal predecessors. Thus, on the reasonable assumption that the content of any normally formed belief is causally determined by its antecedent psychological causes, according to (NS3) each relevant type can have only one content for its output belief.[22] This makes trouble in cases in which the proposition believed dictates the truth-ratio of all process types leading only to it. In such cases the reliability of the relevant type is settled by the mere identity of the belief. Thus, the relevant type of a process leading to any necessary truth must be perfectly reliable. The relevant type of any process leading to any necessary falsehood must be perfectly unreliable. Also perfectly reliable would be the relevant types of all processes leading to any self-confirming belief, such as the belief that someone believes something. The relevant type of the following beliefs would be perfectly unreliable: the belief that there are no beliefs, and the belief that nothing is caused. Since it seems clear that in all of these cases the beliefs can have a level of justification that is other than the implied extreme, these examples run counter to (NS3).

The problems for reliabilist theories built on (NS3) are not confined to beliefs in necessities, impossibilities, or the relatively unusual beliefs just mentioned. Suppose that Jones looks very carefully at a tree and forms the belief that it is a beech on the basis of seeing features which are in fact distinctive to beech trees. As long as experience of such features happens to help to prompt Jones to believe that it is a beech tree, it does not matter to (NS3) why they do so. It can be for good reasons, for bad reasons, or for no reason at all. Recall (R), which tells us that the reliability of a type is determined by the long run truth-ratio of its output when it functions under typical conditions. In the normal worlds used to evaluate the reliability of Jones's tree-identifying process, nothing other than a beech tree presents Jones with exactly the features that initiate the causal process leading to his belief.[23] This by itself is enough for the theory to imply that Jones's belief is justified, regardless of how much information he happens to have about the look of beech trees. Since the highly specific causal factors that led to his belief in fact are indicative of only beech trees, his belief must be justified, according to this theory. In the worlds that determine the

---

[22] Strictly speaking, the assumption may imply only that the "narrow" content of the beliefs resulting from a given relevant type will be the same. No point made here depends on the difference between narrow and broad content. Also, see note 17 above concerning the completeness of psychological explanation.

[23] It is safe to assume that many of our clear vivid experiences of complex ordinary things like trees are produced only by these same ordinary things in all situations of the sort we typically encounter. Holograms, hallucinations, and perfect pictures are, at most, highly atypical.

reliability of the relevant type, only beeches cause the sort of experience that led to his belief that a beech tree is nearby. So this maximally specific type is maximally reliable. Reliabilist theories based on (NS3) thus are unable to distinguish the epistemic status of lucky guesses that happen to be based on distinctive features from expert judgments based on well-understood classifications.

An additional problem is that (NS3) yields a version of reliabilism that is not in keeping with the spirit of process reliabilism. As we have just seen, (NS3) often renders irrelevant the details of the process intervening between an input and a resulting belief. In particular, suppose that Jones and Smith both respond to the same features of a visual input with the belief that there is an elm tree present. Suppose that this input will occur only when there is an elm tree present—it is a distinctive look of an elm leaf, say, the visual appearance of a particular quantity of tiny notches around its edge. Finally, suppose that Smith knows what she is seeing, while Jones is applying some ridiculous and unjustified sort of numerology to the topic. Jones plucks from thin air the idea that the magic number for elms is nine. Jones gets a nine for the tree whose leaf he beholds by counting the number of those distinctive elm notches along the edge of a leaf, and dividing by six, his "tree number". Given (NS3), the relevant types for their processes are maximally specific. These types are thoroughly reliable since nothing other than an elm would cause just that input in any significant fraction of nearby worlds. The fact that one of the two knows what elms look like and the other does not and the fact that one process goes through a silly application of superstitious nonsense do not affect the reliability of the maximally specific types (NS3) specifies.[24] It is just this sort of difference that process reliabilism is supposed to make matter. It is supposed to be sensitive to the possibility that the process one person uses is not generally reliable while the one the other uses is generally reliable, even if in the case at hand both people happen to begin their processes by noticing what is in fact an extremely reliable indicator of the right answer. In other words, process reliability theories are supposed to appeal to much broader relevant types.

D. Categories from Science

Ralph Baergen discusses several examples, explaining what reliabilists might say about them. By generalizing from his remarks it is possible to devise another way reliabilists might appeal to science to solve the generality problem.

---

[24] One might think that the fact that Jones relies on unjustified background beliefs has some bearing on this example. That thought seems right. But (NS3) ignores this fact and suggests nothing about how to make use of it in defending a process reliabilist theory. See note 13.

The Generality Problem for Reliabilism

It is also a second way of attempting to cash out Alston's remark that only one process type is "actually operative" in belief formation.

One example, discussed in the literature by Richard Feldman, concerns a person who sees something on a distant hill.[25] She forms the belief that what she sees is an animal and the belief that it is a mountain-goat. Feldman points out that the more general belief may well be better justified than the more specific one. So, he concludes that reliabilists must find a way to distinguish between the types of processes that cause the beliefs.

Baergen proposes a way to do this.[26] He appeals to David Marr's theory of vision, which holds that in classifying objects on the basis of visual perception, we generate a model of the object which "is compared to descriptions in a sort of catalogue. This catalogue is arranged in levels, so that rough categorizations take place at the lower levels, followed by more fine-grained discriminations at higher levels."[27] Baergen suggests that we make use of this idea in identifying relevant types:

Our account of processes might well reflect this by saying that rough categorizations are generated by different process[es] than those yielding fine-grained categorizations. Applied to Feldman's case, the mountain-goat belief is generated by a different process than that which generated the animal-belief, for they involve different levels of categorization. Also, the process that generated the animal-belief is likely to be more reliable, for there are likely to be fewer nearby situations in which this generates a false belief than there are for the mountain-goat process. So, Reliabilism *can* provide intuitively correct results here.[28]

No doubt reliabilists can state a rule of relevance that produces the intuitively correct results "here". But reliabilism needs a fully general rule. Baergen reports part of a theory of vision that implies that perceptual classifications result from processes that are organized by levels of generality of the resulting beliefs. He suggests that reliabilists can identify relevant types in some way that plays on this fact. However, Baergen does not make clear how to build upon this example to develop a general account of relevant types.

---

[25] "Reliability and Justification", *The Monist*, 68 (1985): 159–74. The example is discussed on pp. 164 f.

[26] Ralph Baergen, *Contemporary Epistemology* (Fort Worth, Harcourt Brace, 1995), p. 99. Contrary to what Baergen says, Feldman does not assert that the processes are of the same type. He merely points out the undesirable consequence of the proposition that they are of the same type. It is notable that this sort of example shows that common sense process types, like the visual belief-forming process, do not produce beliefs of equal justification even when relativized to a fully detailed specification of the external circumstances.   [27] *Contemporary Epistemology*, p. 100.

[28] *Contemporary Epistemology*, p. 100.

One possibility, suggested by Baergen's use of psychology, is that the relevant types are the types that are invoked by the best psychological theories of belief formation. The idea here is that while any token belongs to numerous types that are psychologically real, only one of those types will enter into the best psychological theory that explains the resulting belief. That type is the relevant type. Marr's theory may have been used to illustrate how this might apply in the case of visual belief formation.

We can formulate this idea as follows:

NS4. The relevant type for any belief-forming process token t is the psychological kind that is part of the best psychological explanation of the belief that results from t.

It may be that Alston had something like (NS4) in mind when he said that only one type was "actually operative".

(NS4) rests on the dubious assumption that there is a unique "best" psychological explanation for each belief. The value of an explanation depends upon the use to which it is put. A very specific and narrow explanation might have greater value for some purposes, while a broader explanation might have greater value for other purposes.[29]

Even if (NS4) did identify unique types, it would not be possible to evaluate its implications for process reliabilism without knowing what those types are. There is no good reason to think that the types that are of greatest value for psychological explanation are uniformly helpful to reliabilist theories of justification.

To see why types that are particularly useful for psychological explanation might not be of much help to reliabilists, consider the types Baergen mentions. His proposal ties the relevant types for classificatory beliefs based on visual perception to the level of generality of the resulting belief, and he suggests, plausibly, that a type that produces relatively general beliefs is more reliable than types that produce more specific beliefs. A version of process reliabilism making use of this idea would thus make more general classificatory beliefs better justified than more specific classifications. That is an unacceptable result. Sometimes, a belief applying a broader classification is less well justified than is a belief applying a narrower one. For instance, Jones might use a visual basis for both his belief that the tree he is near is an elm tree and his belief that the tree he is near is a deciduous tree. He can be less well justified in believing the latter, despite its applying a broader classification. This might be true because Jones

---

[29] Compare the water boiling example above. There seems to be no reason to think that the explanation at one level of generality is necessarily better than an explanation at any other level.

does not realize that all elms are deciduous and has just a shaky grip on visual cues to deciduous trees, but he has good training in recognizing elms. Similarly, a person may know at a glance that a thing she sees is a whale, but be less well justified in her belief that it is a mammal. Thus, sometimes the more general belief is the more justified, and sometimes not. So the generality of a visually based classificatory belief does not determine a relevant type that yields a satisfactory version of reliabilism. There is, then, no reason to think that the particular scientific classifications Baergen mentions yield types that are entirely helpful to reliabilism.

Although science does provide the tools to narrow the candidates for relevant types, there is no good reason to think that scientific classifications provide the tools for solving the generality problem.

IV. Solutions without a Necessary and Sufficient Condition

Some philosophers have responded to the generality problem by explicitly denying that the problem requires a general resolution. We will examine two such responses in this section.

A. Constraints

Frederick Schmitt proposes five constraints on which process types are relevant, and then appeals to the constraints in describing problem cases.[30] According to Schmitt, "relevant processes are cognitive processes".[31] His constraints require, among other things, that relevant types are salient, that they are folk psychological process types, and that tokens of the same type are intrinsically similar.

These constraints are not meant to compose what Schmitt calls a "criterion of relevance": a necessary and sufficient condition for relevant types. Schmitt believes that no such criterion is needed. Instead, the constraints are supposed to identify the sorts of factors that we take to matter when we make judgments about justification.

To explain why no criterion of relevance is needed, Schmitt writes:

[W]e have intuitions about which processes are relevant. In judging whether a subject is justified in an inferential belief, we check to see which inferential process the subject exercises—e.g., whether it is induction from sufficiently many instances or affirming the consequent. We have the intuition that these are the relevant processes to consider. In the

---

[30] *Knowledge and Belief* (New York, Routledge, Chapman, and Hall, 1992), Chapter VI.
[31] *Knowledge and Belief*, p. 169.

case of perceptual belief, we check which environmental conditions obtain—whether it is sunny or foggy—and whether the subject is careful and attentive in perception or quick and distracted. Here again we have intuitions about which processes are relevant. Reliabilism may explain why perceptual or inferential beliefs are justified or unjustified by relying on these intuitions.[32]

The existence of these intuitions does not relieve process reliabilists of the responsibility to provide an explanation of their invocation of relevance. Granting that the intuitions exist, the question that we have been asking remains to be answered: According to reliabilism, which type must be reliable for a particular belief to be justified?

Furthermore, Schmitt is mistaken about exactly what intuitions we do have. Schmitt says that "we have intuitions about which processes are relevant". Since Schmitt is addressing the generality problem, this claim seems intended to imply that 'relevant' in the reliabilist use of the 'the relevant type of the process' has some intuitive application to examples. But that is not so. The reliabilist use of 'the relevant type' is entirely technical. The expression might as well have been 'the type that determines justification according to the philosophical theory known as "reliabilism"'. No one has pre-analytic intuitions about this topic. It is up to reliability theorists to assign reference to the term from scratch.

Philosophers and others do make intuitive judgments about which features in examples are "relevant" to the justificatory status of beliefs. Schmitt is entirely right to say that in evaluating inferential beliefs we are inclined to judge relevant the pattern of inference followed, and in evaluating perceptual beliefs we judge the environmental conditions and attentiveness of the perceiver to be relevant. We also judge to be relevant the quality and quantity of evidence the believer has. We typically judge to be irrelevant the day of the week on which the belief is formed and the color of the believer's socks. These are not intuitions about which process types are relevant. They are intuitions directly about what determines a belief's epistemic justification.

The existence of intuitions about which factors are relevant to justification does not eliminate reliabilism's need for a theory of relevant types. The constraints Schmitt describes do not do this on their own. They provide a variety of conflicting criteria. In his discussion of cases, Schmitt gives the constraints differing weights so as to achieve the desired result.[33] Perhaps one can, by

---

[32] *Knowledge and Belief*, pp. 141–2.

[33] For example, Schmitt says about an example that one constraint, which favors a broad relevant type, outweighs two others that favor a narrower type (p. 171). In another case, the existence of two constraints favoring a narrower type is said to outweigh one pointing in a different direction (p. 157).

weighing one factor heavily in one case, a different factor heavily in another, manipulate the constraints in a way that seems to give reliabilism acceptable results. But this is no victory for reliabilism. One could equally well say that the justification of a belief is a function of epistemically irrelevant factors such as the duration of the token of the cognitive process that caused it, the distance of the proximate external cause of the process from the center of the earth, and the amount of energy the process consumed. By *ad hoc* weighting of these factors, one could get acceptable results. The theory, nevertheless, has no merit.

A set of flexible constraints does not solve the generality problem. There are, of course, terms in our language whose application is governed by a set of flexible and varying factors. For example, when we say that someone is a "good athlete", there are a variety of factors that enter into our evaluations. They might include speed, strength, and endurance, among other things. But there is no fixed weight uniformly given to these factors. In different contexts these different factors may be weighed differently and it would be a mistake to ask for some fixed ranking of the importance of these various factors in evaluations of athletic ability. Although Schmitt does not say this, it is possible that he intends to propose that evaluations of processes as reliable work in somewhat the same way.[34] We turn in the next section to a proposal along these lines.

B. Context

Mark Heller contends that the demand for "a general principle for selecting the correct level of generality [for relevant types] . . . is unreasonable".[35] He thinks that contextual factors determine relevant types and thereby solve the generality problem. Heller elaborates his claims about the role of context as follows:

'Reliable' is a perfectly ordinary word that in perfectly ordinary situations is applied to tokens which are instances of several types, where those types have different degrees of reliability. Yet we somehow manage to use this word without difficulty in ordinary discourse.[36]

Heller says that the primary task of his paper is to defend the claim that 'reliable' is richly sensitive to the evaluator's context. This much is unobjectionable. The word 'reliable' surely is context sensitive. That is, whether or not a thing is accurately called 'reliable' depends in part upon the standards set by the context of the ascription. These standards vary, depending for instance on

---

[34] Schmitt does say that relevance is a "messy, more contextual affair" than some might think (p. 159).
[35] "The Simple Solution to the Problem of Generality", *Nous*, 29 (1995): 501–15. The quotation is from p. 502.   [36] "The Simple Solution to the Problem of Generality", p. 502.

how important it is to rely on the thing that is said to be reliable. This is at most a first step toward solving the generality problem. We need to see how context sensitivity helps with the identification of the relevant type.[37]

Heller does not claim just that the standards for the application of 'reliable' are context dependent. He makes the further claim that we readily understand applications of 'reliable' to process tokens that are instances of many types. Thus, when a person says "that process is reliable", the person can refer to a process token and say something true. The person's statement is true provided the contextually determined type for that token is truly said to be 'reliable' in the context of attribution. If Heller is right, then context determines two features of our predications of 'reliable' to tokens. One has to do with the standard for the strength of reliability required for the term to apply in the context. That feature is of no help in determining the relevant type. The other feature has to do with the identification of the type that must meet those standards. We will refer to these latter types as 'contextually determined types'. Thus, a phrase of the form 'the process leading to S's belief that p' is supposed to have, relative to a context, a contextually determined type.

A solution to the generality problem can be constructed from these thoughts. The proposal that we shall formulate combines Heller's contentions about the context dependence of the word 'reliable' with the epistemic contextualist view that the standard for assessing the truth value of knowledge and justification attributions is dependent on the attributor's context.[38]

C. In any context, C, if a person says something of the form 'S knows p' or 'S is justified in believing p', the relevant type of the belief-forming process is the contextually determined type for the phrase 'the process leading to S's belief that p' relative to context C.

(C) embodies the idea that the description 'the process leading to S's belief that p' has a contextually determined process type. (C) puts that idea to

---

[37] Ernest Sosa suggests a contextualist response to the generality problem in *Knowledge in Perspective: Selected Essays in Epistemology* (Cambridge, Cambridge University Press, 1991). Sosa suggests in a programmatic way that relevant types are ones that can "be usefully generalized upon by us as the epistemic community of the" believer (p. 284). Sosa does not elaborate upon this idea, which is a small part of a complex theory. What he does say does not seem to identify a unique type, since multiple types may be "usefully generalized upon".

[38] Although the following thesis is suggested by much of what Heller writes, it goes beyond the explicit proposals in Heller's paper. Also, it makes no use of passages suggesting that a relevant alternative approach to a theory of knowledge solves the generality problem. We see no plausibility in this latter suggestion on its own, and no way to incorporate into it the central theme of Heller's paper concerning the importance for solving the generality problem of the context sensitivity of 'reliable'.

The Generality Problem for Reliabilism

the service of reliabilism by identifying contextually determined types with the relevant types needed to fill out reliabilist theories of knowledge and justification.

A fundamental objection to (C) is that contextual factors do not typically yield one determinate process type for the phrase 'the process leading to S's belief that p'. As a result, reliabilist theories built upon principle (C) will not yield the correct truth value for many clearly determinate attributions of knowledge or justification.

There are some situations in which phrases referring to process tokens apparently work in the way Heller describes. For example, suppose Jones says, "I have three ways to start my old jalopy: first, shifting into gear while rolling it down a hill; second, jump-starting it; and third, praying and then turning the key. Only the first two usually work." Suppose that Jones then starts his car by jump-starting it. He remarks:

P. "The process by which I just started my car is reliable."

Here, Jones's explicit mention of the three types serves to limit drastically the types under consideration. The token mentioned in (P) is of one of those types only. So, this is a case in which 'reliable' is explicitly predicated of a process token and we have no problem in understanding what type must be reliable for the predication to be true.

In typical knowledge attributions, however, no contextual narrowing of candidate process types occurs. If it did, then when a person said that someone knows something, there would typically be a range of contextually salient process types such that the token process leading to the person's belief instantiated only one. But this is plainly not the case for most knowledge attributions. Ordinarily, no class of types of belief-forming processes will have been made contextually salient. And nothing else about typical contexts isolates any one type. So, it is just not true that in the context of knowledge attributions there are contextually determined types for the phrase 'the process that caused this belief'.

To see that this is so, consider our initial example in which Smith comes to know that there is a maple tree nearby by seeing it there. Suppose that Jones, who is sitting in the room with Smith, says:

K. "Smith knows that there is a maple tree nearby."

If Heller's version of reliabilism is to work, there must be, relative to the context of Jones's remark, some contextually determined type for the phrase 'the process that caused Smith's belief'. What would that type be? Nothing beyond the speaker's intentions seems to narrow the candidate pool in this sort of example. Perhaps Jones would be thinking of something like perception of familiar objects at a reasonable distance, or perhaps to something narrower, such as visual perception of familiar well-lit trees from a reasonable distance. Perhaps Jones would not have any type of belief-forming process in mind. After all, he did not say anything about belief-forming processes and there is no reason to think that he was having any thoughts about them. So, there is no reason to think that in this sort of mundane example, there is such a thing as the contextually determined type for the phrase 'the process that caused Smith's belief'. Moreover, there is no reason to think that the truth value of Jones's attribution of knowledge to Smith depends in any way on which, if any, of these types Jones has in mind.

Furthermore, even if an attributor of knowledge does have some belief-forming process types in mind, the attributor's thoughts do not identify relevant types in a way that is uniformly helpful to reliabilists. An attributor of knowledge may be mistaken about the reasons for a person's belief, and thus may be thinking about process types that the subject's token process doesn't even exemplify. For example, suppose that Jones witnesses Smith identify a bird as being of a certain species after Smith has had only the briefest glimpse of it under poor lighting conditions. Jones says that Smith's belief is unjustified and so Smith lacks knowledge. Jones does have in mind some process type for Smith's belief, something like forming a bird classifying belief on the basis of a brief glimpse in poor lighting conditions. Suppose, however, that Smith has formed her belief on the basis of hearing the bird's song, an identification method that Jones has not even thought of. Moreover, Smith does have knowledge as a result. If process reliabilism is anywhere close to the truth about knowledge and justification, it is the reliability of some process type that Smith actually underwent that matters here. So, the generality problem must be solved by appeal to facts about the processes actually involved in the formation of the belief, not by appeal to the possibly mistaken thoughts about those processes in the minds of knowledge attributors.

(C) is incorrect. There simply are no contextually determined types in many, perhaps most, typical contexts in which knowledge and justification claims have a clear truth value. It is true that context helps to determine the standards a process type must meet to be correctly described as "reliable". But the attributor's context comes nowhere near to picking out a relevant type of each belief-forming process, and the process types that are salient to the attributor can be entirely irrelevant to the truth of knowledge claims.

This section has focused on common sense types of belief-forming processes. There are also the many scientific types that classify each belief-forming process. It is clear that nothing about typical contexts of belief, or typical contexts of attribution of knowledge or justification, uniformly singles out one of them. Since our minds are rarely scientifically oriented, speakers' intentions are even less likely to narrow down the scientific types. Nothing else about a context of utterance does so either. Thus, context does not solve the generality problem.

VI. Conclusion

That is the full variety of existing approaches to disposing of the generality problem. In the absence of a brand new idea about relevant types, the problem looks insoluble. Consequently, process reliability theories of justification and knowledge look hopeless.[39]

Afterword

1. The generality problem for reliabilism bears some affinity to the reference class problem. The latter is a problem for interpreting probability ascriptions to single events—e.g., "The probability that Mudslinger will win the next Belmont Stakes is one in a hundred." It seems that sentences like this have truth conditions that are partly determined by a frequency of correlation of the members of some pair of appropriate kinds—the "reference classes". (The pertinent aspects of the problem remain the same in an interpretation that uses propensities of members of the appropriate classes to correlate, rather than frequencies of actual association.) Perhaps one in a hundred of the horses with Mudslinger's win/loss record have won races that have the popular status of the Belmont Stakes. So if the classes whose members are of those two kinds are the reference classes for the claim made by this sentence, then it is true. Perhaps it is also the case that Mudslinger has won the one race that he ran which was of the exact length of the Belmont. If the reference classes are ones containing only Mudslinger and races of this length, then the sentence is false. The horse and the race are of many other kinds as well. Those who seek to interpret such sentences by use of kinds therefore must identify which of the kinds involved has the correlation that determines the truth-value of such sentences.

---

[39] An earlier version of this paper was presented at a symposium at the American Philosophical Association in December, 1996. We are grateful to William Alston for his comments. We are also grateful to Ralph Baergen and John Bennett for comments on earlier drafts.

Earl Conee and Richard Feldman

This reference class problem is clearly not the same problem as the generality problem. The topics of interpretation are different. The generality problem is about reliability theories concerning claims of the form

1. S's belief B is epistemically justified at t.

These are not explicitly about probability of any sort. One way to unite the issues is this. A reliability theorist might assert that such claims have the same truth conditions as ones of this form:

2. There is a high probability that S's belief B at t is true.

Whatever solution is proposed to the reference class problem can be applied to the latter sort of sentence directly, and to the former indirectly.

As there is no established solution to the reference class problem, there is no decisive way to assess how well this proposal works. But we see ample grounds for pessimism. One problem is that any plausible interpretation of (2) will have to be sensitive to details of ascriptive context that are intuitively irrelevant to (1). Here are two examples.

First, suppose that Smith is known by us to have reliably accurate beliefs on some particular topic. Suppose that we learn about a belief of Smith's, B1, only that it is one of Smith's beliefs on the topic. We claim that there is a high probability that B1 is true. This claim seems to be a correct probability assertion. Yet suppose too that Smith has been given strong though spurious grounds for doubting each of his beliefs on the topic in question. Then it is false that Smith's belief B1 is justified at the time.

And second, suppose that we have virtually conclusive grounds for thinking that Jones's belief, B2, is false. On this basis we can truthfully deny that there is a high probability that B2 is true. Yet, by any reasonable standard for justification, it is consistent with this denial that Jones is epistemically justified in believing B2. More generally, explicit probability assertions about a person's beliefs seem to depend for their truth on features of the speaker's context. These are features of the belief that do not derive from the reliability of belief-forming process types, and do not associate closely with justified belief. So this way to unite the reference class problem and the generality problem lacks promise.

We should make one other point about the connection. We have heard it argued that the generality problem must have a good solution. The reason given is that the reference class problem obviously must have some solution, and the generality problem is analogous. It is contended that the reference class problem must have a solution because people often make single case probability judgments with understanding and confidence. Since these judgments clearly

The Generality Problem for Reliabilism

turn on some facts about reference class correlations (or propensities), there must be some way in which suitable reference classes are determined. Specifying how this is done is no doubt difficult, but in principle it must have a solution. Likewise, people make justification judgments with understanding and confidence. These are clearly determined by some fact about truth-conduciveness of associated types. So although the task may likewise be difficult, in principle a solution must exist.

The point at which this reasoning is plainly contestable is the claim that justification judgments depend in some way on something's truth-conduciveness. Epistemic justification is basically a matter of the kind of reasonableness that is determined by evidence. Reasonable belief need not tend toward truth. So judgments about justification can be understood, and correct, without depending for their truth on something truth-conducive.

Furthermore, even if justification is connected to truth in some notable way and there is some solution to the reference class problem, there is no good reason to think that reliabilists can make use of that solution to construct a satisfactory reliabilist theory. There is no good reason to think that exactly those beliefs that can be said in some context to be probably true are justified.

2. Process reliabilists do not have to specify a single relevant type for each belief. Most generally, what they must do is to specify some reliability rating associated with each belief. One way a process reliabilist might specify a reliability rating, without identifying a single relevant type, takes two steps. The first step is to specify multiple relevant process types for each belief. The second step is to specify some combinatorial technique that uses the various reliabilities of the specified types to yield a reliability rating for each belief. (An unpublished manuscript by Allen Plug explores this possibility.) Another alternative is to specify a combinatorial technique that does all of the work. That is, the technique takes the reliabilities of all of the types tokened by the process, and yields a reliability rating for the belief.

Nothing that we know of makes either of these alternatives appear to be more promising than the search for a single relevant type. In fact, they appear less promising. To identify a finite number of relevant types for a given belief-forming process, one would at least have to know approximately where to look. Yet, as things stand, common sense types of numerous varieties have some appeal to reliabilists, and so do scientifically identified types. The field seems wide open. And finding a combinatorial technique that gets a reliability rating out of some multiplicity of types and is plausibly associated with the belief's level of justification seems as formidable a task as finding a single relevant type.

This project would seem worth attempting only if there were some intuitive motivation for thinking that some limited number of types are definitely the relevant ones, in that justification is intuitively some function of their reliability. As things stand, there is no good reason to think that justification correlates with any function from the reliability of any restricted set of process types.

Likewise, the task of combining the reliabilities of all of the seemingly unlimited number of types that are tokened by a belief-forming process so as to get a plausible reliability rating seems technically forbidding. By including arbitrarily gerrymandered types, we can identify as many types as we like for each process, with as many different degrees of reliability as we like. Perhaps some metaphysical limit on "real" types can be cited that would make the work more manageable. But again, we see no intuitive grounds for optimism about the project. It seems hopeless to us.

3. Speaking of apparently hopeless alternatives that nonetheless deserve some mention, there are three other candidate bearers of reliability, beyond the process types and mechanisms of belief formation that are discussed in the paper. First, there are persons. A person can be a more or less reliable believer at any given time. This fact is of no assistance in solving the generality problem, though. It makes no distinctions among the beliefs formed or sustained by a single believer at a single time. Yet these beliefs can vary greatly in justification.

Second, philosophers sometimes appeal to mental "faculties". These seem to be broad capacities to perform mental tasks, like perceiving and imagining. If there are anything like these faculties, perhaps they are somewhat finer grained. For instance, perhaps the faculty used in forming visual beliefs is distinct from the faculty used in forming tactile beliefs. These faculties could well vary in reliability. So some distinctions in reliability would be available to distinguish the justification of beliefs. But still, each person's visual faculty, for instance, would have some overall reliability at any given time. Yet clearly, various visual beliefs formed at the time by the person using the faculty could differ greatly in justification. So an appeal to the reliability of faculties seems hopeless too.

Lastly, there is the idea that a belief is justified exactly when the basis on which the belief is formed or sustained is reliable. This idea has the advantage of using a relatively clear bearer of reliability. We see no fundamental obscurity in the notion of a belief's basis. Indeed, we make primitive use of this concept in our account of well-founded belief in "Evidentialism" (Chapter 4 in this volume; see also section 4 below). There is a serious question about how the reliability is to be determined, however. Suppose first that multiple beliefs can

The Generality Problem for Reliabilism

have the same basis. This is a natural view. People frequently take themselves to base many judgments on a single belief. If so, then perhaps the reliability of S's basis for believing B is determined by the truth-conduciveness of the basis with regard to all of the propositions that are identically based. This makes for a bad theory of justification. From a single basis, a person might infer both some biased and unjustified conclusion as well as some obvious and well-justified conclusion. The general reliability of the basis would have the theory overrate the justification of the biased beliefs and underrate the justification of the obvious inference.

Suppose instead that the exact basis of any given belief is a basis for that one belief only. This is defensible. Perhaps the basis of a belief includes the particular application of conceptual competence that is employed in the believing of a given proposition. If each belief has its own basis, then the theory is subject to a version of the single case problem. The actual truth frequency of a basis is always either one hundred per cent or zero per cent. This will rarely correspond to the level of the belief's justification. Similarly, the tendency of the basis toward truth can diverge from the strength of the belief's justification. A lucky guess that a tree is a maple, based on a clear perception of what is in fact a distinctive maple shape of its leaves, will be unjustified. This is so, in spite of the fact that the same belief on the same basis is true under all likely counterfactual conditions. Thus, a reliability theory of justification using this third bearer of reliability has poor prospects as well.

4. There is a significant difference between a proposition that one is epistemically justified in believing and a belief that one holds in a way that is epistemically justified. We have sought to accommodate that difference with our distinction between a justified attitude of belief, as characterized by EJ, and a well-founded belief, as characterized by WF (from "Evidentialism", Chapter 4 in this volume). What WF requires of a well-founded belief is that the belief be based on justifying and undefeated evidence.

This primitive use of a basing relation might be thought to encumber our views with a generality problem. It might be held that a basis for a belief is a mental cause of the belief. Suppose that B1 has some mental cause. In general, there will be numerous other mental causally sufficient conditions for B1. The question might be raised as to which of the causally sufficient mental conditions for a belief is the relevant one to determine whether that belief is well-founded.

We need not single out one mental cause of a belief as the relevant one. The idea used in WF is that one has a well-founded belief if it is believed on some basis or other that is epistemically okay. Presumably the basis is a cause of the belief. (Actually, one of us doubts that causation is necessary for basing, but we can set this doubt aside for present purposes.) In any event, what makes a basis epistemically okay is that the evidence that it includes is sufficient to justify the attitude of believing, and that this evidence is not overridden by other evidence the person has. As long as any one basis for a person's belief has that epistemic status, the belief is well-founded. This is so, no matter what other mental causally sufficient conditions also happen to exist for the belief.

5. Ernest Sosa has pointed out to us (in conversation) that evidentialism faces a sorting problem, and that reliabilists and other theorists can make use of any evidentialist solution to the problem.

The sorting problem for evidentialism is this. Some but not all perceptual experiences provide justification for corresponding beliefs about the external world, some but not all inductive inferences are good ones, and some but not all memories justify the remembered proposition. A complete evidentialist theory will say what separates the justification-conferring evidence from evidence that fails to justify. It will classify together experiences that justify external world beliefs and distinguish them from experiences that do not; it will classify together good inductive evidence and distinguish it from inductive evidence that is not good; and so forth.

Reliability theorists (and others) can say that the belief-forming processes involving the experiences that evidentialists say confer a particular kind of perceptual justification constitute one relevant process type; the belief-forming processes involved in the inductive inferences that evidentialists say confer a particular kind of inductive justification constitute another relevant type; and so forth. In whatever way evidentialists complete their account of the justifying types of evidence, reliabilists can say that the corresponding process types are the whole story about the relevant types.

This prospective solution to the generality problem has liabilities. For one thing, the evidentially selected classes may not form reliable types. Evil demons duplicate our internal mental life and our beliefs in some very different possible worlds. Intuitively, these demons give their victims beliefs that both have the same evidence that ours have and are as often justified. But the processes by which the victims' external world beliefs are induced tend to produce virtually all falsehoods in such possible worlds. So the reliability of the relevant process types would be very low, assuming that reliability in a world is measured by the truth frequencies or the truth tendencies of the relevant types there.

The Generality Problem for Reliabilism

This difficulty for reliabilism may arise in the actual world. It may be that evidentialists will single out one or more classes of evidentially supported beliefs that actually contain mostly falsehoods. For instance, it is not out of the question that ordinary beliefs embody hidden metaphysical errors. Perhaps routine perceptual beliefs have false implications about the continuing existence of identical material objects, because nothing survives any change of its parts. In an evidentialist view, these beliefs would still be supported by ordinary evidence.

We do not advocate any such metaphysics. The point of the example is to illustrate an advantageous neutrality of evidentialism on such issues. By an evidentialist standard, it does not matter if some such possibility of obscurely false beliefs is actual. The beliefs are justified by fitting the perceptual evidence, however infrequently the belief-forming processes tend to produce truths. This seems to us to be the intuitively correct result. In contrast, theories that rely on reliability are in trouble if the truth tendencies of ordinary beliefs are much worse than people usually think.

Furthermore, the classes of beliefs that are backed by what evidentialists identify as a unified kind of justifying evidence may not form "natural kinds". Reliabilists who aspire to naturalism may be unable simply to proclaim a single relevant type for the processes yielding beliefs in an evidentialist class. For instance, it may be that there is no "natural" unity to the mental states and processes that bring it about that someone has justifying perceptual evidence that something is blue. An evidentialist can say that this evidence consists in something appearing blue to someone with any of various batches of empirical information about circumstances of viewing that show a thing's true colors. There may be no underlying physical, biological, or psychological unity to the variety of background evidence that a person may have that in one way or another contributes to making a certain sort of visual experience sufficient to justify the belief. Likewise, instances of possession of the various relevant bodies of background information need not have any common causal tendency. The only unity to be found may be the evidential role, and the epistemic classifications that derive from it. Naturalists about relevant kinds will not be able to use this sort of grouping.

Finally, it is worth repeating that the reliability of the class need not work out as reliabilists require. Even if reliabilists are willing to forgo naturalism and adopt any evidentialist classification at all as a relevant kind, they have what they need only if the reliability of the kind matches its degree of justification. This is a contingent matter. There is no assurance that the needed match exists.

7
The Ethics of Belief
Richard Feldman

In this paper I will address a few of the many questions that fall under the general heading of "the ethics of belief." In section I I will discuss the adequacy of what has come to be known as the "deontological conception of epistemic justification" in the light of our apparent lack of voluntary control over what we believe. In section II I'll defend an evidentialist view about what we ought to believe. And in section III I will briefly discuss apparent conflicts between epistemic considerations and moral or other considerations.

I. Epistemic Deontologism[1]

A. The Problem

Our talk about epistemic matters parallels our talk about ethical matters in noteworthy ways. In the case of ethics, we say that a person *ought* to perform a certain action, that someone *should* not do a certain thing, that people have *obligations* to act in some ways, that they have *rights* and *duties*, and that they deserve *praise* or *blame* for what they have done. We make seemingly analogous epistemic judgments about beliefs. We say that a typical well-informed contemporary American ought to believe that the Earth revolves around the Sun and should not believe that the Earth is flat. We say that a person has a right to believe one thing and perhaps a duty to refrain from believing something else. We sometimes praise those who believe the things they should and we criticize

---

[1] This section is a shortened version of my paper, "Voluntary Belief and Epistemic Evaluation", in Matthias Steup (ed.), *Knowledge, Truth, and Duty: Essays on Epistemic Justification, Responsibility, and Virtue* (Oxford: Oxford University Press, 2001), pp. 77–92.

those who fail in their believings. We can describe all these judgments as *deontological judgments about beliefs*.

In "The Deontological Conception of Epistemic Justification," William Alston says that the most natural way to understand epistemic justification is deontological.[2] By this he means that it is to be understood in terms of epistemic "obligation, permission, requirement, blame, and the like."[3] He regards "*requirement, prohibition,* and *permission* as the basic deontological terms" and the other terms as derivative ones.[4] Alston eventually argues that deontological conceptions are in the end ill-suited to epistemic purposes.[5] Recently, Alvin Plantinga and Alvin Goldman have independently argued that the viability of a deontological conception of epistemic justification is crucial to the debate between internalists and externalists about epistemic justification.[6] Goldman thinks that a central, but mistaken, line of support for internalist theories begins with the assumption of a deontological account of justification. Plantinga also argues that internalism derives much of its support from a deontological view of justification.[7] The merit of the deontological view of epistemic justification thus is of considerable epistemological significance to contemporary epistemology.

A central problem that both Plantinga and Alston find with deontological judgments about beliefs is that they presuppose that we have voluntary control over what we believe. Yet, reflection on our mental lives suggests that we have no such control. Alston writes of one particular deontological analysis:

…this conception of epistemic justification is viable only if beliefs are sufficiently under voluntary control to render such concepts as *requirement, permission, obligation, reproach,* and *blame* applicable to them. By the time honored principle that "Ought implies can", one can be obliged to do A only if one has an effective choice as to whether to do A.[8]

---

[2] William Alston, "The Deontological Conception of Epistemic Justification," *Philosophical Perspectives*, 2 (1988): 257–99. See especially p. 258. Reprinted in William Alston, *Epistemic Justification* (Ithaca, NY: Cornell University Press, 1989).

[3] "The Deontological Conception of Epistemic Justification," p. 257.   [4] Ibid.

[5] The most prominent advocate of this sort of analysis is Roderick Chisholm. He defends this view as recently as in his 1991 paper, "Firth and the Ethics of Belief," *Philosophy and Phenomenological Research*, 50 (1991): 119–28. For a thorough list of Chisholm's publications on this topic, see Susan Haack, "'The Ethics of Belief' Reconsidered," in Lewis E. Hahn (ed.), *The Philosophy of Roderick Chisholm* (La Salle: Open Court, 1997), pp. 129–44. See especially footnote 2. See also Hilary Kornblith, "Justified Belief and Epistemically Responsible Action," *Philosophical Review*, 92 (1983): 33–48 for an influential discussion of the idea that a belief is epistemically justified provided it is formed in an epistemically responsible way.

[6] See Alvin Plantinga, *Warrant: The Current Debate* (Oxford and New York: Oxford University Press, 1993) and Alvin Goldman, "Internalism Exposed," *Journal of Philosophy*, 96 (1999): 271–93.

[7] *Warrant: The Current Debate*, Chapter 1.

[8] "The Deontological Conception of Epistemic Justification," p. 259.

Richard Feldman

He goes on to argue that we don't have an effective choice over what we believe. In the process of objecting to Chisholm's views about justification, Plantinga says of a particular proposition that "...whether or not I accept it is simply not up to me; but then accepting this proposition cannot be a way in which I can fulfill my obligation to the truth, or, indeed, *any* obligation..."[9] Thus, according to Plantinga, our lack of control over beliefs implies that they are not the sort of thing that can be a matter of obligation, and this undermines Chisholm's deontological conception of epistemic justification. Matthias Steup presents a similar argument, though he goes on to defend the deontological conception on the grounds that belief is voluntary.[10]

For the purposes of the discussion that follows it will be helpful to distinguish two elements of the arguments just presented. Their target is a deontological conception of justification, a conception according to which epistemic justification is to be understood or analyzed in terms of the deontological concepts of obligation, requirement, and the like. This conception is "viable", in Alston's terms, only if belief is sufficiently under our voluntary control. Presumably, the deontological conception is viable only if it can be true that we are required to believe things, that we ought not believe other things, and so on. That is, the deontological conception of epistemic justification is viable only if deontological judgments about beliefs are sometimes true. My goal in what follows is to argue that deontological judgments are sometimes true and that good sense can be made of the idea that we can have epistemic requirements, obligations, and the like. I will not be arguing for the further claim that epistemic justification should be analyzed in deontological terms.

We can formulate the key part of the argument at issue in the following way:

The Voluntarism Argument

1. If deontological judgments about beliefs are true, then people have voluntary control over their beliefs.
2. People do not have voluntary control over their beliefs.
3. Deontological judgments about beliefs are not true.

Epistemologists have three kinds of response to this argument open to them: (i) they can argue that we do have the requisite sort of control over our beliefs, thereby rejecting premise (2); (ii) they can argue that deontological judgments

---

[9] *Warrant: The Current Debate*, p. 38.

[10] Matthias Steup, "The Concept of Epistemic Justification," Chapter 4 of *Contemporary Epistemology* (Upper Saddle River: Prentice-Hall, 1996).

The Ethics of Belief

do not have voluntarist implications, thereby rejecting premise (1); or (iii) they can accept the argument and admit that the familiar deontological terms of epistemic appraisal really are inapplicable.[11] This in itself is a surprising conclusion, whether or not a deontological analysis of justification is acceptable.

I will discuss response (i) in section B below and response (ii) in section C. I will not discuss response (iii) except in passing and by implication.

B. Doxastic Voluntarism

In this section I will examine some arguments for doxastic voluntarism and some arguments against it. I will eventually defend a version of doxastic voluntarism and I will also argue that this fact is of absolutely no epistemological significance and that it does nothing to help resolve the voluntarism puzzle. Although some philosophers have argued that it is a conceptual impossibility that anyone form a belief voluntarily, I will not discuss that view.[12] Instead, I will examine the claim that it is a contingent matter of fact that we lack that ability.

B1. The Argument for Involuntarism

Alston has given the most thorough defense of the contingent inability thesis, the thesis that as a contingent matter of fact people are not able to acquire beliefs voluntarily. Alston's paper includes an excellent survey of a variety of notions of voluntary control. For each type, he argues that we lack that sort of control over beliefs. (Alston does admit that there is one very weak notion of control that does apply to belief. But he contends that this sort of control does not provide an adequate basis for a good response to the Voluntarism Argument.)

Alston begins by discussing *basic voluntary control*.[13] We have basic voluntary control over those actions that we can "just do." Simple bodily motions are the prime examples. I can just raise my hand, close my eyes, and bend my knee. Some people, but not I, can wriggle their ears and curl their tongue. Alston correctly says that forming a belief is not like that. We can't just do it at will.

---

[11] This last alternative implies that either epistemic justification is not to be analyzed in deontological terms or else that epistemic justification is itself inapplicable to our beliefs, just like the other deontological epistemic terms.

[12] For defenses of the conceptual impossibility claim, see Bernard Williams, "Deciding to Believe," *Problems of the Self* (Cambridge: Cambridge University Press, 1973), Jonathan Bennett, "Why Is Belief Involuntary?," *Analysis*, 50 (1990) and Dion Scott-Kakures, "On Belief and the Captivity of the Will," *Philosophy and Phenomenological Research*, 53 (1993). For discussion of Williams, see Barbara Winters, "Believing at Will," *Journal of Philosophy*, 76 (1979). For a discussion of Scott-Kakures' article, see Dana Radcliffe, "Scott-Kakures on Believing at Will," *Philosophy and Phenomenological Research*, 57, 1 (1997).

[13] "The Deontological Conception of Epistemic Justification," Section III, pp. 263–8.

Alston turns next to *nonbasic immediate voluntary control*.[14] One has this sort of control over the things one can do right away by doing something else, typically something over which one has basic voluntary control. Standard examples are opening doors and turning on lights. We can, in typical circumstances, do these things simply by moving our bodies in the appropriate ways. There's vagueness here concerning what counts as "right away" but that vagueness is in no way problematic. This is because the boundary between nonbasic immediate voluntary control and the next weaker kind of control, *long range voluntary control*, is acceptably imprecise.[15] The sorts of things over which we have long range voluntary control are the sorts of things we can do over time by doing other things. Perhaps painting my house is an example. Or, more precisely, I have long range voluntary control over what color my house is because I can do things like paint it. Finally, there is *indirect voluntary influence*.[16] This is the kind of control we have when we can undertake a course of action that may affect some condition over the long term. Perhaps a person has indirect voluntary influence over the condition of her heart, since diet and exercise (courses of action we can more directly control) can affect it.

Alston claims that we have only this weakest sort of control over our beliefs. One can engage in a course of action for the purpose of inculcating or losing a particular belief. Consider my belief that the Earth is not flat. There's nothing I can do to get myself to stop believing that right away. It's not like shutting the door or turning out the lights. And there's nothing much I can do long range to control it either. I might enroll in the Flat Earth Society, read conspiracy literature asserting that satellite photos are all phony, and so on. Perhaps this will help rid me of my belief. Alston would agree that it might. But this gets us, at most, indirect voluntary influence, and this is not the sort of effective voluntary control required to refute the Voluntarism Argument.[17]

I believe that, for the most part, what Alston says is right. However, I will argue that we have considerably more control over some of our beliefs than Alston acknowledges. Still, this control does not undermine the basic idea behind the Voluntarism Argument, although it may show that the argument needs reformulation.

B2. *An Argument for Doxastic Voluntarism*

My argument for doxastic voluntarism begins with the assumption that there are states of the world over which people have nonbasic voluntary control.

---

[14] See Section IV, pp. 268–74.   [15] See Section V, pp. 274–7.   [16] See Section VI, pp. 277–83.
[17] Perhaps this point suggests that both (2) and the consequent of (1) should be about *effective* voluntary control.

The Ethics of Belief

For example, I have nonbasic voluntary control over whether the lights in my office are on. All I have to do is move in a certain way to get the lights on or off. And I can do this. The next step of the argument notes that my belief about whether the lights are on tracks their actual state almost perfectly. As a result, I have a similar amount of control over whether I believe that the lights are on. All I have to do is move a certain way and then I'll have the relevant belief. More generally, when I have control over a state of the world and my beliefs about that state track that state, then I have just as much control over my belief about the state as I have over the state itself. Thus, we have nonbasic immediate voluntary control over our beliefs about states of the world over which we have control, provided our beliefs are responsive to those states. Furthermore, if we know that we will respond in some mistaken way to some state of the world over which we have control, we also have control over the resulting (erroneous) belief. So, doxastic voluntarism is true after all. Premise (2) of the Voluntarism Argument is false.

I believe that the existence of nonbasic voluntary control over beliefs can have prudential and moral significance. If the department chair announces that she'll give a raise to all and only those members of the department who in 30 seconds believe that the lights in their office are on, I'll head for the light switch and turn on the lights to make sure I have the desired belief. If the chair perversely announces that the graduate students will be mercilessly tortured—say, by being forced to take additional prelims—unless in 30 seconds I believe that my lights are on, then I'd better make sure that I have that belief. I'm in control.

Thus, we do have control over many of our beliefs. Of course, we don't often exercise this control. That is, we don't often believe things voluntarily. And this leaves this defense of doxastic voluntarism without a great deal of epistemological significance. The central reason for this is that we make deontological epistemic judgments about beliefs that we can't control and these judgments are as routine and commonplace as are judgments about beliefs that we can control. Thus, our ability to control what we believe in the way described here is epistemically insignificant. We can take this into account by reformulating the Voluntarism Argument:

The Voluntarism Argument (Revised)

1. If deontological judgments about beliefs concerning states of the world people can't control are true, then people have (effective) voluntary control over those beliefs.

2. People do not have (effective) voluntary control over those beliefs.

3. Deontological judgments about those beliefs are not true.

This argument is as troubling as the original. It implies that an enormous number of the deontological epistemic judgments we routinely make cannot be true. Furthermore, the argument might be extended to beliefs that we can control but have not formed in this voluntary way. Thus, I don't think that the fact that we have nonbasic immediate voluntary control over some beliefs provides the basis for an effective defense of epistemic deontologism.[18]

B3. A More Robust Form of Doxastic Voluntarism

Compatibilists in the free will debate contend that we voluntarily perform an action when the action has the right sort of cause. A defender of doxastic voluntarism can argue that, analogously, we believe voluntarily when we believe as a result of the right sort of causal process. Roughly, the idea is that when unconstrained deliberation about evidence leads to belief, we believe voluntarily.[19] This is an interesting line of thought, and it is difficult to refute because we lack a fully adequate understanding of what counts as "the right sort of causal process." Still, I think that there are good grounds to reject the idea that the deliberative process that typically leads to belief is the kind of process that makes its product a voluntary action.

A key fact about the clearest cases of voluntary action is that the action is caused by an intention to perform that action. I turn on the lights because I intend to turn on the lights; I type a certain word because I intend to type that word. No doubt there are puzzles about the details of these matters, such as puzzles resulting from the fact that our intentions are not as precise as the resulting actions—I need not have intended to turn on the light in exactly the way I did. But however we deal with these details, the case of belief is dramatically different. We simply don't, in the typical case, form a belief as a result of an intention to form that belief. It may be that in some sense we do control what we believe, in much the way we control other involuntary processes in us. However, epistemic deliberation does not result in effective intentions to believe. Except in rare cases, we don't form intentions to believe. But such intentions are essential to voluntary control.[20] The cases of voluntary belief formation that

---

[18] If this revised argument is strong, then it would also be reasonable to reject deontological analyses of epistemic justification as well.

[19] For a defense of this view, see Matthias Steup, "Doxastic Voluntarism and Epistemic Deontology," *Acta Analytica*, 15 (2000). For a similar view, see James Montmarquet, "The Voluntariness of Belief," *Analysis*, 46 (1986). Bruce Russell endorses Steup's view in "Epistemic and Moral Duty," in Steup (ed.), *Knowledge, Truth, and Duty*.

[20] Perhaps the process by which we formulate intentions and act on their basis can become automated in certain ways, so that voluntary actions need not involve explicit conscious formulations of intentions. Belief formation is not like that either. It does not typically involve the formation of intentions to believe at all.

I described earlier make it easy to see what it really would be like to believe voluntarily. In those cases, I do believe as a result of an intention to believe. But those are, for this very reason, quite unlike ordinary cases.

Furthermore, if this defense of doxastic voluntarism were sound, then it seems that many other plainly involuntary behaviors would also be voluntary. Deliberating about something can result in states other than belief. It can result in desires or panic. If we say that belief is voluntary because it is the outcome of deliberation about evidence, then it is hard to see why we shouldn't say that these other outcomes of deliberation are also voluntary. Yet it is clear that they are not. Again, what seems clearly missing is the right sort of intention.

Thus, I reject this more robust form of doxastic voluntarism. There is good reason to say that the deterministic processes that typically lead to action render those actions voluntary. The processes lead to effective intentions to act. Deliberating about evidence does lead to belief, but not via such intentions. Such deliberation does not make belief voluntary. We need a better response to the Voluntarism Argument.

C. Ought and Can

The second main sort of response to the Voluntarism Argument denies that the deontological judgments about beliefs imply that those beliefs are voluntarily adopted. It denies premise (1) of the argument. It may be that there are differences among the various assertions that I've described as "deontological." I'll focus first on judgments about what one is obligated to believe and what one ought to believe and then discuss other judgments later in the section.

One way to defend deontological epistemic judgments in the light of doxastic involuntarism is to argue that we can have epistemic obligations even though we can't fulfill them (or even if we can't help but fulfill them). This is to deny that "epistemically obligated to" or "epistemically ought to" implies "can". And one way to make this denial plausible is to show that there are other kinds of ought statements that don't imply voluntary control. I will consider several candidates for this other kind of ought.

C1. Contractual Obligations

You can have an obligation to pay your mortgage even if you don't have the money to do so. Perhaps students in a class have an obligation to do the course work even if they are incapable of doing it. Other examples of this sort are rather easy to construct. Perhaps epistemic obligations are analogous to these financial and academic obligations. Though I once defended this view,[21] it now strikes me as an implausible model for epistemic obligations. The obligation to pay one's mortgage and the obligation to do one's course work are contractual obligations, although in the latter case the contract is in some sense implicit. It's difficult to see any basis for saying that we all have some sort of contractual obligation to believe things. Surely no such contract is explicit, and nothing analogous to enrolling in a course establishes an implicit contract.

C2. *Paradigm Obligations*

In a recent paper, Nicholas Wolterstorff says that there are two kinds of obligations, *paradigm* obligations and *responsibility* obligations.[22] Only obligations of the latter sort are associated with voluntariness. As examples of paradigm obligations, he presents:

1. "You ought to be walking on it in two weeks"—said by a physician as he finishes binding up a person's sprained ankle.
2. "That's strange; you ought to be seeing double"—said by a psychologist to his subject while conducting an experiment in perception.

Wolterstorff suggests that epistemic obligations are similar to the obligations described by these sentences. They lack any implication of voluntary control.

No friend of epistemic deontologism should be comforted by the idea that epistemic obligations are like the obligations described by (1)–(2). This is because there are no obligations described by (1)–(2). Sentences (1)–(2) are "ought" sentences; they are not obligation sentences and they cannot be paraphrased in any straightforward way into obligation sentences. Your ankle has no obligation of any sort to heal; you have no "perceptual obligation" to see double. So, if there are epistemic obligations, they are not like the obligations described here, since there are no obligations described here.

Furthermore, the ought sentences Wolterstorff describes are not relevantly like epistemic oughts. (1) and (2) describe normal, or paradigmatic, behavior. Thus, for example, barring unforeseen developments, your ankle will heal in 2 weeks. But I don't think that this carries over to the epistemic case. That is, epistemic oughts don't describe paradigmatic or normal function. Some researchers report that people typically make various unjustified inferences and predictably form unreasonable or erroneous beliefs.[23] Whatever the proper

---

[21] "Epistemic Obligations," *Philosophical Perspectives*, 2 (1988), pp. 240–3.

[22] Nicholas Wolterstorff, "Obligations of Belief: Two Concepts," in Hahn (ed.), *Philosophy of Roderick Chisholm*.

[23] For a discussion of many of the examples allegedly showing that people are irrational and an examination of their philosophical implications, see Edward Stein, *Without Good Reason: The Rationality Debate in Philosophy and Cognitive Science* (Oxford: Clarendon Press, 1996).

The Ethics of Belief

interpretation of this research actually is, it is at least possible that people normally make epistemic errors. It may be that we epistemically ought not do what we normally do. Epistemic oughts are not paradigm oughts.²⁴

C3. Role Oughts

There are oughts that result from one's playing a certain role or having a certain position. Teachers ought to explain things clearly. Parents ought to take care of their kids. Cyclists ought to move in various ways. Incompetent teachers, incapable parents, and untrained cyclists may be unable to do what they ought to do. Similarly, I'd say, forming beliefs is something people do. That is, we form beliefs in response to our experiences in the world. Anyone engaged in this activity ought to do it right. In my view, what they ought to do is to follow their evidence (rather than wishes or fears). I suggest that epistemic oughts are of this sort—they describe the right way to play a certain role. Unlike Wolterstorff's paradigm oughts, these oughts are not based on what's normal or expected. They are based on what's good performance. Furthermore, it is plausible to say that the role of a believer is not one that we have any real choice about taking on. It is our plight to be believers. We ought to do it right. It doesn't matter that in some cases we are unable to do so. Thus, I reject the first premise of the revised Voluntarism Argument. Even in cases in which a believer has no control at all, it makes sense to speak of what he ought to believe and ought not believe.

I think that most, possibly all, of the deontological terms we ordinarily use to evaluate beliefs can be explained in similar terms, although the case for some may be weaker than the case for others. Thus, if the standards of good believing allow either of two attitudes in a given situation, then it will be true that the believer has a *right* to either of those attitudes and that either of them is *permitted*.²⁵ Other attitudes may be *prohibited*. It seems to me reasonable to say that when only one attitude is permitted, then one has an *epistemic obligation* to have that attitude. (I will add a qualification to this claim later in the paper.) It may be that some terms, especially those associated with *praise* and *blame*, are to be reserved for voluntary behavior. Even here, the case is less than perfectly clear, since we do praise and blame people for attributes, such as beauty, that they are unable to control. Thus, I conclude that deontological epistemic judgments can be true even if doxastic voluntarism is false.

---

²⁴ Thus, a researcher might say, while awaiting the subject's reply to a question that nearly everyone misses, "He ought to make the wrong inference here." The use of "ought" here is Wolterstorff's paradigm ought. But to describe the inference as "wrong" is to say that it is not the case that the person epistemically ought to do what the researcher expects him to do.

²⁵ I'll return to some related issues in section II, part A.

C4. Is This Deontology?

I want to contrast the view I'm defending from a different view about epistemic deontologism. Possibly some critics object primarily to the idea that to be epistemically justified in a belief is to do the best that one can do with respect to that belief. Their target really does imply voluntarism. I haven't attempted to defend that view, and I don't think that it is true. I've taken on the much more modest task of defending the legitimacy of the widespread use of deontological language about belief. My contention is that we can have epistemic requirements, permissions, and the like even if voluntarism is false.

In his influential paper on this topic, Alston begins by saying that it is "natural" to understand epistemological terms in a " 'deontological' way, as having to do with obligation, permission, requirement, blame, and the like."[26] As an example of the view he wants to question, he mentions Carl Ginet's view that explains justification in terms of whether one is as confident as one ought to be.[27] But by the end of his paper Alston seems to be directing his attack more narrowly. In his concluding paragraph he characterizes epistemic deontologism as the view that analyzes "epistemic justification in terms of freedom from blame for believing."[28] I haven't attempted to defend this sort of deontologism here. Moreover, I don't think that this more narrowly defined sort of deontologism is so natural or common. My defense is only of the possible truth of the deontological epistemic claims with which Alston began his paper, claims to the effect that people can have epistemic rights, duties, permissions, etc. They can, no matter what the truth about doxastic voluntarism is.[29]

Given that deontological epistemic judgments can be true, I turn next to a view about the conditions under which they are true.

II. Epistemic Oughts

A. Evidentialism

In this section I will defend a variation on William K. Clifford's frequently quoted claim that "It is wrong, always, everywhere, and for anyone to believe

---

[26] "The Deontological Conception of Epistemic Justification," p. 257.   [27] Ibid., p. 259.
[28] Ibid., p. 294.
[29] It is possible that some critics will contend that sentences like "Smith ought to believe that the earth is not flat" are ambiguous between deontological and non-deontological senses. They might then object that I've merely argued for the possible truth of the non-deontological interpretation of the sentence. I don't see any reason to admit that there are multiple senses of this sort. The deontological

The Ethics of Belief

anything upon insufficient evidence."[30] It is not my purpose here to explain or defend the thesis Clifford asserted with these words. My view may differ from Clifford's in any or all of the following ways. First, he may have been making a *moral* evaluation of believing on insufficient evidence.[31] The claim I want to make concerns epistemic rather than moral evaluation. Second, Clifford evaluates believing on insufficient evidence as *wrong* whereas the claim I will defend is that one ought not believe on insufficient evidence. Whether there is a difference between a thing being wrong and being something one ought not do is unclear to me. If there is a difference, it is the latter claim that I want to defend. Third, in the quoted passage Clifford only objects to believing on insufficient evidence. He does not say that one ought to believe when one does have sufficient evidence. However, I do want to make this additional claim. A succinct way of stating my thesis is that one always ought to follow one's evidence. This *evidentialist* thesis is what I will defend.[32]

The following principle provides a preliminary statement of the evidentialist idea:

O1. For any proposition p, time t, and person S, S epistemically ought to have at t the attitude toward p that is supported by S's evidence at t.

The attitude in question can be belief, disbelief, or suspension of judgment.[33] It's important to realize that (O1) does not imply that a person ought to believe a proposition simply because some of the person's evidence supports that proposition. Belief is the attitude to have only if the evidence on balance supports p.

Some philosophers who are generally sympathetic to evidentialism may think that merely having one's evidence on balance support a proposition is insufficient for it to be true that one epistemically ought to believe the proposition.

---

sense of the sentence just mentioned seems to be nothing other than the conjunction of the non-deontological sense with the proposition that it is up to Smith whether Smith does believe the earth is not flat. Obviously, so interpreted, it does imply voluntarism. But the question with which we began was whether the original claim was compatible with voluntarism. I don't think that this compatibility can be ruled out by fiat.

[30] W. K. Clifford, "The Ethics of Belief," reprinted in Louis P. Pojman (ed.), *The Theory of Knowledge*, 2nd edition (Belmont, California: Wadsworth, 1999), pp. 551–4.

[31] In " 'The Ethics of Belief' Reconsidered" Susan Haack argues that Clifford did not distinguish epistemic and moral senses of the key terms.

[32] In "Evidentialism," *Philosophical Studies*, 48 (1985): 15–34 [Ch. 4 in this volume], Earl Conee and I defend the evidentialist thesis that believing a proposition is justified if and only if believing the proposition "fits" one's evidence.

[33] Those who think that beliefs come in degrees may wish to replace this principle by one saying that one ought to believe propositions to the degree that they are supported by their evidence.

Richard Feldman

That evidential support might be exceedingly weak, and some will think that stronger evidence is required. Those who insist on such a condition can interpret (O1) in a way that fits with this idea. On this interpretation, believing p is supported by one's evidence only if the evidence supports p sufficiently well.

There is, however, reason to doubt (O1). Suppose that a person has evidence that conclusively establishes some proposition, q. There are then a huge number, perhaps an infinite number, of obvious logical consequences of q that are also supported by this evidence. For example, the evidence supports q disjoined with every other proposition, or at least every other proposition S understands. (O1) seems to imply that S ought to believe all these disjunctions. Many of these disjunctions will be trivial; many will be of no practical or theoretical interest. It may be that in some sense believing these propositions is justified—the person has good support for them—but it is not true that he *ought* to believe them. To do so would constitute an exceedingly foolish use of S's cognitive resources.[34]

Whether this objection is a good one depends in part upon what exactly goes into believing a proposition. The more dispositional belief is, the less that (O1) demands of us. If the person with conclusive evidence for q can satisfy its demands by being disposed to assent to each of the disjunctions if asked about them, then (O1) doesn't really require that he expend any cognitive resources. He doesn't have to do anything to meet its standards. If, on the other hand, it takes more than that to believe a proposition, then perhaps (O1) is excessive. I'm inclined to think that (O1) does ask too much of us, but I won't argue for that here. Instead, I propose the following refinement that avoids the problem:

O2. For any person S, time t, and proposition p, if S has any doxastic attitude at all toward p at t and S's evidence at t supports p, then S epistemically ought to have the attitude toward p supported by S's evidence at t.

(O2) in effect conjoins three principles: if a person is going to adopt any attitude toward a proposition, then that person ought to believe it if his current evidence supports it, disbelieve it if his current evidence is against it, and suspend judgment about it if his evidence is neutral (or close to neutral). A person might never even consider a proposition and not be about to adopt any attitude toward it. In that case, (O2) does not imply that there is any attitude the person ought to have toward the proposition. Thus, (O2) avoids the problem concerning the use of cognitive resources that (O1) faced. (O2) merely states which attitude to take toward propositions about which you are going to have one

---

[34] Alvin Goldman makes this point in "Epistemics: The Regulative Theory of Cognition," *The Journal of Philosophy*, 75 (1978).

The Ethics of Belief

attitude or another. It does not instruct you to believe logical consequences that you don't entertain or to otherwise squander precious resources.

B. Requirements and Permissions

(O2) helps clear up a confusing issue about whether epistemic principles state what you are required (ought) to believe or what you are permitted to believe. Suppose some unimportant and unconsidered proposition obviously follows from your evidence. For the reasons just stated, this fact conjoined with (O2) doesn't imply that you ought to believe it. But (O2) does imply that if you take any attitude toward the proposition, it ought to be belief. So, it's not just that believing it is permitted. That's the only permissible attitude. It's the one you ought to have if you have any attitude. Thus, no attitude is epistemically required, but only one is epistemically permitted.

(O2) thus rules out the possibility that each of two attitudes toward a proposition is permitted at a time. Some critics might regard this as a mistake. To see whether it is, let's begin by considering a moral analogue of this possibility. On standard views, there are cases of ties in morality: each of two actions is morally permissible and neither is obligatory. It's permissible for me to give my extra money to the Cancer Society and it's permissible to give it to the Heart Association. It's not permissible to spend it frivolously. It follows then, that it is permissible to give my money to the Heart Association and also permissible to refrain from giving my money to the Heart Association. Each of two incompatible actions is thus permissible. This is a consequence of the existence of moral ties. If the epistemic case is similar, then there are situations in which each of two attitudes toward one proposition is permissible. But I think that in the epistemic world, things aren't quite the same. There are no ties, in the relevant sense.

Potential cases of epistemic ties are of three sorts. The first, and easiest to dispose of, are cases in which the evidence for and against a proposition is equally weighty. In that case, evidentialism implies that the sole acceptable attitude is suspending judgment. Neither belief nor disbelief is permitted. That strikes me as the right result.

The second kind of case consists in those in which two competing propositions are equally well supported by the evidence. For example, there is equally good evidence supporting the guilt of each of two suspects for a crime that could have been committed by only one person. Casual reflection might suggest that you could believe that either is guilty, but obviously, not both. In that case, it is permissible to believe that suspect A is guilty and suspect B is not, and it is permissible to believe that suspect B is guilty and A is not. In fact, however, I think that in the situation described you should not believe that either suspect is guilty. Again, if you have an attitude toward these propositions, you should suspend judgment about each, though perhaps not about their disjunction.

There are possible cases like the one just described in which some action is forced on you and it seems that you ought to form a belief about which action to take. Suppose that you know that one of two boxes in front of you has a bomb that is about to explode. You have time to open only one box and disarm the bomb if it's there. You have no reason to prefer one box to the other. Surely you ought not suspend judgment about the location of the bomb and do nothing. That evaluation is correct, but it's correct because you ought not to do nothing. Failing to act would be imprudent, perhaps immoral. But you needn't have a belief about the location of the bomb in order to act. You can simply choose to open one box. And if you are the sort of person who can only pick a box in this case if you have the relevant belief, then there may well be a sense in which you ought to form a belief about where the bomb is (if you can). But the ought here is a prudential or moral ought, not an epistemic ought.[35] You epistemically ought to suspend judgment.

The third and most difficult sort of case to think about is one in which you have some modest amount of evidence supporting a proposition. It's tempting to think that it's permissible to believe the proposition and it's also permissible to suspend judgment about it, on the grounds that belief requires more than just this modest amount of evidence. In support of this line of thought is the idea that believing on only modest amounts of evidence involves taking some epistemic risk. There is no unique amount of risk that is right or rational. Rather, people simply have varying attitudes toward this risk. My own inclination, which I won't defend here, is that you should believe when your evidence is supportive rather than neutral, even if the evidence is not at all decisive. Those who say that one's evidence supports believing a proposition only when that evidence is sufficiently strong will in all probability be faced with borderline cases. In a case in which this modest amount of evidence is slightly in favor of a proposition, they might think that believing it is permissible and that suspending judgment is permissible. Of course, they are not forced to this conclusion, since they might hold that it is simply indeterminate which attitude one is permitted to have and that it is not simply true that either attitude is permitted.[36]

---

[35] Perhaps the reason it seems right to say that "You ought to form the belief *if you can*" is that the "ought" in this judgment is one that does imply "can". This is further evidence that the intended judgment here is not an epistemic judgment.

[36] Hud Hudson helped me to see this point. Notice that philosophers who think that ties are possible can still be evidentialists. That is, they can say that you always follow your evidence and never believe contrary to your evidence. They just think that there are cases in which the evidence leaves open two possibilities and there's nothing else that could eliminate one.

The Ethics of Belief

The evidentialist account of what we ought to believe relies crucially on the notion of evidential support. Analyzing this notion in a fully satisfactory way is no easy task. Among the problems to be worked out is that of determining which logical consequences of a body of evidence are supported by that evidence. There are possible cases in which a person has evidence that implies some proposition, but the connection between that evidence and that consequence is distant and difficult to see. It may be well beyond the intellectual talents of the person. I believe that in such cases the person ought not to believe the consequence. Given his failure to see that it is a consequence, to believe it (barring other reasons to believe it) would be rash. Furthermore, as I understand (O2), it has exactly the right result in this sort of case. The fact that a person's evidence implies some proposition is not sufficient for the evidence to provide evidential support for the proposition. Roughly, only those propositions whose connection to the evidence the person apprehends are actually supported by his evidence. And I think ascertaining this connection is itself an element of the person's evidence. These issues are complex, however, and I will not pursue them further here.

This completes my description of the evidentialist idea that one epistemically ought always to follow one's evidence. I turn now to a defense of this idea.

C. Evidentialism and Epistemic Value

One way to explain why we ought to do something is to show that it is a means to some goal that we have. A similar, but slightly different, way is to show that it is a means to some valuable result. Both alternatives explain what we ought to do instrumentally. To use the former alternative to show that we ought to follow our evidence would require showing that people have some goal—true belief or knowledge, perhaps—and that following their evidence is the proper means toward that goal. If the oughts in question are supposed to be means to goals that people actually have, then it seems that only people who do have the epistemic goals just mentioned would be subject to the relevant epistemic requirements. However, (O2) is not restricted in that way. It says that all people epistemically ought to follow their evidence, not just those who have adopted some specifically epistemic goals.[37]

One might argue that all people naturally have epistemic goals or perhaps that the goal of true belief or knowledge is in some sense an "ideal" goal. I won't pursue those claims here. Instead, I want to defend (O2) by arguing that

---

[37] One could take epistemic oughts to be conditional. To say that one epistemically ought to believe something is to say that if one has epistemic goals, then one ought to believe it.

181

Richard Feldman

following one's evidence is the proper way to achieve something of epistemic value. My approach does not depend upon the assumption that epistemic value is a kind of instrumental value. Of course, the view I'll defend does not imply that beliefs having epistemic value lack any sort of instrumental value.

C1. *True Belief and Epistemic Value*

The dominant source in the literature for discussions of epistemic goals and epistemic value is William James' famous passage:

There are two ways of looking at our duty in the matter of opinion,—ways entirely different, yet ways about whose difference the theory of knowledge seems hitherto to have shown little concern. We *must know the truth*; and *we must avoid error*,—these are our first and great commandments as would-be knowers...[38]

One idea commonly extracted from this is that our epistemic goal is to believe all and only truths.[39] But if this implies that all people actually have the goal of believing all truths, then I doubt that it is true. People's goals are a varied lot, and I doubt that all people have this one. Moreover, believing all truths is obviously an unattainable goal. We simply can't believe all the truths. Furthermore, attaining it is not desirable. As anyone who lived through President Clinton's impeachment trial knows, there are many truths one would prefer not believing (or even considering). So, it is doubtful that believing all truths is an actual, attainable, or desirable goal.

Whatever our goals, it makes sense to suppose that believing truths (or some related state) has epistemic value, that it is a good thing from an epistemic point of view. I turn now to the idea that having true beliefs and avoiding false beliefs has epistemic value and we should follow our evidence because it is the best way to have valuable beliefs. Consider, then, the following principle:

V1. Each person maximizes epistemic value by making it the case that for every proposition p, he or she believes p if p is true and does not believe p if p is false.

One might then argue that people can best maximize epistemic value by following their evidence.

---

[38] William James, "The Will to Believe," reprinted in *The Theory of Knowledge*, 2nd edition, pp. 555–62.

[39] The idea that this is our epistemic goal is widespread. It is the starting point for numerous discussions of a variety of epistemological issues. See, for example, Alston's "The Deontological Conception of [Epistemic] Justification," p. 258 and Richard Foley's *The Theory of Epistemic Rationality* (Cambridge, Massachusetts: Harvard University Press, 1987), p. 8.

The Ethics of Belief

There are a few problems with a defense of (O2) that is based on (V1). For one thing, (V1) would seem better suited to a defense of (O1), since (V1) assigns value to believing all truths, not just to the ones about which one has some attitude or other. Furthermore, the alleged connection between (V1) and (O2) is based on the assumption that following your evidence is the best way to get at the truth. And I just don't see why this is true. If you are in unfortunate circumstances in which the information you have will lead you to falsehoods, following your evidence is *not* the best way to the truth. That is, it is not the most effective way to get at the truth. In these circumstances, ignoring your evidence is a better way to believe (some) truths.

A possible reply to at least the second problem just mentioned for the argument from (V1) to (O2) relies on the claim that while following one's evidence might not be an infallible way to achieve the goal stated in (V1) or even always the most effective way, it is nevertheless the best or most reasonable way to try to have true beliefs. This defense of (O2) is quite similar to the one I will present in section (C3) below and I will discuss it there.

C2. Knowledge and Epistemic Value

What James actually said in his famous passage wasn't that you should believe truths or avoid believing falsehoods. Nor did he say that you should have true belief or the avoidance of false belief as a goal. What he actually said is that our commandment, as would be *knowers*, is to *know* the truth and to avoid error. One might extract from this the idea that what has epistemic value is not mere true belief but rather knowledge. Here's one way to spell out this idea:

V2. Each person maximizes epistemic value by making it the case that for every proposition p, he or she knows p if p is true and knows ~p if p is false.

(V2), like (V1), seems better suited to support something like (O1) than (O2), but I will ignore this point for now. One argument from (V2) to (O2) goes as follows. Given that one can have knowledge only if one has good evidence for what one believes, one can get beliefs with epistemic value only by following one's evidence. In other words, following one's evidence is a necessary condition for getting what (V2) says has epistemic value. If we epistemically ought to do whatever is necessary to obtain this epistemic value, then we epistemically ought to follow our evidence.

The idea that knowledge is what has epistemic value has a certain plausibility. Knowledge is valuable, and it makes sense to think that knowledge is a particularly *epistemic* kind of value. However, the argument from (V2) to (O2) is unsound. The central problem with the argument turns on cases in

Richard Feldman

which a person has strong evidence for a false proposition, f. According to the evidentialist position expressed in (O2), such a person should believe that falsehood. And the argument for (O2) based on (V2) relies on the assumption that the person should adopt the attitude that is necessary for him to have in order to have knowledge. But since f is false, there's an equally good argument for the conclusion that the person ought to believe $\sim f$, since knowledge also requires truth. If adopting an attitude that will yield knowledge is what's valuable, then in such a situation adopting one attitude—believing f—will satisfy one necessary condition for knowledge and adopting a different attitude—believing $\sim f$—will satisfy a different necessary condition for knowledge. (V2) provides no reason to think that one ought to believe f in this case. Thus, it fails to support (O2).

A related point concerns cases in which one has strong evidence for a proposition, but evidence insufficiently strong to yield knowledge. (O2) implies that one ought to believe in such a case. But it can't be that one ought to believe in such a case because that is a means to knowledge. The situation precludes having knowledge, yet (O2) has implications regarding what one ought to do. Again, (V2) fails to provide support for (O2).

C3. Reasonable Belief and Epistemic Value

While true beliefs may have considerable instrumental value, a person who irrationally believes a lot of truths is not doing well epistemically. In contrast, a person who forms a lot of rational but false beliefs is doing well epistemically. While knowledge also has a kind of value, seeing it as the only thing of epistemic value fails to explain what is valuable about forming beliefs that fall short of knowledge. We avoid the problems associated with identifying epistemic value with true belief or with knowledge if instead we say that what have epistemic value are rational beliefs. To do well as a believer, to achieve a kind of epistemic excellence, one must form only rational beliefs. I will discuss a defense of (O2) based on this account of epistemic value in this section.

One way to understand this evidentialist perspective on epistemic value and epistemic oughts is as follows. Consider a person who is contemplating a particular proposition. To carry out the role of being a believer in an epistemically good way, in a way that maximizes epistemic value, the person must adopt a rational attitude toward this proposition. There are other values that beliefs might yield. Some beliefs might have prudential or moral value. They might make people feel good or provide comfort for others. They might help one to undertake risky but beneficial behavior. They might give one self-confidence that can help to advance one's career. But beliefs that are beneficial in these ways can nevertheless fail to be rational. They can lack epistemic value. To achieve epistemic value one must, in each case, follow one's evidence.

Here, then, is a principle about epistemic value that supports (O2):

V3. When adopting (or maintaining) an attitude toward a proposition, p, a person maximizes epistemic value by adopting (or maintaining) a rational attitude toward p.

Given that (V3) specifies what maximizes epistemic value, a believer epistemically ought to form attitudes as directed by (O2): he ought to follow his evidence. This defense of (O2) depends on the substantive epistemological thesis that rationality consists in making one's beliefs conform to one's evidence. This thesis is apparently denied by some, for example some reliabilists. If reliabilism has substantive implications that differ from those of evidentialism, it must be because in some cases it implies that it is rational to form beliefs in the absence of evidential support. I will not undertake a defense of this evidentialist claim here, nor will I discuss the reliabilist alternative.

Anyone who is about to adopt an attitude toward a proposition, p, and who adheres to the dictates of (O2) will get knowledge (of p or of ~p) whenever such knowledge is attainable. If the available evidence is strong enough to yield a belief well-enough justified for knowledge, and the other conditions for knowledge are satisfied, then the person will have knowledge. Where knowledge is not attainable, the person will have reasonable belief. He'll be doing as well as he can, epistemically speaking. By seeking rational belief, then, one will get knowledge where one can. And, of course, unless one is in unfortunate circumstances in which one's evidence frequently leads to false beliefs, anyone who follows (O2) will mostly have true beliefs.

(V3) and (O2) concern themselves with how to maximize epistemic value when adopting an attitude toward a proposition. There are many ways in which one might behave over the long term that will help one to gain knowledge of important facts. The relevant behavior might include enrolling in suitable courses of study, maintaining a healthy life-style to keep one's mind sharp, and cultivating sound inferential habits. Evidentialism is silent about such practices. It focuses on the epistemic value to be obtained immediately from the adoption of an attitude toward a proposition. The way to do that, in every case, is to follow the evidence one has.

At the end of section C1 I mentioned the idea that one might defend (O2) on the grounds that having true beliefs is epistemically valuable and that following one's evidence is the most reasonable way to try to get beliefs that have epistemic value. The current view is that reasonable beliefs are epistemically valuable and that following one's evidence is a perfect means to getting valuable beliefs. There are then two ways to support (O2). The differences between these defenses of (O2) may not be great, but there are two points worthy of note. They can be brought out by considering a person whose evidence supports a great many falsehoods. First, suppose the person follows his evidence. According to both views, this person is believing as he ought. But according to the earlier view his beliefs, being false, lack epistemic value whereas according to the current view they are epistemically valuable. Second, suppose that the person does not follow his evidence. In that case, both views imply that he is not believing as he ought, but the earlier view implies that he is, by luck, achieving epistemically valuable beliefs. In both cases, I find the implications of the current view more appealing. I don't see anything epistemically good about the person who irrationally gets true beliefs. I don't think that it would be correct to say of him that he's achieved epistemic excellence, even though he's done it in an irrational way or merely by luck. Rather, I think he's failed epistemically, not only because he isn't believing as he ought but because he does not have rational beliefs. Of course, there may be some instrumental value in those true beliefs. They may help the person negotiate the world in a better way. But that is a different matter.

D. Three Objections to Evidentialism

D1. *Evidence One Should Have Had*

Consider a person who is negligent about collecting evidence. Suppose that I have the firm belief that

G. Taking ginkgo supplements is a safe and effective way to improve my memory.

I have a modest amount of evidence supporting (G). I then see on the cover of a reputable magazine that it contains a major article about the merits of ginkgo. Rather than read the article, I avoid it for fear that it will undermine a belief I prefer to keep. Thus, I am negligent in collecting evidence; there is evidence I don't have but should have. Furthermore, suppose that if I read the article, I would have acquired strong evidence against (G). Thus, while (G) is supported by the evidence I do have, I should have had additional evidence and I shouldn't believe (G). So, (O2) has the wrong result in this sort of case. It implies that I ought to follow the limited evidence I do have rather than the larger body of evidence I have negligently avoided.[40]

---

[40] Keith DeRose presented an objection along these lines when he commented on a version of this paper presented at the Rutgers Epistemology Conference.

The details of examples such as this one are quite important. There are possible examples in which a person has some good reasons to believe something, but knows that there are available strong considerations to the contrary although he chooses not to make himself familiar with that evidence. Suppose, that the magazine headline in our example is "Ginkgo Shown to be Ineffective." Upon seeing this headline, I immediately stop reading since I don't want evidence like that. I continue to believe (G) on the basis of my old reasons. Surely my conduct in this case is reprehensible. But just as surely, I have acquired evidence against (G) and my belief loses some considerable support the moment I see the title of the article. It gives me good reason to think that there are strong objections to (G), even if I'm not yet in a position to say in any detail what they are. That significantly alters the evidential status of the proposition for me. Given the credibility of the source and the nature of the article title, most likely my overall evidence no longer supports my belief. I no longer ought to believe (G).

Variations on the example are possible. The article might be in a publication whose reliability is entirely unknown to me or in a magazine I know to be thoroughly disreputable. Other variations on the example concern the wording of the title. It could be something neutral such as "Some New Information on Ginkgo." Again I ignore the article. Again, assume that it contains the same devastating objections. In this case, the mere awareness of the existence of the article has much less evidential force. Nevertheless, you might plausibly think that in these cases, or at least some of them, I am terribly negligent in ignoring the article. I shouldn't do that. Had I not done it, I wouldn't have maintained my belief in (G). So, I ought not to have that belief.

The statement of the objection seems to me to state the heart of the reply. The name and source of the message do not provide me with much, if any, reason to stop believing (G).[41] Until I've read the article, it would be bizarre for me to stop believing what's supported by my old evidence. I don't have any reason to. Suppose that instead of negligently ignoring the article, I'm busy and I simply set it aside until I can give it proper attention. There's nothing negligent about this behavior. What should I believe in the meantime? Should I think, "Well, somebody has written something about ginkgo, so I'd better stop believing that it is effective"? I think that the answer is obvious: I shouldn't change for that reason. And this fact doesn't change whether my motives for setting aside the article are laudatory or reprehensible. In every case, the right answer depends

---

[41] One might argue that we all know that magazines usually run articles like this only when they are negative. If that's the case, then seeing the seemingly neutral title does provide me with some evidence against (G). The case is then similar to the first version in which the title is explicitly negative.

upon what evidence I already have, including the evidence about the possible existence of these objections.

No matter what the answers are to questions about how I ought to conduct my inquiry, where I ought to look for evidence, and so on, there always remain the questions, "What should I believe in the meantime?" "What should I believe until I have a chance (or the courage) to look at that new evidence?" It's that natural and central question to which evidentialism provides a good answer.[42]

One might think that when one should look at additional evidence, one should always suspend judgment in the meantime. But that is a clear mistake, as the example above illustrates. You should follow your current evidence. If you do get more evidence, then you should follow the combined evidence you have at that time.

D2. Duty to Gather Evidence

Even if it is true that in the examples just discussed I am believing as I ought given the limited evidence I have, it is plausible to think that there are other epistemic requirements that I ought to fulfill. In particular, in some versions of these cases, I ought to obtain the additional evidence that is available to me. More generally, in a wide variety of cases, it might be thought, one ought to gather additional evidence about the propositions one considers. It's not enough simply to follow the evidence one actually has. Thus, evidentialism overlooks important epistemic oughts. In a recent paper, "The Epistemic Duty to Seek More Evidence," Richard J. Hall and Charles R. Johnson argue that you have an epistemic duty to seek more evidence about every proposition about which you are not certain.[43] While many epistemologists would reject the demanding condition Hall and Johnson describe, it may seem obvious that in many cases you ought to seek evidence regarding propositions about which you will form beliefs. However, the evidentialist view defended here apparently conflicts with this seemingly obvious truth. If the fundamental epistemic goal is just to have reasonable beliefs, then nothing about evidence gathering techniques or the like follows as a means to that goal.[44] This goal just has implications concerning what attitudes we ought to take given the evidence we have.

---

[42] Richard Foley takes a similar approach to epistemic questions. See especially Chapter 1 of *Working without a Net* (Oxford: Oxford University Press, 1993).

[43] See Richard J. Hall and Charles R. Johnson, "The Epistemic Duty to Seek More Evidence," *American Philosophical Quarterly*, 35 (1998): 129–40. Hall and Johnson actually defend the thesis that this remarkable duty follows from the assumption that our goal is to believe all and only true propositions. They do not defend the claim that this is our goal.

[44] Similarly, if the goal is just to now have true beliefs about the propositions about which we are about to form attitudes, then there's no need to gather new evidence.

The Ethics of Belief

By seeking out new evidence concerning some important proposition and then believing what that evidence supports, I don't do a better job of achieving the goal of believing reasonably. I achieve that goal at any moment by believing what is then supported by my evidence. It's surely true that there are times when one would be best off finding new evidence. But this always turns on what options one has, what one cares about, and other non-epistemic factors. As I see it, these are prudential or moral matters, not strictly epistemic matters.

A familiar distinction may help make the evidentialist account seem more attractive. This is the distinction between short-term and long-term goals and the related distinction between synchronic and diachronic rationality. The former concerns questions of rationality at a given moment while the latter concerns rationality over time. Evidentialism is best seen as a theory about synchronic rationality. It holds that the epistemically rational thing to do at any moment is to follow the evidence you have at that moment. It doesn't address questions of how to conduct inquiry over periods of time. Thus, it does not address questions about how to gather evidence, when one ought to seek additional evidence, and so on. In my view these diachronic questions are moral or prudential questions rather than epistemic questions. You should gather more evidence concerning a proposition only when having a true belief about the subject matter of the proposition makes a moral or prudential difference and gathering more evidence is likely to improve your chances of getting it right. Of course, whether you ought to gather such evidence also depends upon what other things you could do with your time. Epistemological considerations simply don't resolve such matters.

There are cases in which one can spend one's time gathering evidence about propositions concerning inconsequential and trivial propositions or about more weighty matters. Evidentialism provides no guidance about what to do. As I see it, this is not a weakness of evidentialism, since such choices are not to be made on epistemic grounds. What topics you ought to investigate depend upon what topics are of interest to you, what investigations can help you to make your own life or the lives of others better, and other such matters. Evidentialism is silent on those moral and prudential issues, and I don't see why it should address them.

D3. *Being Rational by Avoiding Evidence*

The evidentialist principles stated here imply that one can get oneself into a highly rational state by ridding oneself of as much evidence as one can and then suspending judgment about virtually everything that comes to mind. If a person finds a drug or a machine that can erase memories from his brain and arranges to be immersed in a sensory deprivation tank, he'll have very little evidence regarding anything. By believing very little, he'll then be highly rational according to evidentialist standards. Yet, this may seem just the opposite of being rational.[45]

Evidentialists are committed to the view that the person just described would have little evidence regarding anything and would be rational to suspend judgment about nearly everything. But that seems to be exactly the right conclusion. Once the person has lost his evidence, he has no reasons to believe much, and he'd be unreasonable if he did believe things that would have been well justified for him had he been in more normal circumstances. But he's not in normal circumstances and evidentialism concerns itself with assessing what he should believe in the circumstances he is in, not with what he should believe if he were in different circumstances.

Critics might think that he shouldn't get himself in a condition of evidential deprivation in the first place. Evidentialists can agree, though not on evidentialist grounds. By putting himself in those conditions, he's made himself unable to act on behalf of others who may rely on him. Perhaps he morally ought to avoid rendering himself useless in this way. Furthermore, by putting himself in a condition of evidential deprivation, he deprives himself of all the pleasure that comes from experiencing the world. Unless his prior circumstances and future prospects are extremely grim, it is likely to be imprudent to put himself in that situation. Evidentialists can agree with these critical evaluations of this behavior, but these are not epistemic evaluations. They are moral or prudential evaluations of behavior related to the formation of beliefs.

I conclude that objections such as the ones considered here do not undermine the evidentialist view of what we epistemically ought to do. Evidentialism says that when adopting a doxastic attitude toward a proposition, a person epistemically ought to adopt that attitude that is supported by the evidence the person has at that time. How the person came to have that evidence, whether by conscientious inquiry or by avoiding potentially troublesome information, is irrelevant to this epistemic fact. Similarly, how the person ought to proceed in future inquiry is also irrelevant. Evaluations of this behavior can be made, of course, but these evaluations are of a different nature than those made on evidentialist grounds. The evidentialist evaluation assesses whether the attitude formed in the circumstances one is actually in is the attitude one ought to have formed in those circumstances.

---

[45] This objection was suggested to me by Timothy Williamson.

The Ethics of Belief

III. Epistemology and Ethics

There are several questions about the relation of epistemic duties (or oughts) to ethical and other duties. For example, there is in the literature considerable discussion of the idea that there's some important connection between what one is epistemically justified in believing and what one is morally justified in believing. On one side, there is the line of thought suggested by Clifford, according to which believing without epistemic justification is always morally wrong. To defend this thesis, you'd have to argue that such believing is always voluntary or else that involuntary behavior can be morally wrong. I'm not inclined to argue for either of these theses. Other questions concern whether epistemic duties are a "special case" of moral duties and whether there can be cases in which there is a conflict between these different kinds of duties.[46] I won't take up these topics here. I will discuss one puzzling issue in this area.

The question I do want to address can best be raised by attending to a remark Hall and Johnson make in defense of their claim that we have an epistemic duty to seek more evidence for all uncertain propositions. They say that this duty "is probably a pretty weak duty; most moral and prudential duties would trump it in cases of conflict."[47] They quote Chisholm as holding that moral duties always trump epistemic duties. What I want to discuss is whether any sense can be made of the claim that moral duties trump, or do not trump, epistemic duties.

There is no problem with the idea that duties of the same kind can be weighed in importance. For example, a person might have a moral duty to his students to show up for class and a moral duty to his sick child to stay home and care for her. And one might say that one of these duties outweighs, or trumps, the other. The idea here, I take it, is that there is some scale of moral value and that fulfilling one duty contributes more to that value than does fulfilling the other.

What is far less clear is that there is such a thing as *just plain ought*, as opposed to the various kinds of oughts philosophers have succeeded in distinguishing.[48] To understand the issue, it's important to distinguish two very different points. Suppose you accept the view that it is morally wrong to believe on the basis of insufficient evidence. (Set aside worries about voluntarism.) I take it that at most you would think that the fact that a particular action is a case of believing

---

[46] For discussion of the latter question, see Eugene Mills, "The Unity of Justification," *Philosophy and Phenomenological Research*, 58 (1998): 27–50. For discussion of the former question, see Susan Haack, "'The Ethics of Belief' Reconsidered."

[47] "The Epistemic Duty to Seek More Evidence," p. 136.

[48] I learned this way of formulating this question from Owen McLeod's "Just Plain 'Ought'", *The Journal of Ethics*, 5 (2001): 269–91.

on insufficient evidence counts towards its being wrong. As some would put it, it is *prima facie* wrong. This leaves open the possibility that this case of believing on insufficient evidence has other features that count in its favor, morally speaking. It might be a case of being supportive of one's family or disregarding some excusable flaws in others. It might have much to be said for it. I have no trouble at all understanding the idea that we can in principle compare the negative moral value of failing to follow one's evidence to the positive moral value of the other features of the case. But here we are comparing two moral factors to reach an overall moral assessment.

I take it that when people say things such as "Moral oughts trump epistemic oughts" they are not saying that the moral weight of epistemic oughts is less than the moral weight of other moral considerations. I believe that what they are saying is that there is some sort of generic ought that somehow encompasses moral considerations, epistemic considerations, and perhaps others, and then weighs them against one another to come up with an overall assessment. This is not any particular kind of ought. It is *just plain ought*. I take Hall and Johnson to be suggesting that when you epistemically ought to gather more evidence and you morally ought to do something else, the moral ought "wins" and you just plain ought to do that other thing. It's this that I just don't understand. Of course, by this I mean to suggest that no one else understands it either. It makes no sense.

I know of no way to establish that the notion of *just plain ought* makes no sense. But I can give some partial defense of my view by noting that it would be a mistake to assume that there must be such a thing as "just plain ought" simply because there are various kinds of oughts. There needn't be anything meaningful about their combination. To see why, consider an analogy. Suppose a child has two dolls. One is short and squat. The other is tall and thin. The child asks you which doll is "bigger". You are faced with a problem. One doll is taller. The other is wider and, let's assume, more voluminous. The child could be asking which is taller, which is wider, or which is more voluminous. Each of those measures could be expressed by "bigger". We needn't assume that there's any meaningful measure that combines these three, yielding "bigger all things considered." Or, more precisely, we could arbitrarily combine the various measures in any way we like. But it would be a mistake to pick any such measure as what really counts as "overall bigger". It would make no sense to ask whether height trumps width or volume trumps height in assessing overall size. We've disambiguated the word "bigger". There's no putting the senses back together, at least no way that isn't simply arbitrary. There's no such thing as "just plain bigger". There are simply the various bigger-than relations.

The Ethics of Belief

Consider another example. Suppose we are considering the wealth and strength of two people, A and B. A is stronger, B is wealthier. We ought not assume that there's some proper way of combining these two measures into one, which we might call "strealth." We can of course combine measures of strength and wealth in a limitless number of ways. It might be that some combination would in fact best suit our purposes. But the mere fact that there are two measures, wealth and strength, does not guarantee that there is any proper way to combine them to form strealth. The existence of numerical measures of wealth and strength ought not to deceive us here. We could measure one's wealth in rubles and one's strength in terms of the number of grams one can bench press. We could then add those numbers together to get a proposed measure of strealth. But we also could add one's wealth in dollars to the number of pounds one can bench press. That will give a different number. And there are a limitless number of other such sums. Each will yield potential strealth rankings. The different possibilities will have the effect of counting one measure more heavily than the other. If someone were to object to one of these strealth measures on the grounds that it conflicts with the fact that wealth trumps strength in measures of strealth, I think we should say that we have no idea what that person is talking about. We have no independent concept of strealth for which there are correct weightings of the two components.

I think that the same is true of the attempt to compare various kinds of oughts to determine what one just plain ought to do. Suppose that one belief is prudent for me—it will maximize my well-being or what I care about or what is important to me—but it is not a belief I epistemically ought to have since I lack evidence for it. We can understand the idea that forming an unjustified belief might be imprudent, since it might foster a bad habit. So, we can imagine weighing the short-term prudential gain against the long-term prudential cost. But I can see no values to which we could be appealing when we ask whether the overall prudential benefit trumps the epistemic cost.

For each "ought" there is an associated value. We ought, in the relevant sense, to do the thing that maximizes that value, or perhaps something that does well enough in achieving that kind of value. For example, we morally ought to do what maximizes, or produces enough, moral value. We prudentially ought to do what maximizes, or produces enough, prudential value. If there is such a thing as "just plain ought", then there is a value associated with it. The thing we just plain ought to do is the thing that comes out highest, or high enough, according to that measure. It's far from clear what that value would be—it isn't to be identified with any of the more determinate kinds of value and there seems to be no uniquely correct (or range of correct) ways to combine moral, practical, epistemic, and other values. We've disambiguated "ought" and we can't put the various senses back together again. There is no meaningful question about whether epistemic oughts "trump" or are trumped by other oughts.

Stewart Cohen has presented the following objection to this view.[49] Suppose a child comes to her parents with a problem. She is contemplating some action and she's figured out that it is the prudent thing to do but not the moral thing to do. In other words, she realizes that she prudentially ought to do it, but she morally ought not do it. She asks, "What ought I do?" She is clearly looking for a way to resolve the apparent conflict. The view I've defended requires the parents to say that there is no meaningful question here. More precisely, when she uses the word "ought" in her question, she is either using it in one of the disambiguated senses, in which case she already knows the answer to her question, or else she is using it in the sense of "just plain ought", in which case she's not asking a meaningful question. In the latter case, the question is like that of the child who wants to know which doll is really bigger.[50]

It is difficult to resist the inclination to want to give the child advice about how to conduct herself. And there is advice that one might give. The question invites further reflection on whether the moral evaluation is really correct, given that the act is harmful to her. The question also invites further reflection on whether the prudential calculation is really correct, given that immoral behavior is also often imprudent. And in the particular case of a child asking a parent such a question, there is the matter of whether the child will have the parent's approval whichever way she acts. There is, finally, the question of what the parent predicts he or she would do in similar circumstances. Thus, there are several meaningful questions that one might ask in the sort of case Cohen envisions. However, as I see it, none of them amounts to the question of what one just plain ought to do.

IV. Conclusion

I've argued in this paper that deontological judgments about beliefs do not imply doxastic voluntarism. I've also argued that we do have a form of voluntary control over a substantial number of beliefs, but that this fact is of no great significance for epistemology. Epistemic evaluations do not depend upon whether we have or exercise this voluntary control. I've also argued, or asserted,

---

[49] In conversation.

[50] Another possibility is that she is using "ought" in yet another more determinate sense. This option seems irrelevant to the present example.

The Ethics of Belief

that what we epistemically ought to do is follow our evidence: when we have a doxastic attitude toward a proposition, it ought to be the attitude that is supported by the evidence we have. I haven't attempted to say anything here about what evidential support is or what it is to have something as evidence. Those are topics for another occasion. I have claimed that there is nothing more that a person epistemically ought to do than to follow her evidence in this way. In particular, activities such as gathering additional evidence for propositions about which one is uncertain are not among the things one epistemically ought to do, even if they are on other grounds highly desirable. Finally, I've expressed skepticism about the meaningfulness of questions about whether or not epistemological considerations are outweighed by moral or prudential considerations in figuring out what we ought to do all things considered.

The topics I've addressed by no means exhaust the issues that could properly be raised under the heading "the ethics of belief." But I hope to have made some small contribution to our thinking about the specific topics I have addressed.[51]

---

[51] In working on this paper I've benefited greatly from numerous discussions with Earl Conee, John Bennett, Stewart Cohen, Jonathan Vogel, and all the students in my Fall 1998 epistemology seminar. I'm also grateful to John Greco and Matthias Steup for helpful comments. Earlier versions of the paper have been presented at the University of Rochester and at Rutgers University. I'm grateful to the audiences on both occasions and to Keith DeRose for his provocative comments on the latter occasion.

Part III

Developments and Applications

8

The Justification of Introspective Beliefs

Richard Feldman

1. Introduction

Two theses characterize foundationalism. One is that there are beliefs or propositions whose justification does not depend on other beliefs. Beliefs or propositions that have this status are said to be basic or foundationally justified. The second foundationalist thesis is that everything that is non-foundationally justified has that status in virtue of its relation to things that are foundationally justified. A third thesis characterizes what is plausibly described as classical foundationalism. This is the idea that internal (or mental) factors determine which beliefs are justified. In particular, external factors such as contingent reliability or causal connectedness are not among the conditions for justification, unless they are implied by the internal factors.

For foundationalists to have a reasonably well-developed theory, they must deal with at least three issues in a suitable way. First, there should be an account of which beliefs actually have foundational justification. Second, given that foundationally justified beliefs are not justified in virtue of their relations to other beliefs, there should be some account of what it is that makes them justified. And, third, if skepticism is to be avoided, there should be some account of how the foundationally justified beliefs actually manage to justify a significant body of beliefs about the world.

Familiar versions of classical foundationalism hold that propositions or beliefs about one's own current mental states are foundationally justified. Among the reasons offered for holding them to be foundationally justified are the claims that we are infallible with respect to such matters, or that these states are "self-presenting." Foundationalists who limit what is basic to these mental states are faced with a difficult problem when they attempt to explain how beliefs about the external world are justified on their basis. In several recent publications Ernest Sosa has raised, in a characteristically insightful way, a challenge for such versions of classical foundationalism.[1] In this paper I will examine Sosa's arguments and attempt to defend a version of classical foundationalism from his criticism.

2. A Problem for Classical Foundationalism

A. Initial Formulation of the Theory

Classical foundationalists have thought that there are certain qualities of experiences that are in some sense directly present to consciousness. For example, if a person has an experience of a large expanse of redness in her visual field against a sharply contrasting background, then she can know "directly" that she is having such an experience of redness. That she is having such an experience is a paradigmatic example of foundational justification. From this she can infer that there is something red before her. The traditional foundationalist picture has it that all knowledge is ultimately based on this sort of direct knowledge.

Sosa begins his discussion of this topic by quoting from Leibniz and Russell, both of whom explain foundational justification in terms of awareness. The quotation from Russell will suffice for present purposes:

We shall say that we have *acquaintance* with anything of which we are directly aware, without the intermediary of any process of inference or any knowledge of truths.[2]

This quotation suggests a principle of foundational justification concerning things of which we are directly aware. To formulate any such principle clearly, it will be helpful to make some preliminary distinctions among the potential

---

[1] My primary text here is "Privileged Access," to appear in *Consciousness: New Philosophical Essays* edited by Quentin Smith (Oxford University Press, 2003), pp. 273–92. Similar material appears in "Virtue Epistemology," in a Blackwell Great Debates volume, *Epistemic Justification: Internalism vs. Externalism, Foundations vs. Virtues* by Ernest Sosa and Laurence BonJour (Oxford: Blackwell, 2003). A version of "Privileged Access" was presented at the 1999 Eastern Division Meeting of the American Philosophical Association. I was commentator on that occasion, and this paper is derived from the comments presented there.

[2] *Problems of Philosophy* (Oxford University Press, 1997), p. 46. (First published in 1912.)

objects of direct awareness and also among the things that are potential subjects of foundational justification.

One might say that we are directly aware of certain experiences. Alternatively, one might say that we are directly aware of certain properties of experiences. One might also say that we are directly aware of facts about experiences and their properties. Thus, in the example in which the person is presented with a large expanse of redness, one might say that the person is aware of (i) the experience of redness; (ii) the experiential quality, redness; (iii) the fact that she has an experience of redness. It may be that the view can be developed in terms of any one of these options, but which choice is made will affect exactly how the view is formulated. For present purposes, the discussion can most easily proceed in terms of awareness of properties.

There is a clear difference between a person merely being justified in believing a certain proposition and the person believing that proposition justifiably. The former requires only something such as sufficiently good reasons for belief or an available reliable method that would lead to that belief. The person need not actually have formed the belief. The latter requires that the belief actually be formed, either on the basis of those reasons or as a result of that method. We can refer to the former sort of justification as *propositional justification* and to the latter as *doxastic justification*. We can use sentences of the form "S is justified in believing p" to report propositional justification and sentences of the form "S justifiably believes p" and "S's belief that p is justified" to report doxastic justification. At several points later in this paper this distinction will be important.

An initial statement of a foundationalist principle about propositional justification suggested by Russell's remark is:

PJ1. If a person is aware of experiential property F (i.e., has an experience of F-ness), then the person is foundationally justified in believing that he is having an experience with quality F.

Given the terminology adopted here, this principle says that when a person has an experience of a certain sort, the person is justified in believing the corresponding proposition saying that she is having an experience of that sort. This holds whether or not the person actually believes the proposition. We can easily devise a principle about doxastic justification that corresponds to (PJ1):

DJ1. If a person is aware of experiential property F (i.e., has an experience of F-ness), and believes that he is having an experience with property F, then that belief is foundationally justified.

The difference between (PJ1) and (DJ1) will matter later.

Richard Feldman

Principles such as (PJ1) and (DJ1) should help foundationalists answer the questions for foundationalism that were mentioned at the beginning of this paper. In answer to the first question, these principle say that the foundationally justified beliefs are the ones about directly experienced properties of experience. And, in response to the second question, these principles suggest that it is our awareness of these properties that explains why we are justified in believing them to be present.

B. An Ambiguity

Sosa contends that there is a crucial ambiguity in principles such as (PJ1). He writes:

One's consciousness contains experiences that go unnoticed; unnoticed altogether, or at least unnoticed as experiences with an intrinsic experiential character that they nevertheless do have. Just as one automatically jumps one's jumps, smiles one's smiles, and dances one's dances, however, so one experiences one's experiences. And since experiencing is a form of awareness, one is thus in one sense automatically aware of one's experiences, precisely in experiencing them. One is so aware even of experiences that escape one's notice and of which one is hence *un*aware, in another sense. (p. 276)

He goes on to distinguish two kinds of awareness. One he calls "noticing awareness" or "intellectual awareness." The other is mere "experiential awareness." The experiences that escape one's notice are experiences of which one is experientially aware but not noticingly aware. He asks:

Which kind of awareness do [foundationalists] intend: (a) noticing, intellectual awareness, whereby one occurrently believes or judges the thing noticed to be present, as characterized a certain way; or (b) experiential awareness, whereby one is "aware" directly of an experience of a certain specific sort simply in virtue of undergoing it?... That distinction... is important as follows. From the fact that one is e-aware of something it does not follow that one is n-aware of it. (pp. 276–7)

And then immediately after this he adds:

To notice a fact about one's experience at a given time is to believe correctly that it is so, but just a guess will not suffice: it is required that the correct belief be also at a minimum justified, or reasonable, or epistemically appropriate, or some such. (p. 277)

Given this ambiguity in the notion of awareness, there is a potential ambiguity in principles such as (PJ1). It could mean either of the following:

PJ1e. If a person is experientially-aware of experiential property F, then the person is foundationally justified in believing that he is having an experience with property F.

The Justification of Introspective Beliefs

PJ1n.   If a person is noticingly-aware of experiential property F, then the person is foundationally justified in believing that he is having an experience with property F.

Roughly, Sosa thinks that (PJ1e) is false and that (PJ1n) provides no explanation of the non-epistemic conditions in which a belief is foundationally justified. But some refinement of (PJ1n) will help make this point clearer.

To see the problem with (PJ1n), notice that it says in its antecedent that a person is n-aware of a property. But given what Sosa has said about n-awareness, n-awareness is best construed as a propositional attitude. Although one might be e-aware of properties (or experiences), n-awareness amounts to justified true beliefs about those properties. A better statement of the idea behind (PJ1n) is thus something like this:

PJ2n.   If a person is noticingly-aware of the fact that he is having an experience with experiential property F, then the person is foundationally justified in believing that he is having an experience with property F.

Given what Sosa has told us n-awareness is, this amounts to:

PJ3n.   If a person is having an experience with experiential property F, and the person believes that he is having an experience with property F, and he is justified in that belief, then the person is foundationally justified in believing that he is having an experience with property F.

(PJ3n) obviously does not provide a suitable explanation of *why* beliefs about experienced qualities are justified. Its antecedent just says, in part, that the belief is justified. It does not provide non-epistemic sufficient conditions under which the belief is justified.[3] It is clear that noticing-awareness cannot provide foundationalists with any helpful explanation of why beliefs are foundationally justified, since it builds into its antecedent the fact that they are justified.

Sosa uses the "problem of the speckled hen" to illustrate why classical foundationalists cannot successfully appeal to experiencing awareness, as in (PJ1e), in explaining foundational justification. He writes:

Much in the intricate character of our experience can, again, escape our notice, and can even be mischaracterized, as when one takes oneself to be able to tell at a glance that an image has ten speckles although in actual fact it has eleven rather than ten. If the classical foundationalist wishes to have a theory and not just a promissory note, he needs to tell us *which* sorts of features of our states of consciousness are the epistemically

---

[3] (PJ3n) is not a tautology. The consequent says that the belief is *foundationally* justified, and this is not stated in the antecedent.

effective ones, the ones such that it is *by corresponding to them specifically* that our basic beliefs acquire epistemically foundational status. (pp. 277–8)

I think that there may be a problem for (PJ1e) here, but it is not immediately obvious what it is.

What Sosa says is that we miss or mischaracterize some aspects of the "intricate character of our experience." This would apply most directly to a principle that says that all propositions about, or perhaps all beliefs about, features of experience are justified. But (PJ1e) does not say exactly that. It is more restrictive than that. It says that propositions about the properties of experience *of which we are aware* are justified. Furthermore, Sosa's example in which one mistakenly thinks one's image has ten speckles rather than eleven seems to be more relevant to a principle about doxastic justification than to a principle about propositional justification such as (PJ1e).[4]

I believe that if there is a counterexample to (PJ1e) here, it is this: when one has a mental image, sometimes one is e-aware of some of its properties without being justified in believing that one is having an experience with those properties. For example, when one has an image with eleven speckles, one is e-aware of the experience's eleven-speckle property, but not justified in believing that it has that property. Similarly, when one sees a clearly displayed twenty-three sided object, one is aware of the experiential property of twenty-three sidedness, but not justified in believing that property to be instantiated in one's experience.[5] One can be e-aware of properties without being justified in believing them to apply. That is the significance of the case of the speckled hen: one is aware of some definite number of speckles, but not justified in believing that one's image has that number of speckles.

It is possible for classical foundationalists to resist the claim that one is e-aware of twenty-three sidedness or eleven-specklehood in examples like these. They can say these are properties of experience of which we are unaware. However, I think that Sosa's point can be reformulated in response to this sort of reply. In the examples under consideration, a person has an experience of something with twenty-three sides or eleven speckles. These features of experience are right there in plain "view." Either the person is aware of those features or not. If he is, then the cases are counterexamples to (PJ1e). If the person is not

---

[4] Sosa may fully intend this example to apply only to a principle about doxastic justification. I am just trying to see if there is a problem for (PJ1e) suggested by his remarks.

[5] Sosa presents an example along these lines in "Theories of Justification: Old Doctrines Newly Defended," which appears in his collection *Knowledge in Perspective: Selected Essays in Epistemology* (Cambridge University Press, 1991), pp. 108–30. See especially pp. 127–8.

The Justification of Introspective Beliefs

aware of them, then classical foundationalists owe us some explanation of why not. They need to say more about what awareness of properties of experience amounts to. If they accomplish that, they might make plausible the claim, implied by (PJ1e), that all features of experience of which we are aware are "epistemically effective," i.e., all such features make one justified in believing that one is having an experience with those features.

The challenge for foundationalists is thus either to modify (PJ1e) in light of these examples or to explain why they are not counterexamples. The former requires specifying in some informative way which properties of experience make belief in their presence justified. Further, if what results is to be a defense of anything like traditional foundationalism, this must be done without appeal to concepts such as reliability that are foreign to traditional foundationalism. After all, one possible solution would be to say that we are justified in believing our experiences to have the properties that we can reliably identify. Although this sort of reliability is a purely internal fact about a person—the person's beliefs about a certain internal fact are properly correlated with that fact—this is not the sort of theory traditional foundationalists would like.[6]

C. Clarifying the Problem

In the previous section I ignored an important aspect of Sosa's view about foundational justification. He distinguishes three kinds of concepts: indexical, phenomenal, and simple geometric and arithmetic (SGA). The problem he has raised for classical foundationalism concerns SGA concepts.

Indexical concepts about experience occur in thoughts of the form "I am experiencing thusly," where one simply makes demonstrative reference to some feature of experience. If one succeeds in having a thought at all in such a circumstance, that is, if one does make a reference, then the thought is surely true. I think that Sosa is also willing to grant that any such thought is justified.

Phenomenal concepts are concepts that involve a certain sort of recognitional capacity. To have the phenomenal concept of redness, for example, requires the ability to recognize experiences of redness. (It might be better to call this the concept of phenomenal redness.) Sosa writes:

Grasping such a phenomenal concept comes with a certain guarantee of reliability, then, since it is defined in part by sensitivity to the relevant feature of which it is a concept. It is defined in part by the ability to tell when that feature is present and when

---

[6] It's not entirely clear to me why this is so. Perhaps it is because they'd worry that we could too easily be mistaken about which internal facts we are reliable about.

absent in our experiences. So we must be sufficiently reliable in the application of the concept in order to so much as grasp it. (p. 282)

Sosa thus thinks that beliefs involving both indexical and phenomenal concepts come with a certain guarantee of reliability, and perhaps this suffices to explain why all such beliefs are justified. There is, of course, reason to wonder whether classical foundationalists can rest easy with this reliabilist explanation of why such beliefs are justified, but I will not pursue that point here.

Sosa is granting, I believe, that classical foundationalists can formulate a true principle about foundational justification involving beliefs containing indexical and phenomenal concepts. His contention, as we shall see later, is that this acceptable principle does not allow for enough foundational justification. But before turning to his argument for that conclusion, it will be helpful to get clear about exactly what he is conceding to foundationalists.

Recall the distinction between propositional and doxastic justification. Sosa's discussion of the reliability of beliefs involving indexical and phenomenal concepts suggests that he is prepared to concede that when one has a belief about one's experiences that involves one of those concepts, then that belief is justified. This suggests that he is prepared to grant the truth of a principle about doxastic justification along the following lines:

DJ2.   If a person is experientially-aware of property F, and believes that he is having an experience with property F, and refers to property F in this belief by means of an indexical or phenomenal concept, then this belief is foundationally justified.

It is less clear how to apply Sosa's remarks about indexical and phenomenal concepts to principles about propositional justification. Perhaps there is a phenomenal concept that corresponds to each experiential property and we can specify referents for indexical concepts in propositions that no one is entertaining. If so, we might propose:

PJ4.   If a person is experientially-aware of property F, and P is a proposition that refers to property F by means of an indexical or phenomenal concept and says that the person is having an experience with property F, then the person is foundationally justified in believing P.

These are principles that link experiential awareness with foundational justification. They are not trivially true, nor are they uninformative. They do describe some factual conditions on which foundational justification might supervene. Sosa is willing to concede that they might be true because the

The Justification of Introspective Beliefs

concepts they involve come with a built-in assurance of reliability. However, he contends that these principles are not sufficient to explain all the foundational justification that classical foundationalists need. He thinks that there must be foundational justification involving geometric and arithmetic (SGA) concepts. He writes:

> We move beyond such concepts already with the theoretically richer concepts of arithmetic and geometry. When we form beliefs as to whether *these* concepts apply to our present experience, we can easily go wrong.... Classical foundationalists need some such beliefs with arithmetical or geometrical content, since from purely indexical or phenomenal concepts very little could be inferred, even allowing some explanatory induction from the given to the external.... [Has classical foundationalism] explained how we might be justified foundationally in applying arithmetical and geometric concepts to our experience? No, its lack of any such explanation is a serious problem for classical foundationalism. Might it be overcome in due course? I myself cannot see how. (p. 282)

Thus, the problem Sosa raises for classical foundationalism concerns foundational justification for propositions and beliefs involving geometric and arithmetic concepts. He thinks that there is no good way for classical foundationalists to explain why such propositions are foundationally justified, yet some of them must be foundationally justified if classical foundationalists are to account for the knowledge we have of the world around us. The example of the speckled hen illustrates the point. Suppose we expanded (PJ4) to include geometric and arithmetic concepts:

PJ5. If a person is experientially-aware of property F, and P is a proposition that refers to property F by means of an indexical, phenomenal, or SGA concept, and P says that the person is having an experience with property F, then the person is foundationally justified in believing P.

Sosa contends that the case of the speckled hen shows that (PJ5) is false. Perhaps the principle is true for some very simple SGA concepts, such as three-sidedness. But it is not true for twenty-three sidedness or forty-eight-specklehood, SGA features that we cannot simply spot in our experiences. We are experientially aware of these properties, but we are not automatically justified in believing them to be present.

Similar considerations pose a problem for doxastic justification. Suppose we extended (DJ2) to SGA concepts:

DJ3. If a person is experientially-aware of property F, and believes that he is having an experience with property F, and refers to property F in this belief by means of an indexical, phenomenal, or SGA concept, then this belief is foundationally justified.

The problem with (DJ3) is not simply that one can miss or mischaracterize features of experience. In such cases one does not both have an experience with that feature and believe oneself to have it. Hence, such cases are not counterexamples to (DJ3). But it is not too hard to get an example that does the job. If error is possible about the number of speckles, then it is also possible to get it right by guessing, by a pair of errors that fortuitously lead to the truth, or by a thoroughly unreliable method that happens in one rare instance to capture the truth. So (DJ3) is also mistaken.

Thus, Sosa's contention is that if classical foundationalists restrict foundational justification to beliefs and propositions involving indexical and phenomenal concepts, as in (PJ4) and (DJ2), they have too thin a base of foundational justification to support the rest of what we take ourselves to know. They can attempt to expand the base by bringing in SGA concepts, as in (PJ5) and (DJ3), but those principles are false.

One might think that the difference between the simple arithmetical concepts and the complex ones has to do with reliability. Sosa's own proposal is along those lines. But it is important to realize that to appeal to that sort of factor is to appeal to a factor of the sort classical foundationalists, as Sosa is thinking of them, would not allow into their theory. It is an external factor.

3. Sosa's Proposal

A. Safe and Virtuous Beliefs

Sosa formulates his account of foundational justification by focusing on a particular contrast. The contrast is between a case of a foundationally justified introspective judgment about the phenomenal character of experience and an unjustified belief about the phenomenal character of experience. Suppose that a person is presented with an object with forty-eight speckles. The object and its forty-eight speckles are in clear view. Thus, the person has an experience with the phenomenal character of forty-eight speckles. He is, if you like, appeared to forty-eight-specklishly. And suppose that the person does believe, as a result of guessing, that he is having such an experience. That belief is not justified, or at any rate not foundationally justified. Justification does not just emerge from having an experience of this kind. Contrast this with the appearance of three speckles. The belief that one's experience has three speckles is foundationally justified.

The Justification of Introspective Beliefs

Sosa says that to explain the difference we must appeal to more than the following three items:

(a) the phenomenal character of the experiences,
(b) the propositional content of the occurrent thought as one judges the image to contain so many speckles,
(c) the fit between the phenomenal character and the propositional content.

Sosa proposes that the difference between a justified introspective report and an unjustified introspective report is that the former is *safe* and *virtuous*. To say that a judgment is safe is to say that "in the circumstances not easily *would* one believe as one does without being right" (p. 290). And a belief is virtuous provided it is "derived from a way of forming beliefs that is an intellectual virtue, one that in our normal situation for forming such beliefs would tend strongly enough to give us beliefs that are safe" (p. 290).

These distinctions may seem to bring out nicely the difference between an unjustified belief that the image has forty-eight speckles and a justified belief that it has three. The latter belief is quite safe. As a matter of fact, one is quite unlikely to have that belief and be wrong. In contrast, one could easily believe that the image has forty-eight speckles and be wrong. This might happen if there were forty-nine speckles or forty-seven.

B. The Need for Virtuosity

As Sosa points out, merely having a safe belief is not sufficient for that belief to be justified (p. 290). If there is a belief that could not be false, or could not easily be false, then that belief is safe. But a belief might be safe not because of any particular insight or merit of the believer, but because the proposition believed happens to be one that cannot be false. Sosa uses as an example the case of a necessary truth that one believes with little or no justification. If the proposition believed is in fact true, then it could not be false. Hence, one could not easily (or even possibly) believe as one does and be wrong. Such an unjustified belief passes the safety test. For this reason Sosa adds the requirement that the belief be virtuously formed, that the method for forming the belief be one that in normal situations leads to safe beliefs.

Sosa does not point out that unjustified contingent beliefs can also pass the safety test. It is possible that there are facts about our minds that restrict the sorts of phenomenal properties that can be present to us. Suppose, for example, that we just couldn't experience speckled images with a number of speckles near to, but not identical with, forty-eight. Or suppose it is a law of nature that

209

all speckled hens have forty-eight speckles. And suppose that the hens display either all their speckles or none of them. Thus, whenever you think you are having an experience of a forty-eight-speckled hen, you are right. As things actually are, one could not easily be wrong about that. It's a little difficult to avoid complications involving some of the speckles being obscured, but I think that this complication is not relevant to the fundamental point. It is possible that there are propositions about experience that, like the true mathematical beliefs, cannot easily be wrong (regardless of your reasons for holding the belief). Whenever you believe such a proposition, you satisfy the safety condition. However, just as one can believe the true mathematical propositions unjustifiably, one can believe these contingently true propositions about experience unjustifiably. Thus, as Sosa realizes, safety is not enough.

Sosa describes the case in which one unjustifiably believes that one's image has forty-eight speckles as follows:

> One does not know foundationally that one's image contains 48 speckles even if one's image *does* in fact contain 48 speckles, and one's belief hence corresponds precisely to what is then given in one's consciousness. One fails to know in that case because too easily might one have believed that one's image had 48 speckles while it had one more speckle or one less. But that is not so for the belief that one's image has 3 speckles. (p. 290)

The point of the previous paragraph is to show that there are at least possible situations in which a belief like this one is safe, but still not justified.

C. A Problem?

The considerations just advanced put a considerable burden on the virtuousness condition. Sosa must say that the method by which the unjustified believer arrives at the forty-eight-speckle belief is not virtuous. This means that it does not "derive from a way of forming beliefs that... in our normal situation for forming such beliefs would tend strongly enough to give us beliefs that are safe." But suppose that the person just looks at a three-speckled image and thinks "three speckles" and just looks at a forty-eight-speckled image and thinks "forty-eight speckles." Sosa must say that the latter belief, even when it is safe, derives from a different, and less virtuous, way of forming beliefs. Perhaps it does, though this is difficult to assess.

Much here depends on what counts as the "ways of forming beliefs" on which the theory depends. There is considerable flexibility in how ways of forming beliefs might be characterized. If they are characterized narrowly, it may be that the three-speckle belief and the forty-eight-speckle result from different ways. However, in the circumstance in which the forty-eight-speckle

The Justification of Introspective Beliefs

belief is safe, the way in which it is formed must also extend to other beliefs, most of which are not safe. Otherwise, the theory would rule that the forty-eight-speckle belief is both safe and virtuous. If the ways of forming beliefs are characterized in a broader way, it may turn out that both beliefs are formed in the same way. In that case, the theory improperly evaluates the two beliefs as being epistemically alike. Elsewhere, I've expressed doubts about there being a suitable way to spell this idea out with sufficient clarity to generate a theory capable of being evaluated.[7] Sosa does not attempt to deal with these issues in the works under discussion here.[8] To go into these matters here would take us somewhat far afield. I believe that it is fair to say that this is a difficult issue for Sosa's theory, though not fair to claim here that there is no acceptable response or even that Sosa has not provided one.

4. Defending Classical Foundationalism

We can formulate Sosa's problem for classical foundationalism as a challenge to explain the relevant differences in two pairs of examples. Consider the following pair first. In one case a person has an experience of an image with three speckles. The person knows with certainty that she is visually experiencing an image with three speckles. Contrast this with the case in which the person has an experience of an image with forty-eight speckles, and believes, with confidence, that it has forty-eight speckles. But this belief about forty-eight speckles results from guessing or the unjustified implicit assumption that all multi-speckled images have forty-eight speckles. One wants to say that the three-speckle belief is foundationally justified and the forty-eight-speckle belief is not. Reliability of the sort Sosa favors may seem to explain the difference, but what can a classical foundationalist say to explain the difference?

The second pair of cases that needs explanation is this. We cannot tell, just in a glance, that an image has forty-eight speckles. There could be people who, unlike us, can recognize forty-eight speckles. For them, the belief that they are having an experience of forty-eight speckles might be foundationally justified, just like the belief that we are experiencing something three-speckled is foundationally justified for us. This shows that there is not something intrinsic to the proposition itself that determines whether or not it is the subject of foundational

---

[7] "Reliability and Justification," *The Monist*, 68 (1985): 159–74. See also "The Generality Problem for Reliabilism," co-authored with Earl Conee, *Philosophical Studies*, 89 (1998): 1–29 [Ch. 6 in this volume].

[8] See *Knowledge in Perspective*. Sosa suggests that relevant types are ones that can "be usefully generalized upon by us as the epistemic community of the" believers. (p. 284). It is difficult to see how this solves the problem, since multiple types may be "usefully generalized upon."

justification. Something about the believer matters as well. Again, reliability of some sort might seem to be an attractive answer. What can a classical foundationalist say to explain the difference between us and those who can recognize forty-eight speckles?

A. Phenomenal Concepts and SGA Concepts

To have a phenomenal concept of a particular property is, according to Sosa, to be sensitive to the presence of that property. Now, consider the property of experiencing an image containing forty-eight speckles. It is possible for a person to be sensitive to the presence or absence of this property. That is, a person might be able to distinguish experiences involving images with forty-eight speckles from experiences involving images with any other number of speckles. But it does not follow that the person is able to tell how many speckles there are when in fact there are forty-eight. One can know that there is something distinctive about a certain case, and reliably detect the presence of the distinctive feature, without knowing what that distinctive feature is. In the early stages of identifying things, we often are in just this situation. Perhaps a different example will make the point clearer.

The following example pertains to properties of external things, but it could just as easily be applied to features of experiences. When learning to identify different kinds of trees by the shapes of their leaves, one might learn to recognize the various different shapes without learning which kinds of trees have leaves with those different shapes. One can reliably group similar ones together and one could even make up a name for the different kinds of trees. The same thing could be true with respect to the property of being forty-eight-speckled. One might respond differentially to experiences in which forty-eight speckles appear than to other sorts of experiences.

Given Sosa's account of concepts, any person who is sensitive to experiences of forty-eight speckles has what we can describe as a "phenomenal forty-eight-speckle concept." Such a person can believe that he's having an experience of forty-eight speckles, though the person may not be able to put it that way. From the fact that one has the concept, it does not follow that one is sensitive to the concepts that we might have thought entered into it. The phenomenal forty-eight speckles concept is not constructed out of more primitive concepts. One might not in general be sensitive to the presence of forty-eight things in experience—one might not respond differentially to experiences of forty-eight stripes. One might be reliable at recognizing forty-eight speckles, but not so reliable at recognizing being speckled generally. It follows that one could even lack

The Justification of Introspective Beliefs

the phenomenal concept of being speckled. The phenomenal concept is not logically complex. Nothing much follows from it.

Presumably, most of us do not have the phenomenal concept of being forty-eight-speckled, since we are not sensitive to the presence of the property of which it is a concept. We do not respond differentially to forty-eight-speckled images than to forty-seven- or forty-nine-speckled images. We can, of course, believe that an image has forty-eight speckles. Thus, there must be two different "forty-eight-speckle concepts." One is the complex concept constructed out of the simpler concepts of "forty-eight" and "being speckled". Presumably, we all have this concept. Its possession does not require sensitivity to forty-eight speckles. This, I believe, is an SGA concept of the sort Sosa has called to our attention. The other "forty-eight-speckle concept" is a phenomenal concept, and this is one that normal people lack. This follows from the fact that most of us are insensitive to the presence of forty-eight-specklehood.

The same distinction, of course, applies to seemingly simpler concepts. Consider the property of experiencing an image containing three speckles. We can often tell at a glance that we have this property. But there are both the complex three-speckle concept and the phenomenal three-speckle concept. Most of us grasp both of these concepts.

B. Which Beliefs are Foundationally Justified?

These results about concept possession provide the basis for solving the problem for classical foundationalism that Sosa has posed. Classical foundationalists can plausibly deny Sosa's claim that they must go beyond phenomenal concepts in specifying what is foundationally justified. In other words, the reply is that principles about foundational justification restricted to indexical and phenomenal concepts are adequate. Sosa's claim that foundational justification must extend to propositions or beliefs involving SGA concepts is mistaken.

Sosa's claim that more must be foundationally justified gets little defense in his paper, and I can only speculate about why he might think that it is true. One might think that classical foundationalists have no way to explain how any beliefs involving non-phenomenal concepts are justified at all unless they allow that some beliefs involving non-phenomenal concepts are foundationally justified. This thought might gain support from the failure to take into account the distinction just noted between the phenomenal and the complex forty-eight-speckle concept. The way the failure to take note of the distinction supports this thought is as follows. In a certain sense, things look exactly the same to the person who recognizes forty-eight speckles and the person who is not capable of

213

recognizing these features of experience. Their experiences are phenomenally alike. Hence, on classical foundationalist lines, the same phenomenal beliefs are foundationally justified for them. But if what is foundationally justified were limited to phenomenal (and indexical) beliefs, then the same things would be foundationally justified for them. It is clear that nothing concerning forty-eight speckles is justified for the person who is not capable of recognizing this feature of experience. But then it would not be the case that the one who recognizes forty-eight speckles is justified in his belief. Since he is, it follows that there must be some non-phenomenal belief that is foundationally justified. And classical foundationalists have no good way to explain this.

The consequence of the discussion above is that this argument goes wrong in its assumption that the same phenomenal beliefs are justified for the person who can recognize forty-eight speckles and the person who can not. The former has a phenomenal concept that the latter lacks. The former has a foundationally justified belief, involving this concept, that the latter lacks.

For most of us, if we believed that we had an experience of forty-eight speckles, this would not be a foundationally justified belief. We would come to this belief by inferences, perhaps from inferences involved in counting or background information about what the image was an image of and how many speckles things like that have. We could not tell, just by looking, that the SGA concept applied. For people with special abilities, however, it might be that this belief is nearly basic, though not quite. It is a simple inference from the associated phenomenal concept.

Consider again the two pairs of examples that posed the problem for classical foundationalists. One pair raised the question of what the relevant difference is, for normal people, between the three-speckle image and the forty-eight-speckle image. Sosa assumed that since we can tell at a glance that we have an image with three speckles, but not one with forty-eight, the one belief must be foundationally justified but the other not. And he was referring to beliefs involving SGA concepts. However, most of us have a phenomenal three-speckle concept, but not a phenomenal forty-eight-speckle concept. There is, then, a relevant foundationally justified proposition when we experience an image with three speckles but not when we experience an image with forty-eight speckles.

Of course, this foundationally justified proposition does not involve the geometric and arithmetic concepts on which Sosa focuses. But I think that beliefs involving those concepts are not foundationally justified. The normal person's belief involving the SGA three-speckle concept is non-foundationally justified, depending on background information that associates that phenomenal concept with that SGA concept.

The Justification of Introspective Beliefs

Similar considerations help to explain the second pair of examples. A person who has a remarkable ability to tell at a glance that he is experiencing an image with forty-eight speckles differs from ordinary people in two ways. First, he, unlike us, has a phenomenal forty-eight-speckle concept. This gives him foundational justification for that proposition, justification that most of us lack. Second, he has background information that links that phenomenal state to the complex forty-eight-speckle concept. As a result, he is justified in believing that his image has forty-eight speckles, where this belief involves the SGA concept. But this last proposition is not foundationally justified. As noted earlier, the distinction between the two forty-eight-speckle concepts also helps explain the case of a person who can differentiate at a glance an image with forty-eight speckles from other images without knowing how many speckles the image has. This person has the phenomenal forty-eight-speckle concept, but has not associated that concept with the related SGA concept.

I conclude, then, that the principles formulated earlier are adequate to deal with these cases. One of those principles was:

DJ2. If a person is experientially-aware of property F, and believes that he is having an experience with property F, and refers to property F in this belief by means of an indexical or phenomenal concept, then this belief is foundationally justified.

Most of us do not have the phenomenal forty-eight-speckle concept but we do have the phenomenal three-speckle concept. So, via (DJ2) we can justifiably believe the relevant three-speckle proposition but not the relevant forty-eight-speckle proposition. And we can infer from the proposition involving the phenomenal three-speckle concept, and background information, that our image contains three speckles. But the person with the extraordinary talent to recognize forty-eight speckles does have the phenomenal forty-eight-speckle concept. Thus, when the other conditions are satisfied, he can have a belief involving that concept foundationally justified. And that belief and his background information justifies his belief involving the SGA concept.

Things are more complicated when we attempt to apply these considerations about concepts to principles about propositional justification. The principle restricted to indexical and phenomenal concepts was this:

PJ4. If a person is experientially-aware of property F, and P is a proposition that refers to property F by means of an indexical or phenomenal concept and says that the person is having an experience with property F, then the person is foundationally justified in believing P.

215

Richard Feldman

Nothing said so far answers the objection to this. It would seem that (PJ4) implies that we are e-aware of both three speckles and forty-eight speckles in the relevant cases, but that even though we lack the phenomenal concept in the second case, we are justified in believing each proposition. One possibility is to add to the antecedent of the principle a condition requiring that the person have the relevant phenomenal concept. Another possibility is to argue that Sosa is too lenient in his assumptions about which properties we are e-aware of. In the next section I will discuss a variation on this second option. According to this view, there is a kind of awareness that Sosa overlooks.

5. Another Kind of Experience?

Sosa distinguishes experiential-awareness of properties and noticing-awareness of them. The latter involves justified true beliefs about their presence. The former is mere passive awareness of properties of one's experience. It may be, however, that there are distinctions to be drawn among kinds of awareness that do not involve beliefs.

There is a difference between a property merely being present in one's experience and one's attending to (or "noticing," though not in Sosa's sense) that property. There are things that are, as it were, on the periphery of one's experience. The telephone in my office has a red light that comes on when there's a message for me. We recently got new, improved, state of the art telephones. Unfortunately, sometimes callers are taken to the message center without allowing the phone to ring. As a result, sometimes I'll be sitting at my desk concentrating hard on my work. And a time will come when I'll notice, in Sosa's sense, that the light on my phone is on. And I'll also realize that I've been aware of its being on for a while. I was aware, in some sense, of the red on the edge of my visual field, though I did not notice it. So, some qualities of which we have experiential awareness enjoy only peripheral awareness. Things of which we are peripherally aware can be unnoticed. We miss other intrinsic qualities of our experiences for reasons of the sort discussed earlier: we are not able to pick up on them. Being forty-eight-speckled is like this for most of us. Most of us are not able to pick up that property.

This leads me to think that Sosa overlooks in his discussion another kind of experience, something that involves more than mere experiential awareness but is less than, or at any rate different from, noticing as he's described it. We can *attend to* features of experience. We can focus on them. In this sense, I had not attended to the light on my phone. Or, more precisely, I had not attended to

The Justification of Introspective Beliefs

the patch of red in my image. Then I did. And the difference was not just a difference in belief. It was not the case that I just came to believe that I was experiencing red. I could in principle have come to believe that because someone told me that something red was there. What happened was that I attended to the redness, and believed it was there as a result. Attention of this sort need not be purposeful or intentional. It typically just happens.

Sosa seems to mention this sort of thing when he speaks of "attending to" some features of experience (p. 283). And, it may be that classical foundationalists would be better off saying that only features of experience that one attends to are epistemically effective. Merely having a property present to consciousness, mere e-awareness as Sosa interprets it, is not sufficient. This suggests replacing (PJ4) and (DJ2) by principles that build in the condition that the person attend to the feature of experience:

DJ4. If a person is experientially-aware of property F, and attends to this property, and believes that he is having an experience with property F, and refers to property F in this belief by means of an indexical or phenomenal concept, then the person is foundationally justified in believing that he is having an experience with quality F.

PJ6. If a person is experientially-aware of property F, and attends to this property, and P is a proposition that refers to property F by means of an indexical or phenomenal concept and says that the person is having an experience with property F, then the person is foundationally justified in believing P.

We cannot attend in the way required by these principles to phenomenal properties whose concepts we do not understand. That is, if one lacks the phenomenal concept of being forty-eight-speckled, then one cannot attend to that feature of experience.[9] Thus, not all features that are minimally present in the sense sufficient for Sosa's e-awareness are epistemically effective. The epistemically effective features of experience are the ones that we attend to.

Adding the idea of attending to experiences to the picture helps with another point, one not previously mentioned. It seems to me to be a mistake for classical foundationalists to commit themselves to the view that there are certain features of experience such that, whenever they are present to anyone, a person

---

[9] Sosa apparently thinks that we can attend to properties without having the associated phenomenal concept. See *Epistemic Justification*, p. 129, and "Privileged Access," section E. It is true that you can focus your attention on the forty-eight-speckle array, or, say, an image of a twenty-three-sided thing. But I don't understand how you could attend to the phenomenal properties of being forty-eight-speckled or twenty-three-sided without having those phenomenal concepts.

who has the relevant concept is justified in believing that they are present. (PJ5), even with an added condition requiring that the person have the relevant phenomenal concept, implies the following:

If at one time S has an experience with quality F and S is foundationally justified in believing he is having an experience with quality F, then whenever S has an experience with quality F, then S is foundationally justified in believing that he is having an experience with quality F.

There is no more reason for insisting on this thesis than for insisting that if there is one time that I see a robin and I'm justified in believing that I'm seeing a robin, then whenever I see a robin, then I'm justified in believing that I'm seeing a robin. This is to say that merely seeing a robin is not a sufficient condition for the corresponding belief to be justified. Similarly, merely having an experience of a certain sort need not be sufficient for the corresponding belief to be justified. The example about the unnoticed patch of red in my visual field illustrates why. Other examples in which features of experience are difficult to identify because of factors that call our attention away from them or make them difficult to spot illustrate the same point. A richer notion of experience, the one I have tried to capture with the concept of attention, makes for a better classical foundationalist theory.

6. Conclusion

I conclude that foundationalists have the resources to deal with the specific problem concerning foundational justification that Sosa has raised. This is not to say that all is well with foundationalism. There remain hard questions about how to justify as much as seems to be justified on the basis of what is foundationally justified. And there are legitimate questions about whether traditional foundationalists are really entitled to accept Sosa's offering of the assumption that since phenomenal concepts come with a guarantee of reliability, the designated beliefs involving them are foundationally justified.[10] Nevertheless, I believe that if there are the various kinds of concepts that Sosa describes, then foundationalists are able to deal with the problems he raises.

---

[10] In other words, there is doubt that (DJ4) exactly captures the correct foundationalist idea. It could be that a person satisfies the conditions in the antecedent of the principle, but believes that he is having an experience with quality F not directly on the basis of his awareness of the relevant experiential property but rather on the basis of some mistaken inference or assumption. An improved version of the principle will have to appeal to the idea of believing the proposition on the basis of the experience.

9
Having Evidence
Richard Feldman

Although theories about epistemic rationality and justification often appeal to the notion of the evidence a person has at a time, little has been written about what the conditions are under which a person 'has' something as evidence. Philosophers seem to have failed to notice that the implications of their epistemological theories are largely dependent upon how this concept is interpreted. In this paper I will attempt to correct this deficiency. In the first part I will show, by means of several examples, that it is not at all obvious what it is to have something as evidence. I will then show that a wide variety of epistemological theories implicitly or explicitly appeal to an (uninterpreted) concept of evidence possessed. I will then consider a series of possible accounts of evidence possessed and defend a restrictive account that limits the evidence a person has at a time to the things the person is thinking of or aware of at that time.

1.

That there is some question about what evidence a person has at a time can be brought out by consideration of some examples. A good example for our purposes is one used by Alvin Goldman in his defense of a causal theory of knowledge.[1] Goldman says that he knows that Abraham Lincoln was born in 1809, but he has forgotten where he learned this and he no longer has any 'explicit evidence' for this proposition. Goldman took this, when he wrote this essay, to show that knowledge did not require justification. His assumption, then, was that justification does require having evidence, but the unrecalled facts about

---

[1] Alvin Goldman, "A Causal Theory of Knowing", in G. Pappas and M. Swain (eds.), *Essays on Knowledge and Justification* (Ithaca, NY: Cornell University Press, 1978), 83.

the source of one's beliefs do not count as evidence possessed. Thus, he regarded this as a case of knowledge without justification. However, the assumption that he no longer has evidence for his belief about Lincoln is at least questionable. It might be that with some prompting Goldman could bring back to mind information about where he first learned this fact. Perhaps such retrievable information counts as part of the evidence he has *now*, even if he is not thinking of it now.

More generally, people often consciously entertain beliefs that were initially formed on the basis of evidence that they do not, and perhaps cannot, recall. It is unclear whether such evidence counts as part of the evidence they have. Possibly, whether it counts depends upon if, or how easily, it can be recalled. Whether the initial evidence still counts as evidence possessed may well affect the epistemic status of the belief. Unless other currently possessed information makes the belief justified, it seems that the belief is justified only if the currently unconsidered evidence still is evidence possessed by the believer. Of course, one might also hold (contrary to Goldman) that if a belief is originally justified and the belief is retained, then it remains justified even if the evidence is forgotten.

Similar issues arise with respect to perceptual beliefs. Suppose, for example, that an expert bird-watcher sees a bird that she immediately identifies as a scarlet tanager. We can imagine that she does not consciously think of the field marks of these birds when she forms the belief that she sees one. She just looks at the bird and classifies it. Do the stored beliefs she has about the distinguishing features of scarlet tanagers count as part of her current evidence? Does it matter how difficult it would be for her to articulate these facts or call them to mind? Obviously, similar questions arise in the case of nearly any perceptual belief in which one attributes to an object some property that is not 'directly perceptible'. We might put the question this way: when, if ever, do stored background beliefs count as part of the evidence one has at a time?

Again, there are plausible accounts of justification that make the epistemic status of perceptual beliefs depend upon the answers to these questions about evidence possessed. Any account of justification that implies that the expert must currently have as evidence the facts about the field marks makes these questions about evidence possessed immediately relevant to epistemic evaluations. Once again, it is possible to make the questions somewhat less pressing by holding that other things she is currently aware of, or her knowledge that she is an expert, or perhaps even her mere expertise (whatever she knows about it), make her belief justified.

Getting clear about what counts as evidence possessed seems essential to epistemic evaluations of cases in which stored information which does not come to mind counts against something that is supported by the evidence one does consider. Suppose my friend Jones tells me that the hike up to Precarious Peak is not terribly strenuous or dangerous, that it is the sort of thing I can do without undue difficulty. Assume that Jones knows my abilities with respect to these sorts of things and that he seems to be an honest person. On the basis of his testimony, I believe that the hike is something I can do. It seems that it is rational for me to believe this proposition. But suppose I've failed to think about the time Jones told me that I could paddle my canoe down Rapid River, something he knew to be far beyond my abilities. He just gets a kick out of sending people off on grueling expeditions. If you were to say to me, "Remember when Jones lied about the canoe trip?" I'd say "Yes! How could I have failed to think of that?" Once I was reminded of this episode, it would no longer be rational for me to believe that I can complete the hike, unless I had some additional information supporting the view that Jones was not lying this time. But are the facts about the past lie part of my evidence *before* you remind me of them? Whether my belief is justified depends upon the answer. If this stored information is part of my evidence, then my belief is not justified, but if it is not part of my evidence, then the belief is justified.

The general question about evidence possessed suggested by this example is this: when one believes some proposition on the basis of newly acquired evidence and one has stored in memory some counter-evidence that one fails to think of, when, if ever, does this counter-evidence count as part of the evidence one has at the time?

A final example is drawn from recent studies by psychologists that seem to show that people are systematically irrational. Some studies suggest that people regularly violate the conjunction rule of probability theory.[2] For example, when given a description of a person and asked to decide which of two categories the person is most likely in, people often select categories based on representative characteristics, overlooking probabilistic considerations that ought to be decisive. In one series of studies, people were given a description of a typical liberal and politically active woman. Most people, including people trained in statistics, judged that it is more likely that the woman is a feminist bank teller than a bank teller. In giving this response people are saying that her having a conjunctive property—being a bank teller and a feminist—is more

---

[2] These studies are reported in Amos Tversky and Daniel Kahneman, "Judgments of and by Representativeness", in D. Kahneman, P. Slovic, and A. Tversky (eds.), *Judgement under Uncertainty: Heuristics and Biases* (Cambridge: Cambridge University Press, 1982), 84–98. For discussion of this and other examples of apparent irrationality, see Richard Nisbett and Lee Ross, *Human Inference: Strategies and Shortcomings of Social Judgment* (Englewood Cliffs, NJ: Prentice-Hall, 1980).

probable than her having one of the conjuncts—being a bank teller. This response violates the conjunction rule, which says that the probability of a conjunction cannot exceed the probability of one of its conjuncts. It is not implausible to think that beliefs formed in violation of such a fundamental rule are irrational.[3]

The claim that beliefs that violate the conjunction rule, or other basic rules of logic or probability, are irrational rests on assumptions about what evidence people have in these cases and what that evidence supports. Perhaps many people, and surely experts, have stored in memory some evidence that supports the conjunction rule and shows that the evidence they're given about the woman does not support the conclusion most people make. However, just as in the cases described above, since this evidence does not come to mind, it is not clear that it is part of the body of evidence people have *at the time* they form their beliefs.

Moreover, it may be that the evidence people generally do have supports the beliefs they form. It is commonly suggested[4] that people use in these cases a 'representativeness heuristic', according to which it is more probable that something has property A than B if it is more like the typical, or representative, A than it is like the representative B. In the case at hand, the woman described is more like the typical feminist bank teller than she is like the typical bank teller. Hence, people (mistakenly) judge that she is more probably a feminist bank teller than a bank teller.

What complicates our assessment of the rationality of these beliefs is that people may well have evidence supporting the heuristic they use. After all, in a wide variety of cases, using it has probably yielded correct results that were subsequently corroborated. Moreover, the heuristic has considerable intuitive plausibility and may have been given testimonial support for many people. On the other hand, many people have learned the rules of probability or could easily be made to see, on the basis of things they already believe, that the rule leads them astray in cases such as this one. Thus, the rationality of their beliefs apparently depends in part upon exactly what evidence they have, and what the status is of stored but unconsidered facts about probability. If such information is not part of their evidence, then their beliefs may well be rational.

All of these examples are designed to show that in a wide variety of cases there is some question about what evidence a person has at a time and that assessments of rationality or justification depend upon their answers.

---

[3] The view that these and other cases reveal widespread irrationality is defended by Stephen Stich in "Could Man be an Irrational Animal? Some Notes on the Epistemology of Rationality", *Synthese*, 64 (1985), 115–35.

[4] See Tversky and Kahneman, "Judgments of and by Representativeness".

Having Evidence

The general question is when, if ever, a person has as evidence information that is, in some sense, stored in memory but not recalled at the time.

2.

In the previous section I argued that there are difficult questions about exactly what counts as the evidence a person has at a given time and that how these questions are properly answered often has significant implications for which beliefs are rational or justified. My arguments for that second conclusion rested on the assumption that a correct theory about rationality and justification makes these epistemic properties of beliefs a function of the relation the beliefs have to the evidence possessed by the believer. Not all theories about epistemic justification and rationality explicitly refer to evidence possessed, but, as I will show in this section, similar questions arise for nearly any theory about rationality and justification.

The puzzles about evidence possessed arise most clearly for theories that explicitly analyze rationality in terms of evidence possessed. According to one such view, evidentialism, believing p is rational for a person provided believing p (as opposed to disbelieving p or withholding judgment about p) fits the evidence the person has.[5] (I'll say that believing a proposition is rational for a person whenever believing that proposition is epistemically better than disbelieving or suspending judgment about it. Believing something can be rational, then, but less than fully justified, in the sense that is an important necessary condition for knowledge.) Obviously, what counts as the evidence a believer has drastically affects the implications of this view. In the example about the hike, if I have as evidence the fact that Jones has lied about this sort of thing in the past, then believing that the hike is feasible is not rational. But if that is not part of my evidence, then the belief is rational.

What counts as the evidence one has significantly affects the implications of theories that analyze justification in terms of *prima facie* reasons and defeaters.[6] Theories of this sort imply that believing something is rational (or justified) for a person provided the person has good reasons to believe that thing and those reasons are not defeated by other evidence the person has. The relevance of our question about evidence possessed to these theories is obvious.

---

[5] This sort of view is defended in Richard Feldman and Earl Conee, "Evidentialism", *Philosophical Studies*, 48 (1985), 15–34 [Ch. 4 in this volume].

[6] A view of this sort is defended in John Pollock, *Knowledge and Justification* (Princeton: Princeton University Press, 1974).

Similar questions also arise with respect to the theories of justification that Roderick Chisholm defends.[7] It is not necessary here to go into the details of Chisholm's system of definitions. What is crucial to notice for present purposes is that Chisholm defines all the central epistemic concepts in terms of the primitive notion of epistemic preferability. This, Chisholm says, is "an expression that may be used to compare different beliefs with respect to reasonableness."[8] Thus, we may say that believing p is more reasonable for S than believing (or disbelieving or withholding) q. Chisholm attempts to clarify this primitive expression in his system by providing a paraphrase for it. He says that "(believing) p is more reasonable than (believing) q for S at t" provided "S is so situated at t that his intellectual requirement, his responsibility as an intellectual being, is better fulfilled by (believing) p than by (believing) q."[9] Without going into any details about intellectual requirements, we can see easily that our questions about evidence possessed carry over into Chisholm's system. How, exactly, is a person who has failed to think of some relevant information concerning a proposition he is now entertaining situated? Does this stored but unconsidered information enter into our evaluation of his situation and of how he can best fulfill his intellectual requirement? Thus, questions about evidence possessed arise in Chisholm's system as questions about what factors affect assessments of epistemic reasonability.

Similar considerations apply to coherence theories.[10] Coherence theories imply that a belief is justified provided it coheres with one's body of beliefs. But what counts as one's body of beliefs? A coherence theorist could restrict one's body of beliefs to what one is currently thinking of, one's *occurrent* beliefs. But a coherence theorist could also include in one's body of beliefs some or all of the things that are stored in one's mind, the things one believes *dispositionally*. Thus, for example, in the hiking case described above, one may construe my body of beliefs narrowly so that the unconsidered belief about my friend's past lie is excluded, or one may construe my body of beliefs more broadly and include that belief. Believing that I can complete the hike seems to cohere with the narrower body, but not with the broader one. Hence, the implications of coherence theories for this example, as well as many others, depend upon how the relevant body of beliefs is determined. Questions about evidence possessed

---

[7] See, for example, Roderick Chisholm, *Theory of Knowledge* (Englewood Cliffs, NJ: Prentice-Hall, 1977). [8] Ibid. 6.
[9] Ibid. 14.
[10] For defenses of the coherence theory, see Laurence BonJour, *The Structure of Empirical Knowledge* (Cambridge, Mass., and London: Harvard University Press, 1985), and Keith Lehrer, *Knowledge* (Oxford: Oxford University Press, 1974).

arise in coherence theories as questions about what is included in the body of beliefs relative to which coherence, and thus justification, is measured.

It is important to realize that saying that the relevant evidence is limited to what one actually believes is of no help here. It is just as difficult to figure out whether the things stored, perhaps buried, in one's memory are among the things one believes as it is to tell whether they are part of one's evidence. Thus, I find it just as hard to decide whether the facts about the source of my belief about the year of Lincoln's birth, or facts about my friend's past lie, are among my beliefs as it is to decide whether they are included in my evidence.

A question about evidence possessed also arises in connection with at least some reliabilist views about justification. For example, Alvin Goldman claims that a belief is justified provided it is produced by a reliable belief-forming process and the believer has available no alternative reliable process such that, had he used it, he would not have formed the belief in question.[11] The point of introducing the second clause is to deal with defeaters—cases in which a person forms a belief as a result of a reliable process, but has reasons to think that the outputs of that process are not true. The example of the hike described above is just such a case. A question Goldman must face is whether it is *available* to me to infer from the past lie that my friend's testimony about the hike is not trustworthy. Which inferences from which stored but unconsidered beliefs are available at any given time? Thus, questions about evidence possessed arise for this reliability theory as questions about availability.

These considerations show that essentially the same questions about what evidence one has affect numerous theories of epistemic justification. This is just to point out a feature of the theories that needs development, not to say that any of these theories is incorrect. In fact, it will generally be difficult to determine what implications a theory has, and thus difficult to evaluate it, until these questions about evidence possessed are answered. Proposed objections may well rest in part on debatable assumptions about what counts as the evidence a person has at a time.

3.

In this section I will make a few terminological and other preliminary points before, in the following sections, formulating and evaluating several accounts of what it is for a person to have something as evidence at a time.

In what follows I will sometimes refer to pieces of evidence as beliefs, but I do not wish to rule out the possibility that experiences or perceptual states can

---

[11] See Alvin Goldman, "What is Justified Belief?", in G. Pappas (ed.), *Justification and Knowledge* (Dordrecht: Reidel, 1979), 20.

count as evidence as well. I will also speak of the implications of various views about evidence possessed for what is justified, or rational, for a person at a time. As I will use these terms, it can be rational for a person to believe a proposition even though the person does not actually believe it. Similarly, a person can be justified in believing some proposition without believing it. I assume that, roughly, it is justified or rational for a person to believe a proposition when the evidence he has supports that proposition. Whether the person does believe the proposition does not affect this evaluation. There are, of course, senses of these or related terms that apply only to existent beliefs. For example, we say such things as 'Jones justifiably believes p' and this does imply 'Jones believes p'. But these senses of epistemic terms are not the senses under discussion here.

It will be useful to introduce some terminology for the discussion that follows. Let us say that the *total possible evidence* a person has at a time includes all and only the information the person has 'stored in his mind' at the time. This is intended to be a very broad notion. It includes *everything* that one has actively believed and could recall with some prompting. It thus includes past beliefs that were adopted for no good reason. It includes things that could be recalled only with great difficulty. In each of the examples discussed earlier in this paper, all of the items whose evidential status was said to be questionable were clearly part of the total possible evidence.

There are some things that are excluded from one's total possible evidence that are worth mentioning here. Things that one has never learned about, even if they are known by others, are excluded. Things that one once knew but could not recall with any amount of prompting are also excluded. And, finally, things that one does not yet believe, but would first come to believe as a result of prompting, are excluded from the total possible evidence one has at a time. I exclude these items from consideration because the topic here is the evidence a person *has* at a time, and I assume that facts which are completely out of one's cognizance, as these things are, are plainly not part of the evidence one has.

The *total evidence* one has at a time is some part of the total possible evidence one has at that time. Something that is part of one's total possible evidence may fail to be part of one's total (actual) evidence for one (or both) of two reasons. It may fail to meet some psychological accessibility condition and it may fail to meet some epistemic acceptability condition. I will say that any part of one's total possible evidence which satisfies this psychological condition is part of the evidence one has *available*. Evidence which satisfies the epistemic condition will be said to be *acceptable*. That portion of one's total

Having Evidence

possible evidence which is both available and acceptable is the total evidence one has.

My concern here is primarily with the conditions under which evidence is available, but it will be useful to discuss briefly the conditions under which evidence is acceptable. It is possible to hold that the acceptability condition is vacuous and that if something is part of one's total possible evidence, then it is acceptable. Perhaps some coherence theorists hold this. They would then hold that anything which is available is part of the evidence one has. Some simple examples suggest that this view is incorrect. If I believe, for no good reason, that P and I infer (correctly) from this that Q, I don't think we want to say that I 'have' P as evidence for Q. Only things that I believe (or could believe) rationally, or perhaps, with justification, count as part the evidence I have. It seems to me that this is a good reason to include an epistemic acceptability constraint on evidence possessed, but I will not pursue this point here.

There is an alternative way to set up the issue here. I have said that the evidence one has at a time is restricted to what is both available and acceptable. One might say instead that everything that is available is part of the evidence one has, but that what this body of evidence makes rational or justified depends upon the epistemic status of that evidence. On this view, acceptability determines not what counts as evidence possessed but rather what is made rational or justified by the evidence possessed. I think that matters can be spelled out in this second way and that any differences between the views discussed below and (versions of) this second view are purely terminological. Since nothing important turns on this matter, I will continue to assume that there is an epistemic condition on evidence possessed.

One final preliminary point concerns the conditions of adequacy for accounts of epistemic availability. Factors of two different sorts seem relevant. First, we do have some fairly clear intuitions about what evidence a person has at a time, and a theory must not violate those intuitions. It is clear, for example, that I don't have as evidence now facts I have never learned and have never thought about. Any theory that implies otherwise is mistaken. Things that I am consciously aware of now and explicitly use as the basis for some further belief are part of my available evidence, so no adequate account should rule them out. Second, an account of available evidence will contribute to an account of justification and knowledge. Thus, acceptable accounts of available evidence must not preclude our having knowledge or justification in cases in which we clearly do have them. As we will see in the following section, some initially plausible accounts of available evidence have some remarkably implausible implications.

Richard Feldman

4.

I turn now to some views about the conditions under which something is available as evidence. I will begin with the most inclusive or liberal view:

(1) S has p available as evidence at t iff p is included in S's total possible evidence at t.

According to (1), everything one actively believes at a time and every belief that is retrievable from one's memory is part of one's available evidence at that time. (It is unclear whether there are any irretrievable propositions that are in any sense stored in one's memory, but I will not pursue that point here.)

Easily devised examples suggest that (1) is far too inclusive. Some such examples concern the evidential status of childhood memories that could only be recalled with extensive and highly directed prompting. Suppose, for example, that the house I lived in as a young child was painted yellow, but on my own I cannot remember the house and have no testimonial evidence concerning its color. If I were asked its color, I would report honestly that I couldn't remember. If we add to the story the fact that some complex set of prompts will trigger in me a clear memory of the house, and reveal its color, then (1) has the highly counter-intuitive result that I now, prior to the prompt, have as evidence this memory of the house. Coupled with standard theories of justification, (1) yields the implausible result that I am now justified (or at least highly rational) in believing that the house was yellow. In this situation it would be most unfair to claim that I am epistemically irresponsible or blameworthy for failing to make proper use of my evidence or for failing to believe that my house was yellow. Indeed, it seems clear that the epistemically proper thing for me to do is to suspend judgment on most propositions concerning its color. (I may have inductive evidence, about people generally and my family in particular, that lends strong support to some propositions about the color, for example, that it was not painted purple.)

There are variations on this example that add to the implausibility of (1). Suppose that I do have testimonial evidence supporting some false proposition about the color of my house. Suppose, for some reason, my generally honest family has consistently said that the house was white. I have no recollection of the house and dutifully believe that it was white. Again, a complex prompt could trigger a memory of the house and its color. If we couple (1) with plausible theories of justification and rationality, we get the result that I am not justified or rational in believing what my family tells me because I have this defeater available to me. But that result is surely wrong. I am clearly believing exactly what I should believe, given the situation in which I find myself.

Having Evidence

One possible response to these objections to (1) is worth brief consideration. It might be claimed that deeply buried memories are part of one's psychologically available evidence, but that they are not part of one's epistemically adequate evidence. Thus, my claims about what's rational or justified in the examples just discussed are correct, but (1) does not conflict with them.

The view that deeply buried memories are psychologically available but not epistemically adequate is implausible. It is difficult to see how a plausible account of the epistemic adequacy condition could go that would rule these memories out. In the example about the color of my house, it may be that the relevant memory belief about the color of my house was completely justified when it was formed and that it would be justified once it was brought back to mind. So what epistemic adequacy condition could it be that it fails? The only plausible answer to this seems to be that it is not supported by other available evidence. However, without rejecting (1), that is an implausible claim. After all, as the example was described, psychologically associated with this memory were other memories that did support it. So it seems that if (1) is true, then all these other supporting beliefs are also available and thus my belief about the color of my house is adequate as well. So, this defense of (1) fails. I conclude, therefore, that (1) is too inclusive and turn now to a consideration of some more restrictive accounts of available evidence.

There are several ways in which a less inclusive account of available evidence might be developed. One approach begins with an account of the evidence one has for a particular proposition, and then defines one's total available evidence as the combination of all the evidence one has for anything. The following remark from BonJour is suggestive of one possibility along these lines.

> ... a person for whom a belief is inferentially justified need not have explicitly rehearsed the justificatory argument in question to others or even to himself. It is enough that the inference be available to him if the belief is called into question by others or by himself.[12]

Thus, we might propose:

(2) S has p available as evidence relative to q iff S would mention p if S were asked what S's evidence concerning q is.

This proposal has close affinities to the view that a belief is justified just in case one is able to produce, and would produce on demand, an adequate defense of the belief.

---

[12] Laurence BonJour, "Can Empirical Knowledge Have a Foundation?", *American Philosophical Quarterly*, 15 (1978), 2.

Richard Feldman

(2) is a behavioristic proposal that has the defects often found in behavioristic analyses of psychological concepts. The most serious of these is that it excludes from evidence possessed things that should be included. When asked to state my evidence concerning some proposition, I might get very nervous and not be able to state some of the things that I do think of. I might think that the truth wouldn't persuade the questioner, and choose not to state my best reasons. I might find it very embarrassing to reveal my evidence concerning some proposition, and so choose not to state it. Thus, there are many things that seem plainly to be part of a person's evidence concerning some proposition, but which the person might fail to mention if asked for evidence concerning that proposition.

The problem with (2) is its behavioristic character. A proposal similar in spirit to (2) but without the behavioristic element can be constructed. It specifies a condition for having evidence in terms of a disposition to go into other mental states, rather than in terms of a disposition to overt behavior. It can be formulated this way:

(3) S has p available as evidence relative to q iff S would think of p if S were to think about what evidence he has that pertains to q.

This avoids the problems mentioned in connection with (2), but it succumbs to another objection. The proposed account has the weakness that it excludes from the evidence one has relative to a particular proposition other beliefs whose relevance one fails to appreciate. Suppose I consciously believe both p and d, but fail to recognize that d constitutes strong evidence against p. I'd therefore not mention d when asked about my evidence concerning p. Thus, this proposal excludes d from the evidence I possess concerning p and may lead to the result that I am justified in believing p when in fact I surely am not. The problem is that it restricts a person's available evidence concerning some proposition to those things whose relevance the person appreciates. However, it seems clear that there could be available evidence whose relevance is unappreciated by a particular believer.

A way around the problem just mentioned is to characterize one's total body of available evidence, rather than the evidence relative to some specific proposition. The idea is that one's total body of available evidence includes all those things one would think of as evidence for anything. Underlying this proposal is the assumption that everything one has available as evidence would be thought to be pertinent to something or other. Thus,

(4) S has p available as evidence iff there is some proposition q such that S would think of p if S were asked to think about S's evidence relevant to q.

Having Evidence

The sorts of cases that constituted problems for (2) and (3) are not problems for (4). It avoids the behavioristic implications of (2) and does not restrict available evidence to what is seen to be relevant in the way (3) does.

One correctable problem with (4) is that it includes as available evidence things that one has not yet thought of, but would think of for the first time if asked about evidence for some proposition q. The request might stimulate new thoughts, not just prompt the recollection of old ones. (4) is too inclusive for this reason. This problem can be corrected, however, by requiring that everything one has available as evidence at any time is part of one's total possible evidence at that time. Thus,

(5) S has p available as evidence iff (i) p is part of S's total possible evidence and (ii) there is some proposition q such that S would think of p if S were asked to think about S's evidence relevant to q.

(5) seems to me to be the best formulation of this general sort of approach. It is, however, quite clearly unsatisfactory. The problem with (5) is not that it is too restrictive, but rather that it is implausibly inclusive. It is likely to include as evidence possessed nearly every retrievable item in one's total possible evidence. The reason for this is that nearly everything in one's total possible evidence might be mentioned in response to a request for evidence concerning some (possibly very complex) proposition. Suppose Jones has long forgotten that her first grade teacher was named 'Mrs. Potts'. However, if she were asked what evidence she has concerning the proposition that her first grade teacher was named 'Mrs. Potts', a whole set of relevant memories would be recalled. The current proposal implies, perversely, that all these memories were available as evidence prior to the prompt. One could imagine more extreme cases of this sort in which the proposition asked about is extremely long and complex. Indeed, it seems clear that some such request would bring to mind nearly every retrievable memory. This makes (5) just about as inclusive as (1).

The problem with (5) suggests that a better way to analyze available evidence is in terms of what is easily accessible or easily retrievable. The idea here is that some of the things that are included by the previous account are not easily retrievable and therefore are not part of the available evidence. But (5) allowed them in since it included everything that could be recalled in response to any request for evidence, including requests that might be highly suggestive and helpful. Such requests make one able to remember things that otherwise are not easily accessed. Thus, we might propose:

(6) S has p available as evidence at t iff S is currently aware of p or S could easily access a memory of p.

One problem with this view is its vagueness. There seems to be no definite boundary between those memories that are easily accessible and those that are not. However, I don't think that this vagueness is as serious a problem as is a different sort of obscurity in the notion of easy accessibility. Whether a person will think of some fact depends largely upon how the person is prompted or stimulated. If I ask my childhood friend if he remembers the time we spray-painted my neighbor's dog, I may get an embarrassed "Yes." If I ask him if he remembers any of our childhood pranks, this one may fail to come to mind. Is the fact that we spray-painted the dog easily accessible? There seems to be no clear answer. If we say that something can be easily accessed if there is *some* prompt that will bring it rapidly to mind, then almost everything stored in memory is likely to be easily accessible and this view scarcely differs from (5).

I know of no plausible way to modify (6) to avoid the result just discussed. Introducing factors such as speed of recall hardly seem to help. How long it will take a person to recall something depends upon how he is prompted. If I ask the person described a few paragraphs back what the name of her first grade teacher is, I may get no answer or may get the correct answer only after a long time. But if I ask if her first grade teacher was named 'Mrs. Potts', I may get an immediate affirmative response. There seems to be no straightforward notion of speed of recall useful in the present context.

In this section I have considered an extremely inclusive account of available evidence and some proposals designed to achieve a more moderate account. I have argued that all of these views are unsatisfactory. I turn next to the other extreme and a view that limits available evidence to what one is thinking of at the time.

5.

A much more restrictive view about available evidence may be formulated as follows:

(7) S has p available as evidence at t iff S is currently thinking of p.

This view obviously limits what one has available as evidence far more severely than does any of the previously considered proposals. I will evaluate it by considering several objections intended to show that it is too restrictive.

The first objection goes as follows: sometimes a person has some evidence supporting a proposition and believes that proposition even though there is convincing counter-evidence to it that he could have thought about. If he fails to think about this counter-evidence because of inattentiveness, lack of concentration, or some other epistemic failing, then it is not rational for the person to believe that proposition. However, any theory that includes (7) will make it rational for him to believe this proposition since the theory will imply that his available evidence includes only the supporting evidence he does think of. This seems to be an incorrect result and the source of the error is the fact that (7) overly restricts the evidence a person has.

Versions of the example described above about the hike to Precarious Peak illustrate the point of this objection. In that example, I believe something on the basis of some plausible evidence, but I fail to think of some important counter-evidence which I could have thought of. In order to make the case more convincing, let us add that I am quite hasty in forming my opinion that I can complete the hike. I am not reflective and do not give the possibility that my friend is lying any consideration. Isn't it plain that my belief is irrational and thus that (7) overly restricts the evidence I have?

I believe that the answer to these questions is "No." In order to understand why, it is necessary to distinguish two senses of epistemic terms such as 'rational'. (Other epistemic terms have similar senses, but for simplicity I will consider only 'rational' here.) One sort of epistemic appraisal concerns whether believing a particular proposition is rational for a person at a time given exactly the situation the person happens to be in at the time. We may say that this is an assessment of the *current-state epistemic rationality* of believing the proposition. (Analogously, in asking what a person morally ought to do, we look at the situation the person is in and evaluate the options open to him. How he's gotten himself into his current situation is not strictly relevant to the evaluation.)

A second possible epistemic evaluation of a belief has to do with the methods that led to it. We may call this *methodological epistemic rationality*. Beliefs are methodologically rational if and only if they are formed as the result of good epistemic methods. Good methods might include a consideration of all the evidence, careful reflection, and the like.

It is plausible to maintain that my belief that I can complete the hike is methodologically irrational. One might contend that I should think about the feasibility of the hike more carefully and reflect on the reliability of my friend. If I did that, I would remember his past lie, and then perhaps I would not believe that I could complete the hike. Because I didn't do these things, I did not follow rational methods in arriving at this belief, and my belief is methodologically irrational. On the other hand, it is quite reasonable to maintain that my belief is current-state rational. In the situation I am in, in which I have not thought about the counter-evidence, it would be quite irrational for me to believe anything else. The evidence I do have quite clearly supports my belief. Given the situation that I am in, holding the belief is exactly what I should (epistemically) do.

This distinction between methodological and current-state rationality provides the basis for an adequate response to the first objection to (7). The objection was that (7) overly restricted the evidence I had, leading to the incorrect result that my belief that I could complete the hike was rational. My response is that (7) only leads to the result that my belief is current-state rational, and that result is unobjectionable.

Consideration of a variation on the example about the hike provides support for my claims that (7) is not overly restrictive and that my belief is current-state rational. Suppose that the information about the falsity of my friend's claim about the hike is not stored in my memory but rather is contained in a book—*A Pocket Guide to the Difficulty of Hikes in the Precarious Peak Area*—that I have in my pocket. Since I trust my friend, I don't bother to look up the difficulty of the proposed hike in the guidebook. My critics might say, "You should have looked it up. Your belief is irrational since you did not." They may well be right about its methodological rationality, but surely the fact that I could and should have looked it up does not show that my belief is current-state irrational. It does not show that my belief was not supported by the evidence I already had. In the relevant sense I did not yet possess the evidence in the guidebook. (I did physically possess a book from which I could obtain that evidence. There may be some derivative sense of 'have the evidence' in which I did have the evidence in this case. But surely it is not the sense in which we are interested.) The difference between this example and the original one is that in one case the relevant counter-evidence is in a book in my pocket and in the other case it is 'in my head'. In each case I could have 'looked it up' but I didn't. Perhaps my failure to do so constitutes methodological irrationality in each case, but it does not show current-state irrationality in either case. It does not show that I had psychologically available, in the relevant sense, the counter-evidence. (It is available only in the sense that I could have obtained it.) In the two versions of the example my belief is equally current-state rational, and there is no need, in order to account for our intuitive assessments of rationality, to say that the evidence I actually have in the two cases differs. Since it is clear that in the revised case I do not already have the counter-evidence provided by the book, there is no good reason to say that I have (in the relevant sense) the evidence I fail to think of in the original case. So (7) is not shown to be too restrictive by this example.

The intuitive distinction between current-state and methodological rationality can be further clarified by considering judgments about what I should do or believe, rather than judgments about what I did or should have believed. Even if it is true that I should look up the difficulty of the hike in my book, it does not follow that it is irrational for me to believe that I can complete the hike. It may be that the most reasonable thing for me to believe until I look it up is that I can complete the hike. After all, that is what my evidence supports. Moreover, my evidence suggests that the book will say that it is not a difficult hike. It would be a mistake to infer from the fact that I should acquire more evidence that it is most reasonable for me to suspend judgment until I do. It would also be a mistake to hold that the mere fact that I know that there is additional evidence about the hike somehow neutralizes the evidence I already have about its difficulty. So, the fact that I should look up this additional information just does not show that my belief is current-state irrational. Questions about what I should do, or what I should have done, with regard to evidence for a particular belief are independent of questions about the relation that belief has to the evidence I have at any given time.

The final step in my defense of (7) from this first objection is to emphasize that (7) is part of a theory about current-state rationality, not a theory of methodological rationality. Theories about the conditions under which beliefs are current-state rational are theories about the conditions under which beliefs are well-supported by the evidence one has. (7), as well as the other proposals considered here, obviously fill out a crucial element of any such theory. On the other hand, (7) would play no central role in views about what methods one should follow in forming beliefs. Traditional theories of epistemic justification are best construed as theories about current-state justification (or rationality). That is, coherence theories and foundations theories of justification are theories about the relation of beliefs to evidence. They have nothing to say about the methods by which beliefs should be formed or how evidence should be acquired. Such theories do not give directives about what one should think about or how one should go about gathering evidence.

It is unclear to me whether methodological epistemic rationality is an epistemologically central notion at all. Whether believing something is methodologically rational seems to depend largely on practical matters. For example, in the case of my hike to Precarious Peak, whether I should have thought about whether my friend lied in the past about such matters depends largely on a variety of practical issues: how bad would it be if I set off on a hike I couldn't complete? are there other matters to which it is more important for me to direct my attention at the time? These are practical questions. No purely epistemic considerations yield answers to them. This seems to be the case generally. Questions about methodological rationality are practical questions that cannot be answered without information about the agent's goals and preferences. The central epistemological questions, as I understand them, do not concern such practical matters but rather are questions about the relation of beliefs to evidence. (7) forms an important part of an answer to such epistemological questions. Considerations about methodological rationality provide no good reason to reject (7).

I turn now to a second objection to (7). The objection is that if, as (7) implies, available evidence were restricted to what one is thinking of, then many things that surely are known, and therefore justified, would not be known or justified. For example, while listening to a philosophy lecture you still know, and are justified in believing, that Washington, D.C. is the capital of the United States. But (presumably) that wasn't supported by what you were thinking of during the lecture. Hence, (7) is too restrictive.

It surely is true that we attribute knowledge of propositions to people when they are not thinking of those propositions or of any evidence relevant to them. While this appears to conflict with (7), I believe that there is a distinction between occurrent and dispositional senses of epistemic terms and that our ordinary talk can be reconciled with (7) by appeal to this distinction.

It is uncontroversial that there is an occurrent sense of 'believe' or of some closely related term. That is, there clearly are cases in which people think of or consider some proposition and mentally assent to it. We can define occurrent knowledge in terms of this notion of occurrent belief. In this sense of 'know', while thinking about philosophy, one typically does not know that Washington, D.C. is the capital of the United States. We can, however, introduce a dispositional sense of 'know' in which such things are known. That sense might be roughly characterized in terms of the occurrent sense: a person knows a thing dispositionally provided the person would know it occurrently if he thought of it. Since the thought that Washington is the capital would, presumably, be accompanied by an awareness of justifying evidence, this fact can be known dispositionally by most of us. Hence, the intuition that we know simple facts even when we are not thinking of them can be accommodated by the minimalist view of evidence possessed: they are known dispositionally but not occurrently.[13] This objection also fails to refute (7).[14]

---

[13] (7) can also be reconciled with the view that there is one ordinary sense of the word 'know' and that simple facts are known in that sense whether they are thought of or not. One can define this ordinary sense as the disjunction of the occurrent and dispositional senses just described. Interpreting 'know' in this way does not require abandoning (7).

[14] An attractive feature of the view just described is that it enables us to deal with some puzzling cases in which believing each of two incompatible propositions seems to be rational for a person. It may be that each proposition is such that the evidence the person would think of in connection with it

Having Evidence

The suggested account of dispositional knowledge is not exactly right, but I will not propose a more precise account here. The main trouble with it is that there are some things that, intuitively, are not known at all, but would be known if they were considered. That is, there may be some things that I do not know now, but if were to think of them I would then come to believe them, and come to have evidence for them, for the first time. Such propositions satisfy the condition specified, but they are not even dispositionally known. The problem here, similar to those discussed in connection with (2)–(5), is that dispositional knowledge cannot be exactly characterized by means of the counterfactual proposed. I know of no entirely adequate replacement.

Another problem with this account of dispositional knowledge is that it apparently implies that things one could only bring to mind with helpful prompts (such as the color of my childhood house or my first grade teacher's name) are things that are known, because *if* they were thought of (an unlikely occurrence) they would be occurrently known. It seems, however, that in criticizing other accounts I said that such things were not known at all.

I don't think that these are decisive objections. The difficult and obscure dispositional elements enter this theory at a less central and less crucial stage, whereas in (2)–(5) the troublesome dispositional and counterfactual concepts play a crucial role in the definitions of the primary epistemic notions. On my view, in the most fundamental sense, one does not know things such as that Washington is the capital when one is not thinking of them. As a concession to those with the contrary intuition, I admit that there is a less clear dispositional conception of knowledge in which one does know such things. It may be that my view also implies that one also knows, in this same sense, things that one is only likely to recall with suggestive and helpful prompts. I don't believe that that is an intolerable consequence. Indeed, it captures the point expressed when one says, after being reminded of one of these facts, "I knew that."

The difficulty involved in spelling out the dispositional epistemic notions would be troublesome for my view if some central problem in epistemology or philosophy of mind turned on specifying those conceptions precisely. I don't see that any problem does turn on that. Hence, I don't see that this unclarity in my account is a serious defect.

---

is evidence that does support the proposition. The two bodies of evidence may be unconnected in the believer's mind, so that each proposition is considered only in the light of supporting evidence. The proposed view allows us to say that believing each proposition is (dispositionally) rational. Presumably, however, believing their conjunction would not be rational, since, in considering the conjunction, the conflicting evidence would all be brought to mind at once.

One claim made in the response to the second objection to (7) may suggest a third objection. In responding to the objection I said that, typically, if a person who we are inclined to say knows that Washington, D.C. is the capital of the United States were to think about that proposition, he would also think of evidence that supports it. But that claim may not seem clearly true. He may just think of that proposition, but not of other supporting propositions, such as testimony of teachers, friends, or newspaper reporters. We are still inclined to say that he has occurrent knowledge when he does think about this proposition, even though he does not think of supporting evidence. Thus, it seems that (7) is still too restrictive.

This example is similar to the example about Lincoln's birthday mentioned in section 1. I think that the proper reply makes use of the fact, mentioned earlier, that evidence can include things other than beliefs. The fact that one feels a certain way, or that things look a certain way, can also count as evidence. A significant fact about a typical adult who thinks about the propositions in these examples is that the thought is accompanied by a strong feeling of certainty or conviction. It is plausible to think that these feelings carry evidential weight. Indeed, if I have forgotten my initial evidence but still am rational in thinking that Lincoln was born in 1809, or that Washington is the capital, it seems reasonable to suppose that the source of my current rationality is my current conviction or feeling of certainty that accompanies those beliefs. I suggest, therefore, that 'thinking of' in (7) be interpreted in a sufficiently broad way so that it is true that I am thinking of these sorts of facts when I consider propositions. This is not meant to suggest that I am consciously mulling over or saying to myself that I feel certain that Lincoln was born in 1809. It's just that the feeling of certainty is something of which I am conscious. Thus, with 'thinking of' interpreted in this way, I believe that this objection to (7) can be rejected.[15]

I turn now to a final objection to (7). It is based on the claim that (7) underplays the role of background knowledge in determining current-state rationality. Consider again the case of the expert bird-watcher. Upon seeing a bird, the belief that it is a scarlet tanager just comes to mind. She may be conscious of nothing other than the look of the bird and her thought about the kind of bird it is. Of course, she could recite upon request the field marks of that kind of bird, but she need not consciously think of them at the time. What the expert is conscious of may be quite similar to what a novice bird-watcher is conscious of upon seeing the same bird. The novice, however, may not know the field marks

---

[15] My claim here is that the feeling of certainty accompanying a belief may count as available evidence supporting the belief. This does not imply that all such feelings are epistemically adequate or that every belief accompanied by such a feeling is rational.

and may believe the bird is a scarlet tanager because that's the only bird of approximately that color that he knows of. (He may admit, if asked, that it is likely that other birds have similar markings and that he couldn't distinguish them.) It's implausible to hold that their beliefs are of the same epistemic status. It seems reasonable to say that the expert's operative background beliefs make her belief rational, whereas the novice's belief is not rational. However, the extreme view now in question apparently evaluates their beliefs similarly, since they are conscious of the same evidence—the look of the bird—at the time.

There is, I think, very little plausibility to the reply that believing that the bird is a scarlet tanager is not justified for the expert unless she consciously considers the field marks that enabled her to identify it. The argument for this is simple. Suppose that while becoming an expert bird-watcher the subject had consciously gone through the process of identifying the field marks of the bird in view and recalling the list of distinguishing features in the field guide. At that time, the resulting beliefs about the kinds of birds she saw were justified. She no longer needs to go through that process consciously. She can just look at the birds and classify them. It is plainly mistaken to say that her beliefs were rational and justified previously, but no longer are now that she has automated the identification process.

There are, however, two plausible replies to the objection. First, the expert may have feelings of certainty about her identification that help justify her belief in much the way similar feelings help justify memory beliefs. If she lacks the feeling of certainty and her belief seems to her to be just a guess or a hunch, then it is far from clear that the belief is current-state justified.

A second possible response requires interpreting (7) to allow as available evidence more than we have so far acknowledged. The idea is that 'operative' background beliefs, beliefs that are playing an active role in sustaining one's current state, are also being thought of (non-consciously) and thus are available. Some support for this view can be derived from the following considerations. In the case of the bird-watcher, at some earlier time she would not have formed the belief that she was seeing a scarlet tanager when she had a visual presentation of the sort in question. She then learned that birds that looked that way were scarlet tanagers. When first learning to identify birds, she had to repeat consciously the identifying characteristics to herself. That conscious process is no longer necessary for her. It is plausible to think, however, that she is making use of these beliefs when she 'automatically' identifies the bird. The process that previously occurred consciously still occurs, but not consciously. If (7) is interpreted to imply that this additional evidence is available, then (7) does not conflict with our intuitive judgment that the expert's belief is justified.

Richard Feldman

There are, then, two ways in which this final objection to (7) can be met. Admittedly, the second response introduces additional complexity to the theory. Nevertheless, the availability of these two responses shows that a restrictive account of available evidence can be defended from this final objection. My conclusion is that (7), interpreted to include among one's available evidence everything one is thinking of, consciously and perhaps non-consciously, as well as non-belief states of which one is aware, is an adequate view about the evidence available to a person at a time. As far as I can tell, this view is compatible with all the theories of current-state epistemic justification and rationality mentioned in section 2. It also seems to conform to the intuitions that underlie our judgments about rationality and justification in the examples discussed.

The restrictive view about evidence possessed may also have the implication that we are not quite as irrational as Stich[16] and other interpreters of the psychological studies mentioned earlier suggest. One of the facts about those studies, such as the ones about the conjunction rule, is that people fail to consider stored evidence that may be relevant to the beliefs they form. But if questions about rationality are, in their primary sense, questions about how well people's beliefs are supported by the evidence they do have, then it is far from clear that their beliefs are regularly irrational. It may well be that the incomplete and unsystematic evidence that people do have in mind when they form those beliefs supports the beliefs they do form. So, their beliefs may be current-state rational.

Possibly, many of the beliefs discussed in these studies are methodologically irrational because people 'should' think about additional evidence in these cases. Whether this charge of irrationality is appropriate is, as suggested earlier, difficult to assess. Whether people should think more about these matters, and search their memories for evidence against the heuristic they naturally use, depends largely upon their goals and purposes at the time.

This is not to say, however, that people never have beliefs that are current-state irrational, that what they believe is always supported by the evidence they have. In other words, I am not concurring with the view defended by Daniel Dennett that "[i]t is at least *not obvious* that there are any cases of systematically irrational behavior or thinking" or that alleged cases of irrationality "defy description in ordinary terms of belief and desire."[17] It is compatible with my view, and with common-sense, that people sometimes believe things because it

---

[16] Stich, "Could Man be an Irrational Animal?"

[17] Daniel Dennett, "Making Sense of Ourselves", in J. I. Biro and R. W. Shahan (eds.), *Mind, Brain, and Function* (Norman, Okla.: University of Oklahoma Press, 1982), 66–7.

is comforting or reassuring to do so. That is, they sometimes engage in wishful thinking. Typically, though not always, when they do this their beliefs are not well-supported by their evidence and are current-state irrational. So, the view I have defended here is not so charitable as to make all beliefs rational. That, too, I think, is a virtue of the view.[18]

Afterword

A point mentioned near the end of section 2 of "Having Evidence" warrants emphasis. The point is that questions similar to those raised there are likely to arise for any plausible version of any epistemological theory. I will provide two brief illustrations of this here.

Alvin Plantinga defends the view that a belief is warranted provided it results from the proper function of the believer's cognitive system.[19] Presumably, when a cognitive system functions properly, it evaluates newly obtained information in the light of some range of its stored information. But the question of what stored information matters is a close analogue of the problem of evidence possessed. To take one other example, for a causal theory to be plausible, it must include some sort of "no defeater" condition. Thus, it will say that a belief is justified only if it is caused in the right sort of way and is not defeated by other information the believer has. (This is similar to the requirement, mentioned in the paper, that Goldman adds to his reliabilist theory.) Determining what counts as the potentially defeating evidence a believer has is similar to determining what evidence a person has. Thus, these two theories face a problem similar to the problem discussed in this paper.

While the fact that other theories face a similar problem neither vindicates evidentialism nor relieves evidentialists of the burden of providing a solution, it does show that the existence of this problem does not undermine evidentialism. Opponents of evidentialism who find the solutions proposed here unsatisfactory might consider how their preferred theory would deal with comparable issues.

---

[18] I am grateful to Earl Conee, John Heil, Peter Markie, and Paul Weirich for helpful comments on earlier drafts of this paper.

[19] This statement of Plantinga's theory ignores many of the details Plantinga provides. Those details do not affect the point made here. For a full statement of Plantinga's theory, see his *Warrant and Proper Function* (Oxford: Oxford University Press, 1993).

10
The Truth Connection
Earl Conee

1. When you know, there is something that provides you with knowledge. It is something that answers the question—How do you know? If your knowledge is perceptually based, it is plain that the answer to this question is something in support of the known belief to which perception contributes. In cases of learning from books, the answer plainly involves something that reading contributes in support of the known belief. In cases of mathematical knowledge, the answer plainly involves something contributed in support of the known belief by certain sorts of abstract thinking. In general, possessing factual knowledge implies having something available that shows the known proposition to be true. When you possess factual knowledge, the answer to the question—How do you know?—constitutes what is called your *epistemic* justification.[1] Epistemic justification is the sort of justification that is a necessary condition for factual knowledge.

This epistemic sort of justification is closely related to the truth of what is justified. The existence of some special and intimate connection between epistemic justification and truth seems to be beyond reasonable doubt. The goal of the present work is to give an informative account of this relation (hereafter to be called "the truth connection"[2]). Getting a clear view of the sort of justification

---

[1] John Pollock identifies epistemic justification with the answer to the question—How do you know?— in *Contemporary Theories of Knowledge* (Totowa, New Jersey: Rowman and Littlefield, 1986), p. 7.

[2] The term is Stewart Cohen's, from his paper, "Justification and Truth" (*Philosophical Studies*, 46 (1984), pp. 279–95). In a recent paper ("Truth in Epistemology," *Philosophy and Phenomenological Research*, 51 (1991), pp. 99–108) Scott Sturgeon discusses what he calls "the truth connection". What Sturgeon discusses under that description is the following biconditional: S is justified in believing that p iff S is justified in believing that p is true, where the right side of the biconditional is to be understood to express a proposition which genuinely attributes truth to the proposition that p. Sturgeon asserts that this biconditional "*seems* plainly false" (p. 102), and in the end he finds no good reason to

The Truth Connection

that is required for knowledge will facilitate this effort. In fact the nature of the truth connection seems plain, once we see clearly what it connects.

2. Three further considerations beyond the immediate intuitive plausibility of the existence of the truth connection appear to confirm it and to give information about its nature. Stewart Cohen presents two of these considerations in the course of arguing for the problematic nature of the truth connection.[3] One of Cohen's points is based on the quite plausible thesis that a true belief constitutes knowledge only if the belief is connected in some appropriate way to the truth of what is believed. Cohen suggests that the role played in knowledge by the epistemic justification of the known belief is to constitute this required link between the belief and truth.[4] Ernest Sosa asserts much the same thing, writing:

[C]ognitive justification is the sort of justification which distinguishes true belief that is knowledge from true belief that is little more than a lucky guess. This being so, such justification could not possibly turn out to be a property that a belief might possess in complete independence of the truth of its object.[5]

Cohen and Sosa thus suggest that epistemic justification helps to constitute knowledge by bringing about a necessary link between belief and truth. This in turn suggests that the nature of the truth connection is to constitute this link between belief and truth.

Cohen's other point in support of the existence of the truth connection concerns how epistemic justification differs from other sorts of justification that believing can have, such as prudential justification and moral justification. It seems that a distinguishing feature of the epistemic sort of justification is that it always has some direct bearing on the truth of the justified belief.[6] In contrast, considerations that have nothing to do with the truth of a proposition can justify belief in the proposition on nonepistemic grounds. For instance, the prospect of

---

believe it. In effect, additional reasons for doubting it are presented below when cases are described in which believing a certain proposition is rational on epistemic grounds. It can be readily seen that believing another proposition attributing truth to the first need not be likewise rational, and thus not epistemically justified. The epistemically valuable results of the two believings might differ decisively. As will become clear, the sort of truth connection that is identified and defended in the present work supports nothing closer to Sturgeon's biconditional than this: p is epistemically justified to S iff it is evident to S that p is true, where the left side of this biconditional expresses what is argued below to be the actual justification condition on knowledge. According to the present account, it is not any sort of *believing* that has to be justified. Since this is so, the account is not subject to the problems that affect the biconditional which Sturgeon identifies as the truth connection. These problems arise because different believings have different requirements and effects.

[3] Stewart Cohen, "Justification and Truth," op. cit.   [4] Ibid., p. 279.
[5] Ernest Sosa, "The Coherence of Virtue and the Virtue of Coherence: Justification in Epistemology", *Synthese*, 64 (1985), p. 13.   [6] Cohen, op. cit., pp. 279–80.

benefitting from believing a proposition can be enough to make it prudent to believe. Epistemic justification, on the other hand, seems always to concern the truth of the justified belief.

A third reason for thinking that epistemic justification is closely related to truth can be found in work by Roderick Chisholm, Roderick Firth and Paul Moser.[7] The work differs significantly in detail, but it appears to share two underlying ideas. The first is the familiar claim that rational inquiry is a search for the truth.[8] The second shared idea is that a belief is epistemically justified exactly when the belief meets the epistemic standard that evaluates the pursuit of truth. These thoughts imply the existence of a particular sort of close connection between epistemic justification and truth. The thoughts imply that believing a proposition is epistemically justified exactly when the believing satisfies the epistemic standard that governs pursuit of the goal of rational inquiry, i.e., the truth of the matter.

3. The purpose of the present work is to identify the true nature of the truth connection. To this end, there is some preliminary untangling and refocusing to be done.

It will be useful to start with a simple hypothesis concerning the nature of the truth connection. It will be useful to see why this simple hypothesis is incorrect. The hypothesis asserts that the truth connection consists in an entailment relation. The specific claim is that in order for a belief to satisfy the justification condition for knowledge, the justification for the belief must entail it to be true.

This entailment account of the truth connection seems promising. It seems to bear out the three considerations supporting the existence of the truth connection. First, the entailment account has it that any belief that constitutes knowledge is straightforwardly linked to truth. Any known belief is justified. On the entailment account, the belief's justification implies that it is true. This seems to be the sort of link between belief and truth that is intuitively required for knowledge. Second, it is clear that the other sorts of justification that a person can have for believing something, e.g. prudential and moral justification, do not generally entail that the belief is true. Thus, the entailment account confirms the idea that the truth connection is a distinguishing feature of the epistemic sort of justification. And third, if having knowledge-level epistemic justification for a belief entails that the belief is true, then it is not surprising that

---

[7] See Roderick Chisholm, *Theory of Knowledge*, second edition (Prentice-Hall, 1977), pp. 12–15, Roderick Firth, "Epistemic Merit, Intrinsic and Instrumental," *Proceedings and Addresses of the APA*, 55 (1981), pp. 15–17, Paul Moser, *Empirical Justification* (D. Reidel, 1985), Chapter 1.

[8] No platitude should go unchallenged in philosophy. This one is disputed in section 5 below.

The Truth Connection

adopting epistemically justified beliefs is the epistemically sanctioned way to pursue the truth. If the entailment account is correct, then having epistemic justification for a belief guarantees that this pursuit is successful.

Cohen realizes that the entailment account has explanatory assets such as these. Nonetheless he does not regard this account as the right explanation of the truth connection. Cohen contends that the entailment account implies that no one knows anything about the external world.[9]

Strictly speaking, this contention is incorrect. More that the entailment hypothesis is needed in order to derive the conclusion that we have no knowledge of the external world. But the more that is needed is quite plausible. To see this, consider an example. Suppose that you have the belief that someone is speaking. You infer this from your justified belief that Mr. Jones is speaking. Thus, your external world belief that someone is speaking is a belief for which you have an entailing justification, your justified belief that Jones is speaking. However, it is quite plausible that your belief that Jones is speaking must itself be justified in order to justify any other belief. In general, it is quite plausible that a belief can contribute epistemic justification only if the belief is justified. When we consider candidate justifications for entailing justifiers like the belief that Jones is speaking, it becomes plain that at some point there is always a proposition that is justified without being entailed by its justification. In the present instance, the nonentailing justifier may well be your justification for the belief that Jones is speaking. This belief may be justified by the experience of its seeming to you that you hear what you seem to recall to be the sound of Jones's voice. This experience does not necessitate that Jones, or anyone else, is speaking. But it may be all that you have, and all that you need, in favor of the belief that Jones is speaking. Exactly how this justification works is another matter. Theory is needed, and theories abound. But in any plausible view, at some point in the justification of each external world belief that is justified, there is justification without entailment. When this further assumption is added to the assumption that the entailment account is correct, we have a valid argument for the conclusion that no external world belief is well enough justified to be known. They all need nonentailing justification at some point, and the entailment account denies that this need is ever met. The entailment claim is this argument's least plausible assumption. So if the skeptical conclusion is to be avoided, then the entailment account of the truth connection is the best candidate for rejection.

Skepticism aside, the entailment account cannot wholly explain the close connection that holds quite generally between epistemic justification and truth.

---

[9] Cohen, op. cit., p. 280.

Epistemic justification varies in strength. Often we possess just some slight reason for thinking that one of our beliefs is true—a mere clue. Such a reason plainly does not entail the truth of the belief. Yet it is clear that even the flimsiest of epistemic justifications for a belief pertains to the truth of the belief in the same special way as does justification of greater strength. Even a mere clue is a clue about the truth of the matter. Thus, entailment could not be the nature of this general truth connection, whether or not epistemic justification that is strong enough to meet the justification condition on knowledge entails what it justifies.

4. We should reconsider some of the support cited above for the existence of the truth connection. We should critically examine the view that it is epistemic justification that connects belief to truth in the way that the two must be related in any case of knowledge. Gettier cases show that epistemic justification does not really do this. In Gettier cases, a true belief is epistemically justified without being known. This lack of knowledge is attributable to the fact that the person is somehow lucky that the belief turns out to be true. This is widely acknowledged to be an accurate diagnosis as far as it goes, though it is far from clear what is the exact nature of the luck that precludes knowledge. In any event, the *justified* true beliefs in Gettier cases are each, in Sosa's apt phrase, "little more than a lucky guess". Thus, these beliefs are not linked to the truth of the matter in the way that is required for the beliefs to constitute knowledge. This is so in spite of the fact that the beliefs are epistemically justified. So it cannot be that the link between belief and truth that is required for knowledge is provided by the justification condition on knowledge. This justification is present in Gettier cases, where it is precisely the absence of the required link that precludes knowledge.[10]

---

[10] It is noteworthy that in some cases of justified true belief the justification entails the truth of the belief and yet still there is not knowledge. This can be illustrated by a slight variation on Gettier's second example. In his second example the belief that is justified without being known is a belief in this disjunction: Either Jones owns a Ford or Brown is in Barcelona. The believer has plenty of evidence that Jones owns a Ford, but only the second disjunct is the true one and the believer has no evidence that it is true. Suppose instead that the second disjunct is some necessary truth which has the same status. That is, suppose that the necessarily true disjunct is the only true one, and it is not justified. But by luck it happens to be disjoined to the justified false belief that Jones owns a Ford. Under these circumstances, the believer's justification for the proposition that Jones owns a Ford entails the whole disjunction, whatever that justification is. The reason for this is that the presence of the necessarily true second disjunct renders the whole disjunction true under all possible conditions, including all conditions under which the justification for the Ford belief is true. Nonetheless, the disjunction is not known, and this lack of knowledge has the same intuitive explanation. The fact that makes the belief true, a necessary fact as it happens, is not properly linked to belief in the disjunction. The believer is lucky to be right about the disjunction. Thus, even possessing an entailing justification does not imply the existence of the link between belief and truth that is required for knowledge.

The Truth Connection

The same point can be made without using Gettier cases. The thought in support of the truth connection that we have been considering has been casually expressed here as the thought that a link between belief and truth is required for knowledge. But the actual intuition is more accurately stated as follows. Believing a true proposition constitutes knowledge of the proposition only if the psychological state of believing the proposition is properly linked to something that makes the proposition true. The intuitively required link is between the state of believing and a truth-maker for the proposition believed. To see that this is so, it is helpful to compare what is most plausible about causal theories of knowledge with what is most problematic about mathematical knowledge. Causal theories are entirely credible in what they require of perceptual beliefs. It is entirely credible that a perceptually acquired belief is known only if the state of believing it is causally dependent on a fact or event that makes the belief true. This is plausible because it gives a causal account of the required link between belief and truth for cases where the link is present and this causation is clearly operative. In contrast, it is difficult to see how mathematical knowledge is possible, for lack of any credible candidate to provide this same needed link. It is difficult to see how any abstract mathematical fact which might make true a mathematical proposition could be connected in any way, causally or otherwise, to any human being's psychological state of belief in the proposition. Yet such a connection seems to be required for this knowledge to exist. Thus, what we are looking for in both kinds of cases is an appropriate connection between believing and a truth-making fact. The truth connection holds between justification and truth. It is not the connection of believing to a fact that is needed for knowledge, and it does not exclude the luck that haunts the Gettier cases.

This conclusion remains unaffected, even if knowledge-level justification does entail truth. The fully general truth connection still cannot consist in this entailment. Any strength of epistemic justification specially pertains to the truth of what is justified, including cases in which the supported proposition is false and thus lacks any truth-maker. The special relevance to truth of any epistemic justification cannot consist in the justification serving as a link to a truth-maker, since what gets justified does not always have a truth-maker.[11]

5. Two considerations beyond direct intuition still support the existence of the truth connection. There is the point that it seems to be characteristic of epistemic justification in particular, in contrast to other sorts of justification for believing, that it is always pertinent to the truth of what is justified. This point

---

[11] See also note 9 above.

stands scrutiny. When we identify its basis we will have identified the truth connection. But it will be worthwhile first to reconsider the other remaining support for the existence of the truth connection. Recall that it is based on the two thoughts that rational inquiry is a search for truth and that belief is epistemically justified exactly when believing meets the epistemic standard that governs believing in a search for truth. It will be seen that both of these thoughts are based on a mistake. Correcting the mistake reveals that the truth connection is not a relation between truth and epistemic justification for *believing* at all.

Rational inquiry is not a pursuit of mere truth. This is shown by the fact that successful rational inquiry does not consist in believing anything which happens to be true. A lucky guess does not successfully complete a rational inquiry, any more than does a wishful thought which turns out to be accurate. Rather, rational inquiry is a pursuit of *knowledge*. Knowing the truth is always a successful conclusion to rational inquiry. This seems manifest on reflection. The only challenge is to explain why it is so frequently thought that rational inquiry is a pursuit of the truth. Fortunately, this seems to be readily accounted for. In rational inquiry we do seek to believe the truth, though not as the final goal. Whatever is known, is true, and believed. So in rational inquiry we do seek to believe the truth. But not for its own sake. It is sought as a constituent of our goal—the goal of knowing the truth.

Thus, if we are to continue to maintain that beliefs are epistemically justified exactly when they meet the epistemic standard for believing in the course of rational inquiry, the epistemic standard to be met is the standard for a pursuit of knowledge. Believing a proposition in pursuit of knowledge is taking a certain attitude for the sake of a certain goal. If the attitude passes the standard of practical reason for this pursuit, then it has a sort of justification that practical endeavors can have: it is a rationally justified endeavor. Epistemic grounds are grounds pertaining to knowledge. Hence, there is rational justification on epistemic grounds for believing a proposition when believing the proposition is a practically rational way to pursue knowledge. This is not to imply that believing is ever a voluntary endeavor. Rather, it is to assert that believing sometimes serves as a means to an end. Because it does, the rationality of this means can be assessed, whatever the extent of our voluntary control over the means. The rationality of a given means is determined by how well the means appears to work toward gaining the end when it is viewed from the perspective of the person who has the end. A person's perspective is constituted by the evidence that the person possesses.

The content of a claim that someone's belief in a proposition is epistemically justified is that believing the proposition is practically rational for the person on

The Truth Connection

epistemic grounds, i.e. grounds pertaining to a pursuit of knowledge. Theories of practical rationality differ. Any plausible view accommodates the fact that ordinarily the rational way to believe in pursuit of knowledge is to believe in accordance with one's evidence as to the truth of the matter. If one's epistemic goal is to know whether or not a given proposition is true, ordinarily it is rational to believe the proposition just when one's evidence supports the proposition sufficiently strongly to provide the justification needed for knowledge of the proposition. If one's epistemic goal is to maximize one's total stock of knowledge, then again it is ordinarily rational to pursue this goal by believing exactly those propositions that are sufficiently supported by one's evidence. These considerations suggest a certain hypothesis concerning the nature of the truth connection: Believing a proposition is epistemically justified exactly when the person's evidence sufficiently supports the truth of the proposition. In other words, epistemic justification is the sort of justification that justifies believing for the sake of knowing by providing sufficient evidence of truth.

There are unusual circumstances that refute this hypothesis, however. In any plausible view of practical rationality, believing a proposition can be a rational way to pursue knowledge without that belief itself constituting knowledge. Believing can be a practically rational way to pursue knowledge of whether or not the proposition believed is true because of the apparent instrumental value of the believing, at a time when one's evidence does not so much as suggest that the proposition is true. To illustrate this sort of possibility, suppose that you know that Mr. Jones possesses the only conclusive evidence concerning whether or not Smith committed a certain murder, though you do not know what the evidence is or which way it points. You also know that Jones is unwilling to reveal his decisive evidence, except to those who pass his highly reliable lie detector test for having the belief that Smith is innocent. Suppose that these facts about Jones are evident to you as you seek to find out whether or not Smith committed the murder. You possess no evidence that either incriminates or exonerates Smith. In this situation, what you know about Jones gives you epistemic justification for believing that Smith is innocent. Given Jones's evidence, his known dispositions concerning to whom he will reveal it, and your complete lack of other leads, it is rational for you to believe that Smith is innocent in pursuit of knowledge of whether or not Smith is innocent. It is clear to you that in this situation having this belief is the only way for you to get the evidence you need in order to know. Believing that Smith is innocent is thus epistemically justified for you at the time, even though you do not then have evidence that Smith is innocent. This is not to imply that you have the sort of epistemic justification for this belief which is required to know it for a fact.

249

Earl Conee

That sort of justification is something else, something to be discussed shortly. The point of the example is that believing a proposition can be justified for the sake of the characteristically epistemic purpose of knowing whether or not it is true, while the person lacks all evidence that the belief is true.

This shows that the epistemic sort of justification that believing can have does not consist entirely in evidence that the belief is true. Epistemic justification for believing therefore does not have the hypothesized connection to truth. It is not a kind of justification which is provided only by evidence for the truth of the belief. Rather, in general an epistemic reason for believing is an indication that the believing will help in some way in pursuit of knowledge. We have seen that this help may be nothing more than a causal contribution toward gaining knowledge. Because of this, someone may be epistemically justified in believing a proposition while having no evidence that it is true.

A person need not be epistemically justified in believing a proposition for which the person has conclusive evidence. Again the reason is that the believing itself may have foreseen consequences that decisively affect the rationality of believing for the sake of knowing. For instance, one epistemic goal is that of maximizing one's total stock of knowledge. In some technologically advanced visions of the future, complete brain state detection devices exist. Whatever doxastic states a person is in, these devices can reveal their content to someone else. Such a device might be set by its possessor to link its detection of someone's having a particular belief to, say, the detonation of an explosion. Suppose that these detection devices are common in the world of our Mr. Jones, whose epistemic goal is to maximize his knowledge. Suppose further that Jones foresees that his believing of a certain proposition, say, the proposition that some basset hounds eat fruit, has been nefariously contrived to cause a deadly explosion in his vicinity. He sees that a brain state detector has been rigged so that this belief will get him blown up. Hence, his believing this proposition is not epistemically justified, given the mild additional assumption that he also sees at least one alternative future for himself that includes his accumulating more knowledge. Yet we may suppose that Jones has just come to possess conclusive evidence from observation of his own basset hounds for the proposition that some basset hounds eat fruit. Thus, conclusive evidence is not enough to ensure epistemic justification for believing.

Varying the content of the potentially fatal belief enables us to see that the epistemic goal of knowing whether or not a given proposition is true may not be rationally pursued by believing the proposition even in response to conclusive evidence for it. Suppose that Jones knows that the brain state detection device has been set to blow him up in one minute, to be triggered by his believing that he will remain alive for two minutes. If so, then believing that he will remain alive for two minutes is not a rational way for him to pursue the goal of knowing whether or not he will stay alive for two minutes. He sees that his believing it would make it false. Thus, it is not rational for him to believe it, even assuming that all other indications, apart from the explosive potential of the belief, make a thoroughly convincing case for the truth of the proposition that he will remain alive for two minutes, including indications that he will refrain from forming the fatal belief. His goal of knowing whether or not he will remain alive for two minutes cannot be successfully pursued in this situation. In order to know that he will, he would have to believe that he will. This believing would initiate a series of events making the proposition false. Jones realizes all of that. So, in spite of the conclusive evidence that he has for the proposition, his believing it would not be a rational way for him to pursue the goal of knowing whether or not it is true.[12]

Justification for believing is not simply evidence of truth. In fact, we have seen that believing may have this sort of justification by being evidently instrumental in acquiring knowledge which may turn out to be knowledge that the proposition believed is false. Thus, it is doubtful that this sort of justification has any close connection to truth.

6. When we reflect on the justification that is required for knowledge, it still seems to be thoroughly truth-oriented, in spite of the preceding considerations. The answer to the question—How do you know?—is always directly pertinent to the truth of what is known. This view can be consistently borne out. We should distinguish between the justification that has been our recent focus—the epistemic justification that a person can have for *believing* a proposition, and justification of another sort—the epistemic justification that a person can have for a *proposition*,[13] Epistemic justification for believing a proposition is determined

---

[12] Other cases of this sort are discussed in my paper, "Evident but Rationally Unacceptable," *The Australasian Journal of Philosophy*, 65 (1987), pp. 316–26. It is argued there that the epistemically rational attitude for one in Jones's position to take is a suspension of judgment.

[13] This distinction is slightly different from certain other similar distinctions that have been made by philosophers. For instance, it resembles Roderick Firth's distinction between *propositional* and *doxastic* warrant (see Firth's "Are Epistemic Concepts Reducible to Ethical Concepts?", in *Value and Morals*, A. Goldman and J. Kim, eds. (D. Reidel, 1978), p. 218). Firth's doxastic warrant, though it resembles epistemic justification for believing, is unlike the latter in that doxastically warranted believing must be based on warranting evidence. In contrast to this, believing is epistemically justified when it is rational to believe in pursuit of knowledge, whatever the basis on which the belief is adopted. Ralf Kennedy and Charles Chihara (in "The Dutch Book Argument: Its Logical flaws, Its Subjective Sources" (*Philosophical Studies*, 36 (1979), pp. 19–33)) distinguish between "factors which are epistemically relevant to the truth of a given proposition [and those that] are relevant to the rationality of belief in that proposition" (p. 29). This too is similar to the present distinction. But Kennedy and Chihara seem to take prudential considerations generally to contribute to the rationality of belief (e.g. on p. 20), whereas only contributions to a pursuit of knowledge factor into epistemic justification for believing.

by the practical rationality of believing for the sake of knowing. We have seen that this justification for believing is not what is involved in the truth connection. It also turns out not to be the sort of justification that is a necessary condition for knowledge. This can be shown by use of the first case involving Mr. Jones and a potentially fatal belief. A certain proposition is foreseen by Jones to be fatal to belief, since his believing the proposition has been arranged to cause a deadly explosion in close proximity to him. Yet it is a belief which is evident to him. Jones has the epistemic goal of maximizing his knowledge. Because of this, he would not be epistemically justified in believing the proposition under these circumstances. He sees that he would gain more knowledge by surviving to learn many other things. Suppose that unfortunately Jones believes the proposition anyway. Since his observation of his own dogs has shown him that some basset hounds eat fruit, it is clear that Jones knows this proposition to be true during the brief time before he suffers the fatal consequences of his believing it. Thus, Jones has the sort of epistemic justification needed to know the proposition, although his believing it is an epistemic disaster for him. It has a ruinous effect on his effort to maximize what he knows (not to mention how bad it is for his general welfare). This establishes that it is not *believing* that has to be epistemically justified in order to know.

What must be epistemically justified in order to know is not "the belief" in the sense of: the believing of the proposition. It is "the belief" in the sense of: the proposition believed. What gets justified by the answer to the question—How do you know?—is the known proposition, not believing it. This is the justification that is the topic of the truth connection. Hence, it is the propositional sort of epistemic justification that enters into the truth connection.

7. Prepared by a clearer view of the justification in question, we are in a position to identify the nature of the truth connection. A proposition is epistemically justified to someone when it is evident to the person that the proposition is true. It is plausible that only very strong evidence can make a proposition evidently true.[14] It is equally plausible that only evidence contributes to the epistemic justification of a proposition to a person. Any epistemic support a person has for a proposition is some sort of indication to the person that the proposition is true. Indications of the truth of a proposition are evidence for it. The more strongly

---

[14] Perhaps it must be strong enough to override any evidence to the contrary that might possibly accompany it. If so, then only entailing evidence will do. Perhaps only "relevant" counter-evidence must be overridden. This issue concerning the strength of evidence required for knowledge need not be resolved in order to identify the nature of the truth connection.

a proposition's truth is indicated to someone, the better it is epistemically justified to the person. Epistemic justification of a proposition is evidence of its truth. The relation of evidential support is the truth connection.

This evidential account of the truth connection substantiates the view that a constant bearing on truth distinguishes the epistemic sort of justification that is needed to have knowledge from prudential justifications for believing, moral justifications, and the rest. The account asserts that having knowledge-level epistemic justification for a proposition is equivalent to having sufficient evidence that the proposition is true. In contrast to this, no evidential support of a proposition is sufficient for believing the proposition to be morally justified, prudentially justified, or justified in any other way. For instance, the proposition that final preparations are under way for a dental procedure may be one that it is not prudent for our Mr. Jones to believe, even though he is in a dentist's chair possessing conclusive evidential indications that it is true. This may not be prudent for Jones to believe because he realizes that this belief would increase his anxiety, with no benefit. Epistemic support for a proposition indicates that it is true; prudential reasons for believing a proposition are indications that believing it would be prudent. In general, a proposition can be evidently true without being evidently prudent to believe. So epistemically justified propositions are not guaranteed to be prudent to believe. Similar considerations show that believing epistemically justified propositions need not be morally justified, or religiously sanctioned, or justified in any other way. As the cases of the fatal beliefs show, believing need not even be epistemically justified.

The evidential account of the truth connection also substantiates the view that epistemic justification of any strength pertains to the truth of what is justified. It is common to have evidence that provides some epistemic justification for a proposition, without having enough evidence to meet the justification condition on knowledge. This weaker epistemic support makes something less than a conclusive case for the truth of the proposition. But all evidence for a proposition, however weak, is some indication that the proposition is true. Thus, the sort of justification that is constituted by evidence always bears on the truth of what is justified.

8. Evidence is an epistemic concept. An evidential account of the truth connection is not overtly naturalistic. The relation of giving evidence is not obviously within the ontology of any current or prospective science. This might seem problematic. It might be contended that the account is unsatisfactory until the relation of giving evidence receives some acceptable naturalistic reduction.

Earl Conee

It is far from clear where the boundary lies between naturalism and non-naturalism. Invocations of the supernatural are certainly not naturalistic. The evidential account of the truth connection invokes nothing supernatural. Perhaps naturalism does not conclusively prohibit anything else. But sympathetically construed, the guiding idea behind the imposition of naturalistic constraints is that there is something dubious about putative properties and relations that seem not to be reducible to those of present or foreseeable science. Let us take it for granted that this is a reasonable ground for doubt.

It should be acknowledged that no such reduction seems to be in the offing for the relation of giving evidence. But our best evidence favors the view that the relation exists in any case. We make stable confident reflective judgments that attribute the relation of evidential support. These judgments respond to something real. Presumably we are detecting a relation that is part of the natural world. If all naturalistic reductions of the relation fail, this jeopardizes reductionistic versions of naturalism. It does not cast doubt on the existence of the relation. We lack any plausible eliminativist explanation of our reflective attributions of the relation. Without an acceptable eliminativist account, our evidence favors the view that we have evidence.

9. In brief, the truth connection is a link between the epistemic justification that a person can have for a proposition and the truth of that proposition. The justification that is needed for knowledge consists in evidence.[15]

Afterword

1. In "The Truth Connection" I argue that the sort of epistemic justification that is a necessary condition for *S*'s knowing P is *propositional* justification—the known proposition P must be justified to *S*. Having propositional justification for P consists in having undefeated evidence for P. I also argue that what is termed in the paper *S*'s having epistemic justification for *believing* P is not a necessary condition for *S*'s knowing P.

In "Evidentialism" (Chapter 4 in this volume) we contend that the sort of justification that is "characteristically epistemic" and "basic" is the topic of this thesis:

EJ. Doxastic attitude D toward proposition p is epistemically justified for S at t if and only if having D toward p at t fits the evidence that S has at t.

---

[15] Previous drafts of this paper were presented during the 1990 Pacific APA meetings and the 1991 Spring meetings of the Creighton Club. I am grateful for formal comments on those occasions from Stephen Luper-Foy and Carl Ginet, respectively. I am also grateful for comments and questions from Stewart Cohen, Fred Dretske, Richard Feldman, George Mavrodes, and Jack Sanders.

The Truth Connection

(EJ) is about a sort of justification that believing can have. It is reasonable to wonder whether the arguments of "The Truth Connection" in effect show that the (EJ) sort of justification is not a necessary condition for knowledge.

The epistemic justification for believing discussed in "The Truth Connection" is practical in nature. It pertains to the practical rationality of believing for the sake of knowing. I contend in the paper that believing P need not be practically rational in that way in order for P to be known.

(EJ) is not about practical rationality. It is about "justification" in the sense in which being in some proper alignment plays a primary role. (EJ) is about the doxastic attitudes that align with one's circumstances in a way that is epistemically proper. This justification requires no practical payoff, not even for an epistemic end. Concerning this justification for believing, (EJ) in effect tells us that it occurs exactly when one has propositional justification. Believing P is the doxastic attitude that fits with being in the circumstance of having undefeated evidence for P. Since having propositional justification is necessary for knowledge and it implies having this epistemic justification for believing, both are necessary for knowledge.

2. In the course of denying in the present paper that the practical sort of epistemic justification for believing is closely connected to truth, I assert:

R.   Rational inquiry is a pursuit of knowledge.

(R) is defensible, but only if it is generously interpreted. Inquiry can be rational when no epistemic goal is involved. It can be prudentially rational to engage in an inquiry for the purpose of making a show of finding out the truth, while actually aiming for nothing epistemic. What does require an epistemic goal is something that we sometimes call "purely intellectual" inquiry, or just "pure" inquiry. This is the sort of inquiry that is epistemic in nature. So it is helpful to read the "inquiry" in (R) to be about pure inquiry only. This gives us:

R1.   Rational pure inquiry is a pursuit of knowledge.

More interpretation is needed. Some seemingly pure inquiry is rational, even though it cannot be a pursuit of knowledge. There are possible cases in which someone knows in advance that she has no way to gain knowledge whether or not X is true. There are more frequently occurring cases in which it is more reasonable for someone to deny that knowledge of whether or not X is true is available to her than to believe that it is. Either way, it may be that the truth about X is of entirely intellectual interest to the person, and an inquiry by means of which she will enhance her information about the truth of X is clearly available to her. In such a case, it is possible to pursue a rational inquiry into X that is entirely intellectual in purpose.

In its etymological and semantic core, "epistemic" refers to knowledge. So if we take the purity of an inquiry to be its epistemic nature, then in the core sense of "epistemic" such cases may not refute (R1). Rather, they may illustrate circumstances in which rational pure inquiry concerning X is unavailable to someone.

This defends (R1), but it is not the whole story. It is possible in such cases to pursue rationally a sort of inquiry concerning X that is reasonably classified as epistemic. Knowledge is not the only epistemological topic. The study of propositional justification is also part of epistemology. This is fundamentally because propositional justification is an interesting necessary condition for factual knowledge. Propositional justification consists in evidence. In the envisioned circumstances, there is a rational prospect of inquiry yielding new evidence about whether or not X is true. Acquiring this evidence therefore will enhance propositional justification concerning X. When "epistemic" is read broadly enough to include things that relate in this way to knowledge, enhancing propositional justification counts as an epistemic goal. It can be rational to make an inquiry concerning X in pursuit of this broadly epistemic goal, even while knowing that one cannot know the truth of X.

True belief too is an interesting necessary condition for factual knowledge. Its investigation also belongs to epistemology. Read broadly, inquiry can be "pure" and "epistemic" in virtue of the aim to gain this condition for knowledge. So there is a reading of pursuing a "pure" inquiry concerning X on which the pursuit of true belief concerning X counts. Rational inquiry toward this epistemic goal usually requires gathering evidence about X. This is usually the rational route because it is usually the only means that one is epistemically justified in expecting to succeed.

Even for this limited and derivative sort of pure inquiry with the aim of true belief, there is no simple straightforward truth connection. Even for the purpose of gaining a true belief concerning X, it can be rational to believe X when X is actually untrue. For one far-fetched simple example, it might be that you know that a genie will cause your doxastic attitude toward X to be accurate if and only if you believe X now. It might be evident to you that this is your best available means of having a true belief concerning X. Suppose too that X is false. If so, then once you believe X, the genie will give you a true belief concerning X by causing you to disbelieve X instead. Thus, even when the epistemic end is just true belief, false belief can be the rational means.

The Truth Connection

3. "The Ethics of Belief" (Chapter 7 in this volume) defends a thesis about what people epistemically ought to believe.

O2. For any person S, time t, and proposition p, if S has any doxastic attitude at all toward p at t and S's evidence at t supports p, then S epistemically ought to have the attitude toward p supported by S's evidence at t.

One argument for (O2) that receives favorable comments in the paper—though it is not quite endorsed—relies on the following premise:

V3. When adopting (or maintaining) an attitude toward a proposition, p, a person maximizes epistemic value by adopting (or maintaining) a rational attitude toward p.

With the additional assumption that rationality consists in conforming attitudes to evidence, (V3) enables us to infer that it maximizes epistemic value to have the attitude toward a proposition that is supported by one's evidence at the time. Adding that one epistemically ought to maximize epistemic value, (O2) can be derived.

The pursuit of epistemic goals has been discussed here and in the body of "The Truth Connection". Epistemic value has not been mentioned. But some of the considerations that have been addressed to epistemic goals might seem to reflect badly on (V3).

To see this, suppose that we make the assumption about the bearers of epistemic value that is friendliest to (V3): namely, that positive epistemic value is possessed by all and only instances of having the attitude toward a proposition that is supported by one's evidence at the time. Still, it might seem that (V3) cannot be true. For it seems that this epistemic value can be maximized by adopting an attitude that is not supported by one's evidence at the time. An unsupported attitude can causally contribute to a higher total of epistemic value. Here is another example about a genie to make this point. It may be that a genie will keep one from ever again having a supported attitude unless one has an unsupported attitude now, while if one does have an unsupported attitude now, one will have many more supported attitudes later. In this situation, an unsupported attitude maximizes the total of supported attitudes. It seems that there will be possible cases of this sort in which a supported attitude does not maximize epistemic value. Yet (V3) says that supported attitudes always maximize epistemic value.

A defender of (V3) may not have to disagree about the genie example. *Total* epistemic value may not be the intended magnitude. Perhaps the idea behind

Earl Conee

(V3) is more perspicuously rendered in this way:

V3*. When adopting (or maintaining) an attitude toward a proposition, *p*, a person* has an attitude that constitutes a state of affairs having maximal intrinsic epistemic value* by adopting (or maintaining) a rational attitude toward *p*.

That is, it may be that what determines which doxastic attitude toward a proposition is rational is what attains the highest level available of epistemic value that is *intrinsic* to states of affairs consisting in the person having a doxastic attitude in the epistemically relevant circumstances. So although the effects of an attitude contribute to the total epistemic value that the attitude produces, only its constitutive role in yielding intrinsic epistemic value pertains to rationality, not the total epistemic value that it produces. It is plausible that attitudes supported by one's evidence always constitute states having the highest available intrinsic epistemic value. So having such an attitude would be the only way to maximize that value.

Clearly, (V3*) is not subject to the sorts of objections that the genie example illustrates. Those objections trade on extrinsically valuable epistemic contributions.

The argument for (O2) can use (V3*) instead of (V3), after also adjusting the assumption that connects epistemic value to the attitude that one epistemically ought to have. The argument should now claim that the attitude that one epistemically ought to have is the attitude that constitutes a state having maximal intrinsic epistemic value, rather than the attitude that contributes in some way to maximizing epistemic value.

This last change gives rise to doubt. If we sought the nearest epistemic counterpart to consequentialism in ethics, we would hold that one epistemically ought to have attitudes that maximize total value, rather than attitudes that constitute states having the highest intrinsic value. But we should not blindly model the epistemological evaluations on the consequentialist ones. Consequentialism in ethics has its problems, and anyway we lack reason to think that correct epistemic evaluations match their closest ethical counterparts.

A totalizing view does seem most plausible to me here, though. Cases are possible in which one knows that only some unsupported attitude produces the highest total. Sacrificing current intrinsic epistemic value, knowing that this is needed to gain the most of that value eventually, seems to me to be what one ought to do on epistemic grounds.

11

Heeding Misleading Evidence
Earl Conee

A problem about an effect on knowledge of new contrary information offers evidentialism an occasion to do some good. Evidentialism solves the problem simply and without intellectual cost.

The Problem

A story will illustrate the problem. Our protagonist, Professor Smith, sits in his familiar office looking out onto the Olde Quadd. He hears the noon chimes while seeing a drenching rainstorm. It seems clear that Smith thereby knows:

R.   It is raining on the Olde Quadd at noon.

For no particular reason, Smith proceeds to reason about being misled. He thinks:

It is raining out there now. So, (R) is something true. Since (R) is true, any evidence that it is not true, including any testimony that plausibly denies it, is misleading in that it goes against something true.

Thus, Smith uses his knowledge of (R) and what it implies to derive:

C.   If any evidence against (R) ever exists, then it is misleading evidence.

With "misleading evidence" meaning "evidence against a truth", (C) is implied by (R). Smith sees clearly that (R) implies (C). And Smith knows (R). So Smith appears to know (C) too on the basis of this derivation.

Soon Professor Jones enters Smith's office, bent on mischief. Jones tells Smith that no rain has been falling. Rather, their university's film school is practicing a rainy scene on the roof of the building. What Smith has been seeing is

Earl Conee

an effect of what Jones describes as their "incredibly realistic rain machine." Jones displays an earnest demeanor, and Smith is under the false impression that Jones is a pillar of integrity. Jones proceeds to offer spurious but compelling reasons why the film school is using a rain machine on the roof. This ends our story.

Jones's deceit seems capable of overriding Smith's basis for believing (R). Hearing Jones's credible fiction about the film school appears to deprive Smith of justification for believing that it was rain that he saw at noon. If so, then Smith no longer knows (R). Thus it appears that, immediately after Smith correctly infers from (R) that any evidence against it is misleading, Smith loses knowledge of (R) by receiving evidence against it.

Perhaps no such loss could occur. There is reason to think that, given Smith's derivation of (C), his knowledge of (R) would be preserved. We have seen that as Jones begins to speak, Smith appears to know (C), which tells him that any such evidence is misleading. We should suppose that Smith forgets nothing as Jones speaks. In light of this, why does not Smith's knowledge of (C) show him that Jones's assertions are misleading? Why would not he thereby remain justified in believing (R) and continue to know it?

These two arguments give us a philosophical problem.[1] One argument concludes that Smith loses knowledge of (R). Its principal assumption is that as a result of hearing Jones, Smith is no longer justified in believing (R). The other argument concludes that Smith continues to know (R). Its principal assumption is that Smith's knowledge of (C) shows him that Jones's testimony is merely misleading. Each of these assumptions is initially plausible. Our problem is to identify a defect in one of the arguments, while accounting for its plausibility.

The argument for losing knowledge seems the better of the two. Ordinary knowledge rests on a fallible basis. We can see this in examples where what seemed to be knowledge turned out to be a justified false belief. For instance, there is the proposition that energy transmitted in waves requires a medium of transmission. Many of our predecessors had reasons for believing this that were strong and fully justifying. But we now have stronger justification for the conclusion that those reasons turned out to be deceptive. Light waves its way along without any luminiferous ether. The crucial further point for present purposes is that we are just as fallible about this sort of turn of events. Our reasons for believing something that we actually do know can be made to seem to have misled us. This is clearly possible, because instances of our actual failings are

---

[1] In Gilbert Harman's book *Thought* (Princeton: Princeton University Press, 1973) he attributes the original puzzle of this sort to Saul Kripke (p. 148).

Heeding Misleading Evidence

among the things that we are clearly incapable of discovering with certainty. So it is pretty plain that we can lose knowledge by deception.

On the other hand, it is doubtful that an inference to anything like (C) could save us from any such deception about being deceived. (C) is known in our example, if at all, in a way that depends on (R). We have just seen that knowing (R) itself seems inadequate to block the relevant deception from succeeding, because our basis for knowing things like (R) is not sufficiently secure. Since the way that we know (R) is not secure enough to save knowledge of (R), it is obscure how this knowledge could be saved by knowing something else that relies on (R). So we should expect that the argument that fails here is the one for retaining knowledge of (R) by using (C).

Solution

Evidentialism provides a basis for solving this problem.[2] Details aside, the evidentialist view about epistemic justification is that it derives entirely from the evidence possessed. Here is a pertinent evidentialist thesis for our problem:

E. S is epistemically justified in believing at t exactly what is adequately supported by the totality of S's evidence at t, and S knows at t only propositions that S is epistemically justified in believing at t.

As (E) affects our problem it has three important features. First, (E) does not require evidence to be justified in order to provide support. As long as a consideration actually is evidence for someone, it can justify. Second, (E) requires that justifying evidence be possessed at a time in order to justify at that time. Previously justifying evidence counts for nothing, unless it is retained and continues to justify. And third, according to (E) justification of a belief depends on whether the balance of all of a person's evidence favors the belief. So (E) allows that, even though a certain body of evidence would have been enough to justify a belief if it had been all the evidence that the person had on the topic, that same evidence need not justify the belief in the presence of further evidence strongly pointing in the opposite direction.

The utility of (E) for our problem depends partly on the existence of a credible account of what a person's evidence is. Fortunately for present purposes we do not need anything precise or fully articulated. In a word, the best conception of

---

[2] Gilbert Harman (*ibid.*) and Carl Ginet ('Knowing less by knowing more', *Midwest Studies in Philosophy*, vol. 5 (Minneapolis: Minnesota University Press, 1980), pp. 151–61) have offered versions of this sort of answer.

261

evidence for (E) is that of *data*. The data someone has concerning a proposition are the nonderivative indications that the person has of the truth value of the proposition. The commonest examples of data are conscious deliverances of perceptual experience. The data are distinct from any beliefs that the person may have about them. They are our primary bases for forming reasoned beliefs.[3]

With evidence so conceived, a solution to our problem is ready at hand. In our example, the propositions (R) and (C) are clearly not evidence that Professor Smith has. They are not data for him; they are derivative beliefs. So according to (E) they must be supported by evidence to be justified or known. In our example at the initial time (call it "t1"), Smith has evidence for (R) and for (C). While he looks out of his window and sees the rain, his principal evidence bearing on (R) consists in the perceptual data that he receives.[4] Smith has no evidence against (R) at t1. The same perceptual evidence, with the further evidence that Smith gains by reasoning to (C) from (R), gives Smith uncontested evidence for (C) at t1. So, assuming that the support is adequately strong, (E) implies that (R) and (C) are justified for Smith at t1 and (E) allows that Smith knows (R) and (C) at t1.

As soon as Smith has heard from Jones (call this time "t2"), perception of a highly credible report denying (R) has been added to Smith's evidence. Smith recalls at t2 his perceptual data in favor of (R), data which we are supposing were adequate at t1 for Smith to believe with justification and know (R). But according to (E), this fact is not epistemically decisive at t2. (E) implies that Smith still knows only what his new combination of evidence sufficiently supports. The new totality of Smith's evidence does not support (R). Smith's recalled perceptual evidence for (R) is overridden by the new evidence he has consisting in his perception of Jones's compelling story about the rain machine. (E) implies that Smith no longer knows (R).

That is the evidentialist account of why Smith loses knowledge of (R). The argument for the conclusion that Smith retains knowledge of (R) relies on his continuing to know (C) at t2. In our example, Smith's only available reasons for thinking that any evidence against (R) is misleading stem from (R) itself, backed by his evidence for (R). As soon as Smith receives Jones's testimony,

---

[3] Data may be states of affairs that are immediately apprehended, or they may be self-attributions of properties conceptualized in certain ways, or they may be something else entirely. Data as understood here are whatever fills a certain epistemic role, the role of giving primary indications of truth values. All we require is that this is a workable idea of what a person's evidence is.

[4] A full account of the relevant evidence would not be brief. Smith would have to have memories in support of his location of the rain on the Olde Quadd, memories in support of the chiming he hears being a reliable signal of noon, and numerous conceptual memories assuring him of his having adequate competence in applying the concepts involved in (R).

Smith no longer has justifying evidence for (R). (R) must be supported in order for it to support other propositions by derivation. So Smith no longer has justifying evidence for (C). By (E) therefore he no longer has justification for (C) or knowledge of it. So (C) cannot enable Smith to know at t2 that Jones's assertions about a rain machine are misleading.

Using nothing more than (E), an intuitive view of the nature of evidence, and a routine application of the notion of overriding evidence, we gain explanations of why knowledge of (R) is lost and cannot be retained via (C).

Case closed? Not yet. The evidentialist account of the matter implies something peculiar about knowledge of a conditional. It faces other serious published objections as well. And there are two further questionable aspects of the evidentialist line. One concerns a suspect detail in a transition that the account alleges to occur in Smith's evidence as Jones tells his story. The other concerns the contention that Jones's story defeats Smith's evidence for (R), rather than the story's being defeated by an argument involving (C).

A Difficulty about Modus Ponens

The evidentialist account has it that Smith's knowledge of the conditional (C) is lost when he acquires knowledge of its antecedent, because what gives him knowledge of the antecedent also renders the conditional no longer known to him. This is peculiar. Learning the truth of the antecedent of a known conditional normally sets one up to derive knowledge of the consequent by modus ponens. Yet here the evidentialist claims that learning the truth of the antecedent destroys knowledge of the conditional. Is this finally credible?

Carl Ginet supplements his evidentialist response to our problem by presenting other conditionals that clearly have this same remarkable feature.[5] Roy Sorensen also identifies further sorts of conditionals that clearly cannot be used to yield an expansion of knowledge by modus ponens.[6] These other examples refute any suggestion that knowledge of a conditional always permits expansion by modus ponens. But pointing to the existence of analogous cases does not establish the evidentialist solution on this point. The existence of other conditionals with this epistemic property neither shows that (C) has the property nor explains why anything has it.

---

[5] *Op. cit.*, pp. 156–7.
[6] Roy Sorensen, 'Dogmatism, junk knowledge, and conditionals', *The Philosophical Quarterly*, vol. 38, no. 153 (1988), pp. 433–54.

Sorensen sketches what is in effect an explanation of why Smith cannot use (C) to make a modus ponens derivation of new knowledge, when Smith learns (C)'s antecedent. Sorensen's account is brief. He holds that the derivation is unavailable because (C) is not "robust" with respect to its antecedent. This means that it is not the case that the probability of (C) is high, given its antecedent.[7]

For two reasons this is at most a partial explanation. First, the employed notion of probability must be explained in a way that relates it appropriately to knowledge, since knowledge is the epistemic concept in terms of which the problem is formulated. Second and more importantly, we need to be shown that in the particular circumstances of our example (C) is not robust with respect to its antecedent. It is clear that in somewhat different circumstances (C) could have been used in a justified modus ponens inference. For instance, Smith might have been quite reliably forewarned that although some evidence against (R) is forthcoming, all such evidence is bound to be spurious. If this had happened, then (C) would remain known to Smith after hearing Jones's story. So Smith could have made a modus ponens inference from known premises including (C) and thereby come to know that Jones's testimony is misleading evidence. The evidentialist denies that Smith can do this in our original story. Thus, an explanation is needed of the precarious epistemic character of (C) in Smith's particular situation, if an appeal to robustness is to succeed in solving the problem. Sorensen does not explain this.

Evidentialist concepts could be recruited to serve both of these purposes. The notion of probability that defines "robustness" could be identified with the strength of the evidential support. Then in Smith's situation this probability of (C) for Smith is low, when Smith is "given" (C)'s antecedent by learning its truth. This would be the case because any justifying evidence that Smith has for (C) includes evidence for (R), and Smith's learning (C)'s antecedent defeats his support for (R). So (C) is then not strongly supported to him. That contrasts with (C)'s status in a situation where Smith is forewarned about misleading contrary evidence, thus neutralizing the defeating capacity of Jones's testimony against (R). (C) would be "robust" in that situation, that is, (C) would maintain strong support from Smith's evidence when he learns the truth of its antecedent.

An explanation of (C)'s resistance to modus ponens in Smith's circumstances thus could be completed using an evidentialist interpretation of probability. There may be other ways to fill out the explanation. In any case, a purely evidentialist account that bypasses robustness seems preferable. It has the advantages of being conceptually simpler and having more general explanatory

---

[7] Ibid., p. 448.

capabilities. And we shall soon see, without any appeal to robustness, that there is nothing really doubtful about the attribution to Smith of a loss of knowledge of (C) by learning its antecedent.

Cargile's Objections

James Cargile[8] offers three objections to features of the sort of evidentialist solution to our problem that is advocated here. The first is an objection to any account of the situation allowing that Smith knows until he hears from Jones that all evidence against (R) is misleading:

> [W]e seem to have a case in which someone knows that all A's are B's, such that, when he encounters an x that is A (evidence against *h*), he is supposed to *refrain from* concluding that x is B (misleading)! This is spared from sheer inconsistency by the acknowledgment that when he does this—says 'here is an A which I can't class as a B'—he then gives up the claim to know that all A's are B's. But this is inadequate consolation. For our *h*-knower knows as well as we do about his 'knowledge' that all cases of evidence that will appear to him as counting against *h* are misleading, that he must drop this 'knowledge' the minute he encounters a candidate for an instance of it. Some inference ticket this generalization is![9]

This objection contends that the alleged knowledge that all evidence against a known proposition is misleading is too inferentially feeble to be genuine knowledge. It cannot be used to infer anything about its instances because as soon as an instance is encountered, the alleged knowledge is gone.

Cargile's second objection to the evidentialist account of Smith's loss of knowledge of (R) indicates that the account seems to be committed to endorsing a bad policy:

> [W]hat if the agent just refused to be exposed to the misleading defeaters? Suppose the *h*-knower is approached by someone who says he has evidence that looks bad for *h*, and the knower just refuses to hear the evidence on the grounds that he already knows better? On [the evidentialist] answer, this would seem to be justified as long as the mere exposure to the misleading evidence is avoided.[10]

The objection here is the charge that the evidentialist account, by allowing that the knowledge is preserved until defeating evidence is actually received, seems to justify a general shunning of potential counter-evidence to what is taken to be known. Yet this would not be a reasonable practice.

---

[8] James Cargile, 'Justification and misleading defeaters', *Analysis*, vol. 55, no. 3 (1995), pp. 216–20.
[9] *Ibid.*, p. 217. [10] *Ibid.*

Earl Conee

Cargile's final objection amounts to the contention that the evidentialist account does not explain how knowing a proposition is compatible with having a fully reasonable disposition to defer to evidence against the proposition. In support of this Cargile writes:

> Even a distinguished mathematician would concede ... that if his profession agreed that he was mistaken on some point on which he was quite confident, that vast authority would shake him, would cause him to think that he must somehow have got it wrong, and it would be hubris not to grant this. And yet knowing he would do this does not conflict with his ... knowing that he has got it right. [The evidentialist account] does not, I think, succeed in explaining how this can be so.[11]

We are invited to acknowledge that a distinguished mathematician might know, concerning a proposition of which he is actually quite confident, that a particular sort of evidence would bring him to concede that he did not know it. Yet he does know it. The evidentialist account applied here appears to tell us only that the mathematician's getting some such evidence would result in his losing the knowledge. That does not explain how he manages actually to know the proposition, even while also knowing that such counter-evidence could not be reasonably disregarded.

Replies to Cargile's Objections

Cargile's objections merit refutation. First, there is the matter of the power of a certain "inference ticket". The problem is that in the evidentialist view Smith knows (C) only until he encounters a truth-maker for its antecedent. The account has it that knowledge of (C) is thereby lost before it can be used in an inference. This sort of epistemic status is supposed to be too precarious to qualify as genuine knowledge.

When the peculiarities of the case are appreciated, it becomes clear that there is nothing suspicious in the evidentialist account.

In our example Smith knows (C) on a particular basis, and not otherwise. He needs to know (R) in order to know (C). Once Smith no longer knows this inferential basis for (C), he no longer knows (C). Smith ceases to know this basis as a result of the infusion of new evidence he receives by hearing from Jones. The key remarkable fact here is that this event is also one of those misleading cases that (C) is about.

In our example, Smith's hearing from Jones is an "encounter" with something that obviously makes true the antecedent of the conditional in question. Two

---

[11] James Cargile, 'Justification and misleading defeaters', *Analysis*, vol. 55, no. 3 (1995), p. 218.

epistemically significant things happen at once in this peculiar sort of case, where usually there is only one. In this encounter with something clearly making true the antecedent, the antecedent's truth becomes known. That is the usual thing. But here, the previously known conditional proposition, (C), happens to be about evidence concerning the rain on the Olde Quadd at noon. So this encounter is also the acquisition of evidence that pertains to (R), the basis on which (C) itself is known. Since this is so, an encounter of that sort, in addition to showing Smith the truth of the antecedent, happens also to be the acquisition of new and negative evidence about the basis on which the whole conditional was known. And in our example that new evidence is decisively negative. It is not plausible that knowledge of a conditional can survive such an encounter.[12] The basis for knowing the conditional is thereby lost and not replaced. In contrast, ordinarily what is known says nothing about the basis on which it is known.

There is nothing suspiciously feeble in the knowledge of (C) here. In fact, any alleged knowledge that could survive the acquisition of defeating contrary evidence against its basis would have the tenacity of dogma, not knowledge. It is the relationship of the content of the conditional to the basis on which it is known that is peculiar here, not what evidentialism says about the loss of knowledge. So Cargile's first objection fails.

Cargile's second objection to the evidentialist approach is the claim that it would apparently "justify" the unreasonable practice of hiding from any evidence that seems to threaten one's knowledge.

There is an important ambiguity in this charge. (E) is an evidentialist view of the epistemic justification of a belief. This is a sort of justification that helps to make it true that one is in a certain condition, the condition of knowing something. The view is that this sort of justification consists in supporting evidence. It is not justification for doing anything. The view implies nothing about what gives practical justification to conduct, including the conduct of inquiry.

The evidentialist view does leave it open that adequate evidence for knowledge sometimes can be retained by hiding from a threat of contrary evidence. There is one squarely evidentialist limit on this, however. Discerning a mere

---

[12] While seeing the rain, Smith might have considered various sorts of possible evidence against (R), sorts of evidence as much like Jones's immanent testimony as we like. The evidentialist account allows that Smith could know by inference from (C) that any such item of evidence is misleading. (E) allows that Smith's knowledge of (C) can survive all of these purely contemplative encounters with possible instances of its antecedent.

This is another sort of persistence of knowledge of a conditional through "encounters" with instances of its antecedent. It is plausible to attribute a capacity for such persistence to Smith's knowledge of (C) in our example. The evidentialist view is not committed to disputing that.

prospect of new evidence against a proposition is itself gaining some contrary evidence that may undermine the proposition's justification. In our example, merely gleaning that Jones is starting to explain away the appearance of rain might undercut Smith's evidence for (R) before Smith would have any chance to tune Jones out. If so, then Smith would lose the knowledge by the time he was alerted to the fact that it was in jeopardy. So on purely evidentialist grounds it would be too late to hide.

But the general fact remains that if a person does manage to retain justifying evidence, even by evasion or obliviousness, the evidentialist justification condition on knowledge continues to be met.[13] And it should be acknowledged that a general policy of avoiding potentially threatening evidence would be in some important way unreasonable.

This is not problematic. Any tenable account of why the avoidance is an unreasonable practice is compatible with evidentialism. For instance, the avoidance may be unreasonable because engaging in the practice would not tend to maximize knowledge. Ordinarily, knowledge is not introspectively distinguishable from justified false belief. Shunning potential counter-evidence to our seemingly known justified beliefs would sometimes obstruct our learning the falsehood of justified beliefs that turn out not to be known. Perhaps only a thoroughgoing investigation of any prospect of significant counter-evidence to a justified belief can be justifiably expected to maximize knowledge. It is plausible that this would give these thorough investigations a kind of practical justification, toward the epistemic end of maximizing what is known. If so, then evading threatening evidence might be unreasonable in virtue of not having this sort of practical justification for an epistemic purpose.

Thus, an evidentialist can happily agree that shunning counter-evidence is unreasonable on some such grounds. Strictly speaking, though, the evidentialist view of epistemic justification and its relation to knowledge is silent on these questions of conduct. Justification of conduct, including the conduct of inquiry, derives from reasons for acting. It is a topic for a theory of practical reasoning, not a theory of the justification that can give knowledge.

It might seem that things change drastically, if we include in the case that Smith knows at t1:

KR. Smith knows (R).

---

[13] Whether or not the view really allows knowledge to survive the existence of evaded defeating evidence depends in part on how the view answers the question—familiar from defeasibility solutions to the Gettier problem—of when the sheer existence of such evidence acts as a defeater to knowledge.

It might seem that if Smith knows (KR) at tl, then as Jones spins his tale Smith can bear in mind that Jones is denying a known fact, namely (R). Granting that generally knowledge is not introspectively discernible from false justified belief, still, a policy of dismissing evidence against what is *known* to be known seems entirely reasonable.

Knowledge of (KR) turns out not to make a significant difference. Knowledge of (KR) requires justification for (KR). In Smith's situation he has no independent means of assuring himself that he knows (R), apart from whatever access he has to his way of knowing (R). So his evidence for (KR) must at least include his evidence for (R) itself. He cannot have justifying evidence that (R) is known to him, if his evidence conspicuously indicates to him that (R) is untrue.

With this dependence of knowing (KR) on justification for (R), the evidentialist account of how knowledge of (R) itself is lost carries over to imply that knowledge of (KR) is lost, simultaneously and in the same way. Jones's testimony gives Smith a body of evidence which on balance argues against (R). This conspicuous balance of evidence prevents Smith from having justification at t2 for regarding (R) as something known to him. Smith can recall that he believed at t1 that he knew (R), and he can recall his reasons for thinking that this was knowledge. But in light of his total evidence at t2, his perceptual evidence for (R) at t1 is most reasonably regarded by Smith at t2 as having been misleading. Smith at t2 would be most reasonable in thinking that he was mistaken at t1 in believing (KR), because it seems to him at t2 that he was mistaken in believing (R) itself. Thus, even if Smith knows (KR) at t1, at t2 it is no longer knowledge which he might use to dismiss Jones's testimony.

Cargile's last objection tells us that a distinguished mathematician, let us call her "Professor Matthews", could be convinced of a mathematical proposition, let us call it "Q", concerning which she knows that if her colleagues were united in averring that she was mistaken about it, then she would not know it. Yet it may be that she does know (Q). The complaint against the evidentialist account is that it does not explain how all of this can be true.

Cargile does not specify the full content of the evidentialist view to which he objects. So far we have been invoking only (E). (E) states just a necessary condition for knowledge. A problem for evidentialism would arise only if there is no reasonable way to add to (E) to account for the sort of case that Cargile describes.

We can suppose that Professor Matthews knows (Q) on the basis of an argument that justifies (Q) without its constituting an unshakable proof. Assuming this, we can also assume that Matthews knows a certain counterfactual, namely, that if her colleagues were united in disbelieving (Q), then upon

269

learning this she would not know (Q). This is knowing that certain evidence, which it is not just impossible that she will receive, would pivotally weaken her support for (Q).

According to nonskeptical evidentialist accounts of the strength of evidence needed for knowledge, some sort of nonentailing evidence is sufficient. In any such view, the defeasibility by further evidence of the justification that Matthews has for (Q) is compatible with her knowing (Q). Knowing only that some such barely possible defeater would deprive her of knowledge of (Q) is not acknowledging the existence of any actual evidence against (Q). It acknowledges nothing more than a remote possibility of her case for (Q) failing to hold up. Any view of knowledge on which it can be fallibly based allows this sort of possibility. There is no reason to deny that it can be a known possibility. It casts no actual doubt on (Q). The evidence for (Q) can still be strong enough for knowledge.

In this way an evidentialist account can attribute to Matthews the justification needed for her to know (Q) while she knows that, were the exotic possibility to arise of a sincere denial of (Q) by all of her colleagues, she would no longer know (Q). The evidentialist view thus allows knowledge to be accompanied by this sort of rational humility.

Cargile's Approach

Cargile's own explanation of why it is not reasonable for someone in Smith's position to disregard misleading evidence rests on denying epistemic closure principles. Here is a relevant one, catered to Smith's situation:

K. If S concludes that evidence against X is misleading by inferring this from S's knowledge that X is true and that X implies that any evidence against X is misleading, then S knows that evidence against X is misleading.[14]

The denial of closure applies to our case of Professor Smith as follows. Smith knows (R) as he sees the rain from his office. Our story has Smith also inferring (C) from (R) and its implication of (C). In Cargile's view, this inference does not yield knowledge. Any closure principle that implies otherwise is false. Since Smith never knows (C), it is never knowledge that could entitle Smith to dismiss Jones's testimony.

---

[14] *Op. cit.*, pp. 218–19. In Cargile's view, knowledge is not always preserved by inference from known premises, because the justification that is needed to know something justifies in relation to an issue context. If the issue context of an inferred proposition differs from that of the known propositions that are known to imply it, then the inferred proposition may not be known via such an inference.

Heeding Misleading Evidence

Cargile does not say how a denial of closure helps to explain Smith's loss of knowledge of (R). A denial of closure allows us to say that Smith never knows that such testimony is misleading. And it might be thought that once we see that Smith never knows any such thing, we have all we need for it to be just obvious how hearing Jones's story deprives Smith of his knowledge of (R). But in fact something else is needed, something that does so much work that it becomes idle here to deny closure, as we shall soon see.

Evidentialism Borne Out

Among the apparent facts of the case are that Smith knows (R) until he hears from Jones, and that Smith loses this knowledge by hearing from Jones. Nothing in a denial of closure accounts for why Smith does not retain his knowledge of (R) after hearing Jones's story. At most a denial of closure explains why one sort of argument, via a closure principle like (C), cannot be Smith's basis for disregarding Jones's testimony as it bears on (R). This is inadequate. We still need to see why Smith cannot simply retain his knowledge of (R) while accepting Jones's testimony for exactly what it is. We need to see why Smith cannot know all of the following after he hears Jones's story:

(R) is true. My colleague Jones has made a very powerful case against (R). Therefore, although (R) is true, it is also true that Jones has presented strong evidence against it.

The facts of the case include that Jones's testimony is of overpowering rational force. Smith could not keep knowing (R) by thus simply conjoining it to an acknowledgment of the existence of the testimony and its negative evidential relation to (R). But why not? What accounts for the loss of knowledge of (R)? A denial of closure does not help to answer this question.

If we add that Smith knows at a time only what his overall evidence of the time sufficiently supports, then we are in fine shape to answer our current question. We can say that Smith loses knowledge of (R) in virtue of an effect on his overall evidence of hearing the testimony. Once it is heard, Smith's previous evidence is no longer all that he has to go on about (R), and his overall evidence no longer sufficiently supports (R). So he no longer knows (R).

What we have just added is part of the evidentialist principle (E). Invoking this part of (E) may seem to complement the denial of closure in the explanation. But actually it renders the denial superfluous.

To show this, let us suppose that the closure principle (K) is true after all. This just requires us to say out of principle something that we were already assuming is true in the story. Taking (K) for granted, we must say that at least until hearing Jones's story, Smith knows (C) by inference from his knowledge of (R) and his knowledge of the implication of (C) by (R). This makes no trouble for the evidentialist account of Smith's losing knowledge of (R). Once Smith actually hears from Jones, his evidence about (R) is expanded in a way that defeats his recalled sensory support for (R). (E) tells us that with this new body of evidence, Smith no longer knows (R). Smith's knowledge of (R) is one of the premises that engaged the closure principle (K). So when Smith has heard from Jones, with (R) unjustified Smith no longer knows that such evidence misleads, even assuming (K). Therefore, the evidentialist view still allows us to account for the fact that Smith lacks knowledge to dismiss the testimony once he hears what Jones has to say. And (E) tells us that without that, Smith's knowledge of (R) is lost. So a denial of closure adds nothing useful to the explanation.

A Frozen Moment

It might seem that the evidentialist account of the example has passed too quickly over a crucial point in the story. There may be a moment soon after Smith has begun to hear from Jones at which Smith's evidence of rain is still sufficient for him to know (R). At that moment, our evidentialist account allows that Smith still knows that what Jones is telling him is misleading as it bears on (R).

This description of that moment might seem to have an unacceptable implication. Smith's basis for believing (R) has begun to be undermined, and it would be plain to him that there is more of this to come. Thus, it seems that at this point Smith could not reasonably dismiss what Jones is telling him. The evidentialist account therefore seems to be in error about this point in time.

Examining the moment in greater detail dissolves the difficulty. The evidential situation has to be coherently characterized. Either Smith still has what the best version of evidentialism counts as sufficient evidence to know (R), in spite of what Jones has said so far, or not. If not, then there is no optimal evidentialist reason to say that Smith is in a position to dismiss Jones's testimony. We should therefore focus on the other alternative: Smith still has evidence that is good enough to know (R).

It might be that Jones has mentioned a rain machine, but he has not yet made it fully credible that one is currently operating on the building's roof. Smith still has knowledge-level evidence for (R) only if he retains in memory sufficient support for the proposition that a rain machine did not produce the perceptions through which he has just come to believe (R). So we should suppose that at that moment Smith's evidence for (R) remains strong enough to do this.

One more pair of alternatives is important here. Either it is indicated to Smith at this moment that Jones is in the process of substantially enhancing the plausibility of the thought that a rain machine is in operation on the scene so that this may become a defeating alternative to (R), or not. In all likely versions of the example, Smith would discern from Jones's manner that he is starting to assert something amazing. When this is so, the present evidence of forthcoming enhancement is itself further reason to doubt (R). Depending on the strength of the reason, the evidentialist approach might count this reasoned anticipation of potentially undermining evidence as itself sufficient to undermine knowledge. The original account of the lost knowledge would continue to go through.

In search of trouble for the evidentialist account, let us suppose that Smith has no such ground to anticipate the drift of Jones's story. This makes the case unusual. But in order to have a coherent case of the sort that is most threatening to the evidentialist account, we must set aside our normal presumption that Smith is in a position to anticipate in this way.

Thus, we must consider a case in which Smith's memory still provides evidence that is sufficiently strong to outweigh by a wide margin the threat to (R) from Jones's mention of a rain machine. It outweighs the mention by a margin wide enough for Smith to continue to know (R). And we must consider a case in which Smith is being given no indication that defeating evidence is forthcoming.

When we focus on this version of our example, the evidentialist approach can be seen to come out all right. At this moment in this particular sort of example, Smith has much better reason to deny that a rain machine is at work than to believe it. Given the comparison between what we must suppose to be Smith's clear memory of the rain and what we must suppose to be a weak doubt cast on (R) by Jones's initial statements, Jones's initial talk of a rain machine is not worth Smith's taking seriously. (R) is something that Smith's evidence is still strongly supporting, and he has no current indication that Jones's case against (R) will build into something of defeating strength.

The Direction of Defeat

One further question about the evidentialist account is worth considering. Why couldn't Smith use (C) *as evidence* for sticking with (R) when he hears from Jones? That is, why couldn't Smith dismiss Jones's story as misleading on the ground that his evidence includes the fact that all such testimony is misleading? (C) is a derivative belief by Smith, so taking it as evidence is hard to square with

Earl Conee

the conception of evidence as data. But perhaps that is worth revising. After all, this use of (C) seems to allow Smith to preserve what is in fact knowledge. And if evidence is understood in some broader way that includes (C), then Smith's use of (C) at t2 to disregard Jones could be endorsed by a sort of evidentialism, maybe a sort that is preferable to the one we have been considering.[15]

At t2, just after Smith has heard Jones's story about the rain machine, Smith has one or another sort of cognitive access to three quantities of information that have an important epistemic bearing on (R):

1. Propositions asserting Smith's evidence for (R).
2. Propositions asserting Smith's evidence against (R), gained from hearing Jones's case against (R).
3. A factual proposition about misleading evidence, (C).

If at t2 Smith has (1) and (2) as evidence about (R), and has no justification to rely on (C), then it is straightforward that (2) defeats the support of (R) by (1). It is also then straightforward that at t2 Smith is no longer justified in believing (R).

At least until t2, Smith knows (C) by deriving it using (R). Closure principles like (K) imply this, and in any event it seems clear that Smith knows (C) during this phase of our example. It is straightforward that if Smith has continuing knowledge of (C) at t2, then this would entitle Smith at t2 to reject (2) as misleading. If he can legitimately continue to rely on (C) and use it to reject (2), then there is no obstacle to Smith's continuing to know (R) at t2.

(E) on its own does not decide between these alternatives. It could not do so, because it does not say what anyone's evidence is at any time. In particular, (E) does not imply that at t2 Smith's evidence sufficiently supports (C). We have it in the story that Smith did have such evidence until t2. But (E) does not tell us whether or not he still does. So (E) on its own does not account for why it is (2) rather than (C) that can serve as evidence for Smith at t2.

There are two contrary possibilities. One is suggested by our initial formulation of the current issue in terms of Smith's evidence. Perhaps (C) itself qualifies as evidence that Smith has at t2. The other possibility is that at t2 Smith has data that justify believing (C). Investigating this second possibility will make short work of the first. So let us first assume that use of (C) against (2) requires having supporting evidence for (C).

The facts of the example limit Smith's evidence for (C) to data that include justification for (R). Without a justified (R) to help to support (C), Smith has no

---

[15] This is my rendition of a question raised by Stewart Cohen (in correspondence) about an evidentialist solution to the puzzle. I am grateful for this question and for the rest of the extensive correspondence.

evidence for (C) or for any other proposition that argues in favor of rejecting evidence that goes against (R). So, if we also have it that (R) is no longer justified to Smith at t2, then we can use (E) and conclude that Smith does not know (C) at t2. (E) tells us that for Smith to have justification for (R) at t2, he must have sufficient supporting evidence for (R). We get no more from (E) on its own.

With one new principle we can go the rest of the way. We should see first that nothing is on the horizon in support of (R) for Smith at t2 except (1) with the help of (C) to fend off (2). Thus, at t2 Smith has supporting evidence for (R), and hence for (C), only if he has the combination of (1) and (3) functioning in defense of (R).

The dependency relations among Smith's reasons show that this cannot happen. The key further epistemic fact is that a proposition cannot be taken for granted in rebuttal to a criticism of it. Putting this naturally, we have the following principle:

A. If D is a reason for S to doubt X at t, then at t S has no refutation of D that relies on the assumption of X.

(A) asserts nothing more ambitious than a denial of epistemic merit to the mere assumption of a criticized proposition in rebuttal to the criticism. Viewing the matter from the present evidentialist perspective, a reasonably criticized proposition is one against which evidence has been presented. In the present view, the only thing that can help to justify without having its own evidential support is the evidence itself. A proposition such as (C) is not evidence for itself, and we are now assuming that it is not itself evidence. So it needs support to refute anything, or otherwise to function as an epistemic reason. If it is merely assumed or otherwise ultimately relied on, it does not help to justify any thought.

A rejection by Smith at t2 of the force of (2) against (R) would require a violation of (A). A complication might obscure this fact. In this case the target of the criticism, (R), would not be part of the rebuttal itself. (C) would be playing that role. But (C) can be made reasonable for Smith to use to infer the misleading character of (2) at t2 only if (C) is supported. Once again, (C) can be supported for Smith only by a derivation from (R). And this is a derivation by which (R) would *acquire* support, which is otherwise lacking. So (R) would have to be merely assumed in this derivation. Thus, (R) would have to be taken for granted in order to support something else, (C), which would in turn rebut (2), the objection to (R). It is clear that this cannot work. Once a proposition has been reasonably called into doubt, it cannot be merely assumed in order to back up another one in an otherwise unsupported reply. So on the supposition that (C) is not itself evidence for Smith at t2, we see that he cannot use (C) at t2 in support of (R).

We can see that (A) also quickly eliminates our other contrary possibility about the relation of (C) to justifying evidence that Smith has at t2, the possibility that (C) is itself evidence for Smith. At t2 a reasonable objection has been made against (R) to Smith. If (C) were evidence for Smith at that point, then he could simply rely on (C) without further support in order to refute that objection. But (C) is not self-evident. It declares certain evidence misleading. Why should Smith accept it? (C) is unreasonable for Smith to accept in the absence of support, and (R) is Smith's only potential source of such support. As (A) asserts, and manifestly, once (R) has been cast into doubt, wielding (C) against the objection to (R) would not refute the objection. It is better to deny that (C) is evidence and return to the conception of evidence as data, thereby gaining evidentialist grounds for disallowing this violation of (A). Thus, using (A) we can defend the view that (C) is not available to Smith at t2 to argue against the force of (2).[16]

Conclusion

We can be misled out of knowing something. This possibility is not one of the glories of human existence. But it is a fact. It is also a fact that we cannot insulate ourselves from being thus misled by inferring from a known truth that evidence against it is evidence against a truth. That inference, though impeccable, turns out not to do us any good when we need it. This lack of insulation is not a joyous fact, either. But it is another way that things are.

An evidentially based account explains how all of this can be. We are in no position to disregard evidence when it goes strongly against something that we knew, because we have nothing beyond our evidence as our fundamental epistemic basis for disregarding as well as for knowing. When serious doubts arise, there is nothing better that we can do for the sake of knowing than to keep investigating. Fortunately, further inquiry has frequently overcome deception and rarely made things worse. Induction from this fact is encouraging.[17]

---

[16] This explanation relies on an asymmetric epistemic dependency relation among reasons. To account for the justification to Smith, at t2 of (2), rather than (3), the explanation uses the fact that (3) depends on (R) in a way that (R) does not depend on (3). A coherentist who denies the existence of such asymmetric support relations (or denies their justificatory relevance) seems unable to account for the fact that it is the members of the combination—(1), (2), not-(3), and not-(R)—that are justified for Smith at t2. Ignoring this dependency appears to leave no good reason to deny that Smith would be equally reasonable in believing at t2 the propositions—(R), (1), (3) and not-(2). Since in fact this would be an unreasonable refusal to defer to compelling counter-evidence, an inability to account for this constitutes an objection to any such form of coherentism.

[17] I am grateful to James Cargile, Stewart Cohen, Richard Feldman, epistemology discussion group participants at Brown University, and colloquium participants at UC Davis for helpful comments on previous drafts of this work.

12

Making Sense of Skepticism
Richard Feldman and Earl Conee

This paper compares the way evidentialist and non-evidentialist theories deal with skepticism. We first formulate several familiar arguments for skepticism and then argue that non-evidentialist theories of knowledge and justification fail to engage the considerations that underlie these arguments. In contrast, an evidentialist approach to the justification that is required for knowledge best facilitates an appreciation of skeptical arguments. In the final section of the paper we propose an evidentialist theory of knowledge-level justification that enables us to explain both the credibility and the failure of the skeptical arguments.

1. Arguments for Skepticism[1]

The following four arguments are designed to represent the main classic defenses of external world skepticism.[2]

The Possibility of Error Argument (PE)

1. Any belief about the external world could be mistaken.
2. If a belief could be mistaken, then it is not knowledge.

3. Therefore, no belief about the external world is knowledge. (1), (2)

---

[1] Some parts of this section, the next one, and the final one are heavily revised versions of material originally appearing in chapters 6 and 7 of Richard Feldman, *Epistemology* (Englewood Cliffs, NJ: Prentice-Hall, 2003).

[2] We include as "beliefs about the external world" only contingent propositions implying the existence of an external world. Perhaps a belief such as what one expresses by "I exist" or the belief that either it is the case that there is water or it is not the case that there is water cannot be mistaken. But they do not count for present purposes as beliefs about the external world.

(PE) summarizes familiar arguments based on skeptical scenarios. These arguments support premise (1) in the following way. No one has what Descartes termed "certain indications" to distinguish dreams from reality. Anyone could be a victim of an evil demon, a brain in a vat, or the like. So any external world belief could be mistaken. Premise (2) reflects something about the standards for knowledge. We shall return to it later.

(PE) also encapsulates another traditional skeptical argument, the Argument from Illusion. That argument begins with the thought that illusions sometimes fool people about the external world. The argument continues with the claim that illusion is always possible. The conclusion inferred is that no one knows anything about the external world. Like (PE), this reasoning focuses on a possibility of error. In the Argument from Illusion, the error would stem from deceptive perceptual experiences. We will accommodate this feature of the Argument from Illusion when we discuss (PE) below, concentrating on errors that are possible while we have the same basis for belief.

A second argument for skepticism turns on the introspective indistinguishability of any case of true external world belief from some possible cases of false belief. Fallibilist views about knowledge and justification imply that one can have knowledge on the basis of justification that does not entail the known proposition. Presumably, the fundamental basis for external world justification is perceptual experience. There are pairs of possible cases in which someone believes the same external world proposition and things seem the same to the person, yet in one case the proposition is true and in the other it is false. This implies that if one can have external world knowledge on the basis of perceptual experience, then a case in which one has the knowledge can be introspectively the same as a case in which one lacks the knowledge. Our second skeptical argument contends that the consequent of this conditional is false, and so there cannot be such knowledge.

The Introspective Indistinguishability Argument (II)

1. If anyone has knowledge of the external world on the basis of experience, then there can be cases of knowledge that are introspectively indistinguishable from cases of false belief.
2. There cannot be cases of knowledge that are introspectively indistinguishable from cases of false belief.
3. No one has knowledge of the external world on the basis of experience. (1), (2)

4. If anyone has knowledge of the external world, it is on the basis of experience.

5. No one has knowledge of the external world. (3), (4)

(II) also summarizes a traditional skeptical argument, the Argument from Appearance. That argument proceeds from the premise that people have direct awareness of how external things appear to be, and not of how they really are. The argument adds that appearances might be misleading. The inference drawn is that no one has knowledge of the external world. This traditional concern about a possibility of misleading appearances is captured by the possibility that (II) describes of false beliefs with no introspectable difference from true beliefs.

The Transmissibility Argument is a third argument for skepticism. The gist of the argument is this: ordinary beliefs about the external world imply that the skeptical scenarios are false. If one had knowledge in the ordinary cases, and realized that this implication holds, then one could deduce, and thus know, that the skeptical scenarios are false. But, according to the argument, no one knows that the skeptical scenarios are false. So it must be that no one knows the ordinary propositions from which the falsity of the skeptical scenarios could be inferred.

To formulate this argument efficiently, we will let (O) be any ordinary external world proposition that we would typically claim to know and let (SK) be any skeptical hypothesis inconsistent with (O). (O) will then imply that (SK) is false. Let S be any ordinary person who knows that (O) implies that (SK) is false.

The Transmissibility Argument (TK)

1. S cannot know that (SK) is false.
2. (O) implies that (SK) is false, and S knows this.
3. If S knows that (O) is true, and that (O) implies that (SK) is false, then S can know that (SK) is false.

4. S does not know (O). (1)–(3)

One other skeptical argument deserves separate discussion. It relies on the idea that experiential evidence gives no better reason to accept a commonsense view of the world than to accept alternative hypotheses such as that one is dreaming (DR), that one is a brain in a vat (BIV), or that one is deceived by an evil demon (ED). The lack of a better reason to believe a commonsense view is claimed to imply a lack of justification, and hence a lack of knowledge.

The Alternative Hypotheses Argument (AH)

1. The experiences people have provide no better reason to believe ordinary external world propositions than rival skeptical hypotheses, such as (DR), (BIV), and (ED).
2. If experiences do not provide better reason to believe one external world hypothesis than to believe another, then people are not justified in believing the one.

3. People are not justified (and thus do not know) ordinary external world propositions. (1)–(2)

II. Non-Evidentialist Theories

In this section we will briefly describe five non-evidentialist theories of knowledge and justification. Since our goal here is to examine the kinds of resources that these theories make available for dealing with skepticism, we will not present detailed versions.

One of the first non-evidentialist theories to gain widespread recent attention is the causal theory. The basic idea is that one has knowledge when one's belief is causally connected to the facts in the right way. An initial formulation is:

C. S knows p iff S's belief in p is caused by the fact p.

There are cases involving deviant causal chains and bizarre causal links between facts and beliefs in those facts. Such cases prompted a leading defender of the causal theory, Alvin Goldman, to replace (C) with:

C*. S knows p if and only if the fact p is causally connected in an appropriate way with S's believing p.[3]

For present purposes it is not necessary to discuss in detail what counts as an appropriate connection. It will suffice to note that ordinary perception, memory, introspection, and reasoning are among the leading candidates.

The second non-evidentialist theory is the tracking theory. It holds that one has knowledge of a proposition provided one's belief in that proposition tracks the truth of that proposition:

TT. S knows p iff (1) p is true, (2) S believes p, and (3) S's attitude toward p tracks the truth-value of p: if p were not true, then S would not believe p; and if p were true, then S would believe p.

---

[3] "A Causal Theory of Knowing," *Journal of Philosophy*, 64 (1967), 357–72; see p. 369.

Some counterexamples to (TT) involve people who would use a crucially different method to determine what to believe about P, if P were not true. Such examples prompted a leading defender of this theory, Robert Nozick, to propose the following modified version:

TT*. S knows p iff (1) p is true, (2) S believes p, (3) there is a belief forming method M that S used to form the belief in p and (4) when S uses method M to form beliefs about p, S's beliefs about p track the truth of p.[4]

A third non-evidentialist theory is reliabilism. Reliabilism has been developed both as a theory of justification and as a theory of knowledge that omits any justification condition. These differences will not affect the points to be discussed below, and it is slightly simpler to proceed in terms of reliabilist theories of knowledge. In its simplest form, reliabilism is the view that:

R. S knows p iff S's true belief in p results from a reliable belief-forming process.[5]

Reliable belief-forming processes are processes that generally lead to true beliefs.[6] Details about how reliability is measured will not affect the discussion that follows.

A fourth non-evidentialist theory is the proper function theory, championed by Alvin Plantinga.[7] The central idea is:

PF. S knows p iff S's true belief in p results from the proper functioning of S's cognitive system.

A variety of problem cases have led Plantinga to propose that knowledge requires warranted belief, where warrant is something closer to the following:

PF*. A belief is warranted iff (1) it results from the proper functioning of the believer's cognitive system in a suitable environment, (2) the segment of the system that produced the belief is aimed at the truth, and (3) the overall system usually produces true beliefs when it is in a suitable environment.[8]

---

[4] *Philosophical Explanations* (Cambridge, Mass.: Harvard University Press, 1981), 179.
[5] There are a number of bells and whistles that can be introduced into reliabilism. One can add what amounts to a "no-defeaters" clause, holding that one has knowledge only if there is no reliable process that would lead S not to believe p. One could also introduce the distinction between reliable and conditionally reliable belief-forming processes. (See Alvin Goldman, "What is Justified Belief?", in George S. Pappas (ed.), *Justification and Knowledge* (Dordrecht: D. Reidel, 1979), 1–24.) These modifications will not matter in what follows, and we will ignore them here.
[6] See "The Generality Problem for Reliabilism" (Ch. 6) for problems about the bearers of reliability.
[7] See *Warrant and Proper Function* (Oxford: Oxford University Press, 1993).   [8] Ibid. 46–7.

Finally, there is the idea that it is the "safety" of a true belief that makes it knowledge. Ernest Sosa is the leading proponent of this sort of theory.[9] Very roughly, a true belief is safe provided that it is unlikely to be falsely held. Consider, for example, a typical person's belief that he sees a tree. It is quite plausible that this belief is safe, since ordinarily, it would take the sight of a tree for an ordinary person to believe that he sees a tree. Since beliefs in metaphysical and logical truths, as well as laws of nature, may satisfy this condition without being cases of knowledge, Sosa adds an additional condition for knowledge. In one place he suggests:

S. S knows p iff (1) p is true, (2) S's belief in p is safe, and (3) S's belief in p results from a virtuous intellectual method.[10]

III. Contextualism

Non-evidentialist theories of knowledge are often combined with contextualism in an effort to respond to skepticism. Contemporary contextualism in epistemology is primarily a metalinguistic thesis about "knowledge" and its cognates. The contextualist view is that the truth conditions for attributions of "knowledge" vary with the context of the attributer.[11] The capacity of contextualism to deal with skeptical arguments is often cited as one of its principal assets. Typically, contextualists hold that something about contexts in which skeptical arguments are prominent makes true the skeptic's denials of external world "knowledge" attributions, while something about ordinary contexts makes true many ordinary external world "knowledge" attributions.[12]

In what follows we will focus on non-contextualist versions of the non-evidentialist theories discussed in section II. We will argue that these theories do not make sense of skepticism, since they do not make clear why anyone would even be tempted by the arguments for skepticism. Yet people routinely do

---

[9] See "Tracking, Competence, and Knowledge", in Paul K. Moser (ed.), *The Oxford Handbook of Epistemology* (Oxford: Oxford University Press, 2002), 264–86.   [10] Ibid. 275.

[11] Three influential sources are Stewart Cohen, "Contextualism, Skepticism, and the Structure of Reasons", *Philosophical Perspectives*, 13 (1999), 57–89; Keith DeRose, "Solving the Skeptical Problem", *Philosophical Review*, 104 (1995), 1–52; and David Lewis, "Elusive Knowledge", *Australasian Journal of Philosophy*, 74 (1996), 549–67. Cohen defends an evidentialist view, but DeRose and Lewis do not. More recently, Ram Neta has defended a contextualist view about what evidence counts toward justification, in "Contextualism and the Problem of the External World", *Philosophy and Phenomenological Research*, 66/1 (2003), 1–31.

[12] Contextualists can defend an evidentialist theory of knowledge. Those who do can largely agree with the explanation we offer in section VI of why we often satisfy the conditions for knowledge in place in ordinary contexts.

Making Sense of Skepticism

find skeptical arguments tempting. Contextualist versions of these theories offer an explanation. Again, the idea is that in contexts where skepticism is prominent, the truth conditions for "knowledge" attributions are so demanding that ordinary external world beliefs do not meet them. This goes too far. As one of us has argued elsewhere,[13] this is an unwarranted concession to skepticism. The reasons for thinking that skeptics are right when someone is paying attention either to skepticism or to an argument for it are no better than the reasons for thinking that skeptics are right when no one is paying attention to any such thing. Furthermore, external world skepticism can be refuted. As with all enduring disputed positions in philosophy, the skeptical side has been defended with some plausibility. As with the other enduring disputes, there is no need to endorse the conclusions of both sides to make sense of the debate. When all of the arguments for one side can be given their due while denying that any of them is sound, it is most reasonable not to accept that side's conclusion. An evidentialist theory of knowledge can do this for skepticism. That done, there is no good reason also to interpret the skeptic's conclusion so that it says something true, as contextualists do.

Invariantists deny that "knowledge" attributions have contextually varying truth conditions. Our goal here is to argue that invariantist evidentialist theories of knowledge are much better equipped than are the recent non-evidential theories to appreciate the challenge of external world skepticism, and to reply to that challenge. Invariantist evidentialist theories are not only better equipped, they are so well equipped that no explanatory work about skepticism remains for contextualism to accomplish. Invariantist evidentialism provides a fully reasonable assessment of skepticism.[14] By defending all of this, we are not establishing that contextualism is incorrect. We are showing something about what can be done without it.

IV. Non-Evidentialist Theories and Skepticism

Each of the non-evidentialist theories described in section II provides the basis for simple responses to the skeptical arguments.[15] We will briefly describe each of these responses, and then consider some of the issues that arise in assessing

---

[13] Richard Feldman, "Skeptical Problems, Contextualist Solutions", *Philosophical Studies*, 103 (2001), 61–85.

[14] This is not to say that our version of invariantist evidentialism has all the answers. We leave open important issues. But they are not ones where contextualism holds promise.

[15] Defenders of these non-evidentialist theories who also endorse contextualism will say that the responses described in the remainder of this section apply only to attributions of "knowledge" in ordinary contexts. Defenders of these theories who do not endorse contextualism would say that the responses apply to all contexts.

them. We will then turn to a general assessment of the merits of these responses to the arguments. It is worth noting at the outset that evidentialists are likely to agree with non-evidentialists about which premises of these arguments are mistaken. The disagreements concern the reasons for their falsity.

Consider first (PE). All of us will concede that, in some relevant sense, each external world belief could be mistaken. Non-skeptics will, however, contest the other premise:

2. If a belief could be mistaken, then it is not knowledge.

The phrase "could be mistaken" is susceptible to a number of interpretations. According to one, a belief could be mistaken provided it is possible for the belief to be falsely held. Virtually all beliefs in contingent propositions could be mistaken in this sense. This possibility seems just irrelevant to whether the proposition is ever believed under conditions that yield knowledge. It is difficult to see why anyone would accept (2) when it is interpreted in this way.

According to a better interpretation of (2), its antecedent says that it is possible for the belief to be false while holding fixed epistemically relevant aspects of the circumstances. The central idea is that it is possible for the belief to be false while it is believed on its actual basis. Thus, for example, one's belief about what color one is seeing "could be mistaken," if it is possible for that belief to be false when it is held on the basis of the visual experiences, background information about color classifications, and whatever else one uses to determine the color. We will make use of this interpretation of (2) in the remainder of this discussion.

Causal theorists can say that even though a belief on the same basis could have been mistaken, it may actually have the right sort of causal connection to the facts. Tracking theorists can say that it is consistent with this sort of possibility of error that people actually track the truth of the proposition. Reliabilists will be quick to point out that beliefs formed on any given internal basis could be false while caused by reliable processes. Proper function theorists will respond that a belief that results from a properly functioning cognitive system could have been false even if held on the same basis. A safety theorist will observe that a safe method of adopting a true belief need preserve truth only among the sufficiently likely possibilities. This allows for the possibility of false belief using the same virtuous method. Thus, defenders of all these theories will dismiss (2) as obviously false. Knowledge as they characterize it is plainly compatible with the possibility of error.

The initial appeal of the skeptical argument (PE) remains to be understood, however. In particular, there is significant credibility in some thought to the effect that we do not know anything about which we could be mistaken. On its current interpretation, the thought is that one does not know a proposition when it is possible to believe the same proposition falsely on the same basis. This is credible because if one believed the same proposition on the same basis, then things would seem just the same. This duplication of how things seem, accompanied by false belief, appears somehow to undermine the capacity of the basis to give knowledge.

The invariantist versions of the non-evidentialist theories of knowledge neither accommodate this appearance nor explain it away. None of those theories implies a condition for knowledge that is even weakened by the possibility of error on the same basis.[16] None of the theories provides a way to find a plausible error in the impression that this possibility excludes knowledge.[17]

A correct theory of knowledge that is incompatible with premise (2) of (PE) need not readily explain its plausibility. A correct theory need only give some informative account of what knowledge is. However, something about knowledge makes external world skepticism a perennial temptation. It is reasonable to expect that an illuminating account of the conditions that constitute knowledge will shed light on sources of that temptation.

This is a strength that evidentialist theories have. They make the bearing on knowledge of the skeptic's possibility easy to see. Any known proposition must be adequately supported by the person's evidence. It is at least initially credible that the possibility of being a basis for a false belief is a flaw in the evidence. It is clearly reasonable to suspect that justification constituted by flawed evidence is not adequate for knowledge.

It can be acknowledged by evidentialist theorists that this fallibility is an imperfection in the evidence. So the skeptic need not be wrong that the

---

[16] A broadly reliabilist explanation of the credibility of the premise might be attempted. It would have to use a notion of reliability very different from the one employed by reliability theorists. Perhaps the possibility of error shows that the process used is not necessarily completely reliable. This affects how reliable the process is only if accuracy in remote non-actual cases affects the measure of reliability. It is possible for a reliabilist to claim that the plausibility of (PE) derives from assuming wrongly that all possibilities for a process affect its reliability. It is contrary to the spirit of reliabilist theories to allow such factors to affect measures of reliability. Reliabilists emphasize contingent reliability as what is crucial. So anyone who would count such remote factors toward reliability is using something that does not resemble a standard reliabilist condition on knowledge. (We thank John Bennett for his comments on this topic.)

[17] As noted earlier, some contextualists contend that attributions of external world "knowledge" are almost always false in contexts in which skeptical arguments are discussed. Thus, they do not reject (2). For example, Lewis, in "Elusive Knowledge", held that knowledge is not compatible with the possibility of error. However, he claimed that what possibilities there are varies with context. Discussion of skepticism expands the set of possibilities. On his view, then, there is no error, hence no plausible error, in the view that knowledge is incompatible with the possibility of error. Relative to ordinary contexts, in his view, (1) of (PE) is mistaken.

justification has a kind of weakness. The task of opposing (PE) by using an evidential theory is to explain how the evidence manages nonetheless to be adequate for knowledge. In contrast, defenders of invariantist non-evidential theories get no help from their theories in constructing an account of why the possibility of error might even be thought to bear on whether one has knowledge.

Consider next (II). Here non-evidentialists usually object to its second premise:

2. There cannot be cases of knowledge that are introspectively indistinguishable from cases of false belief.

Their reasons for rejecting (2) are almost identical to their reasons for rejecting the disputed premise of (PE). There need not be any introspectable difference between cases in which the right causal connection is present and cases in which it is not. Similarly, cases in which someone tracks the truth, believes as a result of a reliable process, functions properly, or has safe beliefs, can be indistinguishable from cases in which the person does not do these things.

Again, the initial force of the argument is not accounted for. Why would it be thought for a moment that knowledge is excluded by the fact that introspection finds no difference, if knowledge turns on proper causal connection, or truth tracking, or reliably caused belief, or a properly functioning belief-producing mechanism, or safety? The findings of introspection under very different possible circumstances where the belief is false would have no discernible relevance. The skeptic might as well have proclaimed that someone knows that something is true only if the person is the sole cause of its truth. This idea has nothing going for it from the start. We would not expect a satisfactory theory of knowledge to accommodate this idea or to show the reasonable mistake in it. By contrast, the absence of an introspectable difference between the actual case and a possible case of false belief does seem at least threatening to knowledge. Non-evidentialist theories do not help us to understand why.

If what introspection reveals is one's fundamental evidence, or at least a crucial portion of it for external world propositions, then it is no wonder that it matters to knowledge which possibilities introspection allows. If evidence determines justification, then it is no wonder that allowing the falsehood of the belief renders suspect the strength of the justification. Even if non-entailing evidence is enough for knowledge, the skeptic seems to be on to something.

Consider next (AH). All non-evidentialist theories will happily reject premise (2):[18]

2. If experiences do not provide better reason to believe one external world hypothesis than to believe another, then people are not justified in believing the one.

There can be causal connections, truth tracking, reliable belief formation, proper function, and safety, in the absence of better reasons for a hypothesis. Details may matter. We can imagine defenders of the skeptical argument contending that proper function requires evidential support of the sort described in the argument. However, there is plausibility to the claim that people are designed to believe certain propositions even if experience does not provide reasons to believe those propositions. In any case, it is clear that there is no necessary connection between this sort of support by reasons and proper function. So if the proper function theory is correct, then this premise could easily have been false.

Once again, these theories leave us in the dark about the rational attraction of the argument. The comparative strength of one's reasons for accepting ordinary propositions about the world is given no relevance. Yet it seems clearly requisite to knowing about the external world that one's beliefs about it are supported by adequately good reasons. At a minimum, if some extraordinary skeptical possibility is equally reasonable in the presence of ordinary experiences, then people seem to have at best weak reason to accept ordinary thinking on the topic. Having at best weak reason seems to exclude knowing.

Christopher Hill has argued that reliabilists can make good sense of the appeal of an argument like (AH).[19] Our premise (2) spells out the idea that the justification of our external world beliefs requires that one's experiences give better reasons to accept those beliefs than to accept the skeptic's alternatives. Hill's formulation includes a similar premise:

2*. In determining whether a person is justified in believing ordinary external world propositions rather than the skeptical alternatives, it is appropriate to set all non-sensory evidence aside, and to focus exclusively on facts involving the person's sense experiences and their purely sensory characteristics.[20]

---

[18] Or they will happily deny that knowledge requires justification. Either way, the same explanatory weaknesses arise.

[19] In "Process Reliabilism and Cartesian Skepticism", *Philosophy and Phenomenological Research*, 56 (1996), 567–81; reprinted in Keith DeRose and Ted A. Warfield (eds.), *Skepticism: A Contemporary Reader* (Oxford: Oxford University Press, 1999), 115–28.

[20] We have reworded Hill's premise slightly. As Hill understands (2*), considerations of explanatory power or other "superempirical virtues" are set aside. Only the purely sensory characteristics of experiences have any bearing on justification. Hill acknowledges that some philosophers may think

Hill's central contention is that the appeal of (2*) results from conflating the plausible claim

A. If one wishes to determine whether a person is justified in preferring the real world hypothesis to the skeptical alternatives, it is permissible to set all of the person's extramental evidence aside, and focus exclusively on the person's sensory evidence

with the less plausible claim

B. If one wishes to determine whether a person is justified in preferring the real world hypothesis to the skeptical alternatives, it is appropriate to set all of the person's non-sensory evidence aside, and focus exclusively on facts involving the person's sensory experiences and their purely sensory characteristics.

Both (A) and (B) restrict evidence to sensory experiences. (B) further restricts evidential considerations to facts involving sensory characteristics. (A), by contrast, allows consideration of all facts of any sort about sensory evidence, including the reliability of its connection to the truth of external world propositions. One reason why the skeptical argument is supposed to seem compelling, then, is that philosophers slip easily from (A) to (B).

Hill says that "to do full justice to the seductiveness"[21] of the skeptical argument, a deeper explanation is needed. We agree. Conflating (A) and (B) would explain at most the appeal of just those skeptical arguments that turn on which features of experience provide external world evidence. We do not see that any such conflation is needed to find (2*) plausible. But in any case, not all similar skeptical arguments employ anything like (2*). Indeed, our (AH) is not so formulated, and it is difficult to see how anything like (A) and (B) are helpful when applied to (AH). In order to make the corresponding point about (AH), one would have to hold that the quality of the reasons that experience provides for external world beliefs is subject to the counterpart confusion. This would be a confusion about which features of experience are relevant to our reasons. We see no credibility in that suggestion. It is plausible that brains in vats can have the same reasons for their beliefs as those that any ordinary person has, and it is not plausible that their reasons must differ because their beliefs are mostly untrue. There are no good grounds to think that the appeal of (AH) depends on conflating propositions along the lines of (A) and (B).

---

that this restriction "limits the plausibility of the argument", but he chooses to discuss an argument with this premise nevertheless (ibid. 118). His view about what goes wrong with the premise in his argument can be applied to our own formulation of the argument, so we will not discuss further the restriction he imposes.

[21] Ibid. 122–3.

Making Sense of Skepticism

Hill offers a second reliabilist-friendly explanation of the appeal of skepticism. He says that people have two conceptions of evidential support. One of them is an internalist notion, and the other is an externalist notion.[22] According to the externalist concept, an experience provides evidential support for a belief provided there is a reliable cognitive process that begins with the experience and yields the belief. According to the internalist concept, evidential support is understood in terms of influence on subjective probabilities. Since purely sensory features of sense experiences can influence the strength of beliefs about the external world, on this conception they can be evidence for external world propositions. Since brains in vats or victims of deceptive demons adjust their subjective probabilities in light of experiences in just the way in which normal people do, their experiences have the same (internalist) evidential value as the experiences of normal people. But the reliable connections differ, so their experiences do not have the same (externalist) evidential value as the experiences of normal people. In Hill's view, since it is the externalist evidential value that is actually crucial for knowledge, the skeptic's argument fails. Hill says that there is a tendency to confuse these two conceptions of evidential support, and this explains the appeal of the skeptical argument to non-skeptics.

Granting for the sake of argument that there are these two concepts of evidential support,[23] we find here no explanation of the appeal of the skeptical argument. Presumably, the appeal is supposed to derive from our considering the argument while thinking of the internalist notion of evidential support, subjective probability. (The argument obviously has no appeal while thinking of the externalist notion.) However, using the internalist notion, the argument is distinctly unappealing. Both ordinary people and their envatted counterparts find themselves strongly inclined to believe the ordinary external world propositions on the basis of their sensory experiences. None of them has any inclination to believe skeptical hypotheses on the basis of their experiences. Hence, if people were using the internalist notion in thinking about skeptical arguments, they would conclude that the experiences provide vastly better evidential support for ordinary external world beliefs than for skeptical hypotheses. So the skeptical

---

[22] Hill says that this second explanation somehow accounts for the tendency to conflate (A) and (B). We doubt that the existence of two notions of the evidential support relation (the second explanation) can explain a tendency to conflate two accounts of what the evidence is (the first explanation).

[23] We doubt that these are pre-theoretical conceptions of evidential support. In our view, the proposed internalist conception of evidence is an implausible psychological reduction of the relation of evidential support, and the externalist conception is a reliabilist's invention.

argument would obviously fail.[24] This distinction, then, does not help to explain the appeal of skeptical arguments.

What does explain the appeal of skeptical arguments such as (AH), we think, is a reason for thinking that experiential evidence is at best neutral concerning the choice between the competing explanations. The reason is that the explanations all entail the experiential data, and the usual standards for evaluating explanations like simplicity and comprehensiveness do not obviously favor ordinary beliefs.

Once more, evidentialist theories of knowledge at least make sense of the concern. It is initially credible that experience is the ultimate evidence for the nature of the external world. It is initially credible that experiential evidence provides better reason to believe ordinary external world propositions than the skeptical alternatives. If, instead, one's experiential evidence really is at least equally good reason to accept some extraordinary contrary view of the external world, then one's reasons for ordinary thought are correspondingly weak. Philosophical reflection on the alternatives reveals that it is at least not obvious that standard explanations of experience are better explanations. After all, various skeptical scenarios account for all of the experiential data in one way or another, usually with a much leaner ontology. This clearly threatens the capacity of one's experiences to justify ordinary external world beliefs and thus, according to evidential theories, one's ability to have knowledge of the external world.

Even if this threat can be overcome by an evidentialist account of justification, the evidentialist approach faces a challenge. The skeptic has identified something that needs explaining away. A full evidential theory must say how ordinary thinking is best supported by experience. As will be discussed below, we think that when external world skepticism is properly appreciated, accomplishing this explanatory task is the major challenge that such skepticism poses.

Matters become somewhat more complex in the case of (TK). Unlike the other arguments for skepticism considered here, (TK) has a premise that simply asserts a denial of some external world knowledge:

1. S cannot know that (SK) is false.

By contrast, the other arguments derive denials of knowledge from other factors, such as the possibility of error. Of course, things could be said in support of (1), but they are likely to be along the lines of the considerations put forward in the other arguments. (TK) seems to us, therefore, to be a derivative argument and not in need of independent assessment. This, however, runs counter to recent discussions of skepticism, in which (TK) has figured prominently.

---

[24] This point would apply equally well to any less reductive notion of probability that also plainly turns on an internal condition like degree of belief.

Making Sense of Skepticism

In any case, many non-evidentialist theorists will confidently reject (1). Perhaps causal theorists will say that there is an appropriate causal connection between the fact that you are not a brain in a vat and your belief that you are not a brain in a vat. Exactly how this works is not entirely clear, since the causal consequences of one's *not* being a brain in a vat are difficult to discern. But whatever difficulty the causal theory has with this example carries over to beliefs that have no special connection to skeptical issues. One may know that one is not a professional pole-vaulter. Perhaps the fact that one is not a professional pole-vaulter is a cause of this belief, though it is difficult to identify any role that a negative fact like that might have played in causing one's belief. Presumably, the causal theory can be developed in some way that deals with this example, and it will similarly yield the desired result with respect to premise (1) of (TK).

Proper function theory will most likely be developed to yield the result that one's cognitive system is functioning properly when one believes that one is not a brain in a vat. Again, it is not entirely clear why this is true. A typical basis for denying a vat hypothesis would be that it just seems absurd. Though this impression may be a result of properly functioning cognitive mechanisms, it is doubtful that it is a basis for knowing. The idea of proper function is sufficiently obscure to allow a variety of interpretations, at least as it applies to this case. For instance, the evidentially supported acceptance of this belief that we describe in section VI below can be regarded as a proper functioning of our cognitive system.

Details about the formulation of reliabilism will make a difference in its implications concerning (TK). Exactly what processes produce one's belief that one is not a brain in a vat is unclear.[25] We can assume that the belief is true, and that it results from some inferential process involved in the formation of general beliefs about one's place in the world. Perhaps it is a reliable process. Similarly, one's belief that one is not a brain in a vat is safe—one would not easily be wrong about that—and, presumably, it results from a virtuous process. Thus, defenders of all these non-evidentialist theories will reject (1).

The tracking theory was designed in part to provide a different response to the argument than those so far considered. Apparently, many tracksters are convinced that the first premise is true, and thus are motivated to find some other way to avoid the skeptical conclusion. This leads them to deny closure principles, represented in our formulation by premise (3):

3. If S knows that (O) is true, and that (O) implies that (SK) is false, then S can know that (SK) is false.

---

[25] For extensive discussion, see "The Generality Problem for Reliabilism", [Ch. 6 in this volume].

Richard Feldman and Earl Conee

The idea is that people do track ordinary truths but not the denials of skeptical hypotheses. You track the proposition that you have hands, but not the proposition that you are not a handless brain in a vat. You track the former because if it were not true, you would not believe it. But, it is said, if the proposition that you are not a handless brain in a vat were not true, you would still believe it (because you would be the victim of a deceit).

Thus, the tracking theory is supposed to support (1) and deny (3) of (TK).[26] Whether it actually has these results is questionable. What implication the theory has concerning (1) depends in an odd way upon details of the believer's situation. This is partly because there is a generality problem for methods of belief formation.[27] If anything is naturally regarded as the typical method of forming the belief that one is not a brain in a vat ("BIV"), it is something with a fairly broad range of application. It is plausible that one forms the belief because its negation seems absurd. Another possibility is that the process involves seeing how well the belief fits one's well-justified background beliefs. Applied to this case, the method would be something roughly like this: one's noticing the fit (in this case, the lack of fit) between the skeptical possibility and anything approximating the general view of the world incorporated in one's background beliefs about one's situation that one has good reason to accept, while having no positive reason to think that the skeptical possibility is actual.

If the typical method of believing that one is not a BIV is anything like this, then it is at most contingent that the belief fails to track the truth when one uses this method. It might be that the fact about the conditions under which one would have been a BIV, were this to happen, is that one would have been an informed beneficiary of an emergency brain extraction made possible by future medical progress. This seems considerably more realistic than the deceptive envatments that are the stuff of skeptical scenarios. If so, then one would have possessed that background information while envatted. Had one used the same broad "method" of testing the fit of the BIV possibility with justified background beliefs, then in light of one's background knowledge of the medical procedure, one would *not* believe that one was not a BIV. So on these assumptions, the belief *does* track the truth. On the other hand, the belief does not track the truth if one would have been a deceived BIV, were one a BIV.

---

[26] Not all versions of the tracking theory have the same implications. Contextualist versions of the theory hold that whether one has knowledge depends upon whether one tracks the believed proposition through the contextually determined worlds. If worlds in which one is a brain in a vat are not relevant in ordinary contexts, then perhaps this sort of tracking theory will also reject premise (1) and accept (3).

[27] Considerations such as those advanced in "The Generality Problem for Reliabilism" also apply to versions of the tracking theory that appeal to methods of belief formation.

Making Sense of Skepticism

Knowledge that one is not a BIV does not appear to turn on the relative likelihood of these two possibilities. It is the sheer possibility of BIV deception that threatens knowledge. So the tracking theory's account of the truth-value of (1) is implausible. And this makes its account of the force of the argument implausible. The trackster's intended explanation, again, is that people mistakenly accept the closure principle.[28] However, given the tracking theory, a person thinking about the argument who thinks she would be an informed BIV should not be moved by the argument. Such a person should reject premise (1). This is not realistic. Again, it is nothing more than the possibility of being a BIV that gives premise (1) such plausibility as it has.

There are also questions about how successful the other theories are in explaining why some people find (1) plausible. We have noted that a causal theory has some trouble in saying exactly why (1) is false. We have also noted that the trouble is not limited to skeptical possibilities like being a BIV. Whatever turns out to be the best causal theory of why one's belief that one is not now on Mars is knowledge, it is likely that the same explanation will apply to all negative location beliefs that are contrary to perceived fact, including the belief that one is not located in a vat. This will leave the intuitive difference unexplained: Why does it seem clear that one knows that one is not on Mars, but significantly less clear that one knows that one is not in a vat?

Reliability theorists would be hard pressed to find something plausibly thought to be unreliable in the case of the belief that one is not a BIV. Other theorists would be equally challenged to find something improper, or unsafe, in the formation of this belief. Thus, they have little to say about why (1) even seems true to anyone.

Non-evidentialist theories, we conclude, do a poor job of explaining the appeal that skeptical arguments clearly do have.

V. Fundamental Epistemological Questions

Our central contention so far has been that evidentialist theories do a much better job than non-evidentialist theories in making sense of skepticism. Knowledge requires good enough supporting evidence, and skeptical considerations at least cast doubt on whether the evidence we have is good enough. Non-evidentialist theories propose conditions on knowledge that are not even jeopardized by skeptical considerations. It is, of course, open to defenders of non-evidentialist theories to say that the reason people find skepticism

---

[28] Of course, we think it is no mistake to accept some form of the principle.

troubling is that they mistakenly think that knowledge requires strong evidence, and thus they mistakenly find significance in considerations that cast doubt on the quality of their evidence. There is, however, little reason to think that people would make this mistake if knowledge were what these theorists say it is. The mistake surely is not the result of philosophical indoctrination, since beginning philosophy students so often find skeptical considerations compelling without prior exposure to evidentialist writings.

Some philosophers find non-evidentialist theories of knowledge attractive, and not simply because of the easy denials of skepticism that they make available. In some cases, the starting point is to see human knowledge as an instance of some more general phenomenon like having a capacity to make various sorts of highly selective responses. That "knows" has some such broad application is suggested by sentences like "The thermostat knows that it is time to turn the heat on" or "The trees know when to shed their leaves." Presumably, there is no implication here that thermostats and trees have evidence. They just respond in some suitable way to their environment. Human cognitive systems facilitate human welfare largely by enabling people to improve their responses. This encourages the view that knowing is just having some such selective response capacity.

We find this view about knowledge ill-motivated. Sentences like those about the thermostat and the trees are not literally true. These uses of "know" serve approximately the same practical function as do plainly non-literal uses of psychological expressions other than "know", such as, "Nature *abhors* a vacuum," and "Water always *seeks* the lowest level."

In any case, this view of "knows" also misses the most challenging questions that skepticism raises. Suppose that the truth conditions for the word "knows" are conceded to some non-evidentialist theory or other. Important philosophical questions raised by skepticism remain to be addressed. How good are our reasons for believing the things ordinarily believed about the external world? Does the possibility of error, the existence of introspectively indistinguishable situations in which our beliefs are false, or the availability of alternative hypotheses consistent with ordinary experience, show that ordinary reasons are not good enough to justify the beliefs? If not, how do the reasons justify? If so, how do the reasons fall short, and how far short do they fall? Either way, what makes a reason any good at all?

These are the fundamental epistemological questions that are raised by the classic skeptical arguments. The traditional skeptical arguments are formulated as arguments about knowledge largely because it is assumed that knowledge requires good reasons. We see no good reason to deny that assumption. If it is jettisoned, the questions do not go away. Instead, they must be formulated more directly as questions about reasons or justification, not as questions about knowledge.

Making Sense of Skepticism

To confront the philosophical issues raised by external world skepticism, then, one must address questions about the quality of our reasons. Traditionally, this has been done by thinking about knowledge. This tradition warrants our continued adherence. Even if the tradition were abandoned, though, the questions that underlie skepticism would not have been thereby resolved. Philosophers would have to restate them as questions about the quality of the ordinary reasons for external world beliefs. Such philosophers would face the unenviable further task of explaining why an extensive tradition wrongly links these issues so closely to knowledge.

VI. Evidentialist Theories and the Skeptical Arguments

The threat of skeptical arguments is best understood as an attack on the sufficiency of the available justification for ordinary external world beliefs. This in turn is best understood as an attack on the sufficiency of the evidence for those beliefs. Taking the threat this way, it is easy to make sense of skepticism. In doing this, it should first be noted that an evidentialist theory of knowledge is not automatically anti-skeptical. For instance, it is open to an evidentialist to hold that one's basic experiential evidence for a proposition must entail it in order for the proposition to be well enough justified to be known.[29] Then arguments like (PE) and (II) can be used to show that no one has evidence that is this good.[30] Thus, one way that an evidentialist theory of knowledge can make sense of the external world skeptic's central concerns is to substantiate the skeptical conclusion.

This is not the best evidentialist position. A fallibilist evidentialist theory enables us to explain how people have external world knowledge and to account for the appeal of external world skepticism.

External world skeptical arguments give non-skeptical evidentialist theories of knowledge two main assignments. A first task is to give an informative account of the strength of evidence that is needed to have knowledge. Having just some slight reason to believe is insufficient, while having entailing basic evidence is not required. The problem is to identify and defend something in

---

[29] We assume that the entailment relation is construed broadly enough to enable experiential evidence to have entailments.

[30] In general, entailing evidence is insufficient for justification. Any evidence entails all necessary truths. So any reasonable evidential theory will impose other conditions on which evidence is good enough evidence for a given proposition, whether entailed by the evidence or not. Whatever these further conditions are, they can only strengthen the grounds for external world skepticism when added to an entailment requirement.

between. The other principal work for an evidentialist theory is to defend the claim that the evidence people have for their external world beliefs often meets this condition. An adequate defense must accept the constant possibility of external world error on the same basis for belief, and grant the introspective indiscernibility of error on the same basis. Those imperfections in the external world evidence should be shown not to make it too weak for knowledge. Also, some explanation must be given of why concerns about transmissibility and the existence of skeptical hypotheses that are compatible with any experience do not show the evidence to be inadequate.

Concerning the first project, we shall make a proposal that allows fallible reasons to justify sufficiently for knowledge. Then we shall explain the failure of the skeptical arguments and defend the view that the evidence people have for many ordinary propositions about the external world is often adequate.

A. Knowledge-Level Justification

We turn first to the project of stating what sort of justification is needed in order to satisfy the justification condition on knowledge. We conceive of the evidential condition on justification along the lines of the legal standard for conviction in criminal cases, proof beyond a reasonable doubt. The legal notion of proof is weaker than a mathematical proof, but stronger than a good reason to believe. We will call it strong reason to believe. A belief is epistemically justified sufficiently for knowledge, according to the "criminal" standard that we endorse, when one has strong reasons in support of it, no undefeated epistemic reason to doubt it, and no undefeated epistemic reason to believe that one's evidence for it is unreliable. We will use the word "defeater" to refer both to reasons to deny a proposition and to reasons to believe that one's evidence for a proposition is unreliable. The criminal standard is fallible, in that false beliefs can satisfy it. It is an evidentialist standard, in that only evidence plays a role in determining whether a belief is justified.

This assertion of the criminal standard for the justification needed for knowledge is brief and abstract. It asserts, without argument, that certainty is not required for knowledge. It joins the non-evidentialist responses to skepticism in not arguing for its fallibilism.[31] It leaves many important questions about strength of evidence unanswered. According to the criminal standard, knowledge requires strong reasons, but the account leaves open exactly how strong those reasons must be. There is no conspicuously correct fact of this matter.

---

[31] While we do not argue directly that fallibilism is true, we offer below an explanation of why the possibility of error does not defeat justification.

Fortunately, no external world skeptical argument turns on the details of the required strength of evidence. In fact, the difficulty in resolving this indefiniteness can help to explain the difficulty in answering some puzzling questions about knowledge that arise independently of worries about skepticism. For instance, it is quite credible that any ordinary person's visual experiences under ordinary conditions provide evidence enough to justify many common classificatory beliefs.[32] For example, when a typical contemporary adult has typical perception of a car, the person has justifying evidence for the belief that he or she sees a car, and for some beliefs about its color and shape. These are features that it seems people can "just see." But unless one happens to know more than usual about cars, it does not justify precise propositions about the car's weight or age. Why?

The difficulty in resolving this sort of question is an asset of the view. It helps to explain some reasonable disagreements in this area to assume that people are tacitly guided in knowledge attributions by something like our conception of the justification required. For instance, doubts about the identity of what one "just sees," the propositions that are thereby evidentially supported, and the strength of evidence provided, help to account for disputes about what one knows by looking, disputes that intensify when the stakes rise for accuracy.

There is also plenty of room for reasonable dispute among non-skeptics about the extent of testimonial knowledge. For instance, it is not at all clear when testimonial evidence in support of a conclusion is sufficient (in the absence of any reasonable doubt) to satisfy the justification condition on knowledge. Does the believer need evidence of the reliability of the source about the topic of the testimony? Again, the openness of our proposal is an asset, since the extent of testimonial knowledge is likewise not at all clear.

B. The Justification of External World Beliefs

We turn next to the second project. According to our criminal standard, knowledge-level justification requires three things: (1) strong supporting evidence, (2) the absence of undefeated reasons to doubt, and (3) the absence of undefeated reasons to think that one's evidence is unreliable. The goal now is to defend the claim that ordinary beliefs often meet this standard. We will do this largely by showing why the skeptical arguments do not prove otherwise.

---

[32] This is not to say that the perception is by itself sufficient evidence. Background evidence may be required.

It will be useful in the following discussion to treat separately two positions skeptics might defend. According to the first, ordinary experiential evidence is acknowledged to provide better reason to believe ordinary world propositions than to believe skeptical alternatives, but the skeptical possibilities are defeaters for these propositions. So the evidence is strong enough, but defeated, and condition (2) or condition (3) is not satisfied. According to the second skeptical position, our experiential evidence does not even provide better reason to believe ordinary propositions than the skeptical alternatives. On this view, it is condition (1) that is not satisfied.[33]

B1. Skeptical Alternatives as Defeaters

We begin with the first of these positions. One might think that, although ordinary experiences do provide reasons for ordinary beliefs, the skeptical possibilities show that people have epistemic reasons to doubt the propositions about the world that they ordinarily believe, or that people have epistemic reasons to doubt that their ordinary reasons are reliable.

Three of the skeptical arguments can plausibly be interpreted as relying on just this point. Consider first premise (2) of (PE). If people can be mistaken about the external world propositions that they believe, as the skeptical possibilities show, then apparently people have a reason to doubt these external world propositions. The beliefs are therefore not justified and consequently not known. Similarly, premise (2) of (II) seems to rely on this point. The existence of introspectively indistinguishable cases in which ordinary beliefs are false would seem to undermine knowledge because their existence constitutes a defeater.[34] It may be that such credibility as is had by premise (1) of (TK) also relies on this point.

The skeptical possibilities do not show that people have a reason to doubt ordinary propositions. For instance, a BIV hypothesis is not a reason to doubt ordinary beliefs, unless there is reason to believe that the BIV hypothesis is true. A reason to doubt that a proposition is true is a reason to think that something incompatible with the proposition is true. Reason to think, or proof, that a BIV hypothesis is *possible*, while things are introspectively the same, is not a reason to think that a BIV hypothesis is true. By contrast, good reason to think that

---

[33] A third position which skeptics might defend is that our evidence better supports ordinary propositions than skeptical alternatives, but it does not provide strong enough support to satisfy condition (1). Our response to the second view also applies to this alternative.

[34] It is possible to argue that introspective indistinguishability shows that we have no strong reason at all for our ordinary beliefs. Our response to this way of defending (II) is the same as our response to (AH) below.

a proposition is *probable*, to any extent, given one's basic evidence, is at least some slight reason to doubt that the proposition is true.[35] Similarly, the mere possibility that a BIV hypothesis is true is not a defeater by virtue of being a reason to think that ordinary evidence is unreliable.

Thus, the possibility of error on the same basis does not show that the basis fails to justify. Only evidence that supports the actual truth of some contrary proposition, or some undercutting proposition, defeats the justification. In skeptical scenarios, experiential evidence is misleading. But the fact that such deception is possible does not constitute a reason to think that the evidence actually misleads. The fact about what is possible would have to be supplemented with reason to think that the possibility actually obtains. This further requirement is easily overlooked. Some of the appeal of premises in the skeptical arguments results from the understandable mistake of thinking that the skeptical possibilities do provide reasons to doubt the propositions that are ordinarily believed. This argues against (2) of (PE) and (2) of (II).

The understandable mistake just described is one reason that premise (2) of (PE) may seem correct. In addition, there is a truth with which (2) might be confused. The premise can be casually formulated as "When you know, you have to be right." This sentence can express a truth. Although having knowledge-level justification for a belief does not guarantee the truth of that belief, knowledge does guarantee truth. The justification condition itself, however, allows falsehood, and it allows accidental truth of the sort that Gettier cases illustrate. Non-evidential theories of knowledge typically have no separate anti-Gettier condition. Proper causation, proper function, safety, or the like is supposed to exclude Gettier cases while otherwise filling the role filled by justification in an evidential theory. In accounting for how knowledge excludes the possibility of error, a separate condition to deal with the Gettier problem is an asset. Justification is not the only independent condition on knowledge. There is a "fourth condition" on knowledge. We do not have a specific proposal about what the fourth condition is. Our point here is that any solution will rule out as knowledge the "luckily true justified beliefs" that Gettier revealed. A condition that blocks this luck imposes a requirement of something approximating necessity for the truth of the belief. Justification alone does not accomplish this. Thus, when you know, you must satisfy the truth condition and you must satisfy the anti-Gettier condition. These two requirements for knowledge

---

[35] Suppose that a malicious or confused colleague asserts that you are a brain in a vat. Our view implies that either this undermines your knowledge or that this reason for doubt is defeated. We endorse the second disjunct for the most realistic versions of the example, although the details of the case could make the first option correct.

substantiate the intuitive truth that when you know, you have to be right. Thus, we can agree that there is some truth in this claim, without agreeing that justification is incompatible with the possibility of believing falsely on the same basis.[36]

We turn next to (TK). Premise (1) of (TK) denies that one can know the falsehood of skeptical scenarios. Premise (2) asserts that the knower sees the incompatibility of ordinary beliefs with the truth of the skeptical scenarios, and premise (3) is a closure principle connecting knowledge of ordinary beliefs with a capacity to know the falsehood of any proposition incompatible with a known fact.

Again, (TK) is an exceptional skeptical argument, in that its first premise is itself a skeptical proposition. Unlike the other skeptical arguments, (TK) is not clearly an attack on the adequacy of our justification. But the skeptical scenarios seem to function in (TK) in a way that is at least analogous to defeaters of the justification of ordinary beliefs. The alleged inability of people to know the falsehood of the scenarios is supposed to exclude knowledge of ordinary propositions for those who see the conflict between the two. Presumably, the exclusion arises from some vulnerability in ordinary evidence for the ordinary beliefs that makes skeptical scenarios defeaters of that evidence for those who see the conflict.[37]

There is no good reason to accept premise (1) of (TK), though. It is straightforwardly false. One's evidence for ordinary beliefs straightforwardly supports denials that the skeptical possibilities obtain. The evidence for ordinary beliefs argues against any proposition that one sees to conflict with the ordinary beliefs, while one has no new reason to doubt those beliefs or their support. This conspicuous implication by justified ordinary beliefs of the falsehood of the contrary propositions justifies denials of the contrary propositions. Consequently, one is justified in believing that the skeptical scenarios do not obtain. In this way, one can know that the skeptical scenarios are false.

The reasoning described in the previous paragraph seems to us clearly to refute premise (1) of (TK). To see this, it helps to note that this sort of reasoning is the way one usually knows typical facts about how things are not. For instance, this sort of reasoning is the usual way to know that one is not indoors, when according to one's basic experiential evidence one is outdoors. There are always indoor hypotheses that are metaphysically possible in conjunction

---

[36] The need for a fourth condition on knowledge makes room for a new skeptical concern only if there is reason to believe that the anti-Gettier condition cannot be met. There is no such reason. All promising approaches to a fourth condition on knowledge propose contingent conditions that we have good reason to believe actually obtain with roughly the frequency that knowledge appears to exist.

[37] Defenders of (TK) could defend its skeptical premise (1) by claiming that we have no strong grounds at all for our ordinary beliefs. Presumably, an argument such as (AH) would be used to support this contention. For our response, see section (B2).

Making Sense of Skepticism

with one's basic evidence. Still, one's experience and memory argue strongly enough that one is outdoors, and the conspicuous implication that one is not indoors is thereby amply supported. Absent some reason to believe the indoor proposition, it gives no reason to doubt the outdoor belief or the merits of one's evidence for it. The same goes for skeptical propositions, such as allegations of demonic deception. Absent some reason to believe that they are true, they give no reason to doubt ordinary beliefs or the merits of ordinary evidence for them.

Again, a possibility that is allowed by one's basic evidence, and incompatible with P, is not automatically a reason to doubt P. The possibility must have an epistemic status that bears on how things actually are, such as evidence that the possibility obtains, or at least evidence that gives the possibility some positive probability of being true. This fact about reasons to doubt is not just obviously correct. The lack of obviousness has significant explanatory utility. If people are guided by the conception that we defend of the justification needed for knowledge, according to which knowledge requires having no good reason to doubt what is justified, then they can easily be made to worry about any incompatible possibility. It conflicts with P, and there is nothing in the basic evidence anyone has that entails one rather than the other. In those important salient ways, a possibility incompatible with P is exactly like a good reason to doubt P. That can easily seem to be enough to render P unjustified, although it is not. Though this is not obvious, reason to doubt P is evidence that a possibility contrary to P obtains in fact. Evidence of sheer possibility is not that. But again, this is not an inescapable fact. Skeptics who fail to agree and locate reasons to doubt in other possibilities have made no manifest blunder.

We leave open numerous significant issues. There are questions about whether every known probability of error gives rise to a good reason to doubt. For instance, according to current physical theory, a brief time ago there was some minuscule objective chance that any given ordinary object, say, a teacup, would by now have virtually all of its matter dissolved by quantum fluctuations, save for the surface facing a perceiver.[38] Were that terrifically improbable event of dissolution actually to have happened, the perceiver would see, for a moment before its collapse made the cup's decomposition obvious, a mere cup facade, not a cup. Perceivers who know enough current physical theory to know about this objective chance thus seem rationally bound to assign some positive probability to the possibility that the things perceived at any given time are mere facades rather than ordinary objects.

---

[38] The epistemic significance of this sort of physical possibility is discussed in John Hawthorne's monograph, *Knowledge and Lotteries* (Oxford: Oxford University Press, 2003).

Our view of the justification required for knowledge counts any probability for someone of the truth of any known contrary to a proposition as a reason for the person to doubt the proposition. So we seem committed to denying perceptual knowledge by the physically informed of the current existence of ordinary perceived objects.

We have nothing conclusive to say about this. We note that the reason to doubt is an inference from details of current physical theory, and there is inductive reason to doubt that the current theory is the full truth of the matter. It may also be epistemically significant that this sort of physical possibility has never actually occurred to any ordinary macroscopic object, as far as we know. Perhaps the total evidence of the physically informed on balance supports suspension of judgment about the existence of a positive probability of dissolution. This lack of any known case of the phenomenon stands in contrast to lotteries where it is known that some ticket, whose victory was epistemically highly improbable, nonetheless actually wins. It seems clear that lottery cases are not knowledge. Our account implies that there is inadequate justification, because of a reason to doubt. But it may be that not just any sort of basis for probability is a genuine reason to doubt. Perhaps a probability of an event in a reference class that has never been observed, according to an arguably transitional physical theory, does not give reason for doubt that undercuts justification, as do probabilities derived from actual events in the same reference class.

It also may be that those who know about this objective chance do have this minute probability of falsehood as a reason to doubt. So by ordinary perception they do not quite know of the presence of complete solid objects. If this is the case, and if they have no other reason to doubt, then these perceptual beliefs have such splendidly high probability for them, and are otherwise so well supported, that the practical difference of the beliefs from knowledge is nil. Their epistemic difference from knowledge, though notable, may be similarly small. Perhaps lottery beliefs based on high enough probabilities are likewise "almost known." Such issues plainly deserve further investigation.

This completes our discussion of the skeptical arguments other than (AH). Our ordinary beliefs are sufficiently justified for knowledge only if we have no undefeated reasons to doubt them. The three skeptical arguments just considered rely on the assumption that skeptical scenarios provide reasons to doubt. We have argued that they do not.

B2. Skeptical Alternatives and the Strength of the Evidence

Beliefs have knowledge-level justification only if we have strong evidential support for them. The second skeptical position described earlier in this section contends that we lack strong evidence for external world beliefs. Premise (1) of (AH) relies on just this idea. It asserts that ordinary beliefs are not better supported by experience in the first place than are skeptical world views.

Skeptics give no good reason to believe this premise. And the premise does seem initially incredible. It surely seems that a typical full-blown experience of a warm summer day has to turn out somehow to give one better reason to believe that one is actually experiencing a warm summer day than to believe that one is a brain in a vat being fed warm summer day experiences. With premise (1) unsupported, (AH) does not argue successfully against our having external world knowledge.

It is a further worthwhile project to *show* that the premise is mistaken. To do this, some account is needed of what makes experiences provide basic evidence for ordinary beliefs. It seems clear that experiences do this. Explaining how they do so is a difficult project that remains to be accomplished. Two approaches are surveyed below. Each is found wanting, although not without merit. Showing that experiences really do provide basic evidence for ordinary beliefs is the main work that remains to be done to have a complete answer to external world skepticism.

It can seem so clear as to be a fundamental fact that typical experiential evidence is better evidence for ordinary external world beliefs than for any specific skeptical alternative, or for any disjunction of skeptical alternatives. One sort of view endorsing this position can be found in the work of Roderick Chisholm. In his *Theory of Knowledge* Chisholm proposes as fundamental epistemological principles such principles as the following:

If S believes that he perceives something to have a certain property F, then the proposition that he does perceive something to be F, as well as the proposition that there is something that is F, is one that is *reasonable* for S.[39]

Chisholm does not derive this principle from some other more fundamental truths. He seems to assert, as a fundamental epistemological fact, that our perceptual beliefs do support our external world beliefs. More recently, James Pryor has defended a similar view:

My view is that whenever you have an experience as of *p*, you thereby have immediate *prima facie* justification for believing *p*. Your experiences do not, in the same way, give you immediate *prima facie* justification for believing that you are dreaming, or being deceived by an evil demon, or that any of the skeptic's other hypotheses obtain.[40]

---

[39] Roderick Chisholm, *Theory of Knowledge* (Englewood Cliffs, NJ: Prentice-Hall, 1966), 45.

[40] James Pryor, "The Skeptic and the Dogmatist", *Nous*, 34 (2000), 517–49. The quotation is from p. 536.

Richard Feldman and Earl Conee

Chisholm's principle makes the justification of external world beliefs dependent upon one's beliefs about perceptual experiences. Pryor's view makes the justification dependent upon the experiences themselves. As we interpret these views, both hold that it is a fundamental epistemological fact that our experiences, or our beliefs about experiences, provide immediate perceptual justification for our ordinary external world beliefs.

Many details of the Chisholm/Pryor view need to be worked out. A prominent issue concerns exactly which experiences and propositions any such view applies to. An experience of redness, say, may immediately justify (*prima facie*) the belief that there is a red object before one, but the experience of a ponderosa pine will not, for most observers, similarly justify the belief that there is a ponderosa pine present. Some explanation of the difference is needed.[41]

Furthermore, as a response to premise (1) of (AH) this approach is less than fully enlightening. Although it does indeed seem true that ordinary experiences justify propositions about ordinary physical objects better than they justify propositions about what an evil demon is doing, it also seems that there must be some reason why the experiences support the ordinary beliefs and not the rivals. It is not enough to say that the experiences "just do" support certain propositions. Chisholm and Pryor propose plausible general principles.[42] But simply asserting general principles that imply that experiences justify ordinary beliefs does not explain why they do this. We need either some explanation of why the experiences do justify the external world beliefs or some explanation of why the extension of the epistemic support relation turns out to be inexplicable in the relevant cases. Either way, the Chisholm/Pryor response does not complete an evidentialist reply to skepticism until it is itself completed.

A second evidentialist response to (AH) takes a different tack. It holds that the commonsense beliefs enter into better explanations of our experiences then do the skeptical hypotheses. It asserts that this makes the experiences better reason to believe the ordinary world views.[43] This is an initially promising approach. It is surely quite doubtful that the skeptical hypotheses provide explanations that are as good as the explanations provided by ordinary

---

[41] Ernest Sosa raises this issue in his contribution to *Epistemic Justification: Internalism vs. Externalism, Foundations vs. Virtues*, co-authored with Laurence BonJour (Oxford: Blackwell, 2003). See pp. 122 f.

[42] Chisholm's principle needs a "no defeaters" clause. He adds a condition along these lines in a revised principle in *Theory of Knowledge*, 2nd edn. (Englewood Cliffs, NJ: Prentice-Hall, 1977), 78.

[43] Evidentialist denials of premise (1) need not rest on either the claim that it is a brute fact that our experiences provide better reason to believe ordinary external world propositions than to believe skeptical alternatives, or the claim that ordinary beliefs are included in better explanations of experiences than are

beliefs.[44] The evil demon hypothesis, for instance, usually leaves entirely unexplained the existence, powers, and deceptive motives of the demon, and one's own existence. There is no obvious and economical explanation of these things. The alternative explanations bring in a kind of complexity—amazingly sophisticated computers, evil geniuses monitoring our thoughts and inducing lengthy undetected deceptions, implausibly orderly dreams. These explanations seem *ad hoc*, complex, and ridiculous. The pure chance skeptical hypothesis, according to which one's experiences just happen to occur with no causal explanation, implies less that needs explaining. But the apparent orderliness of the experiences and their coherence with memory makes a chance hypothesis seem an extraordinarily weak explanation. The ordinary external world explanation has none of these liabilities. It seems to be best by far, and good enough to justify.

It is well known that this response is not without difficulties.[45] There are important questions about exactly what counts as a better explanation and exactly why the skeptical hypotheses yield inferior explanations. It is also unclear whether it is sufficient for the ordinary beliefs to be justified that the explanation is in fact best (and good enough). It might be required, instead, that the believer realize that it has this status or that the believer's evidence support the proposition that it has this status (whether this proposition is believed or not). It is not implausible to think that our evidence does support this proposition, but we are not able to offer a compelling defense of this claim here.

These are not hopeless difficulties. Evidentialist responses along the lines of the two discussed here show promise of completing the remaining project, that of establishing that our evidence really does support our commonsense beliefs.[46]

---

skeptical hypotheses. If the ordinary beliefs are made "epistemically probable" by the experiences, while skeptical alternatives are not, then the experiences provide better reason for the ordinary propositions than the skeptical alternatives. Of course, the evidentialist utility of this appraisal depends on giving an evidentialist explanation of this epistemic sort of probability. That is no easy task. Since we think that the strength of "epistemic probability" must be explained by the strength of epistemic reasons, rather than vice versa, this sort of third approach does not seem promising to us.

[44] See Jonathan Vogel, "Cartesian Skepticism and Inference to the Best Explanation", *Journal of Philosophy*, 87 (1990), 658–66.

[45] See Richard Fumerton, *Metaepistemology and Skepticism* (Lanham, Md.: Rowman and Littlefield, 1995), 207–14.

[46] Contextualism does not offer any help here. Any contextualist view that gives evidence a justifying role shares the task of saying how ordinary evidence justifies ordinary belief, at least in those contexts in which ordinary "knowledge" attributions are true. Contextualist views that deny evidence this role share the liabilities discussed above for non-evidentialist theories of knowledge in addressing the fundamental issues raised by skepticism.

If no response such as this were to be correct, then skepticism would be true after all. Justifying evidence is required for knowledge. If our evidence about the external world fails to give adequate support for external world propositions, then skepticism is correct.[47]

Evidentialism has the virtue of squarely facing skeptical challenges. It makes best sense of skepticism.

---

[47] There are important matters of relative detail. For instance, if it turns out that statistical evidence is insufficient for knowledge of inductively drawn conclusions, then a variety of commonly accepted external world propositions are not really known. Nothing in our criminal standard of justification for knowledge readily resolves this issue. But it would be a comparatively modest denial of knowledge, and not a version of external world skepticism. Skepticism with regard to the whole past, on the other hand, is clearly a significant form of external world skepticism. It is equally clear that by the criminal standard we have sufficient evidence to know many propositions about the past.

Works Cited

[1] Alston, William, "Internalism and Externalism in Epistemology", *Philosophical Topics*, 14/1 (1986). Reprinted in [5], 185–226.
[2] Alston, William, "Epistemic Circularity", *Philosophy and Phenomenological Research*, 47 (1986), 1–30. Reprinted in [5], 319–49.
[3] Alston, William, "The Deontological Conception of Epistemic Justification", *Philosophical Perspectives*, 2 (1988), 257–99. Reprinted in [5], 115–52.
[4] Alston, William, "An Internalist Externalism", *Synthese*, 74 (1988), 265–83. Reprinted in [5], 227–45.
[5] Alston, William, *Epistemic Justification: Essays in the Theory of Knowledge* (Ithaca, NY: Cornell University Press, 1989).
[6] Alston, William, "Foley's Theory of Epistemic Rationality", *Philosophy and Phenomenological Research*, 50 (1989), 135–47.
[7] Alston, William, *The Reliability of Sense Perception* (Ithaca, NY: Cornell University Press, 1993).
[8] Alston, William, "How to Think about Reliability", *Philosophical Topics*, 23 (Spring 1995), 1–29.
[9] Annis, David, "A Contextualist Theory of Epistemic Justification", *American Philosophical Quarterly*, 15 (1978), 213–19.
[10] Armstrong, David, *Belief, Truth and Knowledge* (Cambridge: Cambridge University Press, 1973).
[11] Audi, Robert, "Memorial Justification", *Philosophical Topics*, 23 (1995), 31–45.
[12] Audi, Robert, *Epistemology: A Contemporary Introduction to the Theory of Knowledge* (New York: Routledge, 1998).
[13] Audi, Robert, "Doxastic Voluntarism and the Ethics of Belief", in Matthias Steup (ed.), *Knowledge, Truth, and Duty: Essays on Epistemic Justification, Responsibility, and Virtue* (Oxford: Oxford University Press, 2001), 93–111.
[14] Baergen, Ralph, *Contemporary Epistemology* (Fort Worth: Harcourt Brace, 1995).
[15] Bennett, Jonathan, "Why Is Belief Involuntary?", *Analysis*, 50 (1990), 87–107.
[16] Bergmann, Michael, "A Dilemma for Internalism", in Thomas Crisp, Matthew Davidson, and Dave Vanderlaan (eds.), *Knowledge and Reality: Essays in Honor of Alvin Plantinga* (Dordrecht: Kluwer, forthcoming).
[17] BonJour, Laurence, "Can Empirical Knowledge Have a Foundation?", *American Philosophical Quarterly*, 15/1 (1978), 1–14.
[18] BonJour, Laurence, "Externalist Theories of Empirical Knowledge", *Midwest Studies in Philosophy*, 5 (1980), 53–73.

Works Cited

[19] BonJour, Laurence, *The Structure of Empirical Knowledge* (Cambridge, Mass.: Harvard University Press, 1985).

[20] BonJour, Laurence, "Externalism/Internalism", in Jonathan Dancy and Ernest Sosa (eds.), *A Companion to Epistemology* (Oxford: Blackwell, 1992), 132–6.

[21] BonJour, Laurence, "The Dialectic of Foundationalism and Coherentism", in John Greco and Ernest Sosa (eds.), *The Blackwell Guide to Epistemology* (Oxford: Blackwell, 1999), 117–42.

[22] Brink, David, *Moral Realism and the Foundations of Ethics* (Cambridge: Cambridge University Press, 1989).

[23] Cargile, James, "Justification and Misleading Defeaters", *Analysis*, 55/3 (1995), 216–20.

[24] Chisholm, Roderick, *Theory of Knowledge* (Englewood Cliffs, NJ: Prentice-Hall, 1st edn. 1966, 2nd edn. 1977, 3rd edn. 1989).

[25] Chisholm, Roderick, *The Problem of the Criterion* (Milwaukee: Marquette University Press, 1973).

[26] Chisholm, Roderick, "Firth and the Ethics of Belief", *Philosophy and Phenomenological Research*, 50 (1991), 119–28.

[27] Clifford, W. K., "The Ethics of Belief", *Contemporary Review* (1877). Reprinted in Clifford, *Lectures and Essays* (London: MacMillan, 1879) and in Louis P. Pojman (ed.), *The Theory of Knowledge*, 2nd edn. (Belmont, Calif.: Wadsworth, 1999), 551–4.

[28] Cohen, L. J., "Can Human Irrationality be Experimentally Demonstrated?", *Behavioral and Brain Sciences*, 4 (1981), 317–70.

[29] Cohen, Stewart, "Justification and Truth", *Philosophical Studies*, 46 (1984), 279–95.

[30] Cohen, Stewart, "Contextualism, Skepticism, and the Structure of Reasons", *Philosophical Perspectives*, 13 (1999), 57–89.

[31] Cohen, Stewart, "Basic Beliefs and the Problem of Easy Knowledge", *Philosophy and Phenomenological Research*, 65 (2002), 309–29.

[32] Cohen, Stewart, and Keith Lehrer, "Justification, Truth, and Coherence", *Synthese*, 55/2 (1983), 191–207. Reprinted in Paul Moser and Arnold Vander Nat (eds.), *Human Knowledge: Classical & Contemporary Approaches* (New York: Oxford University Press, 1987), 325–34.

[33] Conee, Earl, "Propositional Justification", *Philosophical Studies*, 38 (1980), 65–8.

[34] Conee, Earl, "Evident but Rationally Unacceptable", *Australasian Journal of Philosophy*, 65 (1987), 316–26.

[35] Conee, Earl, and Richard Feldman, "Stich and Nisbett on Justifying Inference Rules", *Philosophy of Science*, 50 (1983), 326–31.

[36] Cornman, James, *Skepticism, Justification, and Explanation* (Dordrecht: D. Reidel, 1980).

[37] Dennett, Daniel, "Making Sense of Ourselves", in J. I. Biro and R. W. Shahan (eds.), *Mind, Brain, and Function* (Norman, Okla.: University of Oklahoma Press, 1982), 63–82.

Works Cited

[38] DeRose, Keith, "Solving the Skeptical Problem", *Philosophical Review*, 104 (1995), 1–52. Reprinted in [39], 183–219.

[39] DeRose, Keith, and Ted A. Warfield (eds.), *Skepticism: A Contemporary Reader* (Oxford: Oxford University Press, 1999).

[40] Fantl, Jeremy, and Matthew McGrath, "Evidence, Pragmatics and Justification", *Philosophical Review*, 111 (2002), 67–94.

[41] Feldman, Richard, "Reliability and Justification", *Monist*, 68 (1985), 159–74.

[42] Feldman, Richard, "Schmitt on Reliability, Objectivity, and Justification", *Australasian Journal of Philosophy*, 63 (1985), 354–60.

[43] Feldman, Richard, "Epistemic Obligations", *Philosophical Perspectives*, 2 (1988), 235–56.

[44] Feldman, Richard, "Foley's Subjective Foundationalism", *Philosophy and Phenomenological Research*, 50 (1989), 149–58.

[45] Feldman, Richard, "Proper Functionalism", *Nous*, 27 (1993), 34–50.

[46] Feldman, Richard, "Skeptical Problems, Contextualist Solutions", *Philosophical Studies*, 103 (2001), 61–85.

[47] Feldman, Richard, "Voluntary Belief and Epistemic Evaluation", in Matthias Steup (ed.), *Knowledge, Truth, and Duty: Essays on Epistemic Justification, Responsibility, and Virtue* (Oxford: Oxford University Press, 2001), 77–92.

[48] Feldman, Richard, *Epistemology* (Englewood Cliffs, NJ: Prentice-Hall, 2003).

[49] Firth, Roderick, "Are Epistemic Concepts Reducible to Ethical Concepts?", in Alvin Goldman and Jaegwon Kim (eds.), *Values and Morals* (Dordrecht: D. Reidel, 1978), 215–29.

[50] Firth, Roderick, "Epistemic Merit, Intrinsic and Instrumental", *Proceedings and Addresses of the American Philosophical Association*, 55 (1981), 5–23.

[51] Foley, Richard, *The Theory of Epistemic Rationality* (Cambridge, Mass.: Harvard University Press, 1987).

[52] Foley, Richard, "Reply to Alston, Feldman and Swain", *Philosophy and Phenomenological Research*, 50 (1989), 169–88.

[53] Foley, Richard, *Working without a Net* (Oxford: Oxford University Press, 1993).

[54] Fumerton, Richard, "Metaepistemology and Skepticism", in Michael Roth and Glenn Ross (eds.), *Doubting: Contemporary Perspectives on Skepticism* (Dordrecht: Kluwer, 1990), 57–68.

[55] Fumerton, Richard, *Metaepistemology and Skepticism* (Lanham, Md.: Rowman and Littlefield, 1995).

[56] Gale, Richard, "William James and the Ethics of Belief", *American Philosophical Quarterly*, 17 (1980), 1–14.

[57] Ginet, Carl, *Knowledge, Perception, and Memory* (Dordrecht: D. Reidel, 1975).

[58] Ginet, Carl, "Knowing Less by Knowing More", *Midwest Studies in Philosophy*, 5 (1980), 151–61.

[59] Goldman, Alvin, "A Causal Theory of Knowing", *Journal of Philosophy*, 64 (1967), 357–72. Reprinted in G. Pappas and M. Swain (eds.), *Essays on Knowledge and Justification* (Ithaca, NY: Cornell University Press, 1978), 67–86.

Works Cited

[60] Goldman, Alvin, "Epistemics: The Regulative Theory of Cognition", *Journal of Philosophy*, 75 (1978), 509–23.

[61] Goldman, Alvin, "What is Justified Belief?", in George S. Pappas (ed.), *Justification and Knowledge* (Dordrecht: D. Reidel, 1979), 1–24.

[62] Goldman, Alvin, *Epistemology and Cognition* (Cambridge, Mass.: Harvard University Press, 1986).

[63] Goldman, Alvin, "Internalism Exposed", *Journal of Philosophy*, 96 (1999), 271–93.

[64] Haack, Susan, "'The Ethics of Belief' Reconsidered", in Lewis E. Hahn (ed.), *The Philosophy of Roderick Chisholm* (La Salle, Ill.: Open Court, 1997), 129–44. Reprinted in Matthias Steup (ed.), *Knowledge, Truth, and Duty: Essays on Epistemic Justification, Responsibility, and Virtue* (Oxford: Oxford University Press, 2001), 21–33.

[65] Hall, Richard J., and Charles R. Johnson, "The Epistemic Duty to Seek More Evidence", *American Philosophical Quarterly*, 35 (1998), 129–40.

[66] Harman, Gilbert, *Thought* (Princeton: Princeton University Press, 1973).

[67] Harman, Gilbert, *Change in View* (Cambridge, Mass.: MIT Press, 1986).

[68] Harper, William, "Paper Maché Problems in Epistemology: A Defense of Strong Internalism", *Synthese*, 116 (1998), 27–49.

[69] Hawthorne, John, *Knowledge and Lotteries* (Oxford: Oxford University Press, 2003).

[70] Heil, John, "Believing What One Ought", *Journal of Philosophy*, 80/11 (1983), 752–65.

[71] Heil, John, "Doxastic Agency", *Philosophical Studies*, 43 (1983), 335–64.

[72] Heller, Mark, "The Simple Solution to the Problem of Generality", *Nous*, 29 (1995), 501–15.

[73] Hill, Christopher S., "Process Reliabilism and Cartesian Skepticism", *Philosophy and Phenomenological Research*, 56 (1996), 567–81. Reprinted in [39], 115–28.

[74] Huemer, Michael, *Skepticism and the Veil of Perception* (Lanham, Md.: Rowman and Littlefield, 2001).

[75] James, William, "The Will to Believe". Reprinted in Louis Pojman (ed.), *The Theory of Knowledge*, 3rd edn. (Belmont, Calif.: Wadsworth, 2003), 518–26.

[76] Kennedy, Ralf, and Charles Chihara, "The Dutch Book Argument: Its Logical Flaws, Its Subjective Sources", *Philosophical Studies*, 36 (1979), 19–33.

[77] Keynes, John, *A Treatise on Probability* (London: Macmillan, 1921).

[78] Kitcher, Philip, "The Naturalists Return", *Philosophical Review*, 101 (1992), 53–114.

[79] Kornblith, Hilary, "Beyond Foundationalism and the Coherence Theory", *Journal of Philosophy*, 77 (1980), 597–612.

[80] Kornblith, Hilary, "The Psychological Turn", *Australasian Journal of Philosophy*, 60 (1982), 238–53.

[81] Kornblith, Hilary, "Justified Belief and Epistemically Responsible Action", *Philosophical Review*, 92 (1983), 33–48.

[82] Lehrer, Keith, *Knowledge* (Oxford: Oxford University Press, 1974).

Works Cited

[83] Lewis, David, "Elusive Knowledge", *Australasian Journal of Philosophy*, 74 (1996), 549–67.

[84] Locke, John, *An Essay Concerning Human Understanding*, ed. A. C. Fraser (New York: Dover, 1959).

[85] Lycan, William, *Judgement and Justification* (Cambridge: Cambridge University Press, 1988).

[86] McLeod, Owen, "Just Plain 'Ought'", *Journal of Ethics*, 5 (2001), 269–91.

[87] Mills, Eugene, "The Unity of Justification", *Philosophy and Phenomenological Research*, 58 (1998), 27–50.

[88] Montmarquet, James, "The Voluntariness of Belief", *Analysis*, 46 (1986), 49–53.

[89] Moser, Paul, *Empirical Justification* (Dordrecht: Reidel, 1985).

[90] Moser, Paul, "Realism, Objectivity and Skepticism", in John Greco and Ernest Sosa (eds.), *The Blackwell Guide to Epistemology* (Oxford: Blackwell, 1999), 70–91.

[91] Neta, Ram, "Contextualism and the Problem of the External World", *Philosophy and Phenomenological Research*, 66/1 (2003), 1–31.

[92] Nisbett, Richard, and Lee Ross, *Human Inference: Strategies and Shortcomings of Social Judgment* (Englewood Cliffs, NJ: Prentice-Hall, 1980).

[93] Nozick, Robert, *Philosophical Explanations* (Cambridge, Mass.: Harvard University Press, 1981).

[94] Papineau, David, "Evidentialism Reconsidered", *Nous*, 35 (2001), 239–59.

[95] Plantinga, Alvin, "Is Belief in God Properly Basic?", *Nous*, 15 (1981), 41–51.

[96] Plantinga, Alvin, *Warrant and Proper Function* (Oxford: Oxford University Press, 1993).

[97] Plantinga, Alvin, *Warrant: The Current Debate* (Oxford: Oxford University Press, 1993).

[98] Plantinga, Alvin, "Respondeo ad Feldman", in Jon Kvanvig (ed.), *Warrant in Contemporary Epistemology: Essays in Honor of Plantinga's Theory of Knowledge* (London: Rowman and Littlefield, 1996), 357–61.

[99] Plato, *Euthyphro, Apology, Crito*, trans. F. J. Church (New York: Bobbs-Merrill, 1956).

[100] Pollock, John, *Knowledge and Justification* (Princeton: Princeton University Press, 1974).

[101] Pollock, John, "A Plethora of Epistemological Theories", in George Pappas (ed.), *Justification and Knowledge* (Dordrecht: D. Reidel, 1979), 93–113.

[102] Pollock, John, "Reliability and Justified Belief", *Canadian Journal of Philosophy*, 14 (1984), 103–14.

[103] Pollock, John, *Contemporary Theories of Knowledge* (Totowa, NJ: Rowman and Littlefield, 1986).

[104] Pollock, John, "At the Interface of Philosophy and AI", in John Greco and Ernest Sosa (eds.), *The Blackwell Guide to Epistemology* (Malden, Mass.: Blackwell, 1999), 383–414.

[105] Pryor, James, "The Skeptic and the Dogmatist", *Nous*, 34 (2000), 517–49.

Works Cited

[106] Pryor, James, "Highlights of Recent Epistemology", *British Journal for the Philosophy of Science*, 52 (2001), 95–124.

[107] Quine, W. V. O., "Natural Kinds", in *Ontological Relativity and Other Essays* (New York: Columbia University Press, 1969), 114–38.

[108] Radcliffe, Dana, "Scott-Kakures on Believing at Will", *Philosophy and Phenomenological Research*, 57/1 (1997), 145–51.

[109] Russell, Bertrand, *Problems of Philosophy* (Oxford: Oxford University Press, 1997; first published in 1912).

[110] Russell, Bruce, "Epistemic and Moral Duty", in Matthias Steup (ed.), *Knowledge, Truth, and Duty: Essays on Epistemic Justification, Responsibility, and Virtue* (Oxford: Oxford University Press, 2001), 34–48.

[111] Schmitt, Frederick, "Reliability, Objectivity, and the Background of Justification", *Australasian Journal of Philosophy*, 62 (1984), 1–15.

[112] Schmitt, Frederick, *Knowledge and Belief* (New York: Routledge, Chapman, and Hall, 1992).

[113] Scott-Kakures, Dion, "On Belief and the Captivity of the Will", *Philosophy and Phenomenological Research*, 53 (1993), 77–103.

[114] Senor, Thomas, "Internalist Foundationalism and the Justification of Memory Belief", *Synthese*, 94 (1993), 453–76.

[115] Sorensen, Roy, "Dogmatism, Junk Knowledge, and Conditionals", *Philosophical Quarterly*, 38 (1988), 433–54.

[116] Sosa, Ernest, "The Raft and the Pyramid: Coherence versus Foundationalism in the Theory of Knowledge", *Midwest Studies in Philosophy*, 5 (1980), 3–25. Reprinted in [119], 165–91.

[117] Sosa, Ernest, "The Coherence of Virtue and the Virtue of Coherence: Justification in Epistemology", *Synthese*, 64 (1985), 3–28. Reprinted in [119], 192–214.

[118] Sosa, Ernest, "Beyond Scepticism, to the Best of our Knowledge", *Mind*, 97 (1988), 153–88.

[119] Sosa, Ernest, *Knowledge in Perspective: Selected Essays in Epistemology* (Cambridge: Cambridge University Press, 1991).

[120] Sosa, Ernest, "Theories of Justification: Old Doctrines Newly Defended", in [119], 108–30.

[121] Sosa, Ernest, "Philosophical Skepticism and Epistemic Circularity", *Aristotelian Society Supplement*, 68 (1994), 263–90. Reprinted in [39], 93–114.

[122] Sosa, Ernest, "Skepticism and the Internal/External Divide", in John Greco and Ernest Sosa (eds.), *The Blackwell Guide to Epistemology* (Oxford: Blackwell, 1999), 145–57.

[123] Sosa, Ernest, "Tracking, Competence, and Knowledge", in Paul K. Moser (ed.), *The Oxford Handbook of Epistemology* (Oxford: Oxford University Press, 2002), 264–86.

Works Cited

[124] Sosa, Ernest, "Privileged Access", in Quentin Smith and Aleksander Jokic (eds.), *Consciousness: New Philosophical Perspectives* (Oxford: Oxford University Press, 2003), 273–92.

[125] Sosa, Ernest, "Beyond Internal Foundations to External Virtues", in [126], 97–170.

[126] Sosa, Ernest, and Laurence BonJour, *Epistemic Justification: Internalism vs. Externalism, Foundations vs. Virtues* (Oxford: Blackwell, 2003).

[127] Stein, Edward, *Without Good Reason: The Rationality Debate in Philosophy and Cognitive Science* (Oxford: Clarendon Press, 1996).

[128] Steup, Matthias, *An Introduction to Contemporary Epistemology* (Upper Saddle River, NJ: Prentice-Hall, 1996).

[129] Steup, Matthias, "A Defense of Internalism", in Louis Pojman (ed.), *The Theory of Knowledge: Classical and Contemporary Readings*, 2nd edn. (Belmont, Calif.: Wadsworth, 1999), 373–84.

[130] Steup, Matthias, "Doxastic Voluntarism and Epistemic Deontology", *Acta Analytica*, 15 (2000), 25–56.

[131] Stich, Stephen, "Could Man be an Irrational Animal? Some Notes on the Epistemology of Rationality", *Synthese*, 64 (1985), 115–35.

[132] Stich, Stephen, and Richard Nisbett, "Justification and the Psychology of Human Reasoning", *Philosophy of Science*, 47 (1980), 188–202.

[133] Stroud, Barry, "Skepticism, 'Externalism', and the Goal of Epistemology", in [39], 292–304.

[134] Stroud, Barry, "Understanding Human Knowledge in General", in M. Clay and K. Lehrer (eds.), *Knowledge and Skepticism* (Boulder, Colo.: Westview, 1989), 31–50. Reprinted in Hilary Kornblith (ed.), *Epistemology: Internalism and Externalism* (Oxford: Blackwell, 2001), 126–46.

[135] Sturgeon, Scott, "Truth in Epistemology", *Philosophy and Phenomenological Research*, 51 (1991), 99–108.

[136] Thagard, Paul, "From the Descriptive to the Normative in Psychology and Logic", *Philosophy of Science*, 49 (1982), 24–42.

[137] Tversky, Amos, and Daniel Kahneman, "Judgments of and by Representativeness", in D. Kahneman, P. Slovic, and A. Tversky (eds.), *Judgement under Uncertainty: Heuristics and Biases* (Cambridge: Cambridge University Press, 1982), 84–98.

[138] van Cleve, James, "Epistemic Supervenience and the Circle of Beliefs", *Monist*, 68/1 (1985), 90–104.

[139] Vogel, Jonathan, "Cartesian Skepticism and Inference to the Best Explanation", *Journal of Philosophy*, 87 (1990), 658–66.

[140] Wallis, Charles, "Truth-Ratios, Process, Task, and Knowledge", *Synthese*, 98 (1994), 243–69.

[141] Williams, Bernard, "Deciding to Believe", in *Problems of the Self* (Cambridge: Cambridge University Press, 1973).

Works Cited

[142] Williams, Michael, *Groundless Beliefs* (Oxford: Blackwell, 1977).
[143] Williamson, Timothy, *Knowledge and its Limits* (Oxford: Oxford University Press, 2000).
[144] Winters, Barbara, "Believing at Will", *Journal of Philosophy*, 76 (1979), 243–56.
[145] Wolterstorff, Nicholas, "Obligations of Belief: Two Concepts", in Lewis E. Hahn (ed.), *The Philosophy of Roderick Chisholm* (La Salle, Ill.: Open Court, 1997), 217–38.

Index

access 16, 39, 47–52, 54, 55, 57, 58, 69–75, 81, 226, 231–2, 269, 274
accessibilism 55, 69, 81
acquaintance 200
Alston, William 22–9, 53, 55, 56, 57, 61, 74, 75, 133, 135, 138, 139, 140, 142, 144, 145, 146, 147, 148, 151, 152, 159, 167, 168, 169, 170, 176, 182, 307, 309
analysis 72, 83, 89, 93, 100, 119, 125, 127, 131, 167, 169
Annis, David 49, 50, 307
appearances 15, 20–1, 30, 31, 98, 105–7, 116, 117, 144, 150, 165, 200, 204, 208, 212, 265, 268, 278–9, 285, 300
Armstrong, David 94, 96, 307
Audi, Robert 52, 54, 55, 69, 307
authoritarian theories 118, 128, 129, 133
availability 14, 22, 35, 48–9, 67–70, 80, 81, 87, 116, 118, 126, 185, 187–8, 201, 225–40, 242, 255, 256, 258, 262
awareness 28–9, 40–2, 45, 55, 187, 200–8, 216–18, 236
  direct 201, 279
  experiential 202–7, 215–18
  noticing 202–3, 216

Baergen, Ralph 135, 144, 145, 150, 151, 152, 153, 159, 307
basics 78, 79, 222
basing relation, the 5, 93, 105, 163, 164

basis
  for belief 3, 22, 23, 29, 65, 67, 70, 72, 75, 92–3, 97–8, 99, 105, 118, 146–53, 158, 162–4, 172, 173, 187, 191, 201, 217, 220–2, 227, 233–4, 251, 276, 284–5, 296, 299–300
  for knowledge 31–2, 260–1, 266–7, 278–9
begging the question 11, 17, 19, 29
belief
  dispositional 178
  doxastic limits 87, 100
  occurrent 67, 68, 224, 236
  stored 67, 68, 69, 70, 72, 73, 74, 81, 220
belief-forming processes 5, 49, 94–9, 136–65, 225
  belief-dependent 144, 145
  belief-independent 144, 145
  sustaining 141
  tokens 136–7, 156–7
  types 140–65
Bennett, John 7, 52, 159, 195, 285
Bennett, Jonathan 169, 307
Bergmann, Michael 76, 307
blame, epistemic 61–3, 85, 166–8, 175–6, 228
BonJour, Laurence 54, 55, 75, 90, 96, 97, 98, 99, 200, 224, 229, 304, 307, 308, 313
brains in vats 60, 278, 279, 291, 292, 299, 303
Brink, David 58, 308

Index

Cargile, James 265–7, 269, 270–1, 276, 308
causal theory of knowledge 219, 241, 280, 291, 293
causation 36, 38–9, 135–7, 146–50, 162–4, 172, 247, 250, 252, 256, 257, 280, 286, 291, 299
certainty 211, 278, 296
  feeling of 238, 239
chance 34, 188, 268, 301, 302, 305
Chihara, Charles 251, 310
Chisholm, Roderick 7, 17, 20, 21, 42, 58, 88, 89, 116, 117, 167, 168, 174, 191, 224, 244, 303, 304, 308, 310, 314
circularity 20–9, 125, 127, 128
clairvoyance 96, 97, 98, 99
classifying dispositions 147
Clay, M. 313
Clifford, W. K. 1, 2, 91, 176, 177, 191, 308
closure, epistemic 270, 271, 272, 291, 293, 300
Cohen, L. J. 128, 131, 132, 308
Cohen, Stewart 7, 49, 99, 100, 105, 106, 107, 117, 194, 195, 242, 243, 245, 254, 274, 276, 282, 308
coherence
  explanatory 38, 42
coherence theory 4, 37–46, 51–2, 72–3, 224–5, 227, 235, 273, 276, 305
color judgments 106, 107
competence-performance distinction 131
computational operations 78
concepts
  geometric 207
  indexical 206
  phenomenal 205–8, 212–18
  SGA 205, 207, 208, 213–15
confirmation 38, 72, 98
conjecturalism 20

consequentialism in ethics 258
contextualism 139, 141, 155–7, 282–3, 285, 305
Cornman, James 44, 308
correspondence 132, 274
counterpart propositions 82
current-state, justification
  (*see* justification, current state)

Davidson, Donald 76, 307
defeat
  external 4, 105
  lack of defeat 4, 15, 66, 72, 104, 163, 254, 255, 296, 297, 302
  undercutting 299
demon worlds 140
Dennett, Daniel 240, 308
deontology, epistemic 5, 53, 61, 62, 63, 72, 73, 75, 166–9, 171–7, 194
DeRose, Keith 30, 31, 186, 195, 282, 287, 309
Descartes, René 278
disposition 68, 147, 230, 266
dispositional 43, 55, 56, 67, 68, 69, 178, 236, 237
dispositions 68, 120, 224, 236, 237, 249
dogmatism 267
duty (*see also* obligations) 1, 61, 62, 63, 73, 75, 91, 166, 176, 182, 188, 191, 228

egocentric predicament 133, 134
eliminativism 254
epistemic authority 118, 120, 123
epistemic community 156, 211
epistemic goals 91, 181, 182, 257
epistemic justification
  for a proposition (*see also* justification, propositional), 253
  for believing (*see also* justification, doxastic) 103, 248, 249, 250, 251, 254, 255

epistemic objectivism 130
epistemic ought 174, 175, 180, 181, 184, 188, 192, 194
epistemic priority 31, 32
epistemic regress 48
epistemic responsibility 65
epistemic standards
  deductive 113
  deepest 118, 119, 123
epistemic value 182–6, 257–8
epistemic-support 113, 117
error, possibility of 277–8, 284–5, 296, 299
ethics 58, 88, 90–1, 112, 117, 124, 166–95, 258
evaluation 75, 85, 90, 126, 129, 130, 155, 177, 180, 190, 191–4, 224, 226, 233, 257–8
evidence
  available 185, 227–41
  balance of 21, 269
  basic 17–18, 39–43, 76–8, 113, 199–205, 213–15, 295, 299, 300–5
  bodies of 87, 93, 101, 113–14, 117, 123, 181, 261, 272
  conscious 73, 79
  counter 221, 232–4, 252, 265–70
  deprivation of 190
  entailing 252, 286, 295
  experiential 3, 84, 111, 279, 290, 295, 298, 299, 300, 303
  fitting 94, 95, 96, 98, 99
  forgotten 69, 70, 72
  having 22, 50, 65, 101, 115, 219, 230
  impulsional 65, 66
  misleading 259, 264, 265, 270, 274
  nonentailing 270
  stored 68, 240
  total 112, 226, 227, 269, 302
  total possible 226, 227, 228, 231
  undermining 273
evidential support 65–6, 178, 181, 194–5, 253, 264, 275, 287, 289, 302–3
evil demon 140, 164, 278, 279, 289, 303, 304, 305
experience 2–3, 22, 24, 31, 33, 39–46, 51–2, 54, 59, 64, 74–5, 77–8, 79–80, 84, 98–9, 106–7, 113, 114, 115–16, 137, 146–8, 149–50, 164–5, 190, 200–18, 225–6, 245, 278–80, 284, 287–90, 295–8, 300–5
  religious 111
expertise 67, 220
expertism 121, 122, 123, 124, 127, 132
explanation 11, 32, 37–8, 42, 61, 76, 97–9, 138, 152, 154, 203, 204–5, 211–13, 245–6, 254, 264, 270–2, 276, 279–80, 282–3, 285, 287–90, 293, 304–5
explanations, psychological 146
external internalism 51
externalism 4, 32–8, 46–51, 52, 53–8, 82, 289

fallibilism 260, 270, 285, 295, 296
Fantl, Jeremy 103, 104, 309
Firth, Roderick 88, 91, 167, 244, 251, 308, 309
Foley, Richard 7, 118, 119, 120, 123, 126, 133, 134, 182, 188, 307, 309
foundational coherentism 51
foundationalism 4, 37–52, 78, 113, 117, 199–218, 235
Fumerton, Richard 7, 13, 14, 116, 117, 305, 309
functions 121, 146, 147, 148, 149, 241, 286

Gale, Richard 91, 309
Gettier problem 71, 105, 246, 247, 299

317

Index

Gettier, Edmund 3, 4, 71, 72, 105, 246, 247, 268, 299, 300
Ginet, Carl 62, 176, 254, 261, 263, 309
given, the 39–42, 199–218, 262
Goldman, Alvin 7, 47, 61–2, 67–75, 78–9, 86, 88, 92, 93, 94, 95, 96, 115, 135, 140, 141–5, 148, 167, 178, 219–20, 225, 241, 251, 280, 281, 309, 310
Greco, John 29, 55, 195, 308, 311, 312

Haack, Susan 167, 177, 191, 310
Hahn, Lewis E. 167, 174, 310, 314
Hall, Richard J. 188, 191–2, 310
Harman, Gilbert 69, 260, 261, 310
Harper, William 54, 310
Hawthorne, John 301, 310
Heil, John 85, 91, 241, 310
Heller, Mark 135, 155–7, 310
Hill, Christopher S. 287–9, 310
holism 106–7
Hudson, Hud 180
Huemer, Michael 14, 15, 16, 310
Hume, David 116
hunches 115

illusions 13, 74, 278
inaccessibility 50, 51, 81
incoherence 45
indiscernibility 296
indistinguishability 278, 286, 294, 298
individual subjectivism 118–20, 123, 124, 130, 132, 134
induction 27, 130, 153, 207
  counter 19, 20, 27
  problem of 111
inductivism 113–17
infallible 79, 183, 200
inference ticket 265, 266
inquiry
  pure 255–6
  rational 6, 244, 248, 256

intellectual requirement 88, 89, 224
intentions 118, 157, 159, 172–3
  to believe 172
internalism 4, 35, 37, 46–51, 53–82, 167, 289
  ethical 58
  mentalism 55–8, 81
intrinsic epistemic value 258
introspection 54, 55, 79, 80, 141, 280, 286
intuitions 132, 153–4
invariantism 283, 285, 286
irrationality 221, 222, 234, 240

James, William 91, 182–3, 310
Johnson, Charles R. 188, 191–2, 310
justification
  current state 233–5, 238–41
  criminal standard 296–7, 306
  defeasibility 15, 72–4, 81, 93, 112, 117, 223, 225, 228, 263–74, 296, 298–302
  doxastic 201, 204, 206–8
  factors determining 62–4, 68–9, 74–8
  knowledge-level 103–4, 246, 247, 277, 296–7, 299, 302–3
  moral 243, 244, 253
  nonbasic 78
  practical 267, 268
  propositional 201–8, 215, 254–6
  prima facie 15, 16, 303
  prudential 2, 190, 243, 253
  reflective 24
  subjective 118–20

Kahneman, Daniel 221, 222, 313
Kennedy, Ralf 251, 310
Keynes, John 117, 310
Kim, Jaegwon 88, 251, 309
Kitcher, Philip. 53, 310
knowledge
  a priori 31, 58

direct 200
easy 105–6
justification condition 5, 103–4, 243, 246–7, 253, 268, 296–7
pursuit of 6, 248–51, 255
Kornblith, Hilary 7, 30, 44, 52, 85, 86, 89–90, 92–3, 96, 97, 167, 310, 313
Kripke, Saul 260

Lehrer, Keith 44, 84, 117, 224, 308, 310, 313
Leibniz, Gottfried 200
levels of generality 151
Lewis, C. I. 40
Lewis, David 282, 285, 311
Locke, John 1, 311
logical consequences 60, 78–9, 86–7, 178–9, 181
logical relations 41, 42, 113
lotteries 302
luck 246, 247, 299
Lycan, William 128, 311

Mc Leod, Owen 311
McGrath, Matthew 103, 104, 309
memory 18, 21, 29, 61, 64, 66–72, 105, 106, 140, 141, 164, 189, 221–3, 225, 228–32, 234, 239–40, 272–3, 280, 305
metaphysical errors 165
methodism 17, 19
methodological rationality 233–6
Mills, Eugene 191, 311
moderate realism 29
Montmarquet, James 172, 311
morally ought 190–4, 233
Moser, Paul 22, 29, 117, 244, 282, 308, 311, 312

natural design 129
natural kinds 96, 145, 146, 165

naturalism 128–9, 130–1, 144, 165, 253–4
Neta, Ram 282, 311
Nisbett, Richard 120, 121, 123, 126, 221, 308, 311, 313
normal worlds 149
norms 86, 119, 131, 132
Nozick, Robert 281, 311

objectivity 94, 95, 96
obligation 58, 61–4, 74, 87–9, 90–2, 166–9, 173–6
  epistemic 87–9, 90–2, 173–4
  paradigm 174
observation 37–9, 44–6, 111
obviousness 66, 301
omniscient 127
optimism 162
override 39, 102, 252

Papineau, David 3, 311
Pappas, George 38, 47, 92, 135, 219, 225, 281, 309, 310, 311
particularism 17
perception 21, 26–7, 29, 97–9, 106, 115–16, 140, 151–3, 154, 158, 163, 242, 272, 280, 297, 302–5
perceptual experience 27, 30, 67–8, 74, 97–9, 105, 113, 146–8, 164, 262, 278, 302–5
permission 167, 176, 179, 180, 288
phenomenally 214
Plantinga, Alvin 1, 2, 54, 61, 63, 64, 65, 66, 67, 76, 121, 122, 123, 124, 126, 128, 129, 167, 168, 241, 281, 307, 311
Plato 5, 111, 123, 311
Plug, Allen 161
Pojman, Louis 62, 177, 308, 310, 313
Pollock, John 38, 39, 44, 55, 95, 117, 119, 135, 223, 242, 311
praiseworthy 61–3, 85–6, 166–7, 175

Index

probability
  epistemic 100, 305
  objective 57
  subjective 289
proper function 121–3, 241, 281, 287, 291, 299
prudence 2, 91–2, 112, 171, 180, 184, 189–95, 243–4, 251, 253, 255
Pryor, James 7, 57, 75, 303, 304, 311, 312

Quine, W. V. O., 130, 131, 312

Radcliffe, Dana 169, 312
rationality, (*see also* justification) 112, 114, 118–23, 126–8, 132, 184–6, 189–90, 222, 223, 234–6, 238, 240, 248–51, 257–8
  diachronic 189
  epistemic 112, 117, 118, 134, 219, 233–6
  of belief 119–20, 121–3, 128, 130, 133–4, 184–6
  practical 249, 252, 255
  synchronic 189
realism 29, 148
reason to doubt (*see* justification: defeasibility)
reasonableness 104–5, 161, 189, 224
reasoning 12–13, 22–9, 41, 114–15, 124, 127–8, 131, 141, 262, 300
  good 124, 127, 131
  habits of mind 145
  human limits 84–7
  inferential abilities 77
reasons, (*see also* evidence) 1, 11–16, 19–22, 33–6, 40–3, 50, 60, 63, 66, 104, 128, 131–2, 149, 187, 190, 201, 223, 253, 262, 268, 270, 275, 276, 287, 290, 295, 296–305
  practical 16
  prima facie 223
  skepticism about 11–13

recognition 47–8, 79–80, 146, 205–6, 211–15
recollection (*see* memory)
reference class problem 5, 159–61
reflective equilibrium 18
reflective subjectivism 118
reliabilism 6, 20, 27–8, 33–5, 47–9, 93–101, 112–13, 135–65, 185, 281, 284–91
  generality problem 5, 94–5, 135–65
representativeness heuristic 222
requirements, higher order 74–8
responsibility 65, 67, 86, 89–90, 101, 167, 174, 224
retrievable information 220
rights 166, 176
robustness 264, 265
Ross, Lee 116, 221, 309, 311
rule circularity 19
Russell, Bertrand 200, 201, 312
Russell, Bruce 172, 312

safety 209–10, 282, 284, 286, 287, 299
Schmitt, Frederick 94, 95, 96, 135, 153, 154, 155, 309, 312
Scott-Kakures, Dion 169, 312
seeming evidentialism 15
self-affirmation 19, 20
self-application 35
self-attribution 27, 40, 262
self-defeat 14
self-evidence 29
self-evident 28, 276
self-justification 38, 47
self-presentation 200
self-refutation 13, 14
self-support 35
Senor, Thomas 69, 312
sensory deprivation 190
sensory evidence (*see* evidence experiential) 65, 287, 288
Sider, Ted 7

simplicity 56, 233, 290
skepticism 6, 11–17, 20–2, 29–30, 245, 277–306
Slovic, P. 221, 313
Sorenson, Roy 312
sorting problem 164
Sosa, Ernest 7, 29, 31, 41, 52, 54, 55, 58, 69, 70, 71, 79, 80, 135, 156, 164, 200–18, 243, 246, 282, 304, 308, 311, 312, 313
Stein, Edward 174, 313
Steup, Matthias 54, 55, 62, 166, 168, 172, 195, 307, 309, 310, 312, 313
Stich, Stephen 120, 121, 123, 126, 222, 240, 308, 313
strealth (strength + wealth) 193
Stroud, Barry 30–6, 313
Sturgeon, Scott 242, 243, 313
subjectivism 118, 125, 132, 133
substantiation 40, 41, 43, 45
supernaturalism 121, 123, 124, 126, 128, 129
supervenience 1, 5, 56–8, 73, 75, 81, 101
suspension of judgment 83, 102, 177, 251, 302
Swain, Marshall 133, 219, 309

testimony 16, 29, 79, 98, 101–2, 114–15, 221, 222, 225, 228, 238, 259, 260–73, 297
Thagard, Paul 86, 313

tracking 280, 286, 287, 291, 292, 293
transmissibility 296
truth connection, the 100, 242–56
truth-conduciveness 161, 163
truth-makers 247, 266
truth-orientation 251
truth-ratio 136, 149
truth-seeking 127
Tversky, Amos 221, 222, 313

vagueness 99, 170, 232
van Cleve, James 41, 313
veridicality 98
virtues, intellectual 6, 209–10, 282, 284, 291
Vogel, Jonathan 7, 195, 305, 313
voluntarism, doxastic 5, 84–7, 100, 167–77, 191, 194

Wallis, Charles 135, 142, 313
Warfield, Ted A. 30, 31, 287, 309
warrant 3, 54, 116, 121, 123, 251, 281
well-foundedness 5, 38–9, 93, 94, 96–101, 104, 105, 163, 164
Wettstein, Howard 41
Wierenga, Ed 7
Williams, Bernard 169, 313
Williams, Michael 40–2, 169, 314
Williamson, Timothy 81, 190, 314
Winters, Barbara 169, 314
wishful thinking 105, 129, 141, 241
Wolterstorff, Nicholas 174, 175, 314